Singing Bronze

LUC ROMBOUTS

Singing Bronze

A History of Carillon Music

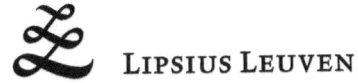
LIPSIUS LEUVEN

With the support of
the Flemish authorities

With the support of
The Guild of Carillonneurs
In North America

Lipsius Leuven is an imprint of Leuven University Press

Original title Zingend Brons. 500 jaar beiaardmuziek in de Lage Landen en de Nieuwe Wereld
Authorized translation from the Dutch language edition published by Davidsfonds / Leuven
© 2010 Dutch language edition by Davidsfonds / Leuven (Belgium)

© 2014 English language edition by Leuven University Press / Universitaire Pers Leuven /
Presses Universitaires de Louvain. Minderbroedersstraat 4, B-3000 Leuven

All rights reserved. Except in those cases expressly determined by law,
no part of this publication may be multiplied, saved in an automated datafile
or made public in any way whatsoever without the express
prior written consent of the publishers.

ISBN 978 90 5867 956 7

D/ 2014 / 1869 / 31

NUR 667

Translation Communicationwise

Design Korpershoek Ontwerpen

Front cover illustration Carillon bells in the St. John's Tower in Gouda (the Netherlands)

Contents

11 Introduction

PART 1 – BELL CULTURES IN ANTIQUITY AND THE MIDDLE AGES

CHAPTER 1 – The magic of old bells

15 A fruit with pith
17 A world of sounds
18 Made in China
21 Jingle Bells
24 Bellmen

CHAPTER 2 – The time of God

27 The daily call to prayer
28 Europe of Bells
30 The appearance of the medieval bell
32 Church doctrine and popular belief
35 Tolling for political ends

CHAPTER 3 – The time of man

39 A day in the city
40 Tolling for special events
43 New bell casting techniques
46 The bell-founder in action

CHAPTER 4 – The bondage of time

49 Clocks in monasteries and cathedrals
52 Measuring time in the open air
55 The signal becomes music

PART 2 – THE OLD CARILLON ART

CHAPTER 5 – **A new musical instrument**

59	*Making music with bells*
61	*The terms* beiaard *and* carillon
62	*Further development of the new musical instrument*
65	*The first founders of carillon bells*

CHAPTER 6 – **Carillon music in a divided land**

71	*Why in the Low Countries?*
74	*Good and bad songs*
78	*Bells as commodity*
80	*The oldest carillon books*

CHAPTER 7 – **Pure bells**

85	*A blind nobleman with a keen sense of hearing*
88	*François Hemony*
90	*The Hemonys' secret*
91	*Pieter Hemony*
94	*The Hemony legacy*

CHAPTER 8 – **Carillon music at the court**

97	*The successors of the Hemonys*
100	*The carillons of Peter the Great*
103	*Carillons for the young Prussians*
105	*Royal extravagance in Portugal*

CHAPTER 9 – **The Bach of the carillon**

109	*Peter Vanden Gheyn, monk and entrepreneur*
111	*Matthias Vanden Gheyn, virtuoso carillonneur*
115	*Andreas Jozef Vanden Gheyn, talented bell-founder*
119	*The descendants of the Vanden Gheyns*

CONTENTS

CHAPTER 10 – **Panorama of the old carillon art**

121	The bells
122	The automatic mechanism
126	Manual playing
127	The carillonneurs
129	The carillon repertoire
133	The audience
135	The fate of the French Low Countries

PART 3 – THE NEW CARILLON ART

CHAPTER 11 – **National Carillon**

139	Carillon music riding the waves of politics
141	The confiscation of bells in the Southern Low Countries
145	Gradual restoration of the bell stock
146	The Northern Republic in the French era
148	Napoleon's bell

CHAPTER 12 – **The carillon as romantic symbol**

149	The carillon, an old instrument
152	Literary interest in bells and carillons
158	The carillon at the service of nationalism

CHAPTER 13 – **In search of the sound of the past**

165	Bell-founding in the 19th century
168	Innovations in keyboard construction
173	Rediscovery of the art of bell tuning

CHAPTER 14 – **A soul in peace, among the stars**

177	A carillonneur with an interest in technique
181	Enchanting Monday evenings
185	The vision of the master
187	An American much interested in carillons

CHAPTER 15 – **The broken bells of Flanders**

191	*War rages over Belgium*
195	*The voice of fallen carillons*
200	*Carillon war in the Netherlands*
205	*Bells of victory*

CHAPTER 16 – **Memorial bells**

207	*A school for carillonneurs*
209	*Carillon sounds across the Atlantic*
214	*Rockefeller and his Belgian carillonneurs*
218	*The race for bigger and heavier*
222	*Contours of a new carillon culture*
225	*New carillons in other parts of the world*

CHAPTER 17 – **New carillon construction in the Old Country**

229	*Belgian and English influence in the Netherlands*
231	*Protectionist reflexes in Belgium*
235	*Malaise among the Belgian bell-founders*
238	*Belgian carillons in the United States*
240	*The Mechelen carillon school during the interwar period*

CHAPTER 18 – **'The bells fight with us'**

249	*Nazi bells*
251	*Carillon music in occupied territory*
256	*The confiscation of bells in Europe*
263	*Liberation*

CHAPTER 19 – **Dutch manufacture versus Carillon Americana**

267	*The return of the bells*
271	*Reconstruction in the Low Countries*
275	*A carillon without bells*
278	*Carillon battle in the Vatican pavilion*

CONTENTS

CHAPTER 20 – Innovations in the Old and the New World

285	*American Beauty*
289	*The American carillon movement*
293	*Acid rain in Europe*
296	*Using the computer*
305	*Carillon music in the East*

CHAPTER 21 – Panorama of the new carillon art

309	*The carillons of the world*
312	*Carillon organizations*
314	*Carillonneurs and their audience*
318	*The diversity of carillon music*
321	*A future for the carillon*

325	Sources and acknowledgements
327	Notes
337	Bibliography
351	Origin of the illustrations
353	Indices

Introduction

Around 1500, something unusual happened in a small region along the North Sea. In the cities of the Low Countries, bells in church and city towers were transformed into musical instruments. And thus the carillon was born, the first musical mass medium in history. A rivalry emerged between the cities for larger instruments, and city governments placed ever-greater demands concerning the sound of the bells and the quality of the playing mechanism. Bell-founders and carillon builders met these challenges with varying degrees of success.

Despite its enormous size, the carillon was fragile. Many instruments fell prey to fire, requisitions and the violence of war. The carillon's existence was most threatened by the social changes and technological innovations of the 19th and 20th centuries. Yet neither the advancing individualization of society, nor compact music players such as radios, record players and mp3 players, could supplant the traditional carillon. Today there are more tower instruments than ever, and in the recent century, especially North America has played an important role in bringing innovation to the art of the carillon. Hundreds of musicians throughout the world still climb the tower stairs to distill an hour of beauty from an instrument that, according to the musical theory of evolution, should have gone extinct along with the Ancien Régime in Europe.

The carillon is by nature a public instrument. It has always adorned or commented on important events, or it has been the product of such. Consequently, this book tells the history of the carillon from the perspective of the social context in which it developed and continues to function. The carillon was witness to 5 centuries of turbulent history in the Low Countries, also called the Netherlands, a territory that largely coincides with the present states of the Netherlands and Belgium, as well as a number of departments in Northern France. The history of the carillon is the story of rivalry between bell-founders, carillon builders and carillonneurs, with in the background larger political, religious, linguistic and military conflicts. Ironically enough, some of these conflicts lifted the art of the carillon to a higher level. Belgian carillon culture, for example, penetrated to the United States of America as a direct outcome of the First World War, and today the carillon remains a musical link between the two countries.

This book also examines the roots of the carillon. The instrument, after all, did not emerge from nowhere, but developed from 1000 years of medieval bell culture and indirectly from the bell cultures of Antiquity. Hence, in this book we will be listening to the jingling bell around the neck of an Old Persian sheep as well as to the ponderous carillons of today that emanate the energy of tons of singing bronze.

Until today, the geographical distribution of the carillon is largely limited to the Netherlands, Belgium and the United States. Even in these core regions, however, the general public is unfamiliar with the instrument. People usually listen to carillon music unconsciously, without knowing exactly what takes place on the inside of the tower. And they know precious little of the rich history of humanity's largest musical instrument. Consequently, this book will reveal a piece of hidden history: the story of musical bells and of the people who developed, played and enjoyed them.

PART ONE

Bell cultures in Antiquity and the Middle Ages

CHAPTER 1

The magic of old bells

A fruit with pith

The bell's history begins in the Bronze Age. With the development of the art of bronze casting around 3000 B.C., humanity took a gigantic step forward. This cast metal had numerous qualities: it was hard yet not breakable, durable yet capable of infinite reuse when remelted. Bronze could be formed into very diverse objects: strong swords, protective shields, useful axes, fireproof kitchenware, refined jewelry, beautiful figurines … and harmonious bells. When in 1200 B.C. bronze began to be replaced by iron as the most important material, this was not because the latter was superior in all respects, but especially because iron was easier to find and thus cheaper. To make bronze, after all, two different metals were needed: copper and tin. Surprisingly enough, nowhere in the world are copper ore and tin ore found in close proximity. Moreover, there were no copper or tin mines in Iran and Iraq, where bronze casting is thought to have originated. Hence, bronze casting was only possible thanks to intensive trade throughout Asia and Europe. Copper and tin were often transported thousands of miles, finally to be smelted together into bronze. Today, bronze remains the preferred metal for the production of bells.

The oldest bronze bells had the shape of a spherical, latticed cage in which a ball was able to freely move back and forth. Archaeological finds reveal that a number of these primordial bells took their inspiration from the pomegranate. In fact, the tops of specimens from Luristan, a mountainous region in West Iran, were decorated with pomegranate leaves. The pomegranate was one of the principal fruits in Antiquity. It was cultivated in Persia and vicinity five thousand years ago, and was a symbol of fertility due to its many seeds encased in a berry-like membrane. The tick of these seeds in a dried pomegranate probably inspired mankind to imitate the fruit in sonorous bronze.

The oldest bell-founder probably used the lost-wax casting technique. He would have first kneaded a clay ball whose circumference equaled the inside of the later crotal bell. Around this, he formed a wax model of the bell. He then molded a clay covering over this, and baked the totality until the clay of the inner and outer

BELL CULTURES IN ANTIQUITY AND THE MIDDLE AGES

Bronze crotal bell in the form of a pomegranate, Luristan, 6th century B.C.

forms dried and hardened. The intervening wax melted and escaped via an opening in the outer form. The mold was now ready. The bell-founder heated a quantity of copper and tin in a ratio of approximately 80/20. When the mixture was liquid enough, he poured it through the opening in the empty mold. After the bronze had cooled and congealed, the bell-founder removed the inner and outer form and the crotal bell was ready. The ball of the crotal bell was cast beforehand and enclosed in the clay inner form during the process of molding the clay. It is impossible to determine where the first bell-founder did his work. However, since Luristan is a region where pomegranates flourish and where bronze casting was first developed, he may very well have lived there.

The crotal bells continued to evolve. The lattices grew together to form a continuous wall with a wide opening at the bottom. In this way, a conic body emerged that we know as the *bell shape*. This shape probably was easier to cast and had the advantage that the ball could be added afterwards by attaching it to the inside of the bell. Still later, the ball evolved to an elongated body that was attached to the head of the bell: the clapper. The clappers of bells that have been preserved were usually made of iron, which indicates that the evolution of the crotal bell to clapper bell could have taken place somewhere at the beginning of the Iron Age, around 1,000 B.C.

A world of sounds

From the colorful primordial soup of hitting, rattling and ringing sounds emerged the 'bell-shaped' bell as the object that best combined a good sound with power, and became the duality of bell and clapper we still know today. The bell with freely suspended clapper is astounding in its simplicity: the swinging movement of the bell brings the clapper in motion, which in turn impacts the bell. Bell and clapper are continually in dynamic interaction and produce a vivid sound to the rhythm of the swinging bell. The bell itself is driven by the external energy of a person, an animal or the wind. In addition to the swinging or tolling technique, stationary bells can also be struck with a separate mallet or other object. This gives the bell-ringer full control of the tempo of the bell signal. Finally, there is a mixed technique that combines both of the previous types: the bell is stationary, but still contains a clapper. The latter is not free to move, but is attached from below to a rope with which it can be pulled towards the wall of the bell. As with the previous technique, this way of playing enables full mastery of the rate at which the bell is struck. Swinging with a free clapper, hitting with a mallet, and striking with a clapper attached to a rope: in the course of history, the bell has always been sounded using one of these three techniques. Later in this book, the third form will play the leading role, since it is the direct forerunner of the carillon.

For bells, the Bronze Age never ended. The best sounding bells are still cast in the expensive alloy, and in the conic form known since Antiquity. The bronze bell has an intimate relationship with the earth's atmosphere. When struck, parts of the bell body begin to vibrate at different rates at the same time, and dozens of partial notes are emitted into the air. The fastest sound waves do not go far and quickly die out, but the slower waves carry across large distances and move the air for a longer time. As the high partial notes fade, the resonance of the bell becomes thinner and more transparent. When the sound has almost disappeared, the lowest tone – the fundamental – continues to resound for a time until the bronze comes fully to rest and the final sound wave fades from the atmosphere. Most listeners are unable to hear the partial notes separately, but experience a total sound whose character is determined by their pitch and relative strength. The bell sound is, as it were, a color composed of a number of primary colors. The sounding together of this mass of partial notes does not result in dissonance, because good bells produce a clearly recognizable musical note: the strike note or melody note.

The strike note is the bell's big bang, a vivid sound that starts at the moment the bell is struck and disappears immediately to make room for the resonance of the partial notes, which fan out like ripples in water. Strangely enough, the strike note cannot be found in the vibration pattern of the bronze. It is formed in the listener's brain, and thus is a purely psychological phenomenon. We know that it is produced via the interplay of specific partial notes, but no generally accepted explanation has been found yet for its true nature. We do know, however, where this strike note is located: by definition, one octave below the bell's fifth partial tone. The bell sound has a double character thanks to the succession of a vivid strike note and the dying partial notes: it sounds sharp and melodious at the same time; it speaks and it sings. Each bell is a world of sounds, a microcosm unto itself.

The sound of the bell can be compared to the taste of wine. In the bell's strike note, you taste the wine's attack; the partial notes are the various flavors that an experienced taster can distinguish in a sip of wine; these must be brought into mutual harmony and evoke a pleasing and round sensory experience, because thinness of taste or sound is to be avoided. Finally, there is the decay, which lasts a long time in good bells, like the aftertaste of delicious wine. Wine of superior quality becomes better with the years because over time, the various acids, the fruit and the alcohol come to rest, and blend into a homogeneous totality. A bell also sounds better as the years pass. Due to the many years of use, the bronze is brought into vibration millions of times, causing the atoms in the bell wall to travel microscopically small distances, resulting in the crystal structure of the bronze becoming more balanced. The casting tensions become smaller and the bell develops a gentler sound.[1]

We, however, are still long before the time in which the perfect bell was cast. In carillon circles, this is assumed to have taken place only in 1644 A.D.

Made in China

We know from school that important inventions were made in China long before they were 'reinvented' in Europe: the compass, gunpowder, paper and the art of printing. To this list also belongs the bronze bell, because while the rest of the world was still experimenting with small crotals and bells in various materials, China was casting large bronze bells. Thus, the art of casting bells began in China.[2]

China, like the Middle East, also made use of the clapper bell. The *feng-ling* are well known: smaller bells that hung on the roofs of temples and that sounded by the movement of the wind. However, the most typical Chinese bell, the *zhong*, is of a completely different order, and appears to be a separate development, independent of the tradition in the West. The term zhong means 'vessel' or 'kettle', and indeed, the Chinese bell was developed from bronze kitchenware. The zhong played an important role in Chinese society. Around 1000 B.C., an edict was issued that established fixed measurement units throughout the land. The *huang zhong* or yellow bell became the official standard for weight, height, content and pitch. It contained 1,200 millet grains and produced the note f1.

Yellow was the color of the sovereign and thus referred to the divine. The sound produced by the yellow bell was the perfect transposition of the primordial vibration of the world. This tone and the right music guaranteed a harmonious way of life and good government. The zhong was literally the measure of all things. It was the vessel in which the human encountered the divine.

The Chinese were masters in the technique of casting. Chinese bell-founders formed their bells from the outside to the inside, where their colleagues in the Middle East worked from the inside to the outside. They first would create a clay form with the dimensions of the outside of the later bell. This form was dried and baked until it was hard enough to serve as mold. The bell-founder then pressed a soft clay plate against the mold and carefully hammered it to obtain a crisp impression. In this way, various plates were obtained that contained a negative of the outer form. He then created the inner form by scraping down the first clay form until it no longer reflected the outside, but rather the inside of the bell. The bell-founder installed the clay plates at the right place on the inner form, and fastened these. This created an empty space between the inner form and the outer plates in which the bronze could be poured. This so-called clay mold method is no longer used today when casting bells. Statue makers often still make use of it, since it is the best technique for creating large and complicated molds.

The zhong differs strongly from the Western bell. Its body is not round, but has a clear front and back. Both halves are curved, and the sides appear to be glued to each other. The lower edge of each side is not flat, but arched toward the middle, such that the lower point where the arches of the two sides meet forms a sharp angle. The zhong generally is lavishly decorated with texts and ornamentation. A twisting dragon is often depicted on the underside, whose task supposedly was to ward off evil. The body of the bell is embellished with bronze bumps or nipples, ordered in four squares of nine pieces each. The origin of such nipples on Chinese bells is unclear. According to some, they contribute to the sound; others say they are too small to make a difference, and are rather fertility symbols.

The sound of the Chinese bell is as different from the Western bell as Chinese character writing differs from our Latin typeface. In the West, bell-founders always aimed at 'extroverted' bells that were hung at a certain height and that could be heard over a great distance. They sought a brilliant sound with a clear strike note, a long decay and a rich bouquet of partial notes tuned to each other. The Chinese bell is introverted: it originated from the household objects located on the kitchen floor, and when turned over, it remained close to the earth, preferably in the forecourt of a temple or palace. The bronze used in the zhong contained less tin and more lead than the bronze of the Western bell. This limited the range of vibrations, and created a muted and subdued sound. This effect was reinforced by the way in which it was played. The zhong was played by a servant using a wooden hammer. When striking, the soft wood released only a limited amount of energy in the bronze, so that the overtones were scarcely present and the timbre was mainly determined by the fundamental. Due to the dominance of this fundamental, the dissonance of the overtones – which were not in tune with each other – was scarcely noticeable. A thinner wall also gave the zhong a deeper sound than the same-sized Western bell. Given two bells of identical size, the bell with the thinnest wall in fact vibrates the slowest.

The zhong was more than a symbolic sound carrier and symbol of the world order. From the 5th century B.C. onward, it played an important role in Chinese music making. In the worldview of Confucius, music played an important role in government, and numerous texts refer to the ethical dimension of music. Almost self-evidently, bells set the tone in the orchestras composed of string and wind instruments as well as drums. In addition to their divine status, they after all sounded a fixed note. The bells were part of the ancient Chinese orchestra, and numerous small chimes have been preserved, among others in graves. Until a short time ago, the largest known variant was the *bian zhong*, a collection of 16 bells hung in two rows, one above the other. In 1977, however, the history of the bell in China had to be rewritten. In that year, an underground grave was discovered while excavating a site for a factory. Found at the site was the extensive survival kit that Marquis Yi had received after his death in 433 B.C. for his sojourn in the afterlife: weapons, chariots, household furniture, decorative objects, eight concubines and a dog. Two adjoining rooms contained 125 musical instruments, a number of musicians and thirteen dancers – made not of terra cotta, but of flesh and blood. There was also a chime consisting of 65 bells – larger than a contemporary carillon. The bells could be played by five musicians. The largest bell was more than five foot tall and weighed 450 lbs. The tonal range of the chime was not limited to the notes of the Chinese scale: the series was fully chromatic over a distance of five octaves. On the bells were texts that provided an answer to a question that music scholars had been disputing for years: the problem of the dual tonality of the Chinese bell.

When a Chinese bell is struck at different places, different notes are sounded. For a long time, it remained unclear whether this was an accidental outcome of the typical shape of the Chinese bell, or whether it was the result of deliberate design. The inscriptions on the bells of Marquis Yi support the second theory by indicating clearly the two optimum striking points. When the bells are struck on the lower middle, *sui*

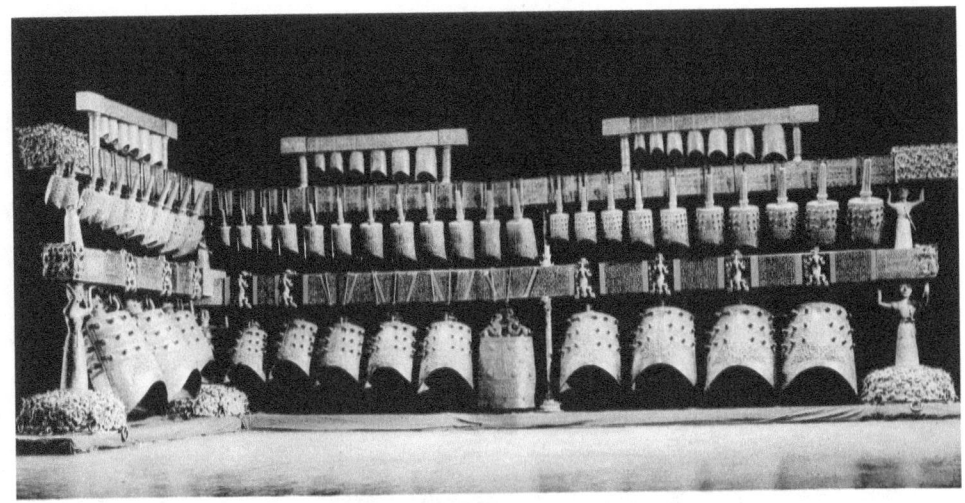

The 65 bell chime of Marquis Yi, about 433 B.C.

sounds. If they are struck close to the left or right edge, a *gu* is sounded, which generally is a minor third, or one and a half notes, above the sui. The clever part of this design is that the two notes interfere minimally with each other: when striking one note, the partial notes of the other note scarcely sound. The world can again acquaint itself with the chime that was intended to revive the dead marquis, because a faithful copy is on a world tour with the Hubei Chime Bells Ensemble. Thus, a new life was given to the refined art of bells that played an important role in the China of the Shang and Chou dynasties, but that came to a halt at the beginning of our calendar. The Chinese chime was a richly decorated branch of the carillon family tree that, however, produced no new offshoots. To uncover the evolution to the carillon, we follow below the main path from crotals and bells in the Middle East.

Jingle Bells

In the first millennium before Christ, jingling crotals and little bells spread quickly, and over time they could be heard in Syria, Palestine, Egypt, the Greek world around the Mediterranean Sea, and the vast Roman Empire. The beneficial properties of bronze were appreciated throughout the entire civilized world. Bronze was the loudest and most resonant material that could be extracted from the earth. It received a sacred status and became associated with eternity. When Horace ascribed eternal value to his own poetry, he called it *aere perennius*, more lasting than bronze.[3]

Iberic-Celtic cult wagon with bells, 5th-1st century B.C.

The Western bell looked less sacred than its big sister from China. Its surface was rough and unadorned, with a normal height of only 1 to 2 inches, with rare exceptions extending to 4 inches. In contrast to the static Chinese bell, the Western clapper bell was a *perpetual motion machine*: always in a state of unrest. It hung on people and animals, and converted the movements of its carrier into sound. Thanks to its freely hanging clapper, it was able to sound on its own, a sound that was tinkling and refreshing, as suggested by its Latin name *tintinnabulum*. Horses, livestock, pets, children, slaves, prisoners, high priests and monarchs: all wore bells. The crotals and bells of Antiquity, despite their wide distribution, were used for very similar purposes, functions that in some cases continue until today.

First, the antique bell served as a tool for localization. In an age in which pastures were not yet systematically parceled into fenced fields, the farmer used animal bells to know where his livestock were at a given moment. The Romans even had a name for the phenomenon: a belled donkey was an *asinus tintinnabulatus*. Analogously, the Romans sometimes also attached a bell to slaves as a means of control. This ancient localization system is still used today in the Swiss Alps, where the cowbell or *trychel* is intended to prevent cows from getting lost in the Alpine meadows. A more recent application are the bells on the horse-drawn sleigh. A sleigh makes little noise on freshly fallen snow, and the tinkling bells warned passers-by of the approaching danger. It is this warning signal that we hear around Christmas in the cheerful sounds of *Jingle Bells*.

The notion 'danger' brings us to the second and main role of the ancient bell: its magic function. In Antiquity, natural phenomena, diseases and death generally were attributed to evil in all of its possible manifestations. Nature gods, the fates, wandering ghosts, the evil eye and others were invisible – yet very present – forces of evil that could be held at bay by producing repetitive sounds. Clapper bells and crotals were obvious amulets: they produced sound and were made of noble bronze.

In wartime, bells were used as an invisible shield: they dangled on the harnesses of horses and not only protected the animal against invisible evil, but could also frighten the enemy if they were not familiar with the noise of ringing bronze. Greeks and Romans hung bells on swords and lances to make them sound frightening.

Bells were also used in times of peace. King Solomon and Emperor Augustus had bells hung on the roofs of their respective temples that sounded with the motion of the wind. In the interior of temples, bronze gongs or bells were sounded to keep the incense pure, and in some temples, the sound of bronze was a means to interpret the counsel of the oracle. Wind chimes were suspended on the branches of trees to purify the air. Animal bells not only localized, but also protected. And bells also did their work at sea: Indian sailors hung bells on their ships to ward off sea monsters, a technique that always worked.

Bells and crotals accompanied people throughout their lives, and created a protective aura around their wearer. Children, rocking horses and other toys were so armed in order to ward off the evil eye. Men hung bells on their belt or garments, and women wore bells around the neck or on the ears.

When death approached, the bell received special significance. At this most vulnerable moment in the human life cycle, it spared the dying person from evil. It also continued to play this role after death. Bells have been found in Greek and Roman graves that were meant to protect the dead in their journey to the hereafter. For the Egyptians, bells were thought to contain a soul: they were sometimes wrapped in cloth before being placed with the mummified dead.

In addition to the grand story of life, the bell also began to play a role in the practical ordering of everyday life. In Greek and Roman cities, the sound of a bell signaled the important events of the day. For the Greeks, these were chiefly the marketplace, the meetings on the agora, and sacrifices in the temple; for the Romans, these also included the opening of the public baths and the start of the games. The sound of the bell was also used in the home. In the great Roman villas, the sound of bells called the slaves of the house to work. The signal function of the bell was also expressed in the names given to it. In addition to its general name *kodon*, the Greeks also called it *semantron* or 'sign'. The Romans, in addition to the playful *tintinnabulum*, also used the serious term *signum*.

This book will treat only the bell cultures of Asia and Europe. We may not forget, however, that simultaneously, bells and crotals of wood, pottery and diverse metals, including bronze, were also used in the African hinterland and in pre-Columbian America. Here again, bells were used in function of magic and the sacred. Which causes us to conclude that the bell has roots throughout the world, and that these different developments probably came about independently of one another. In very diverse locations, the bell has developed into the ideal medium for strong auditory communication. In our search for the origin of the carillon, we will further examine the Eurasian branch.

Bellmen

There is no clearly detectable break between the pre-Christian and Christian use of the bell. Christians probably initially used the object in the same way as their pagan ancestors and contemporaries. After Christians were allowed to openly profess their faith, bells became loaded with Christian meaning and symbolism, and they were recuperated in the same way as other pre-Christian customs and symbols. Thus, the status of the bell evolved from magical to sacred, terms whose meanings in fact are nearly the same.

The earliest use of the bell in a purely Christian context can be traced back to Egypt. Christianity spread quickly in the desert area in the east of the Roman Empire, which led to the emergence of the Coptic Church. A number of Coptic believers withdrew into the desert to lead an ascetic life. One of these was Anthony. He settled in Wadi Natrun, where he was joined by like-minded hermits. Anthony was tormented many times by the devil, who presented him with diverse temptations. He was able to withstand these satanic temptations thanks to prayer and a bell that he sounded with his hand. It is also said that he used this bell to drive out a demon in a pig. Christian iconography depicts St. Anthony the Great with a bell, a pig and a staff that ends at the top with a T-shaped cross, the so-called Cross of Tau or St. Anthony's Cross. He sometimes has the bell in his hand, sometimes it hangs on his staff or around the neck of the pig. Coptic bells have been discovered in Egypt, but it is not clear whether they were used to order life in the first monastic communities, or whether their use was limited to warding off evil.

A century after Anthony, a similar confrontation between good and evil took place at the western edge of Europe. The Englishman Patrick traveled to Ireland on behalf of Pope Celestine I to convert the population to Christianity. In 441, while fasting on the summit of Mount Croagh Patrick, he was attacked by reptiles, black birds and demons, and he prayed to God for help. God immediately placed a bell at his feet, which Patrick sounded with all his force, causing the birds to take flight. The snakes, however, remained until he threw the bell at them. Whereupon they disappeared into the lake Log Na Deanham, and left Ireland for good (in fact, the Emerald Isle has been free of snakes since the end of the ice age). Patrick became the patron saint of Ireland and is depicted with a bell, a staff with a T-shaped cross, and a Bible. The National Museum of Ireland in Dublin houses two bells that supposedly belonged to him. The *Black Bell of St. Patrick* reportedly has been blackened by the fire from hell during Patrick's battle with the demons. The other is called the *Bell of St. Patrick's Will* and was buried together with the Saint, but re-excavated a half century later. It is preserved in an eleventh-century reliquary.

After the Christianization of Ireland, Patrick's followers went to the mainland – armed with staff, Bible and bell – to proclaim the faith, especially at the boundaries of the earlier empire where Christianity had penetrated the least. Their bells supported them in their militant proclamation of the teachings of Christ. These were carried on a ring-shaped handle and sounded with the hand. The bells were made of bent iron sheets riveted together with nails, which gave them the appearance of sheep or cowbells. Some bells were dipped in liquid bronze to improve their sound and protect them from rusting. By contemporary standards, the Irish hand bells did not look attractive, but they were handy while traveling due to their light weight. Tradition has it that they possessed miraculous powers: they held evil at bay and healed the sick. Supported by the sound of their hand bells, Irish monks established monasteries in the whole of Western Europe. The immense influence of Irish monasticism on Western European Christian culture is illustrated by the fact that the term *clock* and its variants in other languages were derived from the Celtic word *clogga*, which means 'object to strike'.

Nevertheless, like the Chinese bell, the bells of the first monks are located on a side branch of the carillon family tree. Both the Egyptian and early Irish forms of monasticism focused on asceticism and preaching that was often performed individually, such that there was no need for large bells to organize a community. Hence, the Celtic bells must be late offshoots of the evil-repelling bells of Antiquity, with the difference that the bells were no longer dangled passively on the body, but were actively sounded with the hand. There was also the new dimension of drawing attention to the message of the preaching. Dispelling gave way to attracting. The passionate Irish missionaries were the distant precursors to the bellmen who in some cities even today call inhabitants together for announcements of major importance.

In a following phase, the bell would evolve from an individual attribute to a means of communication within communities. The small clapper bell will continue to grow and result in the Christian church bell.

CHAPTER 2

The time of God

The daily call to prayer

The origin of the Latin word for bell *campana* is often linked to the Italian region of Campania. While this claim is uncertain, an important step in the development of the church bell did take place there. In 530, Benedict of Nursia built an abbey on Monte Cassino, a rock along the northern border of Campania. He strove for an orderly and harmonious life within the abbey walls, and to this end, he drew up a number of precepts for his monks. The cornerstone of abbey life was a balanced daily schedule of eight hours work, eight hours prayer and eight hours rest. This daily schedule was demarcated by the monk who was responsible for the signum. He gave the signal for the eight prayer times or canonical hours: Matins, Lauds, Prime, Terce, Sext, None, Vespers and Compline.[4] The signal for Matins was given just after midnight and thus also served as an alarm to wake the monks. Benedict wrote: 'When the signal is given, they <the monks> must rise immediately and haste to attend to the work of God, while maintaining an atmosphere of respect and humility.'[5]

Benedict was not the first to use a signal to convene a community. Also before his time, monks were called together at specific times for group activities such as meals or prayer. Given the silent character of many monastic communities, this calling together did not take place in the literal sense, but use was made of a *signum* or signal. In essence, this was nothing more than the Roman villa bell that formerly summoned the house slaves to work, and the house bell that, many centuries later, mobilized house personnel in upper class residences. The agreed signal, however, was not necessarily a bell: use was made of materials that were available locally, and a gong, a wind instrument or a wooden slat could also serve as signum. Benedict too did not refer to the bell by name.

In the situations where it was clear that a bell was being referred to, it probably was not always sounded with a bell rope. The expression *signum pulsare*, 'hit the bell with force', can in fact refer to the three techniques to sound bells. Initially, they were probably moved by hand, since this was before the time of larger bells and the introduction of the bell rope. Sometimes a fixed hanging bell was struck with a hammer or a clapper, which is suggested by the expression *signum tangere*, 'tap the bell', which St. Caesarius of Arles wrote just before Benedict composed his monastic rule. Striking for that matter was the most natural technique to sound signals other than the bell, such as the semantron used in Greek orthodox monasteries. The Greek orthodox monks announced prayer services by striking with a hammer a long slat of maple or beech suspended over their shoulder or hung in the house of prayer. The practice remains today in monastic communities in the Orthodox Churches of Eastern Europe and the Near East.

Shortly after Benedict's death, the Abbey of Monte Cassino was destroyed by the Lombards. However, his rule lived on and was expanded by Gregory, a monk of his order who was elected Pope in 590. Gregory was a great admirer of Benedict and wrote his biography. Thus, the Rule of Benedict quickly spread to hundreds of other abbeys, and became as it were the constitution for Western European monasticism.

Europe of Bells

According to Church tradition, the church bell made the jump from abbey churches to parish churches under Gregory's immediate successor, Sabinian, who was Pope from 604 to 606. Sabinian is said to have extended the obligation to pray at regular times of the day to include the full community of believers. There are indications, however, that the bell had transcended the limited realm of the monastery and was used as a general call to prayer already during the sixth century. Initially, bells were not hung in a tower, but in a masonry arch on the roof of the church building. As the need to cover greater distances grew, they were installed in church towers, from where they could reach the entire local community. Some historians speculate that the early-medieval towers initially had only a military function, and that they only later were used to house bells. Arguing against this, however, is the fact that the free-standing church towers in Italy are called *campanile*, which suggests that accommodating bells was their main purpose. In the footsteps of spreading Christianity, the church bell conquered ever more territory. A dense network of bells emerged, and over time, almost no inhabited place was free from the sound of bells. The eight canonical prayer times of Benedict were often reduced to seven, with the nocturnal ringing of Matins pushed back to coincide with Lauds.

The definitive anchoring of the church bell as symbol of Christian Europe was realized by the Frankish King Charlemagne. In the final decades of the 8th century, he conquered the greatest part of Western and Central Europe, which he transformed into a centrally governed state, the first world empire since the collapse of the Roman Empire. In 800, he was crowned emperor of the Holy Roman Empire by the Pope.

Charlemagne viewed his imperial status as a sort of priesthood. For him, state and religion coincided, and he imposed Christianity throughout the empire, if necessary by force. In his capitularies or administrative codes, he imposed rules for religious practice and the liturgical use of church bells. His son Louis the Pious convened the Council of Aachen in 816, which imposed the monastic rule of Benedict on all monasteries in the West. The ringing of bells became, as it were, a Christian flag planted on Christianized territory. Around the year 800, the bell became the sound of unified Europe: *Glockeneuropa* or 'Europe of Bells', as the Austrian historian Friedrich Heer so concisely expressed it. After the unified Frankish Empire was split into three by the Treaty of Verdun in 843, and fragmented in the following centuries into a patchwork of large and small principalities, the language of the Christian church bell united a politically divided Europe as an indivisible spiritual space.

The bell spread not only geographically, but also multiplied in the towers themselves. Beginning in the 8th century, there are indications of two or more bells in church towers, making it possible to give more sophisticated signals to the faith community. In the 9th and 10th century, the number of bells per tower increased to ten or twelve, making possible multiple tolling combinations and increasing many times over the number of possible signals. Multiple bells in the same tower could not all simply be called *signum* or *campana*, so bells were given a name that was inscribed in their walls during the production process. Generally, they were named after a saint. The demand for multiple bells in one tower meant a new challenge for the bell-founders, who often still were monks. They now had to design bells with different pitches that harmonized with one another when sounded together. Thus, the harmony of multiple bells brings us a step closer to the phenomenon of bell music, the central theme of this book. In the Christian tradition, for that matter, various tolling combinations were named after Gregorian melodies. The combination d-f-g was named Te Deum, because it corresponded to the first notes of the Te Deum; the combination c-d-e was called a Gloria toll, etc. This symbolism, however, came only later, and around the turn of the millennium, bells probably did not sound harmonious enough for the public to have spontaneously associated them with existing hymns.

The appearance of the medieval bell

Of the high number of bells that sounded throughout Europe during this time, very few have been preserved. Bells were hung in vulnerable locations and were continually threatened by fire and war. Moreover, there was an active market for replacing bells. Bronze was recyclable, and the material contained in discarded bells was reused in the larger or improved bells that replaced them. Bells were primarily replaced after they had cracked due to use. Thus there was a continuous cycle of smelting and recasting, and today we can hear in many bells the vibrations of bronze that once sounded in bells that disappeared hundreds of years ago. Due to the almost complete absence of early medieval bells, we are unable to form an accurate picture of their shape. They probably were modest in size and had the form of an upside down bowl, with broad, rounded shoulders. Indirect evidence for this can be found in the iconography around St. Agatha, a Sicilian woman who died a martyr's death in the 3rd century. Her torture included the cutting off of her breasts. Sculptures and paintings depict the saint holding a platter containing her two severed breasts. The public associated this with bronze bells, and St. Agatha thus became the patron saint of bell-founders. Others saw in this a tray with loaves of bread, such that Agatha also became the patron saint of bakers.

The oldest bell that managed to escape the melting pot or other violent end dates back to the 8th or 9th century. It was discovered in the central Italian village of Canino and is preserved in the Vatican museums. It still has the bowl or egg-shaped form that probably characterized the bells of earlier centuries, but there is modest flare at the lower edge as a precursor to the thick sound rim of later bells. At the top, the former handle of the hand bell has developed into a hanging system with a triple ring. The Canino bell is decorated modestly and bears an inscription. It has a diameter – again very modest – of 39 cm. In later centuries, however, bells increased in size substantially, and at the turn of the millennium, they could weigh approximately 1,000 kg. Examples include the preserved Lullusglocke from 1038 in the Romanesque abbey church of Bad Hersfeld in Hesse, Germany. It has a diameter of 112 cm, has wide shoulders and its waist is almost vertical: this is the so-called *beehive profile* that would be used for a number of centuries. The Lullusglocke sounds shrill and tinny. Its present tolling system is a reconstruction of the probable original system. At that time, a church bell was suspended on a yoke, a horizontal beam that balanced on two transverse beams. A crossbeam was attached to the yoke, to which the bell rope was tied. Miniatures from the 12th century and later also have tolling systems with a crossbeam, still without the bell wheel that later became common. They often depict single bell-ringers sounding two bells at the same time. This means that in the High Middle Ages, most bells were still light enough to be put into motion without great physical effort.

Despite the low number of bells still preserved today, thanks to a certain Theophilus, probably a Benedictine monk of the Helmarshausen Abbey in Hesse, we know quite accurately how bells were cast in the High Middle Ages. Around the year 1100, he wrote a Latin do-it-yourself book on applied arts and crafts: the *Schedula diversarum artium*. This book describes in detail the techniques of painting, goldsmithing, organ building, bell casting and much more. In the chapter on bells, Theophilus describes the three important phases in the production of the bell: the construction of the mold, the casting of the bell and its finishing. It was in essence still the lost-wax casting technique used by bell-founders in Antiquity. At the time of Theophilus, bells were formed 'on the spit'. The bell-founder started his work with an oak spindle that had a conical bulge in the middle. The spindle lay on two wooden blocks and rotated like a spit over a fire, which is why it sometimes was called *the goose*. While a helper rotated the spindle with a crank, the bell-founder added a layer of clay. After drying, he would add additional layers in the same way until its form was large enough to demarcate the profile of the inside of the bell with a chisel (in later bell-founding jargon, this clay interior would be called the *core*). The bell-founder then added thin layers of wax to the core, and also finished these with the chisel, such that a template of the outside wall of the bell was obtained (this later would be called the *false bell*). Texts and decorations – 'letters or flowers', writes Theophilus – could be inscribed on the wax surface. New layers of clay were applied to the false bell (the later *cope*). When the totality was formed, the spindle was removed from the form and in the opening, an iron ring was installed on which the clapper later would hang. The form was placed upright and a wax crown fitted to the bell to later attach it to the yoke. The outside of the form was reinforced with iron hoops to withstand the outward pressure of the liquid bronze. When the form had fully dried, it again was placed on its side, and the interior of the core was further hollowed out. The form was again placed upright, and placed over a fire for a day and a night. This made the clay core and cope more solid, and the wax of the false bell melted away, so that an empty mold was created. To prevent the form from cracking or exploding during casting, it was securely buried in the ground. The second phase was the casting itself. Two strong men operated the bellows, and copper was heated in an oven or casting ladle. When a temperature of 1100 degrees Celsius was obtained, green smoke emerged indicating to the bell-founder that the copper was liquid. This was the moment to quickly add a fifth part of tin. Thanks to its lower melting point, the tin immediately mixed with the copper. The liquid bronze was poured into the empty mold via a hole in the form of the crown. Air and gases were able to escape via two vents. After the form had filled with bronze, there was a wait of a day or longer until the metal congealed. Then the bell was excavated for the third phase of its creation: the finishing. Core and cope were removed, and the bell was again tilted on its side, installed on a horizontal spindle and sanded while being rotated. If the creation of the bell was successful, it could be blessed. Hence, during the process of its creation, the bell undergoes a cycle involving the four elements: it receives its matter from the earth, is formed by fire, is given its mission via the holy water, and finds its ultimate purpose in the air that it fills with sound.

Church doctrine and popular belief

The ritual of blessing the bell was the formal confirmation of its new status.[6] The church bell was no longer a functional signal that announced the hours of prayer, but the messenger of an extroverted Christianity, and a mystical object that God and ministers used to speak to the community of believers. Its sound came from on high. Like God, it was largely invisible, and it was brought into movement from a respectful distance via a bell rope. Bell ringing in these first centuries was the privilege of the priests – insofar as this obligatory effort multiple times per day might be considered a privilege. Like the silver trumpets that brought down the walls of Jericho in the Old Testament, the bronze bells were the voices that proclaimed the good news of the New Testament and vanquished evil. The bronze bell was a symbol for the steadfast preacher, and the clapper was his tongue. The yoke on which it was suspended was the cross on which Christ died, and the bell rope was the connection between heaven and earth. The three strands of the rope referred to the three-fold interpretation of the Holy Scriptures: the historical, the allegorical and the moral.

The blessing rite is documented for the first time in the old Spanish liturgy before the Arab invasion of 712, but it could be significantly older. It was an official church ceremony that was subject to fixed rules. Throughout the centuries, however, variants arose. The ritual exists yet today, albeit in a simplified form since the Second Vatican Council (1962-1965). Like the consecration of a new church, the blessing of bells was reserved to bishops. It consists of washing, various anointments and a blessing with incense. While psalm texts are sung, the bishop prepares for the washing of the bell. He pronounces an invocation over the salt and the water, blesses both, and adds the salt to the water. He then begins to wash the bell with the blessed water. The assisting priests continue the washing, and dry the bell with a pure linen cloth. Then follows the anointing with oil. The bishop applies holy anointing oil to the bell at places often designated with a cross cast into the bell. After a prayer, he anoints it with the same oil at seven places along the lower lip of the bell. Finally, he anoints the inside of the bell at four places with Holy Chrism. The symbolism clearly concerns the sacred numbers four and seven, that together with the first anointing with oil on the cross, make the number twelve. Finally, a vessel is placed under the bell from which

Blessing of a new bell by Monseigneur Honoré Van Waeyenbergh,
St. John Baptist Church, Leuven, Belgium, 16 October 1949

fragrant incense ascends. The incense fills the inside of the bell and ascends via the outer wall to heaven. Consecration of the bell gives it special powers: it will protect the community against thunder, lightning and hail, crashing stones and the burning bombs of the enemy.

The blessing of a bell is similar in a number of ways to the baptism ritual. During the blessing, the bell is protected against contact using a white garment that could be seen as a christening robe. It is given a name as well as a godfather and a godmother, generally people who contributed financially to its casting. The believing community in fact often spoke of the bell's baptism, as if it were a living being. The blessing was the only occasion on which bells were accessible to the public, before they disappeared into the obscurity of the towers. Yet they were almost always decorated with inscriptions, ornaments and images. The indication of their function confirmed the healing effects that were attributed to them. Bells always spoke in the first person. Many old bell inscriptions have survived, among others because they often were copied on the new bells that replaced the old ones. Moreover, over the centuries, historians and bell lovers have saved the inscriptions of bells that have disappeared in the meantime by impressing them into plaster or photographing them. These inscriptions and ornaments constitute an exceptionally rich and reliable source of information on the role played by bells in the society of their time. The best-known bell inscription reads as follows:

> VIVOS VOCO, MORTUOS PLANGO, FULGURA FRANGO
> *I call the living, I mourn the dead, I repel lightning*

The inscription became famous after Friedrich Schiller copied it from a cracked bell taken from the Swiss city of Schaffhausen, and in 1799 used it as motto for his poem *Das Lied von der Glocke*. The core functions of the church bell can be summarized in just a few words: calling, mourning and repelling. The bell called not only to prayer, but also to church attendance. Funeral tolling initially took place during the death throes of a confrere or parishioner, and was an appeal to pray for the salvation of the dying. In later times, funeral tolling sounded only after the death, and the nature of the toll made it clear whether the deceased was a man, woman, child or cleric. From here developed the profitable system where the relatives of the deceased paid for the duration and the volume of the toll, and thus indirectly for the salvation of the deceased. Thus, the sound of the death bells underscored one final time the inequality between people. The third core function, ringing to warn of a storm, was used especially in rural areas, where storms could destroy harvests. When thunderstorms approached, church bells were aggressively sounded to repel the clouds via their deterrent sound or due to the air vibrations produced by the vibrating bronze. There are stories of residents of neighboring towns competing to force the thunderstorms to the other village via their respective bells. And also stories of bell-ringers who were struck by lightning while ringing the bells, since a tower is not a safe place to be during a thunderstorm. Some towns continued to sound bells against hail and lightning until well into the 20th century. The Church itself did not object to this custom, as witnessed by the bell inscriptions and the mention of ringing during storms in the blessing rite. The protective power of bells also covered other dangers. Starting with the major plague in the 14th century, plague bells were hung in the towers to purify the air. Sometimes sage leaves were cast in these bells. Sage has a purifying effect, and it was believed that the herb was beneficial against the plague. Often pilgrim badges made of lead and bearing likenesses of saints were used as a mold for bell decorations. For that matter, the pilgrims who crisscrossed Europe in large numbers during the Middle Ages often purchased little bells while on pilgrimage that would protect them during their return journey.[7] The age-old faith in the magic power of sonorous bronze continued unabated.

Bell and devil of course were sworn enemies. Occasionally the devil would steal a bell or attempt to prevent it from being blessed. Bells, however, resisted every attempt to assail their sacred status: they began to ring of their own accord, flew through the air only to fall in a hole, or were sucked into the depths – together with the cart – during hostile transport. Numerous were the wells, peatlands and bogs from which the local residents thought they heard bells *softly* chiming, most clearly on Christmas Eve. In Europe of Bells, there were almost as many bells tolling underground as above ground.

Tolling for political ends

Between the 11th and 15th century, the Angelus – the best-known Christian toll – emerged in three phases. The Angelus originated in the fight between Christians and Muslims. In 1096, Pope Urban II called upon the people of Christian Europe to pray every day at the signal of the curfew bell for the success of the crusade, the first of a series of military expeditions to liberate the holy City of Jerusalem from the Muslims. Two centuries later, a morning prayer to Mary emerged that found its context in a general desire for peace. People prayed for a Truce of God, a period of peace amid the successive periods of wars and conflicts. The name of Mary appeared more frequently on bells than formerly, and the most used bell inscription of the 12th to the 14th century reads as follows:

O Rex glori(a)e veni cum pace.
O King of Glory, Come with Peace.

Finally, Pope Callixtus III introduced the ringing of the Angelus at noon. The Ottoman army had conquered Constantinople in 1453, and in June 1456 stood before the gates of Belgrade. At that moment, a star appeared in the heavens that later would be called Halley's Comet. Both parties saw in the phenomenon a bad sign: the Ottomans saw a cross, the Christians an Ottoman sword. According to tradition, Pope Callixtus excommunicated the comet and ordered all bells to sound in order to repel the heavenly body. In fact, on 29 June, he introduced tolling at noon to call the believing community to prayer in the face of the Turkish threat. Their prayers were heard, and the Ottoman siege of Belgrade failed. In remote regions of Europe, the papal appeal was heard only after the Turkish defeat, such that tolling at noon was interpreted in these places as a call to give prayers of thanks. This tolling at noon became known by the name *Turkish Bell*.

In the 16th century, morning, noon and evening prayer were combined into the Angelus, which had a specific ringing pattern. First, a light bell was struck in three series of three. The intervals between these series gave sufficient time to pray a Hail Mary or an Our Father. Finally, the Angelus was prayed to the tolling of a heavier bell. In Christian symbolism, tolling at noon referred to the incarnation of Jesus, the evening tolling to his suffering and death, and the morning tolling to his resurrection. Despite the disappearance of the military-political occasion for the prayer, ringing the Angelus remained a strong custom in Catholic regions, among others because the accompanying prayer was encouraged by the granting of indulgences. Around the middle of the 20th century, a prayer during the Angelus was still good for a shortening of one's stay in purgatory by 100 days. A second factor behind the continuance of the Angelus, certainly in rural areas, is the fact that the three tolling and prayer times coincided with the beginning of the working day, the lunch break, and the end of the working day. The Angelus marked the transition between work and rest, and at these moments there was time for a prayer. Thus, the Angelus set the rhythm of daily devotion as well as daily work. In many Catholic churches, the Angelus is still sounded three times per day. Fortunately, in the meantime the Angelus has lost its original militant and Islamophobic connotation.

The tolling of the ancient canonical prayer times could also be the occasion for militant action. On Easter Monday 1282, during the ringing of Vespers, a revolt broke out in Palermo against the French occupying forces. All who were unable to pronounce the word *Cicero* without accent, were killed. In the night of 17/18 May 1302, insurgents in Bruges, at the sounding of Matins, killed all the French encamped in the city except for the lucky ones who were able to pronounce the expression *Schild en*

Jean-François Millet, *L'Angélus*, between 1857 and 1859

vriend or 'Shield and friend'. And in the night of 23/24 August 1572, the ringing of Matins in the Paris church of St. Germain l'Auxerrois gave the starting signal for the notorious St. Bartholomew's Day massacre in which thousands of Huguenots in Paris – and later in the rest of France – were killed.

The Sicilian Vespers, the Bruges Matins and the Paris St. Bartholomew's Day massacre are bloody illustrations of the use of prayer tolling for secular ends. More generally, the canonical time signals quickly came to play a central role in the organization of the medieval city.

CHAPTER 3

The time of man

A day in the city

Medieval cities were more lively than their contemporary counterparts. They were small and densely populated, animals and people intermingled, horses with cart rattled over the streets, street vendors and market traders loudly touted their goods, and bells sounded everywhere. In the beginning, these were almost exclusively the bells of churches, abbeys and monasteries that rang out in endless repetition the cycle of canonical tolling. The city dwellers probably no longer answered the call to prayer en masse, but they nevertheless paid attention to the Benedictine tolling. The fixed pattern of bell signals provided citizens with anchor points to organize their day. And city governments used the bell signals to organize their residents.

In obtaining this authority, the city had to compete with two countervailing powers: the feudal lord and the Church. Most cities in the Low Countries received town privileges between the 11th and 13th century. These included the right to use bell signals to organize the activities of citizens and visitors. After the official granting, a city still had to implement the bell right in practice, which was not self-evident in view of the de facto bell monopoly of the clergy. Initially, the city government often only received authorization from the Church for additional tolling of church bells if the frequency of the canonical hours were not capable of handling all of the city's functions. Sometimes one or more city bells were hung in church towers and were sounded with the permission of the church leaders. As a city became more important, or was able to exert more independence with respect to Church and monarch, it hung its own bells at locations to which only its appointees had access: city gates and city towers.

City towers were present throughout Europe, but the city tower par excellence, the belfry, developed only in Flanders, Artois and Picardy. Sometimes the belfry was integrated into a building with a public function, such as the town hall or the clothmakers' hall, but the purest form was the freestanding tower. The city charters were preserved in the body of the belfry and the city bells hung in the top. The belfry also served as lookout for the city guard. Hence, the belfry contained the eyes and the voice of the city. Each city used its own ringing code, which generally was a mixture of ecclesiastical and civil time signals. Nevertheless, the working day proceeded everywhere according to a similar pattern.[8] Matins was sounded a few hours before sunrise. Most citizens could sleep further, but for some professions such as the copper-founders and butchers, this was the signal to start the working day. At sunrise, the Prime bell – or its civil counterparts the gate bell or work bell – was sounded to start the day for all. The city gates were opened, fires could be kindled in the houses, the merchants displayed their goods, and the craftsmen went to work. In the winter, all could sleep somewhat longer, since the day started only at 7 a.m. Inns opened their doors at the signal of Terce around 9 a.m. At mid-day, the work bell signaled break time. The afternoon shift was announced by the work bell or by the bell that announced None (hence the terms *noon* and *afternoon*). Shorter hours were worked on the day before a public holiday, and the None bell signaled the end of the working day. Most residents stopped their day's work at sunset, when Vespers or the last work bell was sounded. When the gate bell was rung, the city gates were closed. In Antwerp, the gate bell was called the *thief bell*, as a signal for thieves to leave the city in time. Curfew was sounded a few hours later. Fires had to be covered or put out, and all professional activities ceased. Curfew must have been one of the oldest bell instructions. It is documented in England in the 11th century. Around this time, taverns closed their doors and innkeepers reported to the city magistrate with the night's guest list. When the curfew bell was tolled, citizens could no longer appear on the street unless unarmed, with uncovered face and carrying a lantern. The second signal of the curfew bell was the sign for general rest, after which only the footsteps and the hand bell of the night watch were heard in the streets.

Tolling for special events

In addition to the sounding of bells at regular times, bells were also tolled for special occasions. When the city government had news to announce, it rang the Bancloque, which was always the heaviest – and thus the loudest – bell. The Bancloque or *campana banni* was the externalization of the *bannum*, the right of the city government to convene the public. The Bancloque could signal good or bad news, more often the latter. The medieval city after all was continually threatened by fire and violence. A watchman on the city tower would scan the city day and night on the lookout for possible calamity. To announce that all was safe – and that he was still awake – he would blow a horn or clarion at fixed intervals. The sound of a horn was more difficult to imitate by a possible infiltrated enemy than the sound of a bell. If the guard noted a hostile signal, he tolled the Bancloque to call all able-bodied citizens to arm themselves and assemble for the fight. Sometimes the Bancloque was sounded to signal danger, and in Germanic regions, it was called the *Sturmglocke* or *stormklok*. In Roman territories it was called *tocsin* or alarm bell. The second great fear of the medieval city was fire. Most houses in the medieval city were made of wood, and a house fire often became a city fire. The Bancloque summoned residents to join forces to fight the fire, in the interest of the community and themselves. In its function as fire bell, the Bancloque was usually not swung but rather struck. The nervous rhythm of the clapper pulled against the bell wall with a cord or a leather belt was for the public a clear sign that immediate action was needed.

The Bancloque also convened the population in situations other than emergencies. Its toll was a formality that gave decrees legal force after their public reading aloud. The Bancloque invited citizens to public executions, not for the spectacle, but because of the *exemplum*, a demonstration of the fate of residents who violated the law. Citizens who responded late or not at all to the call of the Bancloque risked a penalty or even prison. This also meant that its sound must be audible throughout the territory of the city. For this reason, in 1459 the city government of Antwerp replaced its Bancloque *Orida* ('the gruesome') from 1316 with a new Bancloque Gabriel, which weighed 4,840 kg. Three men were needed to ring it. As the city continued to grow and became one of the largest cities north of the Alps, Carolus was acquired in 1507. The new bell weighed 6.5 tons and required 16 men to ring.

The Bancloque also tolled for joyful events: a princely birth, the election of a new pope, a victory by the ruling monarch in this or that battle, or a visit to the city by the monarch. The admonishing timbre of the Bancloque was then accompanied by the cheerful jingle emitted from all the towers in the city. The collective toll from all corners of the city center gave an extra festive feel, and the more important the event, the more exuberantly and longer the bells were sounded, sometimes for days on end. In contrast to the other tolls, the festive ringing was not a call to action, but only to collective joy. Royal deaths in turn led to days of tolling for the salvation of the important deceased.

Bell-ringers used a special technique to give the collective toll an extra dimension. Instead of swinging the bell back and forth, they attached straps or cords to the underside of the clappers and pulled these against the stationary bells. While the striking of a single bell was the agreed alarm signal in the case of fire, the striking of multiple bells created an exceptionally festive effect. A clever bell-ringer was capable of sounding four bells at a time: he pulled two cords with his hands, while ringing two additional bells with cords attached to his feet. The combination of swinging and striking gave rise to two rhythmic systems that sounded together. When swinging, bell-ringers had no influence on the tempo, which depended solely on the mass of the bell. With striking, however, the bell-ringer had full control of the clapper and he

A chimer with four bells, represented on a capital of the
St. Austrégésile Church in Mouchan, Southern France

could add rhythmic variations as he saw fit. The striking of multiple bells was called *beyaerden* (chiming) and the bell-ringers who used this technique are referred to in the archives as *beyaerders*. City authorities gave the command to *luyden ende beyaerden*, (swing and chime) alternately or simultaneously. Beyaerders were not musicians: they were bell-ringers, tower guards, sextons and gravediggers. Smaller towns also engaged in chiming, usually on church feast days and for commemorative Masses for the dead who had donated an annuity to the parish.

The archives in the principalities of Brabant and Flanders in the Southern Netherlands mention chiming from approximately 1350, but the technique is at least a century older in this region, and was used throughout Europe. In orthodox areas, for that matter, it was the only technique for sounding bells, since swinging was unknown there.

Due to the swinging, striking and chiming in the various towers, the heavens above the late medieval cities and towns must have been saturated with bell sounds. While not every signal was relevant to every resident, all experienced in the same way the bell sounds that emerged from all corners of the city and gave it its spatiality and dynamism. The population not only must have had a high tolerance for this superabundance of public sounds, they undoubtedly also possessed excellent powers of discernment. Despite the fact that bells often combined different functions, citizens managed to flawlessly interpret each sound of a bell based on the combination of pitch, time of day and the sounding technique used. An accurate interpretation for that matter was vital, because the voice of the bell was law.

New bell casting techniques

The intense use of bells left many traces in the accounts of cities and churches. Numerous are the payments for new swinging ropes, ball bearings for yokes, and new bells to replace cracked ones. Hence, a flourishing market in bells developed in the Late Middle Ages, and bell casting outgrew the walls of the monasteries where it was practiced in the early Middle Ages. Bell casting was a city craft, and practitioners continuously improved their casting technique in the face of the higher demands that were placed on bells. Their sound volume – and thus their mass – had to evolve as cities grew, and the required harmony when multiple bells were rung or chimed placed greater demands on the tonal purity of the bell.

Between the 12th and the 15th century, bell casting underwent a number of important innovations.[9] A new type of bell emerged in the 12th century: the *sugarloaf model*. In sharp contrast to the somewhat plump beehive shaped bells of the previous centuries, the sugarloaf model was very slim: the bells had narrow shoulders, a strongly conic shaped body, and a wide sound rim. This radical change in form probably was the result of an innovation in the casting technique that occurred after Theophilus wrote his treatise on bell casting. Where Theophilus formed the false bell in wax, a short time later this was done with less expensive clay, just like the core and the cope. Only on the outside wall of the false bell was a thin layer of wax still applied. A disadvantage of the new technique was that the false bell did not automatically melt, but had to be removed after the core and cope had hardened. For this, the cope had to be lifted temporarily, which was easier in the case of a strong conic form than with the wide, almost vertical beehive shape. The sugarloaf shape remained in our regions only until the 14th century, but in a number of Southern European countries such as Italy and Spain, it remains the dominant bell type today. This can clearly be seen in the shape of the bells, often visibly hanging in the tower windows, and it can also be heard in their short, dry sound.

Another new bell model emerged in Western and Northern Europe in the 14th century. This was the so-called *gothic profile*, which had a squatter form than the sugarloaf model: the width of the bell became larger than its height. It received wide shoulders that seamlessly transitioned to a strong sloping waist; the waist broadened at the bottom into a substantial sound rim. The elegant gothic profile would become the prototype for the later Western European bell profiles.

As long as bell-founders continued to create molds with a chisel on a spit, there could be no talk of a standardized and qualitative profile. This often led to

Bell-founder with a couple of clients. Behaim Codex Kraków, c. 1505

asymmetric bells that resulted in audible beats when sounded. Beats are quickly changing intensities in sound that are heard as a 'wah wah' effect. The solution to this quality problem came from of an unexpected corner: weapon making, especially cannon foundry. Explorers brought gunpowder from China to Europe around 1300, and canons were produced in the West not long thereafter. These were made by bell-founders. Bronze after all appeared to be the most suitable material for the production of artillery, on the understanding that bronze cannons contained 10% tin instead of the bell's 20%. Higher levels of tin would make the bronze harder, and less flexible, and thus the cannon could explode under pressure. With a view toward maximum accuracy, the mold for the barrel was symmetrically modeled using a wooden template. Presumably – because there is no absolute proof – this innovation found its way from artillery making to bell casting. Close inspection of historical bells reveals that from the middle of the 14th century, most bells were formed using templates. While being rotated on the spit, the clay core was finished with an inner template that had the form of the inside of the bell. The false bell was added to this, which in turn was formed to the measurements of the outer template that represented the outer profile of the bell. The use of fixed templates of various sizes was a first step in the direction of the industrialization of the craft of bell-founding. From now on, good bells could be copied, and it became possible to cast bells with a predictable pitch. In the meantime, bell-founders had also acquired the practice of no longer forming wax letters and ornamental bands by hand, but casting them in wooden molds, so that here again, pure handwork made way for standardization.

The last major change to the bell casting process gradually took place in the 15th and 16th centuries. As the bells to be cast became larger, it became technically more difficult to form them on a horizontal spit. So bell-founders created them on a vertical axis, around which the template rotated. The new technique had the big advantage that the bell mold did not need to be tilted regularly, and it could be constructed in the casting pit itself.

The bell-founder in action

Together with the bell's increasing weight, the problem of transporting the bell from foundry to customer also increased. Hence, bell-founders began to cast their products close to their final destination. The material for the casting was purchased directly by the church or city government, and expense records give us accurate insight into what a bell-founder needed to complete his work. The customer had cartloads of clay brought in for the molds, piles of bricks for the construction of the oven and the inside of the core, hundreds of eggs with which a paste was made to isolate the clay of the core and the false bell from each other, hemp and iron hoops to reinforce the cope, branches and charcoal to keep the oven burning, strips of bacon to keep the boiling bronze pure and liquid, candles to allow work to continue at night, and wine and beer for the bell-founder and his helpers. Not mentioned in the accounts, probably because available free of charge, was the horse manure used to thin the clay. If a new bell was replacing an existing one, for example because it had cracked, this bronze was used first. When the new bell had to be larger than the previous one, or if no existing bell was available, a collection was made, often with horse and cart, to gather material from the local population. After all, who wouldn't want to contribute their tin, copper or bronze articles to the collective voice of their city or parish? If there was insufficient existing material, new ore was purchased. The best tin came from English Cornwall, while copper was transported from among others Germany and Sweden.

When all the material was on site, the actual work could begin, and the public was allowed to witness the genesis of their new bell. The bell-founder and his team of local helpers constructed a temporary bell foundry in the churchyard, preferably as close as possible to the tower. A casting pit was excavated and an oven built alongside the graves. Then the bell mold was constructed, on a spit or directly in the casting pit. This preparatory work could take weeks. When the bell mold had disappeared into the ground and the earth had been firmly tamped, the oven was ignited to heat the collected metals into liquid bronze. The workmen operating the bellows to bring the oven to the required temperature were lavishly foreseen with beverages. When the bronze was liquid, the moment was right for the casting, and the assembled community looked on as their new bell was born. According to a stubborn tradition, the sound of a bell could be improved if precious metals were added to the bell metal, and wealthy spectators were known to throw gold and silver coins in the sprue. In fact, gold and silver do not have a favorable effect on the sound of bronze, but the dignitaries at least were able to foster the illusion of donating to a good cause. The liquid bronze found its way from the sprue to the bell mold underground. If everything went according to plan, the public would break into the Te Deum out of gratitude for a successful casting. After the casting, the bell would cool in the ground for several days before it was excavated. Inspection could reveal defects: sometimes the metal used was impure – certainly after a local collection – and sometimes the bronze was insufficiently fluid during the casting. Hence, the bronze could be porous or contain casting defects, with possible negative consequences for the sound of the new bell. The risk of a failed casting or a rejected bell always lay with the bell-founder, who was required to redo his work at his own expense.

The most important bell-founder in the latter days of the Middle Ages was the Dutchman Geert van Wou (ca. 1450-1527). Van Wou was from 's-Hertogenbosch, but

Salvator, represented on the bourdon Geert van Wou cast for the Utrecht Dom Tower (1505)

established his foundry in Kampen in Gelderland. His name is especially associated with the impressive peals he chiefly delivered to German-speaking areas. His masterpiece was the Gloriosa for the cathedral of the central German city of Erfurt. He cast the bell on the Domberg during the night of 7/8 July 1497. At 11 tons, it was the largest bell of its time. The scholar Athanasius Kircher called it *omnium campanarum regina*, the queen of all bells. The casting work of the Gloriosa is magnificent, and its full, dark timbre with strike note 'e' echoes long in the air and the mind of the listener.

To experience the total sound of a European city five centuries ago, you need to visit Utrecht in the Netherlands. In 1505, Geert van Wou delivered a series of thirteen heavy swinging and chime bells for the Utrecht cathedral tower, together good for 62,128 pounds.[10] The bells spanned one and a half octaves. The ambitious intention can be read on the wall of Salvator, the 16,454-pound bourdon or bass bell:

SALVATOR DICOR CIEO TEMPLUMQUE FORUMQUE AETHERA
TARTAREAS AC STYGIAS TENEBRAS VENTOS ASTRIGEROS CLANGORE
SONI DIAPASON PERQUE NEMUS SED MENTES JUVENUMQUE
SENUM SUM PENETRANS VOCE SOLIDA DULCORE LATENTI TALIS
HONOR NEC POST CONDITA TECTA FUIT
GERHARDUS DE WOU ME FECIT ANNO DOMINI MCCCCCV

Redeemer is my name. With the sound of my fundamental, I shake church and world, heaven and the icy and dark underworld, the star-bearing winds and the forests; but with my heavy voice, permeated with hidden loveliness, I also penetrate the minds of young and old. There has been no glory such as this since the time houses were built.
Geert van Wou made me in the year of our Lord 1505.

The heaviest six bells have been preserved, and the seven others, which in the 17th century were recast into a new carillon, were replaced by modern replicas in 1982. The thirteen bells are regularly rung manually by members of the Utrecht Bell Ringers Guild. It is scarcely conceivable that the overwhelming sonority of these thirty tons of bronze finds its deepest origin in the humble crotal bell that mimicked the seeds of the pomegranate.

A time was specified for everything in the medieval city, and this time was marked by bells. But how did the ringers know when to sound the bells? Who told *them* the time?

CHAPTER 4

The bondage of time

Clocks in monasteries and cathedrals

The increasing use of bells contributed to a new experience of day and night. The gradual lapse of time that was principally determined by the course of the sun, made way for punctual time indication to the rhythm of the bells. The bell-ringers, however, needed the help of sundials or water clocks to know when it was time to ring the bells. Especially the ringing of Matins was a thankless task. Since the bell had to be sounded in the middle of the night, the bell-ringing monk could not make use of a sundial. Moreover, he himself needed an audible signal to wake up. This problem was solved by the monastery alarm, which sounded a bell at the appropriate hour. The earliest monastery alarms were water clocks that generated an audible signal. At the end of the 13th century, however, a revolutionary new timekeeper emerged: the clockwork.

This new invention used the energy of a weight suspended on a rope. The rope was coiled around a pulley on which the escape wheel, a vertical gear, was mounted. When the escape wheel rotated, it caused the cams, axles, levers and gears to move, which in turn controlled the time signals such as rotating hands or a struck bell. To indicate the time, the escape wheel did not need to rotate continuously, but rather in small, discrete steps. To this end, its movement was kept under control by the teeth of the escapement. In the oldest timepieces, the escapement was a so-called verge. A vertical shaft next to the escape wheel rotated to the left and right, due to two teeth on the spindle blocking the escape wheel briefly and then releasing it again. The familiar ticking sound of mechanical clocks was caused by the engagement of the escape wheel with the teeth. Escape wheel and verge functioned in perfect symbiosis: the verge caused the escape wheel to rotate forward bit by bit, and at the same time, the discrete movements of the escape wheel ensured that the verge continued to oscillate. The rate of this movement determined the rate of the clock and was regulated by the foliot or balance. This was a horizontal bar located at the top of the verge. A small weight hung on each of the two arms of the foliot. These could be shifted in or out by the clock keeper to adjust the speed of the clock.

Two clockworks, one of which with a forestroke of five bells. Detail from a French version of Heinrich Suso's *Horologium Sapientiae*, 2nd half of the 15th century.

The mechanical clock is one of the most marvelous devices invented by humanity. The dream of the *perpetuum mobile*, a device that stays in motion forever and generates its own energy, was almost achieved. The clock's only limitation was the length of the rope on which the weight hung. When the rope with the weight was fully unrolled, the human energy of the tower watchman was needed to rewind it around the pulley.

The oldest indications of clockworks come from English cathedrals in the last quarter of the 13th century. The clockwork quickly received a place in allegorical literature. Dante in his *Divine Comedy* described a heavenly wheel in which the holy ones were seated, an experience like a watch with cogs that produces heavenly sounds: *tin tin sonando con sì dolce nota* [11]. In 1334, the German monk and mystic Heinrich Suso wrote a contemplative booklet titled *Horologium Sapientiae*, 'The Clock of Wisdom', in which he described a splendid clock with bells that emitted a heavenly sound. These enchanting timepieces were not simply poetic or mystical fantasies. The clockwork had quickly developed from a simple alarm clock to a miracle of refinement that informed the viewer of the time of day, Church feast days, the phases of the moon, the position of constellations and planets, and much more. Levers and cogs brought to life figures from biblical history and the world of mythology. The ingenious mechanism was seen as a representation of the cosmic clockwork of the Creator. And time was elevated to music, since bells played a melody every hour.

The earliest reliable mention of an existing melody linked to a clock dates back to 1404. In this year, in the monastery of Windesheim close to Deventer in the Netherlands, Brother Hendrik Loder constructed a clock with seven bells and installed it on the staircase to the dormitory, just in front of the sexton's room. With the help of an iron wheel, each morning the chime would play the Gregorian sequence *Sancti Spiritus Adsit nobis gratia* to awake the monks and place them in the appropriate state of mind.[12]

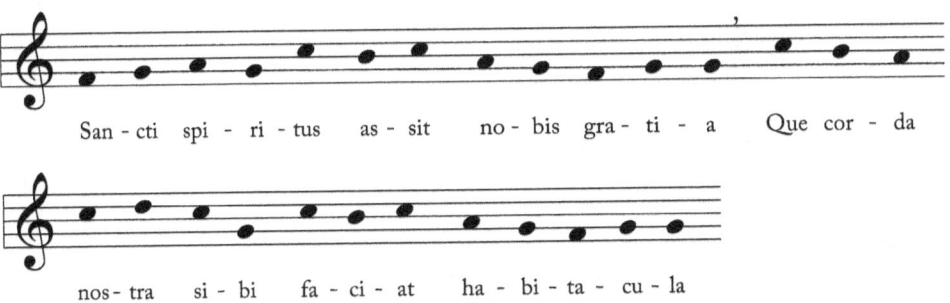

The extension of a monastery alarm to include a musical chime is not illogical, because at the time Hendrik Loder manufactured his clock, monks had been playing music on bells for four centuries.[13] Dozens of miniatures from the 9th to the 15th century depict chime players sounding a series of three to eight bells with hammers, sometimes solo, sometimes together with singers, an organ or string instruments. King David often plays the chime in the first letters of Psalm 80 and Psalm 150, with one of the verses reading: *Laudate eum in cymbalis bene sonantibus* ('praise Him with harmonious cymbals'). A cymbalum originally referred to a cymbal or copper rod, but later also came to mean 'bell', and the plural cymbala thus meant 'chime'. Cymbala players can be seen on the Romanesque and early Gothic capitals of the cathedrals of Chartres and Autun, and the abbey churches of Cluny and Vézelay.

The cymbala also existed in reality. From the 11th to the 14th century, monks wrote treatises with theoretical observations and practical tips on the sizes and weights of cymbala bells. The use of cymbala in churches and monasteries was a pan-European phenomenon. Since the most recent miniatures with cymbalas date from the 15th century, the room instrument presumably died out around this time. The sole specimens that remain are two series of seven and four bells that were excavated in 1906 in the cemetery of the Church of the Nativity in Bethlehem.[14] Many questions remain concerning the use of the cymbala. While the instrument is an extinct offshoot of the carillon family tree, it probably inspired the earliest clockmakers to give their refined mechanisms a musical voice. The vaulted ceilings of the late medieval churches and monasteries must have been ideal acoustic environments for the sound of cymbalas and clockworks that musically decorated the passage of time.

Measuring time in the open air

The mechanical signaling of time in open air came later than it did in the monasteries, and initially was primarily a phenomenon associated with cities. In the countryside, nature continued to function as a time indicator. Moreover, agriculture was less time-based than was work in the city. The tower clock brought with it the advantage of the objective working day, and broke the power and the arbitrariness of the work bell, which was under the control of the guild.[15] In addition to industry, trade was also guided by the clock. The emerging capitalism in the late medieval cities made time a scarce commodity, which brought with it the necessity to measure it. When some time later, the financial markets of Bruges, Antwerp and Amsterdam emerged, bell and clock were essential parts of the trading in shares – as they still are today.

Thanks to its objective regularity, the mechanical clock brought about a revolution in the experience of time: the transition from unequal to equal hours. For thousands of years, humanity had lived according to natural time, which divided the time between sunrise and sunset into 12 hours. For this reason, an hour in the summer was approximately twice as long as an hour in the winter. With the clockwork, time became punctual. This term is perhaps not well chosen when referring to the oldest tower clocks, which were still very inaccurate. Deviations of a half hour per day were more the rule than the exception. Consequently, most towers were equipped with a

The jaquemarts Manten and Kalle striking the time on the Halle Tower in Kortrijk. Free reconstruction by Frans Van Immerseel from 1961.

sundial with which the clock could be calibrated regularly. The tower watchman raised the weights of the clock a few times per day, and a clockmaker or blacksmith would regularly visit the tower. City accounts make continuous mention of maintenance and repair work being done on the clocks. The clock would only gain a certain degree of precision when Christiaan Huygens obtained a patent in 1657 on the pendulum as alternative to the foliot in regulating the speed of the clockwork.

Despite its teething problems, the tower clock quickly spread throughout Europe. The first clocks in towers must have been produced in England and Northern Italy. The technology of the tower clock evolved less quickly than that of the refined monastery clocks. The first clocks were small, and indicated the exact hour to the tower watchman so that he could strike the hour bell at the correct time. After a time, clockworks could be made that directly set in motion a large hammer, as this was also done in the room clocks. The clockwork grew in size, since it had to be robust enough to lift and release the hammer. The tower watchman was dismissed of his task of striking the hour, and from the middle of the 14th century, he was replaced in many cities by a robot that struck the hour clock on the outside of the tower.[16] Most robots were made of wood and had the form of a man in military attire, but biblical or picturesque figures can also be seen such as Adam and Eve, a savage and a fool. The best-known bell-striker or *jaquemart* was Manten on the Belfry of Kortrijk. After the Battle of Westrozebeke in 1382, Burgundian Duke Philip the Bold had it and the clock removed from the tower and taken as spoils of war to Dijon, where an updated version is still active today. There are various theories concerning the origin of the word *jaquemart*, with the combination of Jacques with *marteau* ('hammer') perhaps being the most plausible. In England they are called clock-jacks. Jaquemarts appeared in most regions of Europe, in tower clocks as well as astronomical clocks.

The giant tower clocks still had no hands on the outside of the tower, and in the beginning, the sounding of the hour was their only time signal. For this reason, in some places the sounding of the hour was repeated to give local residents two opportunities per hour to count the strikes. Later a warning signal was introduced: the forestroke. The clock first activated a lighter bell to draw attention to the coming striking of the hour. An undated bell hangs in St. Martin's Basilica in the Brabant city of Halle with the name Katharina, which introduces itself as follows:

> SI TER ADDIS HORA TIBI VENIT HUC
> *Count to three, and you will hear the hour.*

Whenever Katharina sounded three times, the residents of Halle could prepare themselves for the coming sounding of the hour.[17] Gradually a code developed to also indicate every quarter hour. One strike was given on the first quarter, two strikes on the half hour, three strikes on the third quarter, and on the hour, four strikes were sounded, followed by the sounding of the hour on a larger bell. During the course of the 14th century, the forestroke was expanded to two bells in some cities. The highest bell was struck first, followed by the lowest, such that 'ding-dong' was sounded. When the two forestroke bells were approximately two notes or a third apart, a pleasant, consonant motif was sounded that reminded one of the cry of the cuckoo.

The cuckoo motif developed out of an archetypal time and warning signal, with the most striking manifestation being the cuckoo clock that emerged around 1730 in the Black Forest. The motif can still be heard today in doorbells, accompanying announcements from speakers, and as siren on ambulances.

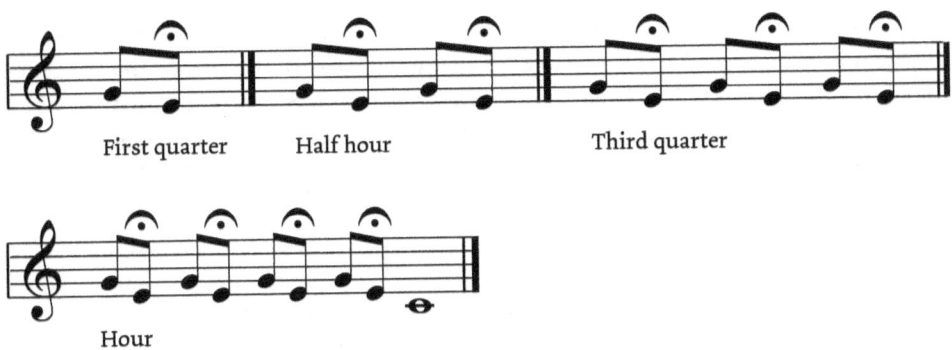

The signal becomes music

In the Low Countries, the cuckoo motif was not the end of the story. From 1372, the Mechelen St. Rumbold's Cathedral sounded a forestroke of three bells, which of course offered more melodic possibilities than the cuckoo.[18] The number of forestroke bells increased gradually during the following century. In 1479, Geert van Wou added six bells to the clock in the Dom Tower of Utrecht, which was enough to play existing melodies. The earliest report of a bell melody in open air, however, comes from the Norbertine Park Abbey close to Leuven. In 1479, Abbot Theodoor van Tuldel had an *antiludium* or forestroke installed in the church tower that each hour played the Gregorian hymn *Inviolata, integra et casta es Maria*, 'Mary, inviolate, spotless and pure art thou'. Since the first phrase of the Marian hymn needs only the notes c, d, e and f, the forestroke probably contained only four bells.[19]

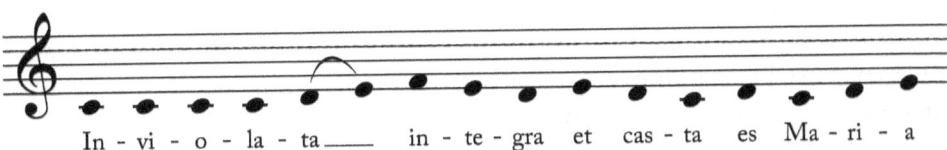

Time had become music, and thanks to the new forestroke, the abbey more than ever was bathed in the aura of the sacred. The musical information of the first outdoor forestrokes was contained on a number of parallel mounted wooden wheels, with one wheel needed per bell. Cams were located on the outer edge of each wheel that during rotation lifted the hammers and let them fall against the bell. By 1501, it was possible to program two melodies per hour. In this year, clockmaster Jan Van Spiere improved the forestroke on the town hall of Oudenaarde, which then probably contained seven bells. On the hour, the sequence for Pentecost *Veni Spiritus Sancte* was sounded, and on the half hour, *Peccatores* was played, by which probably was meant the sequence for Easter *Victimae Paschali Laudes*. Five years later, Van Spiere expanded the forestroke to eight bells, and *Salve Regina* was played on the hour. *Peccatores* continued to be played on the half hour.[20] In 1515, Van Spiere went a step further. For the Church of Our Lady in Deinze, he delivered two *wielen* ('wheels') for the forestroke. The first wheel played music for the Easter Season: *Regina Coeli* on the hour, and *Victimae Paschali Laudes* on the half hour. The second wheel contained a program with music for Advent: *Conditor alme siderum* for the hour and *Benedicamus Domino* for the half hour.[21] The separate wheels per bell thus made way for a wider barrel with pins for all bells. The musical program could be changed by exchanging the barrels.

The atmosphere in cities in the Southern Netherlands gradually was filled with music that accompanied the progression of time, for the moment still with a modest number of 4 to 10 *appeelkens* or alerting bells. They were called *scellen* or *clockxkins* and were rather small bells that formed an independent series in addition to the heavier swinging bells. In both abbeys and city towers, the forestrokes played Gregorian melodies, which were well suited to a limited number of bells due to their restricted tonal range. What's more, their monophony, modal tonalities and quiet melodic progression fit perfectly the musical limitations of the bells with their strong overtones and unavoidable decay time. The most important motivation for this choice of repertoire, however, was not musical, but spiritual in nature. Citizens of the Late Middle Ages believed that they would achieve eternal salvation more quickly if they could come in contact with the sacred while on earth. They prayed in front of the images of saints and touched them, they traversed Europe on pilgrimages, and even buried their dead as close as possible to – or even in – the church. Church music on bells could now immerse an entire city in a sacred atmosphere, and served to teach and edify its residents.

After the introduction of the tower clock around 1300, the manual sounding of time was, strictly speaking, no longer needed for civil and Church use. Thus one might expect that the acoustic landscape in the European cities would become more structured and sober. The opposite appeared to be the case: bell-ringers continued to ring the gate, vesper and other bells, and the Angelus enjoyed rising popularity. Moreover, bell signals not based on time such as the Bancloque and alarm bell remained necessary, and beyaerders continued to indulge themselves at Church and secular events. And the musical forestroke was added in the Low Countries along the North Sea around 1500. The carillon was not far away.

PART TWO

The old carillon art

CHAPTER 5

A new musical instrument

Making music with bells

In March 1478, the residents of the Northern French – but at the time Flemish – city of Dunkirk heard something very special. The Bruges poet and chronicler Anthonis De Roovere recounts: 'At this time, a young bell-ringer by the name of Jan van Bevere lived in Dunkirk. He played a variety of existing songs, hymns, sequences, a Kyrie Eleison and all the ecclesiastical chants on his bells. Never before had something like this been heard: it was a great innovation in honor of God.'[22] Thus, Jan van Bevere must have been a bell-ringer whose chiming technique was so good that he could play existing melodies on his own. This would only have been possible if he had at least 6 to 8 bells and a construction that brought together the clapper ropes. De Roovere provides no more details, hence it is not certain that Van Bevere was already making music on a 'real' baton keyboard, an essential element of the carillon as a music instrument. What is important, however, is that the author describes the playing of existing melodies as an innovation.

In Antwerp as well, music hung in the air at that time. Around 1480, the north tower of the Church of our Lady was high enough to accommodate church bells. A rhymed chronicle by a monk from St. Michael's Abbey in Antwerp states that the activity of *beijaerden* began in 1480, and that it was something that was learned from a fool from Aalst who would have invented this manner of playing.[23] While the term 'fool' was used often at the time, among others in the popular jesters literature, the story quickly spread that the musical instrument typical of the Low Countries was invented by a man from Aalst who was not in full possession of his faculties.[24] This story had become so popular in the 18th century that Utrecht carillonneur Johan Fischer felt obliged to comment in detail on the story and relativize it in the introduction to his *Verhandeling van de klokken en het klokke-spel [Treatise on bells and bell playing]*.[25] The strength of the myth should not blind us to what actually took place around 1480. As was the case in the message from Dunkirk, the Antwerp chronicle clearly speaks of an innovation. What's more, there are indications that the man from Aalst introduced his new playing technique in several locations. In the spring of 1483, he probably was active in Hulst, a city less than twenty miles west of Antwerp. In fact, on 1 May of that year, the authorities paid an allowance to Jan, the *bayaerdere* of Aalst, for providing initiation and training to local *bayaerdere* Cornelis Praet.[26]

The above-mentioned chronicle from St. Michael's Abbey in Antwerp also includes some technical information. In an entry under the year 1482, it was stated that in Antwerp, people had begun playing bells by pulling ropes with batons.[27] The mention of the term 'batons' suggests the presence of a keyboard, which is supported by the fact that on 30 December 1482, the church government appointed a certain Eliseus as *beyaerder* or chimer.[28] A formal appointment meant that chiming had become a skill that could no longer be exercised by one or more bell-ringers. It is not certain whether Eliseus had access to a keyboard, because the batons in question could have been vertical levers that pulled the clapper ropes. We only speak of carillon playing when the clapper ropes have been connected to horizontal batons or slats that are pushed downward. Thus, the essential element is the transition from *pulling* to *pushing*. Despite the absence of a formal mention of a keyboard, an important development in bell music must have taken place around 1480. In addition to the innovations at Dunkirk and Antwerp, there was the musical forestroke in Park Abbey from 1478. Everything appears to indicate that melodies were played for the first time on tower bells around 1480, automatically as well as manually.

Around 1500, beyaerders also applied their chiming technique on the smaller bells of the forestroke. In 1498, chiming took place on the forestroke bells of the St. Rumbold's Tower in Mechelen[29], and in 1505, in 's-Hertogenbosch an unknown number of forestroke bells were equipped with clappers to make them suitable for chiming.[30] Chimers undoubtedly found more musical possibilities in forestroke bells than in the larger church bells. They hung close to one another in the vicinity of the clock, which made them easier to connect to a playing structure. They had lighter clappers, which made possible more varied and virtuoso playing. And they generally were cast as a coherent musical series, where church bells often were heterogeneous with respect to weight and sound character.

The first clear indication of a carillon keyboard came in 1510 in Oudenaarde. We met Jan Van Spiere earlier, the clever clockmaker who had been busy for a number of years expanding and refining the clock and the forestroke of the town hall. In 1510, he further expanded the forestroke to nine bells, and enhanced the clock with jaquemarts in the form of Adam, Eve and a coiling snake. He also hung a clapper in each of the nine bells with straps, so that they could be chimed. And finally he installed a keyboard ('a keyboard in the tower to chime').[31] Van Spiere's keyboard was probably an early variation of the present 'primitive' baton keyboards that still exist, among others in the South of France. There, keyboards with wide slats continue to be used that can be pushed downward with the full hand. This type of keyboard for that matter was also used in the oldest organs.

Hence, from 1510, bells were played in Oudenaarde by pushing on keyboard batons or slats. It, however, would be imprudent to declare Jan Van Spiere the inventor of the carillon. The city accounts speak not of an innovation, but rather limit themselves to a neutral registration of the task of Van Spiere, as if he were doing something routine. What's more, a linguistic analysis of the word *beiaard*, the Flemish term for the carillon, makes clear that the carillon keyboard was not an invention, but rather the result of a development that took a number of centuries to complete.

The terms beiaard *and* carillon

The word *beiaard* makes a rather inglorious entree in the literature. It appears for the first time around 1260 in the animal epic *Van den vos Reynaerde*. In the scene in question, Reynaert the fox entices the tomcat Tybeert to enter the house of a priest at night with the promise of mice to be caught. The tomcat gets caught in a trap and thus awakes the priest and his wife. When cornered by the priest, he pounces on his attacker, severely damaging the latter's private parts: 'and jumped up between the priest's legs, at the purse that has no seam, and pulled out the one thing with which the *beyaert* is struck.'[32] These verses were censored for years in editions due to their obscene connotation. Nevertheless they provide – in addition to risqué entertainment – important insight into the history of the carillon. They show after all that the noun *beyaert* was already being used in relation to bells more than two centuries before the development of the instrument with the same name. We can conclude from this that the technique of rhythmic chiming occurred with the help of a construction that was already called *beyaert* in the 13th century and that it must be considered the forerunner of the later carillon keyboard. Only from the late 15th century on was this construction used for melodic chiming.

None of these primitive carillon constructions have been preserved. We nevertheless can form an idea of how they looked. Chiming is still done in the traditional manner in a number of European regions, and based on this, we are able to form a picture of the art of chiming in the Low Countries during the Late Middle Ages. Today chimers are active among others in the Swiss canton of Valais, the South of France, Valencia, the Balkans and Russia. They succeed in playing multiple bells using various tricks: they fasten clapper cords to each other and bind the totality to a wooden pole that is held in the hand, or they bring cords together in a wooden framework in order to be able to pull them from a single point. Large clappers are pulled with primitive pedals. There is little standardization in this manner of chiming: sometimes multiple players chime together, sometimes one person is located in the bell-chamber who plays all the bells while sitting or standing.

The linguistic origin of the notorious word *beiaard* is still unclear.³³ Some hear an onomatopoeia, while others postulate a link with the old stem *baren* or *beren* ('to bear'), which would mean 'to produce sound'. Still others claim that *beyaerden* has the same root as *beide* ('both') and thus would originally have meant the striking of two bells with clappers. The most plausible explanation is based on a hypothetical Middle Dutch verb *beien* that is related to the French *battre* and the English *to beat*. A *beyaert* thus would be a device to strike, and the terms *beyaerden* and *beyaerder* would be derived from this. Interesting in this hypothesis is the analogy with the French *batteler*, which refers to the traditional *beyaerden* or chiming, as well as to playing the carillon.

Surprisingly, the origin of the French word *carillon* can also be found in the antics of the sly fox Reynaert. One day Reynaert enters a church together with the wolf Primaut. Reynaert gets the wolf drunk and encourages him to play on the bells. The wolf grabs the cords and plays *à glaz, à treble, à carenon* (verse 3341). *Le glas* would later become the term in France for the peal of a bell as a sign of mourning. *Treble* is to chime with three bells. This must have been a popular technique, which appears in other texts as *tribouler* and *trézeler*. The term *carenon* refers to the sounding of four bells, and may have its source in the late Latin *quadriglio(nem)*. Due to a shift in meaning, the term *carillon* later came to take on the meaning it has today. The popular hypothesis that *carillon* initially was a forestroke of four bells is refuted by the source material. No historical text uses the term *carillon* to refer to a forestroke, while *carillonner* is mentioned often in archival texts in the sense of to chime bells.

Further development of the new musical instrument

During the course of the 16th century, the new bell arrangement developed further into a full-fledged musical instrument. In archival texts, the traditional plural form *beyaerders* makes way for the singular, which indicates that one person played all the bells. In the Southern Low Countries, the carillon player was called *beyaerder* or *beyaertmeester*, in the North, *beyerman* or *beyermeester*. From 1530, the verb *beyaerden* was increasingly replaced in city accounts by 'playing on the bells', which clearly refers to a musical event. The pursuit of greater playing quality could be seen in Leuven, where in 1525 the first known carillon competition in history took place. The city government purchased a forestroke of eight or nine bells from Mechelen bellfounder Peter Waghevens for the clock on St. Peter's Church, and organized a contest to determine who was best suited to play the new bells. Butcher Willem Hershals provided a fatted ram as prize for the best three participants.³⁴

The construction of the instrument was improved. The city archives of various cities in the Low Countries indicate that the improvements themselves were not

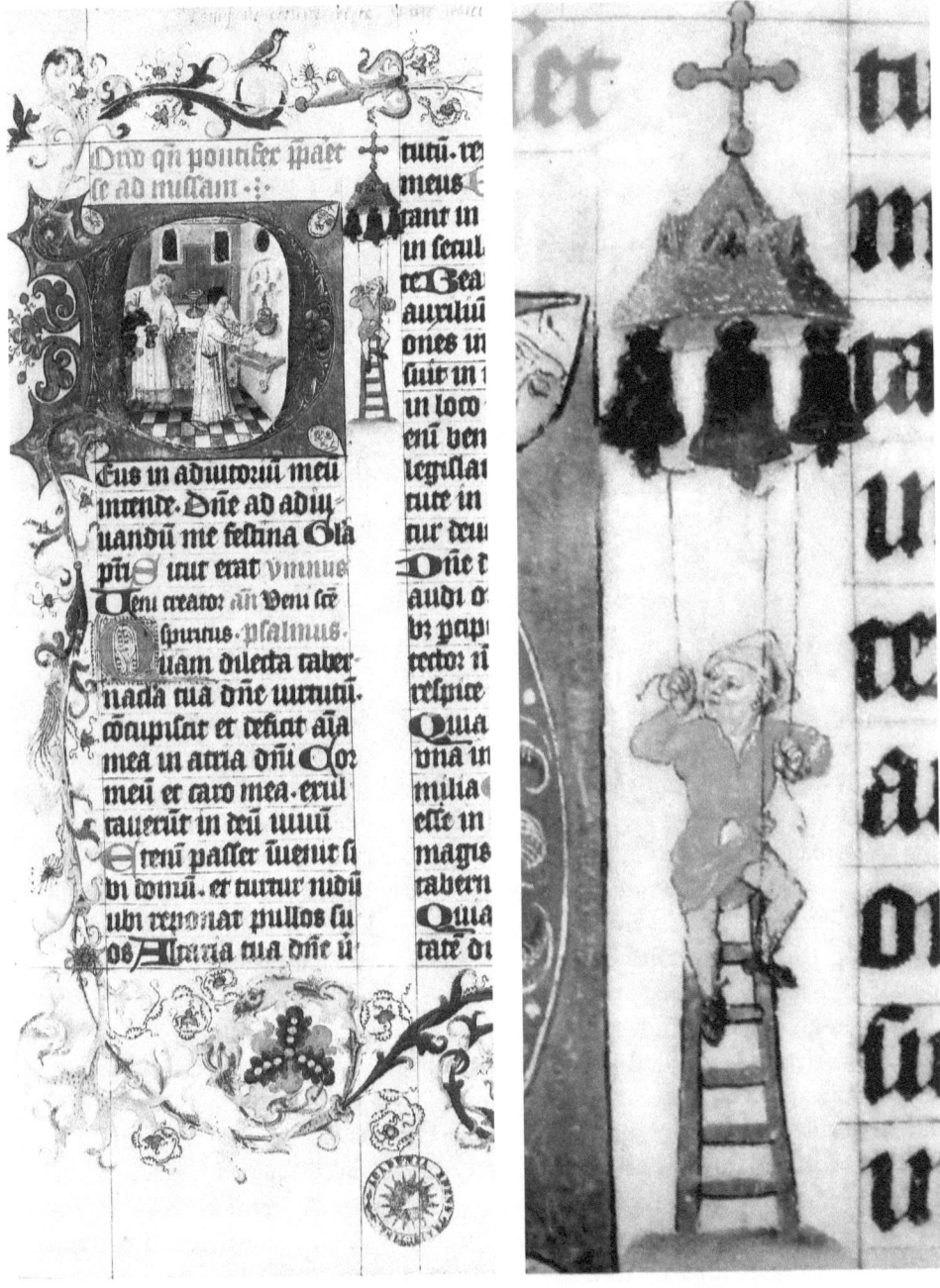

Chimer on three bells; the clappers are not pulled directly, but via intermediate wires. Detail from Pontificale of the Master of Katharina van Kleef, ca. 1450.

Playing drum, constructed by Hans Neurenberg for the New Reformed Church in Hattem, the Netherlands (1635). This is one of the last examples of a drum with slats in wrought iron.

gradually distributed from a central point of origin, but rather that they took place in a more crisscross fashion in the principalities of Flanders, Brabant and Liège. In 1531, the forestroke at Hasselt in Liège received a keyboard with twelve *spiecken*, which possibly indicates the narrow keyboard batons as are still used today. In 1546, a new forestroke was installed in St. Martin's Church in Kortrijk with presumably thirteen bells, including 'the clavier, the pedals and the chains', which indicates the addition of a pedal board for the heaviest bells.[35]

The automatic chiming mechanism was also further improved. In 1526, Leuven priest Henricke Vekenstyl was paid for his help *van den sange ghestelt opten voerslach*, which appears to indicate that Leuven in this year had a mechanical drum with exchangeable pins.[36] Six years later, we obtain certainty concerning the existence of a programmable drum in Hoorn in the County of Holland.[37] There, in 1532, a mechanical drum was installed that made it possible to program different melodies on the 10 bells of the forestroke. The mechanical drums of this time consisted of two hoops connected to each other by several wrought-iron bands. The bands were punctured with holes in which pins were fitted. By periodically changing the location of the pins, the carillonneur or clock-master could program the mechanical drum so that the public regularly was able to hear a new musical program. In 1549, the wooden pins in Hasselt were replaced by iron ones with a screw thread.[38]

A new important development took place around 1550 with regard to the carillon, namely the integration of church bells and forestroke bells into a single instrument. Until then, two groups of bells were located in the towers: heavy church bells that were chimed in the traditional manner and a series of lighter bells that served as forestroke and could be played via a keyboard. Around the middle of the 16th century, the church bells were also connected to the keyboard. Thus, the three functions of tolling, forestroke and playing by keyboard were integrated into a single instrument, and this was no longer called a *voorslagh* but *beyaerd*.[39] The number of bells in the carillon increased further to approximately 20 at the end of the 16th century.

The new musical instrument could always be heard in the public space, and carillonneurs could not practice or learn a new repertoire without the city's population bearing witness. As the musical requirements of carillon playing increased, so did the seriousness of this problem. A solution was found in the creation of the practice keyboard, a replica of a carillon keyboard for indoor use. In 1587, a practice carillon with seventeen bells was installed at the orphanage of Nivelles, so that the local carillonneur could teach one of the orphans. In 1588, the city government of Utrecht made available to the city carillonneur a keyboard with which to teach students. When the Swiss doctor Thomas Platter visited Antwerp on 24 August 1599, he encountered a practice keyboard that was connected to bells of clay with wooden clappers. Thus, the first practice keyboards were equipped with small bells and not yet with metal sounding bars, as would become common later. The introduction of the practice keyboard made it clear that at the end of the 16th century, the carillon was no longer a simple playing device, but a full-fledged musical instrument that was only played outdoors after the music had been learned indoors.[40]

The first founders of carillon bells

The melodic playing of the carillon placed greater demands on the tone purity of bells than previously was the case. The bell-founders who met this challenge with the greatest success worked in Mechelen.[41] Mechelen owed its dominant position in 16th century carillons, among others, to its favorable location. The city was located on the trade route between Germany and the Southern Low Countries, and thanks to the navigable River Dijle, was linked to a dense inland water network and the North Sea. The central position of Mechelen became official when in 1507, Margaret of Austria became Governor of the Low Countries and settled with her court in the city. There, however, was also a geological reason why the city on the Dijle was so

The *Speeltoren* of Monnickendam, with in the lantern the oldest carillon in the world that still is played by hand (1597)

attractive to bell-founders. Mechelen was located in the Brabant clay region, and clay from Mechelen was very well suited to making molds for bells. The first Mechelen bell-founders involved with carillons were members of the Waghevens family. Hendrik Waghevens (ca. 1420-1483) was the forefather of a dynasty that produced ten bell-founders across three generations. The Waghevens family delivered fine castings, richly decorated in renaissance style. The most successful founders of forestrokes and carillons were two of Hendrik's grandsons, the cousins and competitors Medard (ca. 1492-1557) and Jacob (ca. 1500-1574).[42] Of their carillons, only a carillon of Medard in St. Leonard's Church, Zoutleeuw in East Brabant has stood the test of time, or at least seven of the nine original bells from 1530 have. The bells are not part of the modern carillon in the tower, but hang in the lantern openings as silent museum exhibits. They constitute the oldest series of carillon bells in the world still in existence.[43]

At the beginning of the 16th century, the Waghevens family received serious competition in their hometown from an emigrated bell-founder family. On 17 July 1506, Willem Van den Ghein, from Goirle in the north of the Duchy of Brabant, registered himself as bell-founder in the Mechelen burgher book. He was the oldest of ten Van den Ghein bell-founders who would cast bells in Mechelen until 1697. The most successful carillon makers of the dynasty were Willem's son, grandson and great-grandson, all named Peter.[44] Their work still sounds today above the heads of the inhabitants in a number of Dutch towns. The oldest, still working forestroke hangs in Zierikzee in Zeeland. It consists of 13 bells that came from the carillon that Peter Van den Ghein I cast for the town hall between 1550 and 1554. After these carillon bells were taken out of service, in 1967 they were hung as forestroke at Zuidhavenpoort, one of the three city towers in this small Zeeland city. The oldest carillon still being played with a keyboard hangs in Monnickendam, a small port town near Amsterdam. In 1597, Peter Van den Ghein III delivered a carillon of 15 bells for the recently completed carillon tower of the town hall. Today there are 18. The remains of other forestrokes or carillons of the early Van den Gheins still sound in the towns of Edam, Sint-Maartensdijk and Arnemuiden. It is no accident that we are able to listen to the oldest carillon sounds only in these small towns. They flourished to a certain degree in the 16th century as trade or port cities, but in later centuries, they lacked the financial resources to replace their instruments with larger or better carillons.

The still existing bell series of the Mechelen bell-founders are striking for the impurity of their tone. This is not due to their age, but was largely present at their creation. Nevertheless, most commissioning governments had their purchased bells inspected by a college of experts. These generally were professional musicians such as the local organist or an acknowledged choirmaster. Rejected bells whose sound was too high were retuned under the supervision of a musician by chipping out the bell's inner wall with chisel and hammer. Bells that sounded too low could not be retuned and were recast at the expense of the bell-founder.

The musical demands placed on a carillon were strongly present in the assignment Jacob Waghevens received in 1542 from Tournai. He was required to cast a new carillon of 17 bells to replace a forestroke from 1536 that apparently was unsatisfactory. The contract stipulated that the bells had to be suitable for music with two and three voices.[45] Hence, they had to be pure enough to pleasantly reproduce harmonies. This evidently was a popular requirement at the time, because in the same year 1542 the Maastricht city government also requested that the new bells of the forestroke be able to play polyphonic music[46], and in 1560, Jacques Rieulin from Ath was appointed city carillonneur of Antwerp because he was able to play three and even four simultaneous parts during the exam.[47]

The Tournai contract also mentioned that the bells should have 'a true harmonious sound, and be in proper proportion with respect to the third, fifth and octave, without fault.' Perhaps this passage refers to the mutual relationship between specific bells, but it could also concern the relationship between the partial notes within each bell separately. The phenomenon of partial notes is one of the decisive factors contributing to a bell's musicality, but also one of the most complex domains in the craft of bell making. As is the case with each natural sound source, a bell produces a large number of partial notes that together determine its timbre. In the case of flexible sound bodies such as a string or an air column, the vibrational frequencies of the partial notes are always related to one another according to the simple sequence 1 – 2 – 3 – 4 etc., which results in a harmonious series of partial notes (e.g. a - a - e - a - c sharp - e - g - a etc.). Such a sound is experienced by the human ear as pleasant.

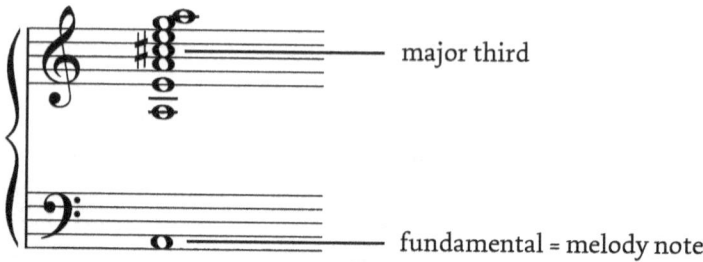

— major third

— fundamental = melody note

When solid objects are caused to vibrate, however, a complicated vibration pattern of partial notes is produced, that do not harmonize with each other and do not result in a distinctive musical note. In their intuitive search for a solid object that approached the musical overtone series, humans developed the bronze bell. Statistical research on bells from the Middle Ages and later reveal that, despite great differences among themselves, the average vibration pattern of the bell tended toward the sequence 1 – 2 – 2.4 – 3 – 4 – etc., which yields as lowest five partial notes: fundamental – prime – minor third – fifth – octave. The strike or melody note of the bell is by definition one octave below the octave partial tone, and thus coincides with the prime partial tone for an average bell. These elements yield a fixed and unwavering pitch as well as a high degree of consonance, and this ratio would later be defined as the ideal vibration pattern for a musical bell. The minor third provided by the conspicuous 2.4 harmonic gives the bell a more serious and somewhat more melancholic character than most other musical sounds in which the first third partial tone is a major third.

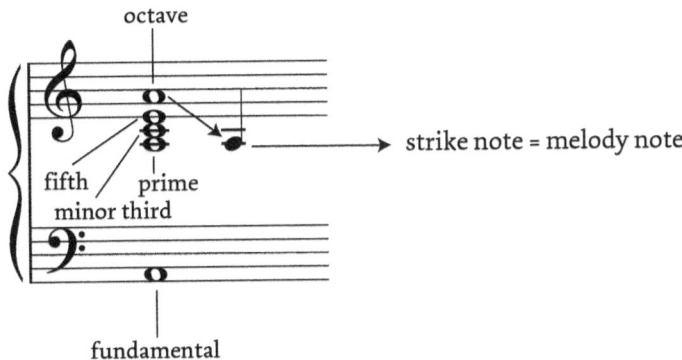

In the 16th century, knowledge of the partial notes of the bell was vague, and the skill of realizing the ideal partial profile in a bell was lacking completely.[48] While the total bell population evidenced on average the ideal partial tone pattern, there were still enormous differences between individual bells in the 16th century, and most bells sounded dissonant *on their own*. When several dissonant bells were required to make music together, various tensions arose between the partial notes of the different bells, which results in so-called beats, the 'wah wah' effect that we also encountered in bells with an asymmetric profile. Audible beats were not annoying by definition for a sonorous church bell, but this was a problem for a bell that was part of a musical series. Hence, the production of carillons brought with it many headaches for bell-founders. Discussions with customers were difficult, and the problems that arose were not easily addressed. Bell-founders and experts knew that they could lower the global pitch of bells by thinning their inner wall, but what they did not have under control was the capricious play of the partial notes. This made the casting of fore-strokes and carillons a risky activity that most bell-founders did not attempt or stopped after a number of disappointing experiences.

Hence, a discrepancy arose in the 16th century between the demands of customers and the expertise of bell-founders. Nevertheless, 16th century city dwellers without a doubt were milder in their judgment of the quality of carillons than we are, with five centuries of carillon history behind us. Otherwise, how could the new musical instrument have spread so quickly throughout the territory of the Low Countries.

CHAPTER 6

Carillon music in a divided land

Why in the Low Countries?

Over a few decades, the carillon spread throughout the Southern Low Countries, and around 1530, it was considered a typical phenomenon for the region. Presumably there initially was a greater concentration in the County of Flanders. In 1531, Bruges historian Jacob De Meyere wrote that the Flemish surpassed all other residents of the Low Countries with their impressive and splendid churches and their large and harmonious bells, on which they played all types of songs, 'just like on cytharas.'[49] Only after 1530 did the carillon penetrate to the northern principalities. The dissemination process was complete by the end of the 16th century. This can be seen among others from the manuscript *Recherche de Plusieurs Singularités* that was compiled between 1583 and 1587 by François Merlin and Jacques Cellier and dedicated by them to King Henry III of France. Page 188 depicts a carillon tower. We see a keyboard with eight manual batons, without pedals, and above it, nine bells. It is the earliest known picture of a carillon keyboard. The caption states that making music with bells using a keyboard is common in the Low Countries and at other places.[50] The latter is not fully correct, because the spread of the carillon stopped abruptly at the edges of the Low Countries and the Prince-Bishopric of Liège, and until the beginning of the twentieth century, there would be few carillons outside this territory.

The question why the carillon came into being in the Southern Low Countries has inspired various authors to highly imaginative explanations. Some sought an explanation in climatological conditions, such as the flat relief that would be favorable to the diffusion of bell sounds, or the cloudy North Sea climate that would have incited residents to cheer up the atmosphere with tower music.[51] Others were of the opinion that the carillon came into being due to the attitude of the residents, whether it be their disposition for devotion that would have inspired them to play sacred music on bells, or their lack of musical taste.[52] The actual explanation lies in an interplay of economic, cultural and technological factors.

In the latter days of the Middle Ages, the County of Flanders and the Duchy of Brabant were one of the most densely populated and most urbanized regions in

Oldest known picture of a carillon keyboard, from *Recherche de Plusieurs Singularités* (1583-1587) by François Merlin and Jacques Cellier

Europe. The cities of Bruges, Ghent and Antwerp were among the largest European trading centers north of the Alps. Industry and trade provided a powerful stimulus for the public measurement of time, and created the financial assets to expand the functional forestroke of the tower clock into a musical carillon. Carillons were prestige objects that city authorities purchased 'for adornment and decoration of the city', and the number of bells and the length of melodies of the forestroke were elements of mutual rivalry.

Periods of economic boom led to a flowering of culture. Around 1500, Flemish polyphony reached a first high point with European celebrities such as Josquin Des Prez, Johannes Ockeghem, Pierre de la Rue, Jacob Obrecht and Heinrich Isaac. The construction of musical instruments was also at a high level in the territory. It is plausible that this favorable cultural climate was conducive to the quick spread of making music with bells. By connecting bells to a keyboard, a primitive percussion instrument was elevated to a keyboard instrument, just as a century earlier, the organ and the clavichord emerged from wind and string instruments.

A third important factor was the technological superiority enjoyed by the Southern Low Countries from the 12th century, especially the County of Flanders.[53] In the fertile coastal region along the North Sea, reclamation techniques were of major importance. Port technology was also present: in these centuries, Bruges was still the most important port north of the Alps. In the coastal areas of Flanders, the wind continually changed in direction and force, which meant extra challenges for the builders of windmills.[54] Windmill construction was based on a technology of gears, pulleys and levers not unlike that of the tower clock and automatic chimes. Above all, however, the weaving industry in the Southern Low Countries was superior. In the Late Middle Ages, the cities of Flanders, Hainault and Brabant developed into the most important textile centers of Europe, with a specialization in luxury clothing and tapestries. There are various indications that the construction technique used for looms had an influence on carillon construction. There is a striking similarity between the medieval loom and the primitive carillon keyboard. Both consist of a wooden construction with a bench, pedals and pulleys. In carillon construction, as in weaving, the term *schering* is used to designate the stretched wire system.[55] The correlation between weaving and the carillon was most clear in the city of Valenciennes in the County of Hainault. The city was one of the most important textile production centers, and with eleven carillons, had an unusually high number of tower instruments. Moreover, a number of weavers in Valenciennes were well-known carillon builders. In 1592, the weavers Augustin and Philippe de Saint-Aubert were called to Mechelen to work on the city carillon. Augustin remained in the city on the Dijle as city carillonneur, and later became city carillonneur in Ypres and Ghent.[56] His fellow townsman and colleague-weaver Jean de Sany became city carillonneur in Brussels in

1606, and there overhauled the carillon in St. Nicholas Church. He was later asked to repair the Mechelen carillon.[57]

An important technological aspect is also the quality of the bells themselves. As Jacob De Meyere wrote, the bells in our regions sounded good. While the bellfounders of the Southern Netherlands had not yet mastered the art of tuning, they were masters of casting. It is almost self-evident that a public familiar with sonorous bells would more quickly arrive at the idea to play music on them than would residents of a region with dry sounding bells such as the Mediterranean Basin.

Thus the carillon emerged in the favorable economic, cultural and technological climate that prevailed in the Southern Low Countries. Intensive contacts with cities in the North ensured the quick spread of the instrument throughout the territory of the Low Countries and the Prince-Bishopric of Liège. It remains unclear why for four centuries carillon culture was scarcely able to penetrate beyond the Low Countries. A possible explanation lies with the instrument's technical complexity. The use of bells as musical instrument was a technological tour de force that could only be realized if three conditions were present: sonorous bells, a reliable playing mechanism and a competent carillonneur. Carillon construction required local expertise that was part of the shared experience of the Low Countries, but that was more difficult to export than portable musical instruments or choir singers.

Good and bad songs

In the 15th century, most principalities where the carillon had spread had achieved political unity under the Dukes of Burgundy, and would remain united under Emperor Charles V. Charles was born in Ghent in 1500, and was educated in Mechelen at the court of his aunt, Margaret. After becoming emperor of a large part of Western Europe and a number of overseas territories, he conducted numerous wars that weighed heavily on the realm's treasury. So, Emperor Charles raised taxes in the rich cities of the Low Countries. In 1537, Ghent, the most rebellious of the Flemish cities, revolted against the central authority. Charles came personally from Spain to put things in order. He hit the residents of his native city where it hurt most. Not only did he have the worst of the rioters executed and the others paraded through the streets with a noose around their necks, he also ordered the removal and confiscation from the belfry of the alarm bell Roland. This fact resonated so long in the collective memory of the residents of Ghent that the story arose that the emperor had chopped Roland into pieces. This would only reinforce the later fame of Bell Roland as mythical alarm bell of Flanders.

Charles managed with some difficulty to preserve the political unity of his empire. He failed, however, in his aspiration to maintain its religious unity. On 31 October 1517, the German Augustinian monk Martin Luther nailed to the door of All Saint's Church in Wittenberg a series of 95 theses in which he protested a number of abuses in the Church. He labeled as superstition a number of Catholic rituals that distracted the attention of believers from the Bible. Despite violent repression on the part of political and Church authorities, Luther's doctrine quickly spread throughout Europe. From 1530, French-Swiss theologian John Calvin propagated from Geneva a stricter variation on this new mindset. According to him, the new doctrine – including the musical expressions thereof – had to be imposed by the government. For Calvin, music was a higher form of prayer, an ideal that could only be achieved if the believing community were able to sing the melodies in the vernacular. This was impossible with the polyphony based on Latin texts that was then present. Calvin recognized the Bible as the sole source of inspiration for church singing. Hence he and his colleagues translated the Psalms of David into rhyme, so that the texts could easily be memorized. The texts were accompanied by simple melodies that followed the words note for note, and that could easily be sung in unison.

The religious developments initially had no impact on the tower music of the cities of the Low Countries. Where the first tower music around 1500 consisted principally of simple Gregorian melodies, a broader repertoire developed after 1520. The increasing number of bells presented greater musical possibilities, and the programmable mechanical drums made possible a varying repertoire. And around 1540, carillonneurs started playing and programming secular melodies. City authorities required their carillonneurs to play mixed programs of spiritual and secular songs 'for the recreation of residents and visitors'.[58] The carillon had evolved into a sort of local radio station, and for the first time in history, bell sounds were no longer exclusively associated with obligations, the pressure of time and religious zeal. The carillons played their cheerful tunes while the public in the cities of the Low Countries became internally divided concerning the true faith and united in their grumbling concerning a monarch who used their money for expensive military campaigns. In 1555, Charles abdicated in Brussels as lord of the Low Countries in favor of his son Philip. From then on, the territory of the Seventeen Provinces would be politically indivisible and always accept the same person as common monarch.

This agreement on paper, however, was quickly overtaken by events on the ground. After agitated Calvinists destroyed Catholic sanctuaries in 1566 in Flanders, Brabant and Holland, King Philip II sent the Duke of Alva to the Low Countries with ten thousand soldiers and unlimited authority. The terror of Alva further instigated the resistance, and resulted in the Eighty Years' War between the Low Countries and Spain. During the initial years, the war fortunes varied, and several cities in the North

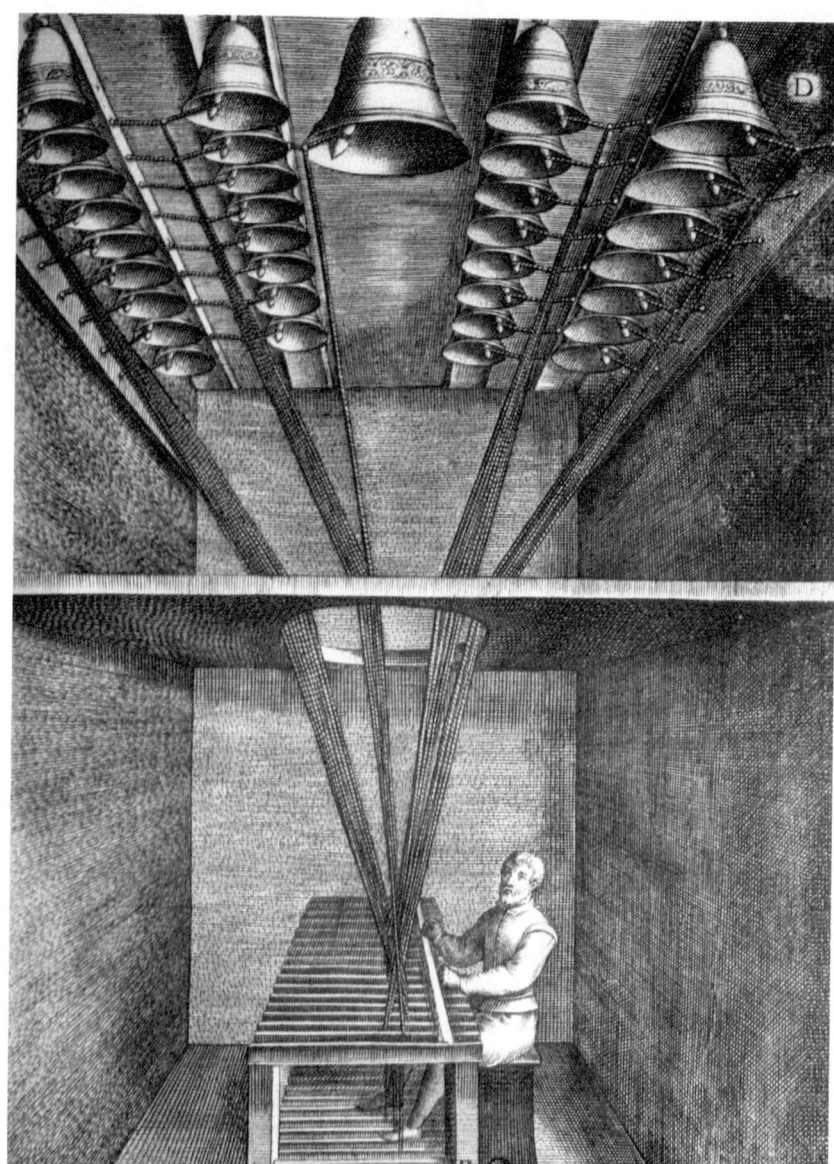

Oldest known picture of a playing carillonneur, from
De Campanis Commentarius (1612) by Angelo Roccha (1545-1620)

and the South were dominated alternately by Calvinist and Spanish rulers. In December 1572, Alva's troops besieged Haarlem, which surrendered only after seven months of fighting and famine. At the start of the siege, the insurgents stopped the automatic playing of the St. Bavo Church, presumably to not interfere with functional signals such as the alarm bell. The day after the capitulation of 12 July 1573, the mechanical drum rotated again after 31 weeks of silence. On the hour, *Gaudeamus omnes in Domino* was played, and on the half hour, *Te Deum laudamus*, Gregorian melodies that confirmed restoration of the Catholic order. The bell music must have sounded bitter to the ears of the insurgents who were led to the scaffold on the Market Square under the carillon tower of St. Bavo.[59] The time was past that carillons could noncommittally play their songs. From now on, carillon music would be a weapon in the fight for faith.

The foundation for the new musical climate was laid by the Council of Trent, which formulated a reply to the challenges of the reformed religions and purified the Church of a number of abuses. On 10 September 1562, the Council pronounced judgment on music in the Church. Henceforth, only spiritual music could be played or sung in churches; polyphonic music was not banned, but had to be simple enough for the words to be understood; music was not to be enjoyed for its own sake, but had to inspire desire in the hearts of believers for celestial harmonies. On 5 September 1563, the Council ruled that sweetish songs (*molliores cantus*) did not belong in the church, and that only serious music fit the simplicity of the Church liturgy. The concrete implementation of the general principles of the Council was left to the synods that would take place in the following years in the various European ecclesiastical provinces. The synods held in the Low Countries also addressed the matter of bell music. While carillons often were not church-related by nature, their sound filled the public space and needed to be brought under control. In 1564, the Synod of Haarlem prohibited bells that were blessed for sacred use from being misused to play licentious and unsuitable songs. A year later, the Synod of Cambrai decreed that no immoral, shameful and folk songs would be played on large and small bells, but that carillonneurs must play Church hymns and songs. Each violation of these rules would be punished. In 1570, the Synod of Mechelen stipulated that singers, organists and carillonneurs could not play licentious, military or tasteless music. Offenders would pay a penalty of ten *stuivers*, which would be allocated by the bishops to a good cause. Multiple violations would result in a prison sentence.[60]

The reformation side also began to censure music in and around the church. In 1566, the psalms were translated by Pastor Peter Dathenus into a form of Dutch that fit Calvin's original Geneva melodies. In the cities that came under Calvinist rule, musical life was thoroughly 'purified'. Organ music was banned as a product of the devil, and polyphonic music was replaced by simple community singing in the vernacular. This evolution was confirmed in a number of reformed synods, such as that of Edam, which in 1586 banned organs and carillons from playing frivolous and worldly songs. The city governments followed the church prescriptions and instructed their carillonneurs to program the mechanical drums to play psalm melodies on the hour. In cities such as Utrecht and Gouda, the carillonneur was required to play only psalm melodies during his Sunday concerts. From this moment, the soundscape in the cities of the Northern Low Countries would be determined for centuries by the stately melodies of the Genevan Psalter.[61]

Around 1580, a number of cities in the Southern Low Countries also briefly came under Calvinist rule. Brussels, Ghent and Antwerp were transformed into small republics with a totalitarian Calvinist regime that prohibited Catholic religious practice. This also had an influence on the carillon repertoire. Antwerp city carillonneur Jacques Rieulin, who in 1560 was appointed by the city government because he could play so artistically in three and four voices, had to modify his repertoire from 8 December 1580. The city government warned him to no longer play any indecent songs, but rather only psalms, spiritual songs and hymns.[62]

Thus an end came to the short period in which carillons freely emitted melodies of all types over the roofs of the city. An echo of this carefree time can be read in *De Tintinnabulis*, the first study on bells in history.[63] Tuscan scholar Hieronymus Magius had heard from his Dutch colleague Aubertus Gifanius that bells in the church towers of the Low Countries were played by musicians and he wrote that during concerts, residents danced and leaped about in utter merriment in their houses and on the city squares. When Magius penned these words in 1571, he was prisoner in an Ottoman cell in Istanbul. He wrote his bell treatise from memory to attract the attention of Western diplomats to his miserable plight. His aim to gain release failed, however, and he was strangled shortly thereafter. From his Turkish cell, Magius was unable to document the new musical climate prevailing in the Low Countries, where there was no longer room for danceable carillon music.

Bells as commodity

The reformation restrained not only bell music, but also formed a threat to the bells themselves. The reformed forces needed resources for the war against the Spanish occupying forces, and no longer felt bound by the time-honored, sacrosanct status of bells. For the followers of Calvin, bells – like images of saints, complicated music and Latin texts – were expressions of the old faith and stood in the way of direct contact by believers with God. The tolling of bells to drive away storm clouds, chase away the devil or to save the souls of the dead was labeled a form of superstition, and only functional ringing was allowed, among others to call believers to church. Bells were systematically removed from church towers in 1578 and 1579.⁶⁴ A part of the stolen goods was melted into artillery, among others in Mechelen and Maastricht. Other bells escaped the melting pot because they were resold, and ended up in various regions of reformed Europe. For this reason, Mechelen bells are still ringing in Germany, Switzerland, Denmark, Sweden, England and Scotland. They all date from before 1578 and clearly were not cast at the request of their reformed owners, since they included Dutch language inscriptions, pictures of Catholic saints and medallions of King Philip II.⁶⁵

Churches in the countryside probably suffered more from the robbery of bells than their urban counterparts, since the latter were better protected and anarchy was given less scope for its destructive work. What's more, heavy city bells were not as easy to remove. Nevertheless, forestrokes and carillons were subject to danger. In 1580, the Abbey of Roozendaal at Mechelen was visited by English reformist soldiers who took with them the clock and the forestroke consisting of nine bells cast by Peter Van den Ghein I. The bells were sold via an Antwerp merchant to St. Martin's Church in the Zeeland fishing village of Arnemuiden, which had the series expanded into a manually playable carillon. We will encounter this modest carillon from Mechelen again later in this story. ⁶⁶

The Spanish soldiers, however, were the equal to their Reformed opponents in the robbery of bells. Numerous bells were shipped to the south, where they were traded, among others in Lisbon. When Antwerp resident Jehan L'hermite visited El Escorial in 1597, he encountered numerous bells there from Northern and Southern Low Country bell-founders Peter Van den Ghein, Jan Tolhuis, Henrick De Borch, Adriaen Steylaert, Steven Butendiick and Jan Zeelstman. Some had been combined into a chime or carillon: 'un tres bel accord de clochettes pour y carillonner ou tribouler à la façon et mode de nostre pays'. According to L'hermite, King Philip himself had a number of bells cast, and he purchased most at the Lisbon bell market.⁶⁷

In many cities and towns, the large-scale robbery of bells resulted in a protracted interruption to the traditional custom of chiming, and in a number of locations, this tradition was never resumed. The old playing technique, however, never died out completely. We learn this among others from the Brabants-Latin dictionary *Etymologicum Teutonicae Linguae* by Corneel Kiliaen from 1599, in which the word *beyaerden* still had three meanings: 'to sound', 'to play on bells' and 'to repeatedly strike bells', which is equivalent to chiming.

The oldest carillon books

Around 1580, the war momentum turned permanently in favor of the insurgents in the North, and the northern provinces separated from Spain. In 1588, under the name of the Republic of the Seven United Netherlands, they became the first republic in the history of Western Europe. The fate of the Southern Low Countries was sealed when on 27 August 1585, the Spanish commander Alexander Farnese took Antwerp after a siege of fourteen months. Antwerp again became a Spanish city, and with the closure of the Scheldt, lost its free access to the sea. More than half of its one hundred thousand residents left the city. Thousands of merchants and intellectuals from cities in Brabant and Flanders also left. They went to the North and would become the dominant class in Amsterdam, Leiden, Haarlem and other Dutch cities. They thus laid the foundation for the Dutch Golden Age, in which also the carillon would flourish. The Southern Low Countries came under the rule of Archdukes Albrecht and Isabella, and enjoyed a period of relative peace and cultural flowering in the first decades of the 17th century. To the extent that the ringing of bells is a measure of popularity, the governors were well loved. When Albrecht died in 1621, bells were rung in all the churches of Brussels for three hours a day, six weeks long.

Carillon music at this time was still largely religious. In 1607, a new synod in Mechelen had reaffirmed the obligation to play religious songs. It was also stated that, if necessary, negotiations must be undertaken with the city government.[68] Thus an ecclesiastical repertoire was also imposed on the city carillonneurs, which is confirmed in the oldest extant sources with carillon music. Both come from Brussels, the residence of the governors.

The oldest manuscript is located in the Bibliothèque nationale de France in Paris. It was written between 1616 and 1633 by Hendrick Claes, a Brussels clockmaker of Mechelen origin.[69] It is a workbook with varied content: medical formulas, detailed drawings of ironwork and tower clocks, a recipe for making cement, family information, account statements, a love letter, and a list of saints who could be successfully invoked against the plague. The 63 compositions contain musical material for a carillon drum. A number of these are traditional Gregorian melodies such as *Veni creator* and *Ave Maris Stella*, which were programmed for the Church feast days. The music always begins with the monophonic melody, which is then enriched with a second voice. The greatest part of the repertoire is profane and consists of both French airs and court dances as well as melodies to texts by Dutch poets Bredero and Hooft. The music sounds static and simple, and has a tonal range of two diatonic octaves and a major third, with the addition of b flat in each octave. This corresponds to a series – somewhat modest for the time – of 19 bells. The manuscript mentions no specific carillon. Hendrick Claes presumably was a clockmaker without much musical

Title page of the carillon book of Brussels city carillonneur Theodoor de Sany (1599-1658)

knowledge who used the treatise as an aid in programming different carillons or forestrokes.

The second carillon programming book was intended for the Brussels city carillon in St. Nicholas Church, which served as city tower. It was compiled by city carillonneur Theodoor de Sany.[70] In 1648, he presented the city government with a manuscript containing 61 melodies for the automatic chimes of St. Nicholas. The repertoire shows similarities to the material in the carillon programming book of Hendrick Claes. De Sany also foresaw melodies on the hour and half-hour for Advent, Lent and the most important Church feast days. These are followed by a number of profane dances and songs, and three melodies from the Requiem Mass that could be used on the occasion of the death of a duke or duchess of Brabant. The old Gregorian themes are first presented monophonically, and thereafter in a variety of three or four-voice settings. The music sounds static and the polyphony must have sounded very unclear on the carillon drum, which was unable to reproduce volume variations. The great preponderance of Church melodies shows that for the Brussels city government, politics and religion were interwoven. The structuring around Church feast days also suggests that De Sany programmed the mechanical drum in the tower at least once a month. We are given no information on the repertoire for manual playing. It is possible that the carillonneur had greater freedom concerning the choice of repertoire for his concerts than was the case for programming the carillon drum.

In contrast to the manuscript of Hendrick Claes, De Sany's book has a very luxurious appearance. The musical part is preceded by elegant drawings and texts that praise the Brussels city carillon, and in particular the automatic chimes that were set up by his father, and that De Sany himself perfected. In a long introduction, De Sany pompously praises the perfection of his carillon, which plays automatically without human intervention, and that exceeds all the tower instruments in the Low Countries in size, artistry and splendor. De Sany hopes that his carillon would be able to offer even more services, now that peace had returned. In this, he is anticipating the Peace of Münster, which later that year would end the Eighty Years' War. The carillonneur then demonstrates the superiority of the Brussels carillon: the instrument had no less than 38 bells with a tonal range of three octaves, and a drum with 7840 holes. He also provides the numbers for eleven other important carillons, which of course were inferior to the Brussels carillon. Finally, there are extensive descriptions and drawings of the marvelous device.

De Sany was also active as a painter, and presumably was the author of an allegorical painting from 1642 that glorifies the city carillon. It depicts the nine muses who present to the Brussels city government a portrait of the god Apollo making music with his lyre on Mount Helicon. Fama floats above, proclaiming that hanging in St. Nicholas Church in Brussels is a carillon that produces melodies as varied as the choir of the muses, and that brings the residents of the city to a halt, as if petrified. Despite the attachment to his carillon, De Sany later left his carillonneur position in Brussels to become city carillonneur in Halle, where after his death in 1658, he was succeeded by his son Michel.

The glorification of the Brussels city carillon marked the close of one and a half centuries in which the carillon emerged, spread geographically throughout the Low Countries, and developed into a sophisticated musical instrument that could play three octaves and, above all, whose automatic play mechanism displayed great ingenuity. The big obstacle to the musical development of the instrument remained the tonal accuracy of the bells. At the moment that De Sany painted the glorification of his Brussels city carillon, however, the first pure sounding carillon was built in the Northern Low Countries.

CHAPTER 7

Pure bells

A blind nobleman with a keen sense of hearing

On 23 August 1638, René Descartes wrote to colleague-scientist Marin Mersenne: 'In Utrecht lives a blind man with a great musical reputation, who regularly plays bells (...). I have seen how he elicits 5 or 6 different sounds on each of the largest bells, without touching them, but only by coming close to their sound rim with his mouth ...'[71] Descartes was living at that time in Utrecht, where he had met the nobleman Jacob van Eyck, city carillonneur and recorder virtuoso. Van Eyck was born blind, but had fabulous hearing, and had demonstrated to the French scientist the physical principle of *resonance*. To do so, he stood close to one of his carillon bells and whistled at precisely the same pitch as one of the partial notes of the bell. The air vibrations produced by the whistle were transferred to the bell, which softly sounded the same pitch. By whistling at different pitches, Van Eyck could cause multiple partial notes of the bell 'to speak'. The blind carillonneur demonstrated the same trick with wine glasses. He tapped a glass and listened to its sound. He then whistled the different partial notes of the glass, to which the glass would always respond with the same partial note.

It is surprising that a man with such a keen sense of hearing would become carillonneur. Making music on untuned or poorly tuned bells must have been a constant torment for him. Hence, he strove to improve the tuning of bells, and became an active adviser in the design of carillons. He told the mathematician Isaac Beeckman that the ideal series of a bell's partial notes consisted of three notes an octave apart, supplemented by a minor third and a pure fifth in the second octave. This was the same series of partial notes that bell-founders had pursued for centuries, seldom with success. Beeckman noted in his *Journal* that Van Eyck had found a way to tune bells according to this ideal series of partial notes. Much depended on the bell having the correct profile: only a broad-shouldered bell could be correctly tuned after it was cast. The blind carillonneur only needed bell-founders to work with him to create a bell with a pure tone. He found them almost twenty years after his appointment as

Jacob van Eyck (ca. 1590-1657), François Hemony (ca. 1609-1667) and Pieter Hemony (1619-1680) testing small bells. Romanticized drawing from W.G. Hofdijk, *Lauwerblaren uit Neêrlands gloriekrans*, 1875.

One of the preserved bells from the carillon of Zutphen

carillonneur in Utrecht, at the moment that the Frenchmen François and Pierre Hemony had arrived in the Low Countries.

The Hemony brothers were born in the small village of Levécourt: François around 1609 and Pierre in 1619.[72] Levécourt was in Bassigny, the region where the Meuse rises. In this small region lived dozens of bell-founders, often linked to one another by familial ties. They were craftsmen without workplace. Around Ash Wednesday, they would leave their village and search for administrators of cities, churches and abbeys that needed bells. Their baggage consisted of a few molds to cast wax letters and decorations, a compass, a ruler and a brochette. This was a wooden or bronze sphere that indicated the proportions of bells of various weights. The remainder of the needed materials and equipment was supplied by their customer to the location of the casting. When the ground froze in the autumn, work could no longer be done, and they returned to their homes. After some time, many bell-founders would settle elsewhere, sometimes far from their place of birth, and thus Bassigny became the cradle of numerous European bell-founder dynasties.

Descendents of the families Causard, Fremy, Jullien, Petit and Plumere established themselves in the Low Countries.

Around 1640, the young Hemony brothers settled in the Rhineland, where they cast bells for churches in the region. In 1641, they cast three church bells for the church in the Twente municipality of Goor. Shortly thereafter, the nearby city of Zutphen decided to install a clock and a carillon in the recently finished Winery Tower.[73] On 1 August 1643, François Hemony was provisionally awarded the work of casting the bells. Shortly thereafter, he moved with his wife Maria Michelin and his brother Pierre to Zutphen to establish a foundry there. In March 1644, the brothers received the official assignment, and two years later, they delivered the instrument. It is very likely that for tuning the bells, they received instructions from Jacob van Eyck. In any case, the bells were approved by the blind carillonneur. The city government was very pleased with the result, and expressed its gratitude to the bell-founders because the resonance of the new instrument surpassed all other carillons in the neighboring cities. Unfortunately, the first purely tuned carillon in history can no longer be heard today, because the Winery Tower went up in flames during the night of 17/18 January 1920. The owner of a neighboring bicycle shop had financial problems and had his business set on fire in order to collect the insurance money.

François Hemony

After the success of his first carillon, François Hemony wrote a letter to the city government of neighboring Deventer, in which he let it be known that its carillon was nothing special, a matter that did not help the reputation of this important city. The bell-founder knew the instrument, because he had visited it in preparation for his work in Zutphen. Hemony made the city government a proposal they could not refuse: he would, at his own risk, cast a new carillon that would surpass all other tower instruments in the Northern Low Countries. The city government sought guidance from the same advisers of the work in Zutphen: Lucas van Lennick and Jacob van Eyck. Van Eyck announced to his co-adviser that, before the start of work, he would like to spend another hour or two with the bell-founder in order to further instruct him. This letter is the only material indication of collaboration between the musician and the bell-founder. In 1647, the Hemony brothers delivered a carillon in Deventer that reinforced their growing fame. In the years that followed, many Northern Dutch cities ordered a carillon from the foundry in Zutphen. The Hemonys arrived in the Low Countries at the right time, because in 1648, the Peace of Münster was concluded in which the surrounding states recognized the sovereignty of the Dutch Republic. The carillons made by the Hemonys would add to the prestige of the newborn nation.

The breakthrough in the Southern Low Countries came in 1655.[74] Two carillons hung in the north tower of the Church of Our Lady in Antwerp: one belonging to the church government consisting of 23 bells, and one belonging to the city with 31 bells. The two instruments were played by the same carillonneur. Only the city carillon was equipped with a mechanical drum. It was from 1541, and could play only 17 bells. François Hemony proposed to the City of Antwerp a series of 32 bells tuned to the existing hour bell Gabriel. In May 1655, the bell-founder came to Antwerp with 25 new bells. He installed them in the tower alongside the bells of the existing carillon, and connected them to a keyboard with ropes. This allowed a comparison to be conducted by city government members and a number of experts. Hemony triumphed, because despite the primitive playing mechanism and some rope breakage, the citizens of Antwerp were full of praise for the new bells. The comparison made it even more clear that the existing bells were not in tune with each other and simply sounded bad. So the city government decided to also have the gate bell, the thief bell and two heavy carillon bells recast by Hemony. The two brothers cast the additional four bells only in 1558, and using the existing bourdon Gabriel, created a carillon consisting of 37 bells with a total weight of 38,800 pounds. The city government, in its eagerness, put themselves strongly in debt: the four additional bells alone cost the city approximately 10,000 guilders, with the last payment of 2,271 guilder and 19 stuivers only being made in 1660 after taking out an additional loan. The church government was not to be outdone by the city and already on 1 December 1654, had decided to have a carillon of 32 bells cast by Hemony. Together with the Bancloque Carolus as bourdon and a number of other church bells, the new church carillon contained 37 bells. It weighed 45,500 pounds and was a half note lower than the city carillon that hung above it. The Hemonys also did other business in Antwerp: in 1655, the Norbertine Abbey of St. Michael ordered a carillon.

In November 1655, François received a letter from the mayors of Amsterdam with the request for a meeting. A Hemony instrument already hung in the Regulierstoren, but the city was considering the purchase of additional carillons. François went to Amsterdam, where he was offered the position of official city bell and artillery founder. The city was prepared to give him a foundry free of charge and as only condition, stated that he must deliver good products for a fair price. Hemony accepted the proposal and was given premises along the Molenpad next to the Keizersgracht. From then on, the city's existing bell and artillery founder Assuerus Koster was limited to casting cannons. Pierre did not follow his brother and would go his own way, more about which later.

Amsterdam was in full expansion at this time. The city's population had increased in 50 years' time from 30,000 to more than 150,000, and it absorbed this population explosion via four successive urbanization projects. The so-called *stadsuitleg* or city expansion resulted in the famous web of canals that so strongly defines the appearance of the City on the Amstel until today. It was also a time of ambitious building projects. A number of decades earlier, the Westerkerk and Zuiderkerk, both designed by city architect Hendrick De Keyser, were completed, and when Hemony settled in Amsterdam, an impressive new town hall on the Dam Square was nearing completion. François Hemony would crown the new cityscape with three new carillons that were housed in the towers of Zuiderkerk, Westerkerk and Oudekerk. A number of years later, an instrument would follow for the dome of the new town hall.

In his old age, the great poet Joost van den Vondel heard the sound of the city change, and in 1661 wrote the poem *Op 't Klokmusyk van Amsterdam*, which made a poetic link between the new carillons and the city's infrastructure work. As erudite poet, he took inspiration from Greek mythology. He compared the new carillons with the wondrous lyre of the hero Amphion, who helped build the ramparts of the city Thebes: Amphion's music had the power to attract stones and stack them on each other. In the same way, the City on the Amstel reached its completion – as a new Thebes – to the harmonious sounds of its carillons. According to Vondel's poem, no music could compete with the bells of Hemony, 'the eternal honor of Lorraine', when played by the hands and feet of city carillonneur Salomon Verbeek.

The Amsterdam carillons were a magnificent reference for the new city bell-founder, and every Northern Dutch city now wanted at least one Hemony instrument within its walls. In the South, François Hemony sold carillons for Averbode Abbey and St. Nicholas Church in Brussels. And with Hemony instruments for Mainz and Hamburg, the carillon took its first steps into Central Europe.

The Hemonys' secret

What exactly was the secret to François Hemony's success?[75] What particular technique had he developed together with his brother and Jacob van Eyck to flawlessly extract the ideal series of partial notes from the bronze? First, there was the realization that it is impossible to create a perfect bell by casting alone. During the casting and cooling process of bronze, unpredictable processes take place that always cause the final bell to deviate somewhat from its model, the false bell. For this reason, after casting, a carillon bell must always receive a 'finishing touch' to obtain the correct series of partial notes. Where bell-founders previously only tuned their bells after a negative evaluation and when the bell already hung in the tower, the Hemonys tuned their bells beforehand by turning them in the foundry. Thanks to various eyewitness accounts, we know the broad outlines of the technique François Hemony used in his

Amsterdam workshop. He cast the bell slightly too thick, causing it to sound a bit too high. A thicker wall after all results in higher frequency vibrations. The additional wall thickness gave the bell-founder a so-called *tuning margin*. He then placed the bell on a lathe and had it rotated by five to six men. Hemony turned the inside of the bell at various heights with a chisel in order to tune down the lowest five partial notes. Since tuning was only possible by removing bronze, this process was irreversible. Hence, Hemony had to stop turning when a partial note obtained the desired frequency. This moment was determined using an ingenious method. As a reference for tuning, Hemony used a series of tuning bars. He tuned a partial note until a bar began to sympathetically vibrate due to the resonance. Because the shrill sound of the turning overpowered the soft hum of the bar, Hemony built in a means of visual control. He had the bar covered with sand beforehand, and immediately stopped turning when the grains began to dance on the bar. Thanks to Van Eyck and his own experience, Hemony knew at which position on the bell wall each partial note dropped the most in response to thinning of the wall. Because most partial notes are correlated to each other, retuning one partial note also affects the others to one degree or another. Hence, tuning a bell is a game of anticipation and compensation, a form of tightrope walking with the bell.

François Hemony and his younger brother tuned the partial notes of their bells according to the minor third chord that Jacob van Eyck had determined as the ideal for consonant bells. They tuned their partial notes, and the tone series of their carillons in their totality, not according to the present well-tempered tuning, which subdivides the octave into twelve identical half tones, but they rather used the mean tone temperament that was common in their time. This is an adaptation of just intonation, in which all intervals are derived from simple fractions such as 1/2, 1/3, etc. In mean tone temperament, only the major thirds remain pure and the other intervals are adjusted to allow playing music in more keys than is possible with just intonation. As a result, however, sharped notes are no longer the same as the corresponding flatted notes, so that a choice always has to be made for 'chromatic' bells. Consequently, carillons tuned using mean tone temperament only sound pure in keys with a maximum of three sharps or two flats. Subject to this limitation, the Hemonys tuned their bells with a precision that would only be equaled after the Second World War.

Pieter Hemony

While François was renewing the carillon landscape in the North, younger brother Pierre, who in the meantime had changed his name to Pieter, was trying his luck in the South. In 1658, he cast for Tongerlo Abbey his first carillon as independent bell-

Pieter Hemony's Large Triumphant, commonly known as *Roland*

founder. He then moved to Ghent to cast church bells for St. Nicholas Church in Ghent, and for the Ename Abbey close to Oudenaarde. During his stay in Ghent, the city government ordered from him a new carillon for the belfry.[76] It needed to catch up, since it was saddled with an old instrument with 18 Waghevens bells, while the

St. Bavo Tower on the other side of the square had had a 32-bell carillon for twenty years. Hemony contractually promised to deliver an instrument that would be unrivaled anywhere in the land in terms of perfection and that would sound as pure as his instruments in Antwerp and Tongerlo. The bell-founder received all the needed facilities and could use the bell metal from the Waghevens carillon and the old Roland. On 16 June 1659, Hemony shattered the famous tocsin, which already after the third hit crumbled into 71 pieces. When complete, the 37 bells of the new carillon received high praise, and the city government placed an additional order for three *Triumphants* to serve as swinging bells and as additional bass bells in the carillon. This would make the new Ghent city carillon with 40 bells and a total weight of more than 60,000 Ghent pounds the largest and heaviest tower instrument of its time. In the summer of 1660, Hemony cast the three Triumphants. The heaviest of these – which would quickly receive the popular name Roland – weighed 13,973 Ghent pounds (or 13,400 lbs.). It was the heaviest bell that Pieter or his brother had ever cast. During inspection, the experts noted that the new Triumphants sounded less sonorous than the three swinging bells in St. Bavo Church on the other side of the square. Hemony was reminded that in his contract for the Triumphants he had promised that better bells would not be found anywhere in the land. The city government appointed new experts, and Hemony finally had to help an expert in tuning the third Triumphant. When bystanders noted that in removing bell metal for tuning it began to sound dissonant, the expert was ordered to immediately stop the work and limit himself to providing written advice to the bell-founder. The city government stubbornly continued to refuse to pay the balance, which amounted to more than 5,000 guilders. Years later, in 1676, Hemony would finally summon the Ghent officials before the Court of Flanders. This was followed by a series of reciprocal accusations and threats, but in the end, Hemony never got his way. Thus the City of Ghent never fully paid for the Hemony carillon of which it is now rightly so proud.

At the time Pieter Hemony summoned the Ghent dignitaries before the court, he had long since left the city. In the summer of 1664, he had joined his brother François in the city foundry of Amsterdam. In the meantime François had become a widower and was suffering from malaria. Together the brothers cast carillons for the completed Amsterdam town hall, the Dom Tower in Utrecht and St. Gertrude's Tower in Stockholm. The city council of Maastricht bought an existing instrument for the dome of the city hall. The brothers occasionally interrupted bell casting for long periods because they were too busy casting cannons for the benefit of the republic. In the meantime it had become the most important sea power in the world, and in the '50s and '60s had fought two wars against England over trade hegemony at sea. After the death of François in 1667, Pieter succeeded him as bell and artillery founder for the city, and he became guardian of his children François Jr. and Margareta.

Pieter remained unmarried. We know quite a bit about the last years of his life via 28 extant letters that he wrote to a client who had become a good friend: Antoine De Loose, prelate of St. Salvator Abbey in Ename. When De Loose, by order of the Pope, had built a new official residence with tower in his abbey, Hemony supplied three swinging bells and a light carillon of 27 bells. After Pieter returned to Amsterdam, De Loose continued to expand his carillon: he ordered a number of both heavier and smaller bells, finally bringing the total number of bells in the instrument to 35. Hemony's letters to the abbot are interspersed with personal elements such as his immense Catholic faith – in his Amsterdam house, Hemony had a furnished oratory at his disposal – and complaints concerning his waning health. The letters from De Loose have not been preserved, but based on Hemony's letters, the abbot must have asked the bell-founder a number of times for details concerning his famous tuning technique. Hemony's answer was always vague and evasive. On 24 June 1677, he wrote that his approach to tuning was like that of a doctor. He feels the patient's pulse and prescribes something. If it works, he continues to prescribe the same thing. The bell-founder listens, and at the places where the deviation is the greatest, he turns the bell. He listens again, and his ear tells him where to turn. A month later, the bell-founder wrote the abbot that he was no longer able to make the forms or cast the bells. This was all being done by his student and grandnephew Mammertus ('Mammes') Fremy, descendant of a Lorraine bell-founder family that had settled in Winterswijk. Hemony gave the instructions and still tuned the bells himself. He hoped that over time, his student would also learn how to tune. In subsequent letters, Hemony spoke increasingly about his declining health. In February 1680, De Loose received a short letter from Margareta Hemony, who lived with her uncle and did the housekeeping. She told him that her uncle had died, and sent him by ship in Hemony's name a small set of liturgical bells in gratitude for the affection and favors he had received from the abbot.

The Hemony legacy

After their deaths, François and Pieter Hemony became known in carillon circles as the *Stradivarii of the carillon*. Of the 51 carillons that they cast together or separately, 30 are entirely or partially extant today: 24 in the Netherlands and 6 in Belgium. The four Hemony instruments outside the Low Countries have been lost. A downside of their success is the fact that nearly all Flemish and Dutch carillons from before their time have been lost. Every city wanted a Hemony carillon, and to make the new instrument affordable, the material from the old bells was usually used to cast the new carillon.

The Hemonys did not make the carillon apparatus themselves, but rather called upon a clockmaker or a specialist carillon builder. They often worked with

Putto playing a carillon keyboard, from a Hemony bell at Kampen, the Netherlands

Juriaen Sprakel, the talented mechanic who presumably had recommended them in Zutphen at the beginning of their career: advice that would have far-reaching consequences for the carillon.

The Hemonys took great care in making their bells. Not only did their bells have a high degree of consonance and internal tranquility due to accurate tuning according to the ideal minor third chord, they also had scarcely any casting defects such as unevenness or porous parts. Great attention was given to texts and decorations. The larger Hemony bells contained Latin texts. Sometimes this was a confident pronouncement on the quality of their work:

> DVLCIOR E NOSTRIS RESONAT TINNITIBVS AER
> *The sounds of our bells sweeten the air*

Sometimes they used the then motto of the Republic:

> CONCORDIA RES PARVAE CRESCVNT
> *Where there is harmony, small things grow*

They usually selected psalm fragments that sung the majesty of the Creator, among which the well-known verse from Psalm 150:

> LAVDATE DOMINVM IN CYMBALIS BENE SONANTIBVS
> *Praise the Lord with resounding cymbals*

The psalm texts came from the Catholic Vulgate translation, but were accepted by their Reformed clients without a problem. On larger bells, the brothers usually applied a frieze of a centaur robbing a naked lady. The second and best-known frieze shows five putti or angels playing bells in various ways. One of them is playing a carillon keyboard and another is measuring the purity of the bell's sound using a tuning bar. The two friezes were the visual trademark of the Hemonys, and until the beginning of the 19th century, carillon makers in the Low Countries took them over to give their bells a Hemony appearance.

There was, however, one weak point in the Hemonys' work: the sonority of the smallest bells. The ever-greater range of their bell series gave rise to the need for smaller and smaller bells, and over time a natural limit was reached. The pitch of a bell is determined by its diameter at the bottom of the sound rim. This means that a bell that sounds an octave higher than another bell is half as wide at the bottom. Since weight evolves in three dimensions, the second bell is eight times lighter than the first ($8 = 2^3$). This simple law is called *dynamic similarity*. To prevent their high bells from weighing only a few hundred grams and not being audible from the ground, the Hemony brothers made their small bells thicker and wider, so that their vibration frequency was greater and their sound higher. This made possible a minimum weight of 11 to 18 lbs. This special profile, however, made the small or treble bells difficult to tune. Yet, despite their thicker profile, they often had a 'thin' sound and a short decay time. Only a century later would a bell-founder succeed in casting small bells with good sonority.

Thanks to the collaboration between a blind Dutch carillonneur and two French immigrant bell-founders, the carillon had won a place in the pantheon of recognized musical instruments. It was by no means certain, however, that the coming generations would be able to deliver instruments of the same quality. This question was also a concern to Abbot De Loose. After the death of her uncle, Margareta Hemony wrote to the abbot to tell him that Hemony's grandnephew Fremy was the best workman at the bell-foundry, but she doubted whether her uncle had ever taught him the tuning technique. She hoped he had been able to adequately observe his tuning work in the foundry. It would quickly become clear whether Mammes had been initiated in what Margareta called *the ultimate secret*, the secret of the pure bell.

CHAPTER 8

Carillon music at the court

The successors of the Hemonys

François and Pieter Hemony had purified the Low Countries of unpleasing carillon sounds. Most important city towers now housed a carillon that sounded as melodious as any other musical instrument. Foreigners visiting the cities in the region listened with astonishment to the public instruments that offered them daily musical delight. Moreover, some foreign monarchs saw the carillon as a potential means of support for their political or religious objectives, or as a – somewhat oversize – enrichment of their cabinet of curiosities. There was, however, one problem: it was unclear whether the new bell-founders equaled the quality of the Hemonys. This resulted in interesting projects with uncertain outcomes.

Pieter Hemony was succeeded as bell and artillery founder of Amsterdam by his apprentice Mammes Fremy. The city government required him to move the foundry to the workplace of Gerard Koster – which came free with his death in 1679 – and began charging him rent. Mammes started an association with his older brother Claude, but the two soon split. In 1682, Mammes received an order for a new carillon for St. James' Tower in The Hague. He evidently took on the project in his own name, and at a certain moment the city officials heard that not Mammes, but Claude would have been the official city bell-founder of Amsterdam. The city government believed the erroneous message, labeled Mammes an impostor, and withdrew the work assignment. Pieter Hemony's best student died two years later, without being able to demonstrate whether he had learned from his uncle the secret of tuning bells.[77] His brother Claude became city bell-founder of Amsterdam. When The Hague relaunched the project around 1683, it would not go to him, but to a bell-founder from the Spanish Netherlands, Melchior De Haze from Antwerp.

De Haze was held in high esteem, because in addition to bell-founder, he was mint master of the lord.[78] Moreover, he had already successfully competed against Pieter Hemony: in 1675, the city government of Bruges had preferred him to Hemony for the new carillon for its belfry. And they were very satisfied with the instrument. He – surprisingly – had mastered the tuning technique, which caused

Angel playing a carillon. Detail from the ode on Melchior De Haze (1632-1697) by François-Didier de Sevin.

some researchers to conclude that he must have been a student of the Hemonys at one time. An ode by Antwerp Minim brother and ode specialist François-Didier de Sevin rates his work even higher than that of Hemony ('Altius Emoniis Aeribus aera sonant').

The city government of The Hague remained critical, and the city's carillon became a long ordeal for De Haze. The bell-founder had contractually promised that the new carillon for St. James' Tower would be equal to the Hemony instrument of the Amsterdam town hall. When the carillon was hung in the tower at the beginning of

1687, this guarantee came back to haunt him. One of the inspectors noted that the difference with the instrument in Amsterdam was as clear as night and day. Especially Delft city carillonneur Dirck Scholl wrote very sarcastically about the tuning and sonority of the bells. In response to which De Haze wrote him a bitter letter in which he asserted that he had other, more profitable things to do than casting bells, but that his love for the art compelled him, especially since this art might be lost after the death of the Hemonys. He, however, would take the secret of bell casting with him to his grave, because he was planning to destroy all his papers before his death. Experts haggled for five years and De Haze continued to recast bells, until Claude Fremy again arrived on the scene and was commissioned to recast the De Haze carillon. This, however, never happened, and the bell series by De Haze remained in the tower. A number of its bells still exist today. An analysis of these bells shows that while De Haze tuned correctly, his bells had numerous casting defects that impaired their ability to vibrate and gave them a rather dull sound when compared to the instruments of the Hemonys. The fact that De Haze had problems with the casting technique could also be seen from an earlier experience in Bruges: while the bells were approved, his mechanical drum was not accepted by the city, even after three castings.

Fremy and De Haze also confronted one another in Alkmaar. In 1684, the city government ordered from Fremy a carillon for the Waagtoren. The work was delayed because several bells broke while being tuned. When the instrument was complete, successive experts contradicted one another, until Melchior De Haze was hired in 1687 to put things right. The city approved his work, and asked him to make a second instrument for St. Lawrence Church. The two De Haze carillons still sound today across the city center of Alkmaar. Despite his proven incompetence, Fremy succeeded in selling carillons to Riga and Prague. The carillon in the Loreto Convent in Prague presumably consists of rejected bells from Alkmaar, and its dubious sound can still be heard today. In his own country, Fremy delivered a carillon for Leeuwarden. This instrument was later retuned, so that it is not possible to assess its original quality.

The work of De Haze also found its way to other countries, including three carillons for Spanish palaces: he sold carillons for El Escorial and for the Prado Palace in Madrid, and the royal palace of Aranjuez also received a De Haze instrument. According to some sources, this instrument was removed by the Count of Monterey, the Governor General of the Spanish Netherlands, from the palace of the Dukes of Brabant in Brussels to present as a gift to the King of Spain upon his return to Spain in 1675. None of the three instruments has survived. Fortunately, De Haze's final export product survived the test of time. In 1695, he sold a carillon to Count Johann Ernst van Thun und Hohenstein, Prince-Archbishop of Salzburg. Johann Ernst was a major builder, and had a number of churches constructed that transformed Salzburg into the brilliant baroque city that it remains today. He wished to purchase a carillon for the tower of his palace, the *neue Residenz*, with the proceeds from his shares in the East India Company. His intermediary J.B. Guillelmi first consulted Claude Fremy in Amsterdam. When Fremy was judged too expensive, Guillelmi visited Melchior De Haze in Antwerp. He had a series of 35 carillon bells ready and told his visitor that this was the most beautiful set of bells he had ever cast: he had made them for his own enjoyment at a time when he had no assignments, and thus was able to take his time. He added that others were also interested: the mayor of Amsterdam had already come to hear the bells. In response, Guillelmi asked the Prince-Archbishop to decide quickly, because De Haze was the best bell-founder in the world and was ready to sell his only available bell series to others. Johann Ernst took the bait. Bells, keyboard, clappers and other accessories were carefully wrapped in straw, packed in three crates, and transported to Salzburg in two carts. When the shipment arrived in the archiepiscopal city two months later, there was no one there capable of installing the carillon in the tower. Fitters in the Southern Low Countries were contacted, but they refused or set excessive conditions. Not knowing what else to do, the archbishop had local contractors cast the mechanical drum and install the instrument. In the meantime, he had time to increase the height of tower of the neue Residenz from four to six levels and – as culmination – to install at the top an open lantern for the carillon. The fitters didn't know what to do with the keyboard, and only the automatic mechanism was put into operation. The instrument played for the first time in 1705, nine years after the bells arrived in Salzburg. The bell music of Salzburg received the name *Monatmusiken*, since the music was reprogrammed each month. At the end of the 18th century, court Kapellmeister Michael Haydn composed a number of melodies for the carillon. After three hundred years, the Salzburg carillon of Melchior De Haze still plays three times per day, and is successfully promoted as a worthy musical attraction for the numerous tourists who visit the city.[79]

De Haze had already died by the time the Salzburg carillon was ready to be played. He died in 1697 without successor. He left behind a daughter Maria and a son-in-law with whom he quarreled due to the younger man's violent character. Nevertheless, after the death of the bell-founder, son-in-law Jeronimo Lenaerts became administrator of his estate. It is unlikely that Melchior De Haze passed on to his son-in-law the secret of tuning bells.

The carillons of Peter the Great

Two years after De Haze, his Amsterdam rival Claude Fremy died. He was survived by his widow Catherine ten Wege and four underage children. Catherine continued the foundry with the help of 66 year old Claes Noorden, a former foreman of François

Hemony. A few months later, she ensured the survival of the foundry by marrying Jan Albert de Grave, an artillery founder of German origin. Amazingly enough, the duo Noorden and De Grave cast brilliant carillons from the start. This is likely due to the craftsmanship of Amsterdam organist and carillonneur Sybrand van Noordt, who assisted the bell-founders in tuning the bells.[80] Noorden and De Grave restored the splendor of the Amsterdam bell and artillery foundry, and contributed to the export of carillons. They received their most prestigious order in 1702, from Moscow.

This order was remarkable, because Russia had a significant indigenous tradition of bell-founders and chimers.[81] Russian bell-chimers played on untuned bells, as had been common in the Low Countries in earlier times. During the Middle Ages, the playing of bells was imported from the West, which can be seen among others from the fact that *kolokol*, the Russian word for 'bell', is derived from the Celtic *glogga*. The sound of chiming bells fit the Russian soul, and it supplanted the wooden semantron that was the custom in the Russian orthodox liturgy. The Russians call chiming *zvon*. The most sophisticated form is the *trezvon*, in which one or more chimers play three bell registers at the same time: quick sound clusters in the small bells above a foundation of sound provided by heavy bells with, in between, a filler by bells of average size. Echoes of Russian bell playing can be heard in the music of Mussorgsky, Rimsky-Korsakov and other Russian composers. Rachmaninov, with the choral symphony *Kolokola* ('The bells'), composed a grand sound fresco in honor of Russian bell-playing – even if the text is a Russian translation of *The Bells*, a poem by Edgar Allen Poe about church bells in New York. Russian bell-founders surpassed their Western colleagues in the size of their bells. Movie lovers undoubtedly know the impressive final scene of Tarkovsky's movie *Andrei Rublev*, in which an enormous bell is cast under the direction of a young bell-founder according to the secret formula of his deceased father. The reality was no less spectacular. A 64-ton bell hangs in the Ivan the Great Bell Tower in the Kremlin complex, and on the square in front of the tower stands the *Tsar Kolokol* or king of bells, a colossus with an incredible weight of approximately 445,000 lbs. The bell was cast in 1735 for the Ivan the Great Bell Tower, but was never installed because, during an immense fire, a piece of the bell broke off while it was still in the casting pit.

Tsar Peter the Great imported a new sound into Russia. He wanted to modernize his kingdom and transform it into a Western style state. In 1697 and 1698, together with thirty companions, he traveled one and a half years throughout Europe to become acquainted with Western politics, technology and culture. He learned many useful things, especially in Amsterdam and surroundings: he studied shipbuilding at the East India Company, which at the time owned the largest shipyard in the world; he spoke with technicians, scholars and artists, and frequented taverns. All of this took place to the rhythm of the always present music of Hemony bells in five

Amsterdam towers. Four years after his long trip, the Tsar ordered from Noorden and De Grave three forestrokes or carillons for the Kremlin. Thus, bell music was also a part of the Western culture that Peter the Great wanted to introduce to his compatriots. Little is known about the type and use of these instruments that have disappeared in the meantime.

The Cathedral of St. Peter and St. Paul in St. Petersburg

Shortly after installation of the Dutch carillons in the Kremlin, Peter started construction of a new capital in the north, at the place where the Neva River empties into the Baltic Sea. St. Petersburg became Russia's window to the West. The city received canals like Amsterdam, and was built by Western architects in a Baroque style inspired by Dutch and Scandinavian examples. In the garden of his Peterhof Palace, the Tsar had a cascade and fountains constructed. The Prussian carillonneur and technician Johann Christian Förster designed a series of crystal bells that were sounded by the movement of water. One of St. Petersburg's most impressive buildings was the Peter and Paul Fortress intended to protect the city against the threat from Sweden. From within the fortress rose a cathedral with a tower and a 400-foot needle-shaped gilded steeple as a beacon for travelers entering the city via the river. In 1717, Peter ordered a Dutch carillon with baton keyboard for this tower. Presumably the bells were cast by Jan Albert de Grave, who had continued to cast bells alone after the death of his partner Claes Noorden in 1716. The instrument had 35 bells and was played daily by Förster and a number of young Russians being trained by him. The residents of St. Petersburg, however, were not able to enjoy the carillon for long. On 29 April 1756, around 11 p.m., lightning struck the slender steeple. The tower appeared to be undamaged, but a smoldering flame slowly crawled from the top of the steeple downwards. In the morning, only the ruins of the tower and carillon remained.

Carillons for the young Prussians

Peter's neighbor, Frederick III, Elector of Brandenburg and Duke of Prussia, had grand plans. Frederick wished to become king, and after some military and political haggling with Emperor Leopold I of the Holy Roman Empire, he succeeded. In 1701, in Königsberg (present Kaliningrad), he crowned himself Frederick I, *King in Prussia*. He was unable to say 'of Prussia' since he only ruled over the eastern part of Prussia. Unofficially he was referred to as *Krumme Fritz* due to a spinal injury he sustained in a coach accident as a child. Thanks to the connections of his Dutch mother, Countess Louise Henriette of Nassau, he could be cared for in IJsselstein close to Utrecht. During his stay in Holland, the young prince and his brother had ample opportunity to visit and listen to the sounds of Amsterdam. One day he would do something with a carillon.[82]

Frederick loved art and grandeur, and with the prospect of becoming king within reach, he had Berlin beautified into a dignified monarchical capital. The city's showpiece was the expansion of the *Stadtschloss*. The design foresaw a plaza surrounded by a cathedral, a palace, horse stables and a slender three hundred twenty-two foot tower to house the royal mint. The tower would be crowned with a carillon that among others would serve to musically announce the changing of the guard. In 1700, he ordered his official bell and artillery founder Johann Jacobi to cast a carillon with 37 bells. Two years later, the bells were ready, needing only to be tuned, which would be done with hammer and chisel. Thus, the wait began for completion of the tower. When it was two thirds complete, cracks appeared and it began to tilt. The situation could not be righted, and the decision was taken to demolish the mint tower. Architect Andreas Schlüter was dismissed, and he went to St. Petersburg, where he was able to work for Tsar Peter. King Frederick died in 1713, leaving behind an incomplete *Stadtschloss* and a mountain of debt. He was never able to hear his carillon – fortunately, as quickly would become clear.

Frederick's son and successor Frederick William reorganized government spending in favor of defense. He built up a powerful army of 80,000, which earned him the nickname *Soldier King*, and he created Prussia as it would later be known: well-organized and overarmed. In contrast to his father, he disliked art, the sciences and any form of finery. He halted his father's megalomaniac construction projects and disbanded the court chapel. Frederick William, however, did have a plan for the bells gathering dust in Jacobi's foundry. Before his enthronement, he had been on several study trips to the Dutch Republic and, like his father, he was a great admirer of all things Dutch. He purchased the carillon and donated it to the Parochialkirche, his Berlin parish church. The monarch was a strict Calvinist, and saw in bell music a means to exhort the residents to piety. The bells were inspected and found to be inadequate. Jacobi was forced to recast twenty bells. When organist Johann Martin gave the inauguration concert on New Year's Day 1715, the bells still sounded out of tune. So a sample of the bronze was sent to Jan Albert de Grave in Amsterdam, who replied that the bronze used was unsuitable for bells. In the meantime, the patience of King Frederick William had been exhausted, and in April 1717, he wrote the church government, asking it to purchase – within the year – a quality carillon from Holland and to install it in the tower. The church government hastened to Amsterdam to negotiate with De Grave, and a contract was signed on 16 June. The bell-founder went to work immediately in order to have the bells ready before the waterways to Berlin froze shut. They were cast and tuned for the most part on 10 August, and on 10 and 11 September they were approved by experts, after which they were weighed, packed and insured against robbery by Swedish pirates. On 4 October, the cargo was loaded at Amsterdam to arrive in Berlin by the end of the month. The Dutchman Arnold Carsseboom assembled the instrument, and on November 1717, seventeen years after the start of the project, the carillon – to everyone's satisfaction – sounded through the streets of Berlin. The instrument received intense use. The automatic mechanism was reprogrammed fifteen times per year, so that it accurately adorned the time of the year. It sounded eight times per hour and played principally psalms and chorales, in accordance with the wishes of the Soldier King.

    The entwining of piety and militarism that characterized Frederick William was also prominent in the nearby city of Potsdam, where the King had his summer residence. Frederick William developed Potsdam into a garrison city and had a church built there for the benefit of citizens and soldiers. For the tower, he ordered an automatic carillon of 35 bells from De Grave that received an excellent evaluation from the experts. Arnold Carsseboom installed the bells, which were first heard on 1 January 1722. The building developed cracks after a number of years, presumably due to its swampy foundation. The bells were taken from the tower and the building demolished to make room for a new garrison church with an almost 300-foot tall tower according to the Dutch model. The King brought in Dutch workmen who built a Dutch neighborhood with canals and brick houses. At the King's request, Arnold Carsseboom added five bass bells and a keyboard to the carillon. Every 7.5 minutes a variety of music was automatically played: in addition to the classical chorales and psalms, various dances were also programmed on the drum. After the death of a king, funeral music was programmed to play for an entire year. In 1797, at the request of Queen Louise, *Lobe den Herrn* was programmed to play on the hour, and on the half hour, the song *Üb' immer Treu und Redlichkeit*, a slow version of Papageno's aria *Ein Mädchen oder Weibchen* from Mozart's *Magic Flute*. The text refers to the rigorous Prussian military ethos, and the song grew into the official Prussian folk song. From this year, the two melodies sounded over Potsdam unchanged, further increasing the carillon's fame.

Royal extravagance in Portugal

The largest carillon project of the time – and until today – was realized in Portugal.[83] At its origin lay a fertility problem with sensitive political overtones. King John V of Portugal, surnamed the Magnanimous, was still without child in 1711, after more than two years of marriage. On the advice of a Franciscan monk, he made a pact with God: if God would grant him an heir, as thanks, he would erect a Franciscan monastery. God did his work, and that same year the infanta Barbara was born. King John more than fulfilled his promise, because instead of a modest Franciscan monastery, he had built in Mafra – a small village not far from Lisbon – a complex that would rival El Escorial and the buildings of the Vatican. The complex comprising nearly 900 rooms included a monastery for 300 monks, a church with six organs, a magnificent library with 40,000 volumes, and a huge palace. King John was able to pay for this with the 20% profits he received on the gold ore that had recently been discovered in Brazil.

It is said that shortly before 1730, King John traveled to the Southern Low Countries where he became acquainted with carillon music. He asked his steward, the Marquis of Abrantes, how much such a carillon might cost. When the latter stated the price of 400 contos, adding that this indeed was quite a bit of money, the King was said to have replied that it was cheaper than he thought. Because his church had two towers, he ordered two carillons, one from Willem Witlockx in Antwerp, and one from Liège bell-founder Nicolas Levache. The inauguration of the still incomplete building complex had to take place on 22 October 1730, the King's 41st birthday. The bells of Levache were ready first, and after unloading from the boat, were transported to the palace on ox carts, escorted by 400 soldiers. Due to the bumpy roads, they had their hands full keeping the heavy bells on the carts. Work continued day and night on the north tower, so that the Levache carillon could be played on the King's birthday. The Witlockx bells only arrived two years later. The loading in Antwerp was not without problems. The captain refused to load the bells until he received a guarantee that possible damage to his vessel due to bells colliding against the wall would be reimbursed.

Mafra was indeed a huge project. The Levache carillon in the north tower had 45 bells with as bourdon, an 8-ton f sharp. The Witlockx carillon consisted of 47 bells and – with a 9-ton bourdon sounding f – was even a half tone lower. Each carillon weighed approximately 97,000 lbs. The clappers and connectors were elegantly decorated, and the carillons were lavishly embellished with putti and allegorical figures. Especially the automatic mechanisms were astounding. Each instrument had two mechanical drums, cast by Gilles De Beefe from Liège. Moreover, the four giant music boxes were spring drums, able to store twice as much musical information than was usual. One of the drums in the north tower even contained three 'music tracks', which

Clockwork of the Levache carillon in the north tower of the Royal palace of Mafra

was unique in the world. The drums were equipped with a reserve weight, so that they could continue to play while the main weight was being rewound. It is possible that the second tower only played when the mechanical drums of the first tower were being reprogrammed. This ensured uninterrupted music for the monarch, his court and the monks. All could clearly hear that the Witlockx carillon was much superior to the Levache instrument: it was properly tuned and had magnificent, sonorous bass bells. Nicolas Levache had also attempted to tune his bells, but the result was poor by any standard. After the arrival of the Witlockx carillon, his carillon was probably scarcely played. Nicolas Levache himself must have enjoyed Portugal, because he and his brother settled there as bell-founders.

Willem Witlockx mastered bell casting to a high degree and was a reasonably good bell-tuner, things he could have learned from his older fellow townsman Melchior De Haze, supplemented with his own experience as ivory turner.[84] In most of the extant documents, he comes across as somewhat unreliable and opportunistic. His self-centeredness can be seen in the gaudy self-portrait that he cast on his large bells. His social status was confirmed by his appointment in 1723 as director of the Royal Cannon Foundry at Mechelen. Willem Witlockx died a wealthy man in 1733.

After his death, an excellent bell-founder tradition continued in the Southern Low Countries, which had been under Austrian rule since 1713. Joris Dumery, from Hove near Enghien, had learned the craft of bell-founding from his uncle Alexis Jullien, a bell-founder from Lorraine who had settled in Weert. After working a short time in Antwerp, Dumery was asked to cast a new carillon for the City of Bruges.[85] Lightning had struck the belfry on 30 April 1741. In the subsequent fire, the carillon of De Haze as well as the Holy Blood bell of Witlockx were destroyed. Dumery moved permanently to Bruges and cast for the city a new Holy Blood Bell and the heavy carillon that until today sets the mood in the city. Like De Haze and Witlockx, Dumery was a capable carillon and bell-founder, able to reasonably tune his bells without, however, achieving the tone purity of the Hemonys.

In the Dutch Republic, the death of Jan Albert de Grave in 1729 marked a temporary end to a high point in bell casting. The only bell-founder who still ventured to cast carillons was artillery and bell-founder Nicolaes Derck from Hoorn. Despite his ignorance of tuning, he succeeded in selling to three trading cities on the Baltic Sea: Copenhagen, Danzig and St. Petersburg. The instrument for St. Petersburg was to replace the carillon destroyed by lightning in 1756.[86] Tsarina Elisabeth, daughter of Peter the Great, wanted a new Dutch carillon for the yet-to-be-rebuilt tower of the cathedral, and placed an order with clockmaker Barend Oortkras of The Hague. In 1761, he with five helpers and 37 Derck bells traveled to St. Petersburg, where they saw that the rebuilding of the tower had not yet begun. Oortkras remained in St. Petersburg, awaiting completion of the tower. He would never see Holland again: three years later, he died in the Russian capital, ruined and bitter over local opposition to his ideas. The instrument was finally installed in 1776 by a German clockmaker, but was not well received. Over the years, some of the Dutch bells were even replaced by Russian bells – Tsar Peter no doubt turning over in his large grave in the Cathedral of St. Peter and St. Paul.

CHAPTER 9

The Bach of the carillon

Peter Vanden Gheyn, monk and entrepreneur

Should something like a bell-founder gene exist, it was certainly present in the Vanden Gheyn family. When Willem Van den Ghein settled in Mechelen as bell-founder in 1506, he could not have known that he would found a dynasty of bell-founders that would remain active until well into the 20th century. The career of the Vanden Gheyns, however, was not always a bed of roses.[87] After the golden age of the 16th century, when the Van den Gheins cast the first carillons, Mechelen entered a period of economic recession, and the family moved on. In 1655, Andries Vanden Gheyn settled near Sint-Truiden, only to depart a few years later to settle in Tienen. In this city at the eastern edge of Brabant, the bell-founder dynasty was continued by his son Peter and his grandson Andries.[88]

Andries was more of a local bell-founder, but in 1725 he received an important assignment. The city government of nearby Leuven wished to update its carillon, and concluded a contract with the Tienen bell-founder for delivery of an instrument that had to be better than the Witlockx carillon in his own city and of quality equal to the carillon of Pieter Hemony in Diest. Vanden Gheyn cast the smaller bells in his foundry in Tienen, and then moved to Leuven where he set up a foundry to cast the bass bells. The 40 bells were inspected in September 1728. The inspectors rejected nine. After Vanden Gheyn recast the bells, the instrument was approved, though it was not entirely satisfactory. The young bell-founder died shortly thereafter, probably in 1730. His wife Elisabeth Peeters was left behind with an unmanaged bell foundry and five children, including one newborn. Fortunately, the deceased bell-founder had a younger sibling who was an Alexian brother in Tienen.[89] Brother Peter Vanden Gheyn left the monastery on 11 April 1732 to help his sister-in-law and temporarily become bell-founder. This step was not irreconcilable with his status as Alexian. To fulfil their tasks, especially spiritual healthcare, the Alexians were not bound by *stabilitas loci* and consequently they often lived outside the monastery for a time. Surprisingly, Peter had mastered the art of bell tuning, something he could not have learned from his father or his older brother, since they themselves did not possess this skill.

18th century view on the central square of Leuven, with the city carillon in the St. Peter's Tower

Perhaps Peter received help in tuning from his nephew Matthijs, who already at a young age had evidenced exceptional musical ability. Since the foundry had no references, Peter first cast a carillon as stock. On 8 June 1734, Elisabeth announced in the *Gazette van Antwerpen* that she had a new carillon for sale with 32 bells. In the same year, the church government of St. James' Church in Antwerp, the church where Rubens is buried, purchased a carillon from Vanden Gheyn. The instrument cost 3,715.16 guilders, but the church government itself had to pay only 21.18 guilders. The parishioners had been generous in donating for the instrument, and Peter Vanden Gheyn used the bronze from the old bells.[90]

In 1735, Peter finished a contract that had been concluded with his brother Andries: the delivery of a new carillon for St. Rumbold's Church in Steenokkerzeel.[91] Peter delivered 21 new bells and retuned six existing bells. Elisabeth in the meantime took on young Matheus van Frachem, son of the local sexton, as lodger so that he could learn keyboard and carillon playing from her son Matthijs, who was then 14. In the same year, Brother Peter delivered a bell series for the town hall tower of Veere in Zeeland, and a new instrument for the church tower in Nieuwpoort. This last purchase, however, was vetoed by the emperor's minister in Brussels. He could not understand why necessary repair work to the streets and port infrastructure of Nieuwpoort dragged on, while the city appeared to have enough resources to purchase a carillon. In the end, the city was reprimanded, but the order could proceed.[92]

Peter was then called to Nijmegen, where the city government was facing serious problems.[93] It had given the order for a new carillon for St. Stephen's Tower to Liège bell-founder Jean-Baptiste Levache, the brother of Nicolas, who had cast one of the large carillons for Mafra. Jean-Baptiste had recommended himself to the city government using the work of his brother as reference. The city government had given him and his helper all the facilities needed to complete the work, but after two attempts, the results were poor. Not knowing what else to do, the Nijmegen authorities contacted Peter Vanden Gheyn, who completed the work together with then seventeen-year-old Matthijs. They retuned 18 of the heaviest Levache bells and recast the false sounding treble bells. The inspection committee declared that the bells corresponded fully with the views of François Hemony, the best of all bell-founders. This success increased Vanden Gheyn's confidence, because on 11 October 1740, Elisabeth announced in the *Gazette van Antwerpen* that she had in the foundry a three-octave carillon that was played daily to the pleasure of music lovers, and that in terms of tone and resonance was equal to the best works of the famous Hemony. Perhaps strengthened by the recent successes, in 1740 she sent a request to the city government of Mechelen to again establish a foundry there. Mechelen was not interested.

Matthias Vanden Gheyn, virtuoso carillonneur

Elisabeth's oldest son Matthijs – who for the rest of this book will be referred to by his known official first name of Matthias – did not wish to succeed his father as bell-founder.[94] He had demonstrated great musical ability from childhood, and at 20 years of age was appointed as organist of St. Peter's Church in Leuven. Four years later, in June 1745, Karel Peeters, who as a city carillonneur played the bells at St. Peter's Church, died. The Leuven city government appealed via the *Gazette van Antwerpen* of 18 June for all interested parties to present themselves for the vacant position;

candidates were given access to the carillon beforehand in order to become familiar with the instrument. On 1 July, five candidates presented themselves: the city carillonneurs of Soignies and Dendermonde and three Leuven organists, including Matthias Vanden Gheyn. The sequence of the playing had been determined by a lot. The jury, who had taken its place in the large hall on the second floor of the town hall, did not know the sequence in which the candidates would play. To exclude possible collusion with the members of the jury, the city authorities forbade the candidates from playing a prelude or striking any bells before playing the required works. The candidates were required to play four pieces: *Les folies d'Espagne*, *Les Bergeries* (probably the harpsichord piece by François Couperin), a *capriccio* and an *andante*. The jury was harsh on four participants, and announced that candidate five gave the best performance by far. Number five turned out to be Matthias Vanden Gheyn, who was then unanimously elected as new city carillonneur of Leuven. The city offered the young musician a contract containing a number of unusual conditions. He was required to pay the fees of the three members of the jury and contribute 25 pattacons or silver coins for a new canopy in St. Peter's Church. And he was required to retune the poorly tuned carillon bells of his father at his own expense or recast them if necessary. After protest on the part of Vanden Gheyn, this article was weakened to the upgrading of only the small bells. Furthermore, the carillonneur could not appoint a substitute, unless he announced this beforehand. Each violation would result in a penalty being deducted from his salary.

Matthias quickly achieved a reputation as a great musician on the organ and on the carillon. His biographer, the jurist and musician Xavier van Elewyck, recounts that the Archbishop of Mechelen, after a Mass in the Leuven St. Peter's Church, refused to leave the church until Vanden Gheyn had finished his *sortie* on the organ. Older citizens of Leuven told Van Elewyck that Vanden Gheyn would walk to the Market Square one hour before his Sunday carillon concert, elegantly dressed in black habit with white tie, pants and jacket in black silk, gold rings on his shoes, a tricorn on his head and a cane with knob in hand. He would talk with the audience some twenty minutes, and imperceptibly look around to see whether people from outside Leuven had come to listen to him. He would then disappear into the tower, change his clothes, play a number of preludes, and further regale the audience a half hour long with virtuoso and original improvisations. After the concert, he would again change his clothes, slowly descend the tower stairs, and once outside, shake the hands of the bystanders who had waited for him. His success is even more amazing when you know that he was forced to play on the flawed carillon of his father.

The virtuosity of Matthias Vanden Gheyn is highlighted in a memorable story that musicologist Charles Burney wrote while traveling through Leuven in the summer of 1772. At this time, the post of chapel master of St. Peter's Church was held by

Romanticized 19th century portrait of Matthias Vanden Gheyn (1721-1785) on the facade of the city hall of Leuven

violinist Willem Gommaar Kennis, according to Burney 'the most remarkable performer on the violin in point of execution, not only of Lovain, but of all this part of the world'.[95] Burney wrote that the solos of Kennis were so difficult that no one dared to play them but the composer himself. However, the local carillonneur – Burney wrongly referred to him as *Scheppen* – was jealous of the renowned violinist and bet him that he could play one of his most difficult solos on bells. A jury judged the carillonneur the winner, and he won much praise for being able to bring a difficult undertaking to a successful conclusion. Burney mentioned this anecdote especially for his English readers to demonstrate how highly bell music is regarded in the Low Countries. And he concludes the story stating that in every city, residents tell foreigners that their carillon is better than all the others.

Matthias Vanden Gheyn was also a successful composer. His *Fondements de la basse continue* was published in Leuven, and a bundle of divertimenti for harpsichord was published in London. Vanden Gheyn, however, also wrote music specifically for the carillon. In 1862, Xavier van Elewyck found at various locations in Leuven unpublished scores of the Leuven carillonneur. With the manuscripts, Van Elewyck discovered two handwritten copies of eleven preludes, which he rightly identified as carillon music. He copied the preludes and published two of them. Thanks to Van

Elewyck's copy, carillonneurs discovered the eleven preludes in the 20th century and included them in their standard repertoire. The copy, however, contained many copy errors and incorrect interpretations. These were corrected in Dutch and American publications as much as possible, but without much guidance on which to base these corrections. This confusion continued until the autograph of the preludes was found in 1995. This document is written in the recognizable hand of Matthias Vanden Gheyn and is clearly the composer's copy, given the numerous deletions and corrections. Vanden Gheyn's preludes are festive pieces that provide an uninterrupted stream of music with a series of scale runs, broken chords, harmonious progressions and echo-effects in all conceivable variants and combinations, all to a propulsive rhythm of bass notes.[96]

Beginning of Matthias Vanden Gheyn's prelude n° 7 for carillon

The collection of preludes by Vanden Gheyn is the earliest known music specifically written for carillon: music that uses the full range of the then existing carillons and that is easier to play on a baton keyboard than on the keys of a harpsichord or piano. They are not autonomous concert pieces, but virtuoso opening pages that as it were bubble up at the moment of the playing itself. They give the performer the opportunity to familiarize listeners with the sound of the carillon and draw their attention to the repertory work that follows.

Due to the strong cadence and harmonic logic of the preludes, in carillon circles Matthias Vanden Gheyn is referred to as the *Bach of the carillon*. The number of his offspring brought him even closer to the German master: he was father to 17 children. To maintain the large family, the Vanden Gheyn family ran a textile shop. Van Elewyck was told that Vanden Gheyn composed off the cuff on the counter of the shop while his wife served the customers. His eleven preludes may have been composed in this way.

Andreas Jozef Vanden Gheyn, talented bell-founder

Given the professional direction taken by his older brother Matthias, the pressure to take over the foundry fell to his younger brother Andries – the third Vanden Gheyn with this name. We will call him Andreas Jozef to distinguish him from his great-grandfather, father and son with the same name. Mother Elisabeth died in 1745, but uncle Peter Vanden Gheyn in the meantime had educated his youngest nephew to be an excellent bell-founder. In 1751, Andreas Jozef delivered his opus 1 in Hasselt in the Prince-Bishopric of Liège.[97] The city had been without carillon since 1725, when a thunderstorm erupted above the city. Despite the diligent ringing of bells, lightning struck the tower of St. Quintin's Church – which by the way was cited as a reason not to pay the bell-ringers. In 1728, a new thunderstorm finished the job. Pastor Sigers then championed for a new carillon that would increase the piety of the people and encourage believers to attend church to listen to the word of God. The city concluded a contract with a traveling bell-founder from Lorraine, Antoine Bernard. When the work was complete in 1731, 15 of the 40 bells were rejected. Bernard went back to work, but remained unable to convince a team of new inspectors. The case dragged on until Bernard died three years later. The bells were stored in the city barn and Hasselt was deprived of carillon music for years. When lightning struck the tower again in 1751, the city decided to fully renovate the steeple and finally attend to the issue of a new carillon. Matthias Vanden Gheyn was called to Hasselt for advice, and his brother Andreas, then 24 years of age, could deliver his first instrument. The young bell-founder inscribed on the heaviest of the new bells a text that more than illustrated his faith in his own abilities:

ACTA VIRUM PROBANT
AD MAJOREM DEI GLORIAM
ANNO 1751 ME ET ADHUC 27 CAMP(ANAS). REFUDIT ET
RESTANTES CORREXIT.
HASSELETI AETATIS SUAE 24: OPE(RE) (PR)IMA. ANDREAS JOS.
VAN DEN GHEYN LOVANIENSIS

A man is judged by his deeds.
To the greater glory of God.
In 1751, Andreas Jozef Vanden Gheyn of Leuven recast me and 27 other bells
and retuned the rest. At Hasselt, 24 years of age. Opus I.

The first sentence often appears on Flemish harpsichords from the same period, and it places Andreas Jozef's first carillon in the line of full-fledged musical instruments. The self-assured tone is scarcely tempered by the second sentence, the familiar Jesuit motto that attributes his glory to God. Young Andreas gave his first carillon an opus number, which shows that he did not see himself as a craftsman, but rather as a genuine artist. The inspectors and administrators of the city shared the bell-founder's boast, and a local poet wrote a triumphal poem of more than 300 verses about the new carillon.[98] The unknown poet invites all who suffer from sickness or melancholy to come to Hasselt, because the sounds of the carillon will heal all. He then compares the Hasselt carillon to 24 other carillons in the North and South, and deems it superior to all of them. At the end, the poet extols the economic virtues of the new tower instrument: peasants will drink more when they hear the carillon and shops will do better business. And finally the carillon plays for all, the poor as well as the rich. Nothing is left of the increased piety hoped for by pastor Sigers a quarter century earlier.

In 1754, the young bell-founder delivered his opus 2 for the belfry at Sint-Truiden to replace a failed instrument by Nicolas Legros of Liège. In the same year, he replaced an inferior carillon by the same bell-founder in St. Lambert's Cathedral in Liège. Brother Peter guided the business aspects of these projects, but after the project in Liège, he judged that his task was complete. He returned to the anonymity of the Alexian Monastery in Tienen, where he died in 1770 at the age of 72. He left behind several delightful carillons in which he placed his own role in the background. Almost all of his bells were signed only with his surname.

His nephew Andreas Jozef enjoyed success after success. In 1759, he helped out the Oudenaarde city government by replacing an out-of-tune carillon by Tournai bell-founder Jean-Baptiste Barbieux with an instrument that, as agreed, sounded as beautiful as the Hemony carillon in the nearby Abbey of Ename. He also successfully completed restoration work in the Northern Low Countries. In Goes as well as

Nijkerk, he retuned and recast failed carillons of Alexius Petit, a bell-founder from Lorraine who operated a foundry in Someren in North Brabant. In Nijkerk, the farmers made their horses available to hoist the bells into the tower, on the condition that the carillon would play each Monday morning during the market. And the tradition continues until today.[99] In 1775, the city of Schoonhoven ordered a new carillon from Vanden Gheyn, and sent the Waghevens bells from the old carillon to Leuven as raw material, together with one of its *memorabilia*: a cannon that had been used on the ship of Olivier Van Noort, the first Dutchman to sail around the world. The city government asked Vanden Gheyn to cast the following inscription into the bourdon: 'My voice, that sounded hoarse for the Courageous Van Noort, after a long rest now sounds a beautiful chord.'[100]

Vanden Gheyn delivered the two smallest bells free of charge. The Schoonhoven city government was so elated that in September 1776, it sent a letter to the bell-founder stating that next spring, when the salmon were at their best, he would receive a smoked Schoonhoven salmon as a sign of gratitude. Vanden Gheyn received the promised shipment in the spring of the following year, with best wishes and 'bon appetit' from the city government.[101] Vanden Gheyn was the first bell-founder from the Low Countries to sell carillons in France. His opus 6 was ordered by François Gilbert, Abbot of the Abbey of Bonnefond in the Pyrenees, and opus 12 was delivered to the Benedictine Abbey of Liessies in the North of France.

In view of the overall success of the products of Vanden Gheyn, it is surprising that the Leuven town council never took the effort to replace the inferior city carillon of father Vanden Gheyn with an instrument by his talented son. Another Leuven tower did receive a Vanden Gheyn carillon. In 1776, Adriaan de Renesse van Baer, Abbot of St. Gertrude's Abbey, received an important inheritance from his deceased brother. He used part of the money to purchase a new carillon. Vanden Gheyn's opus 21 was ready in October 1778. Before being hung in the tower, the bells were suspended in the inner garden of the abbey between two chestnut trees, so that the prelate, who suffered from a chronic sickness, could see them from his room. In this temporary arrangement, they were played by Frans De Prins, who shortly thereafter was appointed abbey carillonneur. De Renesse commissioned his carillonneur to program the mechanical drum with new arias two times per year, and these were to be submitted to him beforehand for approval. For the rest, De Prins was required to play on many Church feast days and on the eves thereof. The duration of the concerts was set at 'three arias'. If we assume that De Prins had to play approximately thirty minutes, as was common at that time, we may also assume that he embellished the arias with diverse variations, and that he played long preludes, as Matthias Vanden Gheyn had done.[102]

Andreas Jozef Vanden Gheyn would deliver 23 opus numbers: all harmonious carillons that were quite light in weight and in tone. Vanden Gheyn tuned his bells

Bourdon of the carillon of Schoonhoven, the Netherlands,
cast by Andreas Jozef Vanden Gheyn (1727-1793)

slightly less precisely than the Hemonys, but he remained well within the limits of musical acceptability. He presumably used tuning bars for this, as was normal since the Hemonys. The quality of his small bells was much better than those of the Hemony brothers. More than his famous predecessors, he deviated from the principle of dynamic similarity, the law according to which very high bells would be extremely light. He cast his highest bells larger and thicker, which allowed greater volume while retaining the pitch. Hence, Vanden Gheyn cast bells that sounded nearly an octave higher than those of the Hemonys.

The instruments of Andreas Jozef Vanden Gheyn were the result of consultation and an exchange of experiences with his older brother Matthias, who served as advisor several times. Both brothers must have complemented one another well, because like Matthias, Andreas Jozef was also both a skilled bell-founder and a musician. He was organist at St. Michael's Church, which was located close to his foundry on Tiensestraat. Matthias and Andreas raised their children to follow in their footsteps. This, however, turned out differently than planned.

The descendants of the Vanden Gheyns

Matthias chose from among his numerous offspring his son Joost to succeed him as organist and carillonneur. At the age of twenty, Joost was given a first opportunity to prove himself as carillonneur. At the end of 1771, the Mechelen city organist and carillonneur Jan Jozef Colfs died, and the Mechelen city government posted a vacancy for a new organist-carillonneur. The Royal Board of Finance had stipulated that the chosen candidate must pay 1,000 guilders, an amount the city would forward to the government to pay down a loan. A few days before the contest, on 28 April 1772, a bidding war erupted between the candidates, after which the city government decided to postpone the exam. Finally, on 16 May, Jan Baptist Kieckens, the carillonneur from the Abbey of Tongerlo, was appointed as new city carillonneur and organist. He had offered 2,100 guilders, 100 guilders more than Matthias Vanden Gheyn had bid for his son Joost Thomas.[103]

After this negative experience in Mechelen, Matthias ensured the future of his son in Leuven. In 1777, he received from the city government the commitment that when he died, Joost would succeed him as city carillonneur. A number of his other children would be given important social positions. The best known of his descendants was great-great grandson canon Gabriel Van den Gheyn, archivist for the Diocese of Ghent and author of several historical publications. Canon Van den Gheyn was curator of St. Bavo Cathedral in Ghent when in 1934, the infamous theft of two panels of the Adoration of the Mystic Lamb by Hubert and Jan Van Eyck took place.

Until today he is considered one of the most mentioned protagonists in the unsolved saga of the Just Judges.

Andreas Jozef was succeeded by the younger of his two sons, André Louis, who from 1775, at 17 years of age, had helped his father in the foundry. For unknown reasons, in 1783 André Louis went to Nivelles, where the city government placed a foundry at his disposal free of charge. Only in 1792, a year before the death of his father, did he return to Leuven to continue bell casting there. The bells of André Louis show that he had not learned the bell tuning technique from his father. Thus an end came to the first major golden age of carillon building in the Low Countries.

Soon the skill of bell tuning would no longer be an important concern in our regions: a political storm was brewing with huge consequences for bells and carillon playing. But let's first take a look back on the golden age that we soon will leave behind.

CHAPTER 10

Panorama of the old carillon art

The number of carillons had reached a first high point around 1790. The Southern Low Countries were more densely inhabited with carillons than the Republic in the north, which can be explained by the fact that the Catholic South, in addition to the city carillons also included a large number of church and abbey carillons. Large cities had 5 or more carillons. According to what we now know, more than 100 carillons must have been heard in the Austrian Low Countries, and slightly less than 100 in the Dutch Republic. Together with an estimated 50 carillons in French Flanders and other areas in Europe, this amounts to some 250 singing towers worldwide. Only after the Second World War would this number be surpassed.

The bells

The carillon went through a profound evolution in the first three centuries of its existence. The number of bells in a carillon evolved from approximately twenty around 1600 to nearly twice this number at the end of the 18th century. Most carillons developed into all-in-one instruments with bells that were used for tolling, striking the hour, automatic playing and manual playing. The price of bells remained quite stable over the years. Most bell-founders asked 15 *stuivers* or slightly more per pound for a finished bell, with small bells being more expensive per pound than large bells (each city had its own pound, but in general a pound was somewhat less than a half kilo). If the customer provided old bells or other objects as bell metal, their value was deducted from the purchase price at a rate of approximately 10 stuivers or a half guilder per pound. To obtain the required money, city and church governments took out loans, levied additional taxes or organized collections among local residents. Occasionally a benefactor would make a contribution. The price depended on the number of bells and their weight, the size of the drum, transportation costs, and the rates charged by the individual bell-founder. A carillon cost between 5,000 and 20,000 guilders, which represented a huge investment for an abbey or for a city with on average much fewer residents than today. Since a carillon was a major investment,

Death riding a horse. Ornament on a Jullien bell in the carillon of Lier.

church and city governments appointed a board of experts to assess the quality of the work delivered. This was always done for the bells, often also for the carillon drum, and almost never for the keyboard and the system of connections. The numerous reported disputes between experts and bell-founders show that assessing the tuning of bells in a time without electronic measuring instruments was quite subjective. A number of experts played a somewhat dubious role in evaluating instruments: some were uncritical, probably because they did not know enough about the overtone structure of bells; others were needlessly strict because the bell-founder had included in the contract a standard formulation that the new carillon must be better than any other carillon in the Low Countries.

The automatic mechanism

The carillon drum and the clock were the most expensive items when purchasing a carillon.[104] We are well informed concerning the technical details of the complex carillon drum via the extant accounting records and a number of programming manuals that carillonneurs bequeathed to their successors. In addition to the Brussels programming books by Claes and De Sany, which were discussed above, we have two

Pins on the drum of the city carillon of Antwerp

documents from Ghent: a programming book with instructions by Fr. Philippus Wijckaert, who at the end of the 17th century programmed the Ghent belfry carillon, and a concise programming manual by J. Damman, presumably the same Damman who played the Baudelo carillon in Ghent. From Antwerp, there is an extant programming manual by city carillonneur Jan De Gruytters, and 109 worksheets with programmable music by Jan De Gruytters and his son Amandus. This collection contains music that sounded from the Church of Our Lady from 17 November 1740 to 19 September 1804.

The first playing mechanisms consisted of wooden wheels with fixed cams. During the course of the 16th century, these made way for wrought-iron hoops with in between, a number of wrought-iron slats that were drilled with holes. Around 1645, Jan van Call, a clockmaker from Nijmegen, developed a drum with a continuous surface that was cast as a single piece. Important to the casting of a drum was the right choice of materials. A drum that was too soft, could warp when subject to protracted use; material that was too hard, made drilling the thousands of drum holes a major chore. For this reason, most drums were cast in brass, an alloy of copper and zinc. Often drums were cast by bell-founders, but regularly also by specialized brass casters or watchmakers.

The system used in the carillon drum was quite simple. The mechanical drum was equipped with holes in which pins were inserted according to the pattern of the programmed music. Thus, pinning and re-pinning the carillon drum was digital programming avant-la-lettre, with the pins as 'ones' and the rest of drum surface as 'zeros' or unused memory. Each time the drum turned, the pins passed below a bed of levers. A lever pushed upward by a pin pulled a wire that in turn lifted a playing hammer. When the lever again fell to its normal position, the hammer fell against the outside wall of the bell. Immediately after the strike, a long spring lifted the hammer back to its original position, so that the sound of the bell would not be damped. The hammers hung on the outside of the bells, with the striking body at the bottom. In the Dutch Republic, many carillons hung in the lantern openings of the towers, with the hammers visible on the outside. In this way, the public could not only hear the mechanism, but could also *see* it playing from the street. The transition from vertical to horizontal wire between drum and hammer was handled by so-called *tuymelaers* or tumblers, L-shaped levers that hinged on a fulcrum. Holes were drilled in the two arms of the tumblers with which to attach the wires. The rotating speed of the drum was determined by a weight that was connected to the drum with a cable. Often a discarded cannon or a former millstone was used as weight. To keep the system in motion, the tower watchman had to raise the weight with a crank once or twice per day. The carillonneur could vary the tempo of the programmed music somewhat using a rotating reel with four metal plates attached to the drum. By changing the angle of the plates, he could modify the air resistance, which had an effect on the rotating speed of the drum. In many towers, the metal wind plates took the shape of swans with wings spread. No explanation has been found to date for what the swans symbolize.

City authorities wished to provide the city with a maximum of music, and to keep the periods of intervening silence as short as possible. The automatic drums were often repeated up to eight times per hour. Thus, local residents were reminded every seven and a half minutes of the passage of time, day and night, year round. The music followed a natural hierarchy: that played on the hour was the longest, followed by that played on the half hour; the two remaining quarters were limited to a single musical phrase and the so-called *klik* ('click') between the four quarters was only a scale figure or some other fantasia.

Not only the frequency, but also the length of the programmed music gradually increased. To increase the memory of the carillons, larger diameter drums were produced, allowing the addition of more rows with holes. In 1748, Jan and Antoon D'hondt created the largest music box in history, the still active drum of the belfry in Bruges. It has a diameter of two meters, and contains 250 rows of holes or drum measures, allowing more than five minutes of music to be played per hour. It contains

30,500 drum holes and weighs 9,000 kg. Around 1712, Antwerp clockmaker Hendrick Joltrain found a way to increase the memory capacity of the drum without increasing its diameter. He added intervening columns of holes to the surface of the drum, and had it rotate twice per hour instead of once. Joltrain used his invention for the first time in 1712 on the Jullien carillon in the St. Gummarus Tower in Lier. This revolutionary drum containing a total of 22,180 holes, good for ten minutes of music per hour, is still in use. Ten minutes of music per hour meant for the public four hours of music per 24-hour period, without the carillonneur even playing a note.

The aim was not only more music per hour, but also more complex music that approximated the performance of the carillonneur as closely as possible. In order to repeat notes quickly despite the slow hammer movement, frequently-used bells were equipped with multiple hammers, as many as six in the belfry of Bruges. A greater number of hammers required more columns, thus the drums became broader. In order to program all possible rhythms, the carillonneur had different types of pins available that could occupy each position between two holes. Repetitions of notes that were possible with the same hammer were handled by pins with a double or triple jaw. There often was also a separate series of pins for playing triplets and music written in 3/4 or 6/8 time such as gigues. If this series was not available, a carillonneur had to program measures in three, using classic pins. A musical measure was then programmed over the drum measure, a technique that was called *couperen*. As a programming tool, the carillonneur used a special lath that was placed on the drum and that indicated the corresponding bell per column. Programming was often done by two people: the carillonneur placed the right pins in the right holes, and a helper screwed them into the inside of the drum.

The programming sheets of father and son De Gruytters from Antwerp offer a fascinating look at the concrete practice of programming a carillon: in contrast to the prestigious programming books of Theodoor de Sany and Filip Wyckaert, they were used during the fieldwork in the tower. They contained numbered notes, deletions, additions, dates and other comments. The Antwerp mechanical drum had pins that could subdivide a drum measure into 24 and 36 parts. This made possible embellishments that accurately reflected the trills and mordents used extensively in baroque keyboard music. Carillonneurs Aeneas Veldkamp from The Hague and Joachim Hess from Delft went even further and used different hammers on a single bell to produce a tremolo effect on the bell.

Manual playing

While the archives provide good information concerning the automatic playing mechanisms of the old carillon, we have very little information on manual playing.[105] It appears that the ancien regime placed greater importance on mechanical carillon playing than on the musical performance of the carillonneur. This perhaps is due to the fascination our ancestors had with machines, devices that moved of their own accord and were able to produce music without human intervention. There are also fewer traces of keyboards in the towers than for the carillon drums. Carillon drum mechanisms that no longer worked often remained in the tower for reasons of cost, usually with the most recent program as a souvenir of the now-silent tower music. Discarded keyboards, however, ended up on the scrapheap or in the wood stove of this or that city worker, and today no more than ten keyboards survive from the period 1650-1800.

The keyboards for manual playing developed out of the primitive playing constructions of the former chimers and were initially made by local craftsmen. Only in the 18th century did bell-founders such as Andreas Jozef Vanden Gheyn produce them themselves. The dimensions and layout of the extant keyboards vary greatly. They, however, do share a number of characteristics. Independent of the weight and thus the absolute pitch of the bell series, a keyboard almost always started with C in the bass register. The pedal board covered just over an octave and extended down to d_1 or e_1. In total, an 18th century keyboard covered just over three octaves, depending on the number of bells. A striking difference between the North and South was the construction of the pedal board. The fulcrum of the keys in the so-called Flemish pedal board was in the keyboard, while the Dutch pedal keys hinged under the bench of the carillonneur. Presumably this later – less ergonomic – construction was influenced by organ building.

There are indications that at some locations, principally in the South, the connection between keyboard and clappers was realized by tumblers, such as those used on the carillon drum. The hinged tumblers, however, resulted in too much resistance for smooth carillon playing, and a simpler connection without moving parts – called a *schering* – was more often used for manual playing, certainly in the Northern Netherlands. The original form of the schering can be seen clearly in the picture of the Antwerp carillon that first appeared in the book *De Campanis Commentarius* by Angelo Roccha from 1612, and which was re-engraved several times. The carillon builder attached a wire to the underside of the clapper and stretched it horizontally by attaching it to a fixed point such as a wall or a wooden post. This so-called clapper wire was connected with a vertical wire to a keyboard baton. Whenever the carillonneur depressed a keyboard baton, the keyboard wire pulled on the clapper wire, which further tightened and pulled the clapper against the bell. After a time, this system was perfected by interrupting the clapper wire with a ring, which became the intersection of three wires. This type of connection had no hinged parts and thus was simple and smooth. On the other hand, it was not easy to install a carillon in such a way that all wires crossed at the same angle. This was possible in a large bell-chamber where the bells could be hung in rows, but in small towers where the bells hung around the window openings and there was insufficient wall space to optimally hang the wires, various intermediate connections were needed. Consequently, most bell-chambers resembled a spider web, with a motley tangle of vertical wires that emerged from the floor, horizontal or oblique wires that ran to the clappers and the walls, intermediate and support wires that ensured that all bells could be reached, and intermediate rings that kept the totality in equilibrium. In between these ran the wires for the carillon drum, connected finally to the hammers of automatic playing mechanism. Since all the angles in the wire connections of the schering were not the same, many baton keyboards had an uneven touch across the keys, which of course had a negative effect on playability. Moreover, the wires had the tendency to continue to swing after the attack, which made playing fast passages difficult. While in principle the carillon was already a touch-sensitive percussion instrument, this lack of control over the clapper strike meant that most instruments had a limited dynamic range. Until into the 18th century, manually played carillon music probably did not sound much different from the best programmed music.

The carillonneurs

Once a new carillon was hung in the tower and ready to be played, the owner had to find a suitable carillonneur. In the beginning, they were usually recruited from the local population. The residing carillonneur sometimes was given the additional task of training one or more students to succeed him. From the second half of the 17th century, most church and city governments gave priority to quality over local sentiment, and a vacancy was usually published in several newspapers. Vacancies attracted musicians from all regions of the Low Countries. There was, however, little interchange of carillon playing talent between North and South. The musical practices in the Reformed Republic and the Catholic Southern Low Countries probably had grown too far apart for active exchange to be possible. City and church governments appointed a jury of musicians who themselves were not carillonneurs. This shows that in these centuries, the carillon was considered a full-fledged keyboard instrument like the organ and harpsichord.

Because in the North, the functions of carillonneur and organist were often combined, there often was great interest when positions opened up, with sometimes up to twenty candidates. Larger cities after all paid a respectable annual salary of 500 to 1000 guilders. The number of candidates in the South was smaller on average than in the North: this usually concerned only the position of carillonneur, and for which a yearly salary of 200 to 800 guilders was paid. To this sometimes were added tax advantages, donations in kind such as a cloak, a hat or a pair of shoes, free housing or exemption from civil obligations such as guard duty. As a rule, an appointed carillonneur left his place of residence to settle in the city of his new employer.

Most carillonneurs did not exercise their function full-time. In the 16th century, they often assumed supplemental church-related tasks such as sexton, bell-ringer or gravedigger, or they worked for the city, such as carillonneur Job Adriaansz from Gouda, who in 1590 was responsible for the city's swans.[106] By the 17th and 18th century, however, most carillonneurs were active with their music full-time. In addition to carillonneur, they were organist, violinist, composer, singing teacher or instrument builder. Some, such as Matthias Vanden Gheyn, were traders and others were timekeepers in the church. Several carillonneurs were responsible for the proper functioning of the tower clock. Given the absence of organized social security, carillonneurs almost always remained active until their death.

Even if carillonneurs did not play full-time, they in any case had a busy schedule. In addition to carillon playing, they also had to program the mechanical drum. Due to the ever-growing memory capacity of the drums, this task became increasingly cumbersome and took two or more days. In most cities in the Low Countries in the 17th and 18th century, programming was done monthly, but sometimes more frequently as was the case in Leiden and Brielle, where around 1600, programming was done every two weeks.[107] At the periphery of the carillon region, this was taken to extremes: the carillonneur at Danzig programmed the drums for the town hall and St. Catherine's Church once per week, and even more often during some periods of the year.[108]

The carillonneur, during his fixed recital times, added accents to the continuous soundscape of the programmed bell music. In the cities of the Republic, a carillonneur played on average 150 to 170 times per year, which comes down to three times per week plus a number of feast days.[109] The preferred days for playing were Sundays and market days. In some cities such as Delft, Deventer and Kampen, the carillon was played several times on certain days. Many places celebrated the arrival of spring in May. From 30 April each year, carillonneurs would be playing almost daily until the end of May. The average playing time on the carillons of the North was initially a half hour, but expanded in the 17th century almost everywhere to one hour, probably in parallel with the growing musical possibilities of the carillon. Most concerts took place in the late morning, preferably between 11 and 12, just before the bells were rung for the lunch break.

In the South, the standard length of a concert remained limited to a half hour. The average frequency, however, was higher than in the North, which can be explained by the numerous Catholic feast days that were adorned by both Church and city carillons. Important holidays were announced by a concert on the evening before, and sometimes two concerts were given on the public holiday itself. As a result, the frequency of playing could be as high as 300 times per year, even in smaller cities such as Tienen and Diest.[110] The concerts of the carillonneur emphasized the calendar of Church and secular celebrations, the activities of guilds, chambers of rhetoric and other societal groups, and in this way enhanced the city's social agenda. For large celebrations, carillon playing alternated with music by city pipers and the ringing of bells. There are no direct indications that carillonneurs adapted their repertoire to the time of the year. Whereas the music of the carillon drum was occasionally – but often not – adapted to concrete circumstances, the carillonneurs probably played their known repertoire throughout the year. They created a musical decor in their city, and in this role, they were the precursors of local radio broadcasters.

Thus, carillonneurs in the North and South played year round, even though playing the carillon in winter would have been less than fun. Moreover, the carillonneur was expected to be available on an almost permanent basis. In some cities, the carillonneur was not allowed to leave the city without the prior permission of the authorities. He after all had to be available for unforeseen festive events such as a military victory or – in particular in the Republic – the birth of a child of the stadtholder. Despite the high frequency of playing, nowhere were the playing duties shared between multiple carillonneurs. There are also almost no documented exchanges between carillonneurs of different cities for special concerts.

The carillon repertoire

Today some fifteen collections with music from the heyday of the carillon are extant. This is a high number when we take into account that carillon music was not printed at the time, but only written down by carillonneurs for their own use. All but three come from the Southern Low Countries. In total, the extant manuscripts contain approximately 3,500 pieces, albeit often of short duration and with some duplication between collections. The extant collections of programmed music provide us with the best picture of the concrete practices at a number of carillon towers, since they often give information on the day or month on which the listed pieces were programmed. In the context of the counterreformation in the 17th century, programmed music featured much religious music, even in city towers. This can be seen from the fact that 51 of the 61 pieces in the Brussels carillon programming book by Theodoor de

Sany contain religious music, which was programmed for the appropriate time of the year. The carillon programming book for the Ghent belfry, compiled by Filip Wyckaert around 1685, also contains much spiritual music, such as *Martin Luther is in hell* that was popular among the public of Ghent in 1690 and 1691, judging by the added note *placuit* ('this was pleasing'). Both De Sany and Wyckaert programmed their drums with somewhat static polyphonic settings. The only extant South Dutch collection of programmed music from the 18th century is the bundle with programming sheets of Antwerp city carillonneurs Jan and Amandus De Gruytters (1740-1804). If these documents can be considered as representative for the programmed music of the time, we may conclude that in the 18th century, the goals of moral edification and increased religious zeal had made way for recreation and civil entertainment.

There is no extant programmed music from the North, but other sources reveal that there was less musical freedom in that region, and that even in the 18th century, the music of the carillon drum was still in support of political and religious ends. Psalms continued to be played on the hour, as was done in the 16th century. Since in the meantime, the Republic had become an independent state with a national feeling, the Wilhelmus melody (not the present national anthem Wilhelmus) was often heard emanating from carillon towers. On the carillon of the Waagtoren in Alkmaar, *Het Belegh van Alkmaar* ('The Siege of Alkmaar') was programmed each year on 8 October as a memorial to one of the crucial episodes in the Eighty Years' War. The titles of 941 pieces from Alkmaar have been preserved that would have been played between 1688 and 1727 on the De Haze instrument housed in the Waagtoren. They reveal a mixed picture of psalms, secular songs and dances. In Lutheran regions, bell music in the 18th century was exclusively religious and was characterized by simplicity and austerity. This can be seen from among others the extant music of the Assmus family from Darmstadt (1744-1790) and the collections of programmed music of Theodor Friedrich Gülich (1769-1775) and Johann Ephraim Eggert (1784) from Danzig. The bundles by Gülich occupy a unique place in carillon literature. The musical information is expressed not as notes, but as a sort of tablature for mechanical drum.

Like the programmed music, the extant bundles of manually played music contain no or very little original carillon music. Existing music was usually rewritten and adapted to the technical limitations of playing the carillon. Like the programmed music and standard keyboard music, it was written using two staffs. The upper staff was intended for the melody, played by both hands or fists, and the lower staff for the accompaniment, played by the feet. The music is easily recognizable as carillon music because especially the base line makes illogical jumps in order to remain within the range of the pedal board. From Antwerp, we have the booklet *Beijaert 1728*, a bundle containing Christmas carols, and the book written by Jan De Gruytters in 1746 for his concerts on the two carillons in the Antwerp cathedral tower. Ten years later, a

Les Folies d'Espagne in an arrangement from the Leuven Carillon Manuscript

carillon manuscript was compiled containing music for St. Peter's Church in Leuven. Thus, it presumably would have been written under the supervision of Matthias Vanden Gheyn. Both books contain a common core of popular music that included minuets and marches of legendary generals such as Prince Eugène of Savoye and the Duke of Marlborough, who had fought in the Low Countries. In addition, Jan De Gruytters borrowed material primarily from keyboard music of South-Dutch composers Raick, Fiocco, De Croes and others. The Leuven book in turn more strongly emphasizes the socially supporting role played by the carillon. It contains marches of the Leuven shooter's guilds and ecclesiastical societies, arias in honor of primuses of the university, and music that refers to festive occasions such as the appointment of the abbot of Park Abbey in 1730 and the ceremony marking the start of the digging of the Leuven Canal, performed by Governor Charles Alexander of Lorraine in 1750. It is simple, popular music that was also played by the city pipers and the city organist.

The Leuven carillon manuscript also contains two brilliant variations: extraordinary, genuine carillon music that together with the preludes of Matthias Vanden Gheyn represents the best of the old carillon culture. *Cecilia* is a theme with 7 variations based on a pan-European folk melody known in Flanders as *Ik zag Cecilia komen*. *Les folies d'Espagne* consists of a theme and counterpart, each of which is varied twelve times, good for fifteen minutes of haunting music. The famous melody Les folies d'Espagne, which inspired dozens of composers to write variations for diverse instrumental settings, was also the most often heard melody on the carillons of the Low Countries. It was programmed on mechanical drums and its playing was often required for exams.[111] The melody gave the jury the opportunity to test the virtuosity and the variation talent of candidate carillonneurs.

Musical tastes changed in the 2nd half of the 18th century, which can be seen in two music books of abbey carillonneurs: the carillon and clavier book by Frans De Prins, carillonneur of St. Gertrude's Abbey in Leuven (ca. 1781) and the extensive collection of André Dupont, carillonneur of the Abbey of St. Bertin in St. Omer (1780-1785). Very conspicuous is the absence of religious music in these bundles. In addition to minuets and various Flemish folk songs, Frans De Prins also scored French arias, often from operas that were then the rage in Paris such as *Le maréchal ferrant* by François Philidor and *L'amoureux de quinze ans* by Jean-Paul-Egide Martini. His North French colleague André Dupont played lighthearted songs such as *Le délice des dames*, *Les belles brunes* and *Les plaisirs de bains* for the monks of St. Bertin. Of the nearly four hundred numbers in his book, there is only one piece that is religious by nature, a paltry *Te Deum*, certainly insufficient to guarantee salvation for him and his patrons.

The only extant carillon music from the Northern Low Countries is a collection of music books by father and son Johan and Frederik Berghuys, city carillonneurs of Delft. They date from 1775 to 1816, and contain 1560 numbers, which represents a large portion of the extant old carillon repertoire. Here we encounter for the first time an extensive selection of classical music from other regions of Europe such as Italy, Germany and Austria. The Berghuys repertoire is generally cheerful and musically simple. In most pieces, the pedal part is indicated only by the letter denominations of the corresponding notes.

The material for manual playing confirms the major trends we saw in the programmed music. In the 18th century, the profane repertoire had the absolute upper hand in the Southern Low Countries. The carillonneur played the role of local DJ who presented the popular music of his time to a wide audience. In the Republic, psalm arrangements were the backbone of concerts, but in between there was sufficient room for variety.

Regarding difficulty, most arrangements in the extant carillon books are far below the level of virtuosity reflected in the preludes of Matthias Vanden Gheyn.

The pedal parts are indeed busy by today's standards, but given the relatively short reverberation time of Baroque carillons, this was musically acceptable. The performance practice of 18th century carillonneurs can be reconstructed thanks to the programming sheets of Jan and Amandus De Gruytters. With a view toward efficient programming, father and son De Gruytters wrote out their programmed music note for note, with the addition of a numeric code for the type of pins to be used. If the musical content of this programmed music can be transposed to manual playing, we note that De Gruytters, like his Leuven colleague Matthias Vanden Gheyn, warmed up his audience by playing preludes on the bells. The richly ornamented scores for the carillon drum make one suspect that behind the simple notation of the books for manual playing lie a rich musical praxis of playing preludes, variations and fantasias. Many carillonneurs were also organists and thus were familiar with the technique of playing liturgical melodies using variation techniques or freer fantasia forms.

The audience

One might expect that the richness of bell music in the Low Countries would have inspired poets and writers to poems or diverse lyrical descriptions. This appears not to be the case. Except for a few ad hoc poems on the occasion of a new carillon, there is no known contemplative literature on the instrument from the heyday of the carillon. Since the carillon was a standard part of our cities, carillon music was a common consumption article like food and drink. This was different for travelers: for them, the carillon was something new that gave cities in the Low Countries a special local flavor. Consequently, many travel journals contain impressions and descriptions of carillons from the North and South. Their authors were almost always enthusiastic about the numerous musical towers, which they often climbed out of curiosity.[112]

The traveler who wrote the most about the carillons in the Low Countries, however, was not a fan. English musicologist Charles Burney considered the carillon to be a barbaric musical instrument that would never have been invented in countries with a high music culture such as France, England and Italy. He nevertheless admired a number of carillonneurs. During a stay in Amsterdam in October 1772, he made contact with the blind musician Jacob Potholt. He listened to him admiringly on the organ of the Old Church, and then followed him to the dome of the town hall to watch him play the Hemony bells. Potholt began with a psalm melody, to which he added tasteful variations. To please his visitor, he then played a 15-minute improvisation. Burney was dumbfounded by what he saw and heard. The carillonneur punctuated his improvisation with trills, mordents, runs, triplets and arpeggios: in short, passages that according to Burney would have been difficult to play even with ten fingers.

Potholt always played in three or more voices, and indicated the rhythm with the pedals. He was able to vary the intensity of his sound from forte to piano, and to make trills swell in force and speed. After his improvisation, the carillonneur was sweating so much that he removed all of his clothing except his shirt. He donned a nightcap and rolled up his sleeves, in order to continue playing. In the meantime, he told Burney that after a concert he was so exhausted that he could scarcely speak, and had to go to bed immediately to keep from catching a cold. Burney concluded that the genius of Potholt deserved better than such a barbaric instrument. His description makes it clear that the carillonneurs of the time – or at least the virtuosi among them – did not play with a flat hand, but rather with the closed fist, with the little finger being the point of contact with the baton. When Burney saw the carillonneur of the belfry in Ghent at work some time before, he had already remarked that he played with leather protectors on the little fingers. For that matter, he too played in his shirtsleeves and 'with the collar unbottoned'.

Where Burney still had some admiration for the talent of a number of carillonneurs, the Englishman was unmercifully critical of the automatic carillons. During his stay in Amsterdam, he was scarcely able to recognize music in the sounds of the numerous carillons because the sounds of the bells overlapped with each other. Moreover, the timepieces on the various towers were not calibrated, so the carillons offered him scarcely five minutes of peace each hour. If he would have been forced to listen to such for months on end, he assured his readers, he would begin to hate all music – if he were not already deaf from all the racket. Thus, he had few good memories of Amsterdam, the city 'where little other music is encouraged or attended to, than the jingling of bells, and of ducats.'[113] It is difficult to know whether Burney was writing out of true annoyance, or simply being ironic.

The most famous traveler to get to know the carillon was Wolfgang Amadeus Mozart. In 1765, the Salzburg prodigy made a three-year tour of the European Courts, including a visit of the Low Countries. On 5 September, he climbed with father Leopold and big sister Nannerl one of the singing towers in Ghent. Thanks to Nannerl, who had noted the number of steps in her diary, we know that it was the belfry. The instrument must not have made much of an impression on the Mozarts, because father Leopold writes nothing more about it in his travel book. There is also the question whether nine-year-old Amadeus had the strength to play the stiff batons with sufficient power; and of course, he was still too small to be able to play the pedals. From 6 to 9 September, the Mozarts stayed in Antwerp, where at that moment among others the Flemish folksong *Reuzegom* ('the Giant's song') sounded each hour. Jan De Gruytters had programmed the drum on 12 August, presumably to announce the city procession of 19 August in which a new folkloric giantess would make the rounds. If young Amadeus had used one of the bell tunes he heard there as basis for a compo-

Jan De Gruytters' arrangement of the Flemish folksong *Reuzegom*; it was playing on the carillon of Our Lady Tower when the Mozart family stayed in Antwerp.

sition, this would have been fantastic international promotion for the music instrument of the Low Countries. Unfortunately it didn't happen... Years later, in 1791, Mozart did sing the wondrous qualities of Papageno's carillon in *The Magic Flute*:

> *That sounds so pretty, that sounds so fine!*
> *Never did I hear and see anything like it!*

Perhaps, shortly before his death, Mozart briefly thought back on the Low Countries along the North Sea, that musical land of plenty where towers make music.

The fate of the French Low Countries

The reader may have noticed that this chapter no longer speaks of the French Low Countries, one of the oldest carillon regions. After the annexation of French Flanders to France by Louis XIV in the second half of the 17th century, the political link between this region and the rest of the Southern Low Countries was broken, and it was degraded to a border region on the north side of the French kingdom. It continued to deliver competent carillonneurs, but these often found better work in the Southern Low Countries. The cities and towns of the French Low Countries no longer followed the carillon's ascendance. The region remained densely inhabited with carillons that usually hung in the typical belfries, but these sounded out of tune, because except for the Vanden Gheyn carillon in Liessies Abbey, they were cast by bellfounders from the region who had not mastered the art of tuning. The drum mechanisms were programmed conspicuously less often than in the Low Countries, and at a number of locations the same tune was on the drum so long that it became the standard jingle of the local community. This led to the so-called *Carillons* of Esquelbecq, Bailleul, Douai, Cassel, Cambrai and St. Quentin. In Dunkirk, the folk song *Een kalemanden rok* sounded so long throughout the city that it became known as the *Carillon of Dunkirk*. In later times as well, the residents of the region remained fond of the regular local forestroke. In Arras, a fixed melody sounded on the hour, *le carillon de l'heure*, for which a new text was written each year during carnival time with allusions to local situations. One of the most popular programmed melodies was the *Reuzegom* which was linked to the tradition of the procession giants that was very much alive in this region.[114]

After the establishment of the French republic in 1789, the carillon cultures of the Low Countries and Northern France would once again meet, admittedly under an unlucky star.

PART THREE

The new carillon art

CHAPTER 11

National Carillon

Carillon music riding the waves of politics

Habsburg Emperor Joseph II began his rule of the Austrian Low Countries in 1780. As a follower of the enlightened philosophers who throughout Europe reflected critically on the church, politics and science, he supported renewal, and quickly implemented administrative changes in his empire. These changes met with strong resistance in the Southern Low Countries. The old principalities, which had enjoyed a certain level of autonomy under their former governors, felt muzzled, and the Church was uneasy because Joseph II had abolished the contemplative monastic orders. Rebellious groups – calling themselves patriots – formed in various cities. They received growing support, and central authority weakened quickly. This was the case among others in the city of Diest, where for Easter 1788, the arias of the patriots of Diest and Mons were programmed on the mechanical drum of the Hemony carillon.[115]

In the autumn of 1789, the situation exploded. Encouraged by the popular uprising in Paris that in the summer had resulted in the Storming of the Bastille, the people of the Southern Low Countries went into action and – to the tolling of the storm bells – a revolt broke out that later would be referred to as the Brabant Revolution. When the Great Triumphant known as Roland tolled in the Ghent belfry, the Austrians fired back and hit the second Triumphant Filips in its waist. Until this day, the bell boasts a three-inch hole, which amazingly enough does not affect its sound[116]. In Diest, city carillonneur Jozef De Decker programmed the drum with the *March of the patriots of Leuven*. On 12 December 1789, the Austrians were chased from the territory, and on 11 January 1790, the new rulers proclaimed the United States of the Low Countries (later historiography would tend to speak of the United States of Belgium). More than two centuries after the northern provinces, the Southern Low Countries were now an independent state. In Diest, the *Lied der Eendracht* or Song of Unity rang from the tower. The new rulers, however, were unable to agree on the future of the young nation, and in the same year, 1790, the Austrians reclaimed power. Jozef De Decker was ordered by the Diest city government to promptly remove the patriotic arias from the mechanical drum.

Control over the Southern Low Countries changed again several times in the years that followed. On 22 September 1792, France officially declared itself a republic, and initiated a new calendar. The young republic wished to share its ideals of freedom, equality and fraternity with the rest of Europe, and after the Battle of Jemappes on 6 November 1792, the Southern Low Countries were occupied by France. The new rulers saw in carillon music a powerful promotional tool, and they forced local carillonneurs to add luster to the celebrations of the republic and to musically accompany the dance parties around the liberty tree. In Aalst, they asked city carillonneur Cornelis Schepers to play the republican songs *Marseillaise* and *Carmagnole*, and to program them on the drum. Schepers refused, and only after a stay in prison did he perform the required programming. From then on in Aalst one could hear:

> *Dansons la Carmagnole,*
> *Vive le son du canon!*[117]

Mechelen city carillonneur Gommaar Haverals on the other hand made a virtue of necessity, and so strongly convinced the French of the usefulness of the carillon as republican propaganda tool that they promised him a bell from the Church of Our Lady across the Dijle to complete his carillon in St. Rumbold's Tower. Later, the image of the carillonneur forced to engage in musical collaboration would speak strongly to the romantic soul: it is the tragedy of the clown who must entertain the audience despite his sadness.

The Austrians returned and defeated the French on 18 March 1793 in Neerwinden, at the border of Brabant and Liège. To please its English ally, the city government of Bruges ordered that *God Save the King* and an aria from *Richard the Lionheart* be programmed on the drum of the belfry. After the Battle of Fleurus on 26 June 1794, the French were back in the country, and the city government of Bruges was hastily forced to reverse its decision.[118] In Diest, the mechanical drum also continued to be programmed according to the political season. From Christmas 1794, revolutionary songs sounded every quarter: on the hour, the *Marseillaise*, every quarter, a Picard tune and the *Carmagnole*, and on the half hour, *Ça ira*.

> *Ah! Ça ira, ça ira, ça ira! Les artistocrats à la lanterne!*
> *Ah! Ça ira, ça ira, ça ira! Les artistocrats, on les pendra!*

Ironically, this latter revolutionary song is based on a popular pre-revolutionary contradance called *Le Carillon National*. Queen Marie-Antoinette, in better times, reportedly liked to play this cheerful tune on the harpsichord.

Melody of *Ça ira*, known formerly as *Carillon national*

The confiscation of bells in the Southern Low Countries

In 1795, the Southern Low Countries were officially incorporated into the French Republic and divided into nine departments. A number of laws already in force in France were automatically applied to the captured territory, including the law on church property.[119] In a decree of 2 November 1789, all church property in France was transferred to the state. Bells also became state property, and the state machinery had a keen interest in these objects. Contained in an instruction book on analyzing the bronze of bells could be read 'The bells that populated the churches due to superstition, provide us with a rich supply, a sort of inexhaustible mine to meet our needs'.[120]

The metal needs of the young French Republic were first monetary and later military in nature. The French currency system was reformed in successive stages, and bell bronze, if sufficient copper was added, turned out to be exceptionally useful for the minting of coins. It was durable and suitable for the pressing of sharp images. From 17 May 1790, all bells in the state could be used for the production of coins.

Needs changed, however, and on 23 July 1793, the National Convention placed all bells in the territory at the disposal of the minister of war.

French coin, made from bell bronze

Only hour bells and bells that warned of dangers such as storms and floods were exempt. The French population did not agree with this measure on behalf of freedom, and protested or sabotaged the disassembly of the bells where possible. In the French carillon region, all church and abbey carillons were requisitioned, and at least 30 towers lost their musical voice.[121] Only the abbey carillons of St. Amand and Liessies were spared. The latter instrument survived because the citizens of the nearby city of Avesnes were prepared to relinquish their own carillon if they would receive ownership of the abbey carillon. Despite protest by the residents of Liessies, this was allowed by the Directory, after which the citizens of Avesnes – weapons in hand – went to fetch the Vanden Gheyn bells.

When the Southern Low Countries were declared French territory, the French laws were applied to the nine new departments via decrees and circulars. On 21 February 1795, the ringing of bells for cult purposes was banned, on pain of imprisonment; on 22 July, all external signs of worship such as processions were banned; on 1 October, a number of monasteries were abolished and on 12 December, a writ was issued requiring an inventory to be made of all bells. This last decree found its context in the obligation of the annexed areas to deliver 60 million pounds of bronze to the central government, 'to be used for a more useful purpose, namely in support of the lofty task of freedom for the world', as could be read in a letter to the parish of St. Andrew in Antwerp.[122] The local authorities were in no hurry to submit the requested inventory, and on 8 May 1796, a decree was issued calling for urgent action in the matter; the local authorities would be held responsible for any further delay.

In the autumn, the systematic confiscation of bells was started by firms contracted by the occupying forces. Bells were preferably broken into pieces while still in the towers in order to facilitate their transport. The pieces were transported by horse and cart to central storage locations, to later be shipped to the cannon foundry at Le Creusot in Burgundy where they were used for the nobler goals of artillery and industrial machines. As was the case in France, the residents of the occupied territories did not make it easy for the dismantlers. Local residents alleged that the construction of the tower did not allow the bells to be removed, removed bells were immediately repurchased, swinging bells were connected to the clock in order to exempt them from requisitioning, and bells were hidden and buried, after which the French promised rewards for betraying the location of the hidden bells. The deportation efforts were also hampered by poor organization: the firms hired by the French government to handle the disassembly and the transportation protested because they were paid late, there was discussion concerning the property right of the clappers, and the like.

Given the artistic and promotional value of carillons, these objects were dealt with more cautiously. On 1 April 1797, the French Minister of Finance Dominique Ramel issued a circular in which he requested that the carillons not be destroyed, but be sold in their totality, 'comme ces objects tiennent aux arts'. On 11 August, it was stated that carillons with a high artistic value could remain in their towers. In the meantime, the program requirements for the carillonneurs of the Southern Low Countries continued unabated. In January 1796, Antwerp city carillonneur Amandus De Gruytters received a list with the following requests: *Le Chant du Départ, la Marseillaise, Ça ira, la Carmagnole* and a song with as chorus: 'Nous ne reconnaissons, en détestant les rois, que l'amour des vertues et l'empire des lois! Veillons au salut de l'Empire!' He was requested to limit himself to these songs during his concerts. Yet not all carillons were safe. In Maastricht – which then was not part of the seven northern provinces and thus was occupied territory – there was a serious dispute concerning the artistic value of the Vanden Gheyn Carillon in St. Servatius Church.[123] On 27 January 1798, a commission appointed by the city council advised that the instrument was a masterpiece and thus should not be taken. On 5 August, the authorities of the canton of Maastricht wrote that this qualification probably was based on the number of its bells, the sound quality, and the preconception of the residents of Belgium 'that a tower without carillon is like a body without soul', but that the carillon surely should not be considered an artistic masterpiece. Nevertheless, the authorities allowed the carillon to remain, if only not to deprive the residents of an 'object to which they have always been attached.' In the meantime, the hunt for abbey carillons continued unabated. At first, only the clappers were taken from the carillon in Grimbergen. When the automatic playing mechanism continued to play, the local peasants were commandeered to remove the carillon, and the Witlockx bells were thrown from the tower.[124] When it was the turn of the Hemony carillon at the Abbey of Tongerlo, the French found no local laborers and had workmen come from Antwerp. This gave the monks the time to remove a number of smaller bells, and present them to neighboring churches. Thus only the larger bells fell prey to the regime. The Vanden Gheyn carillon in the Leuven St. Gertrude's Church was preserved, but damaged: the coat of arms of Abbot Adriaan de Renesse van Baer was filed off six bells. This was probably done by local residents, who wished to avoid any association of the instrument with the nobility.

More than three years after the requisition order, many bells still hung in the towers of the Southern Low Countries. When the rural population, exasperated by high taxes, compulsory military service and the harassment of priests, revolted on 18 October 1798, the signal for the rebellion was spread by the tolling of the alarm bell in each successive village, from tower to tower. In each village where the insurgent peasants gained the upper hand, the remaining bells in the churches and monasteries were sounded. Bell ringing was used to pass on signals between the insurgent groups in the Flemish countryside and – after years of silence – no doubt must have had an infectious effect on the local residents. The unpredictable sound coming from

Coat of arms of Abbot Adriaan de Renesse, filed off a Vanden Gheyn bell in St. Gertrude's Church in Leuven

everywhere made the French soldiers nervous, which resulted in dramas, among others in the village of Langemark in West Flanders. On 25 October, the French in Ypres advanced to drive away the peasants who had taken the village. In response, a certain Rosalie Demeersseman rang the alarm bell. When she ignored the French order to stop, the soldiers set fire to the church tower. Rosalie continued to ring and was burnt alive.[125] The cities also became restless. In Antwerp, on 1 December, the government removed the clappers and swinging ropes from the bells of the Church of Our Lady and the parish churches to prevent tolling by rebels.

    The desperate battle on the part of the rural population came to an end after seven weeks when on 5 December, the peasant army was roundly defeated by the

French in Hasselt. Afterwards, the violence of the occupying forces was directed at the bells that had participated in the revolt, and the towers were emptied at a quicker pace. In the spring of 1799, large loads of bells and pieces of bronze arrived in carts at collection areas in the former Bonnefanten convent in Maastricht and the former Crosier monastery in Maaseik. Especially painful was the destruction of the carillon of St. James in Antwerp that began on 22 December 1798. The French tried to smash the bells while still in the tower, but this took longer than anticipated and they had to return multiple times to complete the work. For two months, the residents of the parish were forced to listen to the noisy death throes of the bells of Brother Peter Vanden Gheyn. An estimated thirty carillons in the Southern Low Countries, chiefly from churches and monasteries, were lost during the French occupation.

Gradual restoration of the bell stock

An end came to the violence against bells when the new ruler Napoleon Bonaparte concluded a concordat with Pope Pius VII on 15 July 1801 that provided for freedom of religion and worship. Due to a metal scarcity, restoration of the bells occurred slowly. In 1801, a chronicler in Leuven wrote that only one bell could be sounded in the entire city to celebrate the anniversary of the republic.[126] During the following years, the still remaining bells in cities and villages regularly announced the victories of Napoleon's armies on European battlefields. Gradually bells and carillons that had been hidden during the destructive bell campaign again saw the light of day. The residents of Steenokkerzeel reinstalled the carillon bells of Brother Peter Vanden Gheyn after removing them from under the dung hill where they had hid them. Due to the unfavorable financial position of the abbeys, the monks often sold their recuperated carillon bells. Thus in 1807, the Vanden Gheyn carillon of Val-Saint-Lambert moved to St. Bartholomew's Church in Liège, and in 1819, the Hemony carillon of Averbode arrived at the Collegiate Church of Our Lady at Huy. The Jullien carillon at the Abbey of Postel was sold in 1836 to the municipality of Helmond for the price of 1,000 guilders plus the eleven-bell carillon of Helmond itself.[127] The most important transaction took place at Leuven in 1811.[128] Since 1730, the monks of Park Abbey had possessed a magnificent carillon by Noorden and De Grave from 1712. This very likely was the instrument that the city of Brussels had purchased for the collapsed tower of St. Nicholas Church, which in the end was never rebuilt.[129] The monks were able to preserve the bells from requisitioning by burying them in a nearby farm. After the bells again saw the light of day, in 1811 they offered them via an intermediary to the city of Leuven. A commission of eight musicians first inspected the bells of Andries Vanden Gheyn in the tower of St. Peter's Church and judged them to be unbearably dissonant.

The bells of Noorden and De Grave, installed in the town hall, were considered the best carillon bells the commission members had ever heard. Abbey and city exchanged their bells, and from then on, the harmonious carillon of Noorden and De Grave hung in the crossing tower of St. Peter's Church in Leuven. The monks of Park Abbey probably sold the Andries Vanden Gheyn bells separately.

Trade during the post-French era sometimes brought the bells to unexpected places. A bell by Andries Vanden Gheyn from 1725 somehow ended up in France and now hangs in the chapel of the Palace of Versailles. Other traces of the diaspora undergone by bells and carillons during and after French domination can be found in a number of North French churches, where bells by Pieter Hemony hang that came from the Abbey of Ename that was abolished under Emperor Joseph II. The wordplay motto of Abbot Antoine De Loose can still be read on the bells: *caute, nec dolose* ('cautious, but not sly'). In the decades that followed, a church bell was occasionally discovered that had been forgotten by its savior or whose hiding place under the ground could no longer be found.

The French confiscation of bells was the first in history to be organized by a government and to be methodically executed. It was inspired in the first place by utilitarian considerations, but further fueled by a fanatical hatred of religion. It meant the end to an estimated 100,000 bells in France and the annexed territories. On the other hand, the French contributed to an aspect of the carillon that had been less developed until then, namely the use of the instrument for political ends. As a result, most civilian carillons in the Southern Low Countries escaped the ovens of Le Creusot.

The Northern Republic in the French era

The Northern Republic escaped the bell confiscation campaign that had plagued the South. The state, however, was not immune to the new philosophical and political ideas prevalent at the end of the 18th century, and it too was faced with the whirlpool of reform and revolution. The regime of stadtholders had increasingly begun to assume royal airs, and the regents divided up the administrative positions among their own ranks. This ran up against growing opposition from democratically minded movements that borrowed their thinking from the enlightened ideas of Paris and who, as in the South, were called patriots. In 1787, this resulted in a revolt and for a few months, the Republic was in the hands of the patriots. Supporters of the House of Orange-Nassau struck back with the support of Prussian troops. The honor of Stadtholder William V was restored, and the insurgents fled to the Southern Low Countries and to France. Orange flags were hung in the towers, and everywhere the Wilhelmus was sounded on the carillons.

Eight years later, the patriots were back, but this time with French reinforcements. On 18 January 1795, Stadtholder William fled to Orangist England, and the Batavian Republic was established the next day. This also changed the sound in the cities, such as in Utrecht, where pharmacist Hendrik Keetell recorded all the changes undergone by his city during these years.[130] English troops left the city during the night of 14 and 15 January, and on 16 January, Utrecht surrendered to the French troops. The next day, patriots cheerfully danced, dressed in ribbons, bows and colorful cockades. The Wilhelmus programmed on the carillon of the Dom Tower made way for a patriot's song. On 12 February, the psalm played on the hour was replaced by a secular melody. The new regime would no longer allow one religion to be placed above another. The growing French influence in the Batavian Republic became audible when, on 8 March 1798, the Marseillaise and *Ça ira* were placed on the drum. The swinging bells and carillon of the Dom Tower rang continually to enhance French victories and celebrations.

When in 1806, the Batavian Republic was transformed into a kingdom with Louis Napoleon as monarch, the Utrecht Dom carillon continued to do its promotional work. On 24 April 1808, carillonneur Frederick Nieuwenhuizen had to climb the tower three times to add grandeur to the birth of the king's son with carillon playing. Louis Napoleon took up the causes of the residents of his newly granted kingdom, to the displeasure of Paris. In 1810, his brother Napoleon Bonaparte dissolved the Kingdom of Holland and annexed it to the French Empire. When in the spring of the following year Napoleon and the Empress received a crown prince, the people of Utrecht celebrated with cannons, bells and carillon music, and when the imperial couple visited the bishopric in October, they did it all over again. Napoleon's star, however, was waning. On 30 November 1813, Crown Prince William of Orange landed on Dutch soil in Scheveningen after 18 years of exile, and on 6 December, the Utrecht Dom tower sounded music in his honor.

Thus carillonneurs in the Republic also adapted themselves quickly to the changing political winds. At the end of the day, they were civil servants in service of whomever was in power. Only the extenuating element that carillonneurs from the South could use to justify their actions, namely the protection of the bells they played, did not apply to northern colleagues. No northern Dutch bell was sent to the artillery foundries in France, because at the moment that the Northern Low Countries officially became French territory, the concordat between Napoleon and the Vatican had long since halted the hunt for bells.

Thus, the carillons in the Northern Low Countries were subject to the central authority of the day. With one exception. In the south of the country, one small carillon continued to oppose the occupying forces. In the Zeeland fishing village of Arnemuiden, the automatic carillon continued to play the old Wilhelmus, hour after hour, day after day. Presumably the bells of Peter Van den Ghein were so out of tune that they camouflaged the national song and no one could recognize its political message.[131]

Napoleon's bell

In 1812, Napoleon was driven from Russia – Tchaikovsky in his famous *1812 Overture* had the sounds of the Marseillaise make room for the roar of cannons and the triumphant chiming of the bells of Moscow – and on 18 June 1815, the final defeat at Waterloo followed, where ever since, a cast-iron lion gazes ominously in the direction of France. The lion on the hill was not cast from the bronze of French cannons, as many think.

The former emperor was banned to St. Helena, a small island without bells in the south of the Atlantic Ocean. When an occasional Dutch ship would dock at the small harbor, Napoleon often went to listen to the ship's bell. The sound fueled his homesickness and made him think of the cracked bell of Rueil, close to the castle of Malmaison where he lived. The former emperor thought back to his country, his family and the bell that informed him every day when he was to rise in the morning, when it was time in the afternoon to go to work in Paris, and when the hour had come to rest in the evening. The same bell had convinced him at the time that people needed religion, and would inspire him to conclude the concordat with the Pope. The former emperor told his discussion partner on the island the story of the pastor of Rueil. He had once asked Napoleon to present his church with two new bells to replace the bells lost in the revolution. The emperor agreed, on the condition that the cracked bell remained in the tower. Noting the surprise on the part of the pastor, he said: 'It's an old friend of mine.'[132]

CHAPTER 12

The carillon as romantic symbol

The carillon, an old instrument

In 1815, the Waterloo victors mapped out the Europe of the future in the Habsburg capital of Vienna. One of the most difficult pieces in the political puzzle was the status of the Low Countries. After considering various scenarios, the superpowers decided that the Low Countries on the North Sea would again be united. France was not allowed to keep the South French territory, and the powers that be found it important to protect themselves from the defeated enemy with a strong buffer state in the north. Thus the Kingdom of the Netherlands was created, with as monarch, William I, descendant of the stadtsholder of Orange-Nassau. After a separation of 250 years, the Low Countries were again reunited.

King William had new roads and waterways constructed in the South, and expanded the Port of Antwerp. His freethinking ideas and religious intolerance, however, were unacceptable to the French Catholic elite in the South of the Kingdom. The fermenting revolution was ignited during a performance of the opera *La Muette de Portici* by Daniel Auber in the Brussels la Monnaie theater on 25 August 1830. After hearing the aria *Amour sacré de la patrie*, the bourgeoisie walked out of the theater, and a war broke out in the city that finally led to the expulsion of Dutch troops from the territory, which from then on became known officially as Belgium. It is telling that the revolutionary feelings of 1830 were fed musically in the opera house and no longer from the carillon towers. A new society had formed in which the place of the carillon was not self-evident. There were various causes for this.

First, the carillon towers had lost their local monopolies on indicating the time. While the public indication of time continued, it was no longer required for society to function. More and more households had clocks that we now usually refer to as *grandfather clocks*, and the development of pocket watches in the 18th century made the measurement of time affordable to more people. Thus it was less obvious for a city government to spend considerable resources on local time indication and its musical embellishment. Still later, the development of railways and the postal service would substitute a national time standard for local ones.

In addition to timekeeping, the experience of music also changed thoroughly. Already in the 18th century, the music scene had gradually shifted from outdoors to indoors with the emergence of aristocratic salons, opera houses and concert halls. The 19th century brought with it still wider musical participation in the private sphere. Publishers marketed affordable arrangements of orchestral work and operas, and the piano became a polyvalent musical instrument that made a multitude of music accessible to the living room. It would soon even be possible to use perforated roles to produce mechanical keyboard music. Thus the mechanical drum in the towers received competition from the manual and automatic piano in the music room of the better bourgeoisie who provided for their own musical needs. The lower classes also no longer actively listened to the carefree and noncommittal music of the bells. They needed to focus their attention and energy on the fight for survival, and when they wanted to escape from everyday miseries, they preferred to seek consolation in drinking and paid sexual pleasure rather than in free tower music. Often for that matter they lived in working-class districts at the edge of the city, where the sound of the city carillon did not penetrate. The cities were becoming too large for a collective carillon experience.

Finally, there was also an important musical explanation for the declining popularity of the carillon. The new music simply didn't fit the sound of the old bells. Composers had shaken off the straitjacket of Baroque and Viennese classical music, and wrote adventuresome works that made frequent use of new means of expression such as surprising wanderings to remote keys, and musical phrases that swelled and ebbed in strength. Instrument builders adapted, and built keyboard, string and wind instruments capable of greater expression. The carillon lagged behind these developments: the required sound nuances were scarcely feasible on the stiff keyboards of the time, and impossible on the rigid carillon drum. In addition, carillon arrangements with many key changes were painful to the ears: the harmonious fabric of the previous measures continued to sound while the bells were being played in a new key. The decay of the bells, on the other hand, was too short to acceptably reproduce the sustained sung notes of the popular *bel canto*. Carillon bells were also tuned to the baroque mean tone temperament, which was unsuitable for keys with many sharps or flats. The new musical instruments on the other hand used equal temperament tuning, which divided the octave into twelve equal intervals and thus made possible unlimited modulations into any key. It was also difficult to convincingly reproduce on the carillon the rhetoric and the drama of romantic music, with its slight variations in tempo, expressive delays and rhetorical breaks. These effects obviously could not be reproduced on the mechanical drums, and carillonneurs who frequently made use of them in their concerts often did not achieve the desired effect. Carillon music in fact worked best in an atmosphere of rhythmic and harmonious predictability: it was popular music that the passer-by must be able to enjoy, even if he or she arrived within earshot of the carillon only in the middle of the music. Romantic music on the other hand worked best when the listener was able to follow the musical story from the first note. Thus as a result of the social and musical changes, a new and less natural relationship between people and carillon emerged, which inevitably led to a certain decline. Here again the changes in the North and South did not take place in parallel.

In the Netherlands, a certain cooling in the appreciation for the carillon could be detected already from the middle of the 18th century.[133] In a number of cities and towns, the frequency of the drum programming was reduced from once a month to once every two months or less. The ostentation of the Golden Century was past, and the late Republic was no longer the proud and extroverted global power it once was. This trend continued in the young Kingdom of the Netherlands. The mechanical drums continued to turn, but the programming frequency was further reduced to once per year in the larger cities and occasionally or never in smaller locations. The quality of the music decreased in parallel with its frequency, and it was no accident that from the 19th century, the forestroke was also called a *rammel*, a term that can also mean 'ramshackle', inspired by the irregular character of the programmed music. On the other hand, in places where programming continued, a contemporary repertoire could be heard on the carillon. This can be seen in the extant programmed music from the cities of Kampen, Schiedam and Utrecht.[134] In addition to the perennial psalms, the Dutch carillonneurs also programmed their mechanical drums with music by Mendelssohn, Donizetti, Weber and Rossini, often only a few years after the first performance in the concert hall or opera house. The carillonneurs still played concerts once or twice per week, usually on market days. The traditional Sunday concert disappeared almost completely. The hard work on the unwilling keyboards no doubt would have clashed with the Calvinist principle of Sunday rest. The playing mechanisms were poorly maintained and did not allow virtuoso carillon playing. In some cities, people could no longer be found to perform the task of carillonneur, and often the office was held by non-musicians such as shoemakers, blacksmiths or bicycle mechanics.

Yet a carillonneur lived in a city on the River Waal who knew how to evoke true emotion from his audience, and thus unintentionally wrote a piece of history. In November 1842, Frans Liszt journeyed through the Netherlands via the Waal River. When he docked at the city of Zaltbommel, he heard the Hemony carillon playing from the Hospital Tower. He visited carillonneur Carolus Leenhoff and was impressed with the piano playing of his daughter Suzanne. On his advice, Suzanne went to Paris to study at the conservatory, where she resided with the Manet family. In 1863, she married Eduard, the oldest son of the family, after which she became one of the beloved models of the father of impressionism.[135]

In Belgium, things were not as bad as in the Netherlands. Most cities still programmed their carillons twice per year, and there were still a number of ambitious city carillonneurs, such as Jan Volckerick, who worked in Antwerp as goldsmith and city carillonneur. In 1841, Volckerick wrote a number of *Preludes mélodiques* for the carillon. The pieces manifest numerous changes of tempo and mood, and are interspersed with virtuoso 32nd-note runs. These whimsical works full of effects are almost unplayable as written, and yielded Volckerick the nickname *the Liszt of the carillon*. In his other work, Volckerick followed the musical fashion. He wrote adaptations of opera melodies and in 1845, he programmed a polka on the carillon drum of the Our Lady Tower, scarcely two years after the dance had taken the Paris dance halls by storm. In the same year, the potato harvest failed in Belgium, which inspired poet Theodoor van Rijswijck to write an ironic poem about the polka music from the tower: thanks to the new dance, the people can now decline to a rhythm – one step forward and two steps backwards.

Literary interest in bells and carillons

While 19th century music culture did not lend itself well to the carillon, literary romanticism discovered a reality behind the carillon: for poets and novelists, the old-fashioned instrument was a strong carrier of meaning and ideas. This romantic conceptualization may even have been stimulated by the greater distance that the carillon took with respect to day-to-day life. Romanticism kept the carillon alive until it was rediscovered as a musical instrument at the end of the 19th century.

The carillon's new role found its place in the context of the rediscovery of the bell, which was transformed by European romanticism from signal to symbol. Already at the end of the 18th century, writers had discovered the rich symbolic world of the bell. Between 1795 and 1799, François René de Chateaubriand wrote *Génie du christianisme*, a large-scale apologia for Christianity that was a response to the rational ideas of the enlightenment and the anticlericalism of the French revolution. The work was published in 1802 after Napoleon's concordat with the Pope, and it had a major influence on budding romanticism. Chateaubriand passionately described the transcendent character and the evocative power of church bells, which were capable of simultaneously causing like-minded feelings to be born in thousands of hearts, which through their admonishing nightly tolling were a torment for adulterers, atheists, tyrants and killers, but which also enhanced the joy of major celebrations and joined in the mourning when major disasters struck humanity.[136] In 1799, Friedrich Schiller wrote *Das Lied von der Glocke* ['The Song of the Bell'], a long poem that describes the process of becoming a bell, and compares it with the various stages in human life and the role played in this by the bell. The work was translated multiple times and set to music, and quickly won a place in the canon of German literature. Via Schiller's poem, many generations of German youth have become acquainted with the mystical nature and associative power of the bell.

In 1831, the bell received a place in the art of novel writing thanks to *Notre Dame de Paris* ['The Hunchback of Notre-Dame'], the epic novel by Victor Hugo. With full evocative power, Hugo describes the tolling of the church towers of Paris on Easter morning. His hero, the hunchback bell-ringer Quasimodo, loves his bells as if they were human beings: 'He loved them, he caressed them, he talked to them, he understood them. (...) It was these [bells], however, which had deafened him: but mothers are often fondest of the child which has caused them the greatest pain.' When the bell-ringer has the giant bell Mary rung by his helpers and the tower begins to vibrate due to the movement and the sound, Quasimodo stands before the big bell, waits until it is at its loudest, and pounces on it, as if a strange centaur, half human, half bell, swaying through the bell-chamber.[137]

In August 1837, Hugo visited Belgium for the first time and was introduced to the carillon. Full of admiration, he described his experiences in letters to his wife Adele.[138] Just before the border, in Douai, Hugo drew a picture of the richly decorated belfry. When viewing the result, he could still hear the cheerful music 'springing from [the carillon] as the natural emanation of that mass of bells.' In Mons, he admired the capricious baroque belfry, 'the result of the collision between north and south, between Flanders and Spain.' Hugo viewed Mons as a Flemish city, because for him, Flemish and Belgian were synonymous. Because he would be taking the coach from Mons to Brussels at three in the night on 18 August, he stayed awake and looked toward the town hall square from his room under the star-studded heavens: 'Occasionally a delightful carillon would sound from the giant tower (...) And when the last vibrations of the striking of the hour had sounded, and silence had scarcely returned, a strange and melancholic sound descended from high in the giant tower. It was the void and weakened sound of a horn, no more than two sighs. Then silence again enveloped the city for an hour. The horn was the voice

The belfry of Mons, as sketched by Victor Hugo in 1837

of the night watchman. (...) Sleep could never have given me a dream that would have pleased me more.' In Mechelen, he stood in awe of the clock of St. Rumbold's: 'All of the giant construction was taken up by a clockwork; the weights ascend, the cogs turn, the pendulums swings to-and-fro, the carillon sings. This is life, it has a soul. (...) On certain days a man sits behind a keyboard that I have seen, like Didine sits behind the piano, and plays on the instrument. Imagine that: a four hundred foot high piano, with the entire cathedral as sounding board.' In Mechelen, Hugo also wrote his often-cited poem *Écrit sur une vitre flamande* in which he described the carillon as a paragon of the Flemish people, a people living on the divide between north and south and who celebrated their traditional values:

> J'aime le carillon dans tes cités antiques,
> O vieux pays gardien de tes moeurs domestiques,
> Noble Flandre, où le Nord se réchauffe engourdi
> Au soleil de Castille et s'accouple au Midi!
> (...)

The poem bears as caption *Malines*, the French name for Mechelen. The story goes that Hugo, in his hotel on the Market Square, was kept awake by the carillon of St. Rumbold's, after which he used the diamond in his ring to express his romantic feelings on the window glass of his room. However, the poem in fact describes his nocturnal experience in Mons two nights earlier. In Antwerp, the writer could not get enough of the slender Tower of Our Lady: 'an immense construction, like a miraculous ornament. A titan could live there; a woman would love to wear it around her neck.' He probably had not understood that the bells in the tower were part of two carillons: 'Eighty-two bells! Imagine a carillon that would ring from this beehive.' In Tournai on the occasion of the feast of St. Louis, the residents lit the belfry with colorful oil lamps, and from the tower sounded 'the chattiest, most amusing carillon in the world'. It was a celebration, and 'all bells were in movement, as were the women.' The last Belgian city he visited was Bruges, where he was told that the belfry carillon was known as the most beautiful tower instrument in Belgium.

The enthusiasm of Victor Hugo when writing of Belgium was in stark contrast to the disapproval of Charles Baudelaire when he visited the country in 1864. Only in Mechelen did he feel at home: 'If Mechelen were not in Belgium and not inhabited by Flemish, I would love to live, and especially die, there. So many carillons and bell towers, so much grass in the streets, so many beguines ... ' On reflection, he judged that the carillon in any case was only a passive expression of art: 'Mechanical music in the air. It represents the pleasure of a will-less people (*un peuple automate*) who can only entertain themselves on command. Carillons release the individual from the need to express pleasure.' Baudelaire was alone in these opinions, and his pronouncements probably say more about the misanthropic and melancholic attitude of the poet than about his topic.

Hugo and other writers visiting the new Belgium found the carillon so beautiful because it did not fit with the modern era. The carillon sounded 'old' with its meantone bells in which the new music no longer neatly fit. The carillons that were programmed less than before played the same tune for a long time, which gave rise in poetic souls to a feeling of nostalgia. Due to lack of maintenance, programmed music sounded increasingly irregular and halting, and as wires broke and were no longer repaired, the music gradually faded until it became a sound mist at the border between recognizability and mystery. The deterioration of the music carried with it a form of beauty that made one think of the attractiveness that emanates from ruins. Like weather-beaten and overgrown ruins testified to a grand, but irrevocably vanished past, the vulnerable sounds of the carillon made one dream of times of richness, cultural flowering and the struggle for freedom, in short of an age in which Flanders was great. The carillon fit the fascination the romantic artist had for the past. And the carillon that best embodied this was the Dumery instrument in the belfry of Bruges, the city once referred to as the Venice of the North. Where its Italian sister city slowly sank into the Adriatic Sea, Bruges underwent the opposite: the North Sea had turned its back on Bruges, and the port of Damme, its life vein, was overtaken by land. Bruges' past reverberated in the voice emanating from the oversized tower that emerged from the medieval cloth hall, a tower that cast its shadow of both greatness and fate over squares and streets, and scattered its sounds to the remote corners of the city. The romantic traveler met the carillon of carillons in Bruges.

The carillon of Bruges became famous in the Anglo Saxon world thanks to the most read American poet of the time, Henry Wadsworth Longfellow. He arrived by train in Bruges on 30 May 1842, and took up residence in the hotel *La Fleur de Blé*. The carillon played and the hour bell struck eleven times. The poet wrote:

> *In the ancient town of Bruges,*
> *In the quaint old Flemish city,*
> *As the evening shades descended,*
> *Low and loud and sweetly blended,*
> *Low at times and loud at times,*
> *And changing like a poet's rhymes,*
> *Rang the beautiful wild chimes*
> *From the belfry in the market*
> *Of the ancient town of Bruges.*
> (...)

Visit to the carillon drum of the belfry of Bruges, from *L'illustration* (1898)

The eleven strikes continued to echo in his mind and evoke a range of images. The poet thought that he was the only one who listened to the bells, because it was night, and everyone had been too busy during the day. His thoughts wandered from the bell tower to the 'belfry of his brain', from which verses emerged that no one heard either. The poet hoped that he one day would find someone who would listen to him and relate the verses to his or her own experience, as he himself had done with the carillon at that moment.

> (...)
> *Thus dreamed I, as by night I lay*
> *In Bruges, at the Fleur de Blé,*
> *Listening with a wild delight*
> *To the chimes that, through the night,*
> *Rang their changes from the belfry*
> *Of that quaint old Flemish city.*

The next morning, Longfellow awoke at five in the morning and climbed the belfry. He heard the swallows singing together with the bells, he discovered the canal that as a silver ribbon connected Bruges with the sea, and he saw below the slowly awakening city. At that moment, the belfry came to life:

> (...)
> *Then most musical and solemn, bringing back the olden times,*
> *With their strange, unearthly changes rang the melancholy chimes,*
>
> *Like the psalms from some old cloister, when the nuns sing in the choir;*
> *And the great bell tolled among them, like the chanting of a friar.*
>
> *Visions of the days departed, shadowy phantoms filled my brain;*
> *They who live in history only, seemed to walk the earth again;*
> (...)

The bells of the belfry revived images of Flanders' past, and the poet saw Knights of the Golden Fleece, Italian merchants, Mary of Burgundy and her husband Maximilian, Flemish weavers returning from the Battle of the Golden Spurs, the great Jacob van Artevelde, deadly Spaniards and wailing alarm bells ...

> *Till the bell of Ghent responded o'er lagoon and dike of sand,*
> *'I am Roland! I am Roland! There is victory in the land!'*
> (...)

Then the noise of the city at his feet awoke him from his vision and chased the ghosts from the past back into their grave. Longfellow was the first of a long line of great and minor writers who until today lost their hearts to the beauty of the Bruges carillon: Dante Gabriel Rossetti, Rainer Maria Rilke, Arthur Miller, Tomas Tranströmer and many others.

The carillon at the service of nationalism

Interest in the past was also an item on the political agenda. Throughout Europe, national achievements from the past were dug up from under the dust of centuries to give the peoples of new states a feeling of national identity and patriotic pride. This 'programmatic' nationalism was much stronger in Belgium than in the Netherlands. Since the struggle for freedom under the leadership of William of Orange 250 years earlier, the Netherlands had developed a strong national feeling that had become an *organic* part of the Dutch people. Young Belgium, however, covered a territory that never before had been an autonomous entity. In the eyes of many, it was an artificial political construction, an imposed society made up of two different language groups on the dividing line between Roman and Germanic culture. In Flanders, Orangist groups still longed for a great, unified Netherlands, and in some French language circles, there was the rattachist dream of unification of Belgium with France. Thus the young Belgian State had to demonstrate the country's right to exist, and went in search of connections that promoted the Belgian-ness of its inhabitants. Historiography created national heroes, and with state support, statues were erected in the cities of Belgians from an era in which the country had not yet existed: Ambiorix, Godfrey of Bouillon, Margaret of Austria and many others. With Rubens, Bruegel and the Flemish primitives, a pantheon of Belgian art was established. The French-speaking upper class that ruled the country had no problems seeking the historical roots of Belgium primarily in the Flemish past. In the early years of the kingdom, the use of the French language and a Flemish feel for culture were in fact perfectly compatible. The Belgian nation was given sufficient Germanic roots to differentiate it culturally from its threatening French neighbor to the south. The challenge of course was to transform the presence of two Belgian subcultures from a threat into a strength. We have already read that Victor Hugo, who was favorably disposed to the new country, was part of this effort. Did he not speak in his carillon poem of northern Flanders that warmed itself in the southern sun? Resounding proof of the unity of the Belgian people were the carillons in their cities. Carillons were remnants from the past and could be found both in the Dutch speaking region in the north and in the French speaking region in the south of the country.[139]

The carillon was deployed for the first time in the service of the new country on 20 February 1852. On that evening at the Opéra Comique in Paris, the premiere took place of the opera *Le carillonneur de Bruges* by Albert Grisar, an Antwerp composer who had made his career in Paris. The story of the opera takes place during the Eighty Years' War. Old Bruges city carillonneur Matheus Claes has gone deaf from sadness after the capture of Bruges by the Spanish troops. After a number of changes of fortune and intrigues, Claes with his carillon playing in the belfry gives the signal for the revolt against the Spanish occupying forces. The Spaniards were expelled, and when the national flag again waved from the Bruges belfry, Claes receives his hearing back out of pure joy. Grisar dedicated the opera to Belgian King Leopold I. The Belgian premiere took place in the Leuven city theater in the presence of Princess Charlotte and Princes Leopold and Philippe.[140]

In addition to militant purposes, the carillon was also positioned as something typically Belgian, and three centuries of shared carillon history with the Netherlands and Northern France were shamelessly ignored.[141] According to music historian Edouard Fétis, the carillon developed in Belgium because the Belgians were good instrument makers, skillful as they were in professions requiring patience and precision. In this context, the age-old story of how the carillon originated no longer fit this narrative. Consequently, somewhere between 1830 and 1850 the anonymous crazy man from Aalst was transformed into Bartholomew Coecke, bell-founder living on Lange Zoutstraat in Aalst, and family of two historical figures. He is said to have been the son of Pieter Coecke, court painter for Charles V, and brother-in-law of Dirk Martens, printing press pioneer of the Low Countries.[142] According to the story, Coecke was encouraged by his wife Pharaïlde to cast a complete carillon and connect it to the clock in the belfry. And thus, on Christmas Eve 1487 just before midnight, five minutes of bell music could be heard for the first time. The people of Aalst celebrated enthusiastically, and every city ordered a carillon from Coecke, who quickly became rich. The new myth was also difficult to eradicate. Only well into the 20th century did the romantic story of the Aalst bell-founder and his shrewd young wife fade into the background.

In addition to the carillon, the Ghent alarm-bell Roland also won a prominent place in prose and poetry. When Longfellow stood on the belfry in Bruges, he listened to the bell ringing from Ghent as a call to revolt heard throughout the country. In the revolutionary mood of nineteenth century Europe, the alarm-bell from Ghent even grew into a universal symbol of opposition to enslavement and the deprivation of liberty. Its call could even be heard on the other side of the Atlantic. During the American Civil War, the soldiers of the northern army were encouraged to listen to the voice of the bell from Ghent. It is striking that lyricist Theodore Tilton did not have America's own Liberty Bell, but rather the Ghent bell Roland, rumble across the American plains in the call to freedom – in this case the abolition of slavery in the South.

Whereas from the 20th century, this print by Jos Speybrouck reflects well the 19th century romantic imagery around the carillon.

> *Toll! Roland, toll!*
> *In old St. Bavon's Tower,*
> *At midnight hour,*
> *The great Bell Roland spoke,*
> *And all who slept in Ghent awoke.*
> *(...)*
> *Toll! Roland, toll!*
> *Till Freedom's Flag, wherever waved,*
> *Shall shadow not a man enslaved!*
> *Toll! Roland, toll!*
> *Toll! Roland, toll!*
> *From Northern lake o Southern strand!*
> *(...)*[143]

While the Ghent bell Roland sounded revolt, in Antwerp the carillon cheerfully played. In 1877, the 300-year anniversary of the birth of Peter Paul Rubens was celebrated on the Groenplaats square in Antwerp with an ensemble of choirs, orchestra and carillon. Peter Benoit had the original idea to give a prominent role to the carillon in the oratorio *Vlaanderens kunstroem*, better known as the *Rubenscantate*. The text evokes the image of how the carillon would play in the time in which art and music still flourished in Flanders. And in the future, when all demons and bad spirits would have disappeared, art in Flanders would once again reign supreme, again to the sounds of the carillon. The carillon song from the oratorio would become one of the most popular Flemish songs.[144]

The most beautiful and most intimate pages about bell and carillon came from the pen of Georges Rodenbach. Like many writers of the time, he thought in Flemish and wrote in French. His writing belonged to symbolism, a deepening of Romanticism that sought the reality of things not so much behind, but rather *below* the visible. Georges Rodenbach gave Bruges its ultimate, most aesthetic literary form. Bruges was for him a city that was more dream than reality, a place where weather-beaten stepped gables and mossy walls carried the walker back into the past and where the black Minnewater was the mirror of the human soul. Bruges was the realm of silence, which could be felt most when it was interrupted by the sound of bells. Bells sound throughout Rodenbach's poems: they chime cheerfully, fearfully or sadly; the beguines who hastily proceed along the cobblestones waddle like dark sounding bells; and the sound of the carillon from the upper world reverberates on the motionless surface of the water, under which the inner world lives.

Rodenbach became famous with his short novel *Bruges-la-Morte* that obtained cult status immediately after its publication in 1892, and which definitively enshrined the image of Bruges as reliquary of the Middle Ages at home as well as abroad. In

Bruges-la-Morte, the silent city is a metaphor for the dead wife of the protagonist, and at the same time also a mirror of his own state of mind. Throughout the book, the reader hears pounding bells that become almost a full-fledged character.

In 1896, Rodenbach wrote his final and most important novel, *Le carillonneur*. The work first appeared in installments in magazines, and was published in book form in 1897. The book starts with a carillon competition. The old carillonneur Bavo De Vos had died, and a competition was held to select a new city carillonneur. All of Bruges had assembled on the Market Square in front of the belfry, because not a jury, but the people would decide the winner:

> *The carillon after all is people's music. Elsewhere, in spirited cities, the national feast is marked by fireworks, a picturesque phenomenon that enraptures the soul. In meditative Flanders, amid damp mists incompatible with fire, the carillon takes their place. It is a fireworks show to which one listens.*

The programmed carillon announced the hour:

> *In anticipation, the carillon automatically played the prelude that usually sounded the hour, an airy embroidery, sound bouquets as a farewell gift to fleeting time. Because this is not the carillon's raison d'être: arousing a bit of joy, to mitigate the melancholy of the hour that is now ending?*

On the fourth stroke of the bell, a herald started the competition. The first three participants played contrived melodies, foreign national songs and tunes from operettas. The people initially were left cold, and over time became angry at the musical rape of the belfry's ancient bells. The remaining participants became afraid and withdrew. After a bit of confusion, the herald asked the people if there were other candidates. A man freed himself from the mass and disappeared into the belfry. A few minutes later, the carillon sounded again:

> *Dream music! It came not from the tower, but from much further away, from deep in the heavens, from way back in time. The carillonneur had come up with the idea to play traditional Christmas carols, Flemish Christmas carols that had come from the people and that were mirrors in which they recognized themselves. It was heavy and somewhat sad, like everything that has withstood the centuries. It was ancient, yet understandable to children. (...)*
> *Then cheers suddenly erupted, emotion gushed forth, branches of joy shot upward, took over floor after floor, crawling like black ivy up the tower, and storming the new carillonneur.*

Then the unknown participant played *De Vlaamse Leeuw*, the official anthem of Flanders:

> *The entire market square became inflamed. Everyone joined in the singing.*
> *The sound of the people singing mixed in the air with the song of the bells; and*
> *the soul of Flanders sailed through the air, like the sun between heaven and sea.*

The name of the new city carillonneur was Joris Borluut. He was also a city architect who saw it as his mission to restore the honor of ancient Bruges, and reinstate its old buildings with love and tenderness, without brutal innovations. This brought him into conflict with a number of his fellow citizens who wished to bring back the prosperous Bruges of the Middle Ages by constructing a port. Borluut feared that this would destroy the beauty of the old Bruges, and campaigned against the plan. He was unable to win over the people, and was finally dismissed as city architect. There was only one way out. His final destination was the carillon in the belfry. The tragic hero climbed the tower one last time, and hung himself on the hour bell.[145]

Rodenbach died on Christmas Eve 1898, reportedly surrounded by the tolling of bells. His novels, however, lived on. The opera *Die tote Stadt* by Erich Korngold is based on a theater adaptation of *Bruges-la-Morte*, and in 1913, *Le carillonneur* was adapted into an opera by Xavier Leroux. Rodenbach's indirect influence was also great: somewhat to the displeasure of the residents of Bruges, the image of the dead city became a popular literary topos, with offshoots far into the 20th century.

Despite its symbolist bias, *Le carillonneur* had a number of points of contact with the reality of the times. The construction project against which the carillonneur fought was the Port of Zeebrugge, which the Belgian parliament had approved in 1895. The carillon competition at the beginning of the book was inspired by a similar event that took place at Brussels in 1895. In this year, the city had a light carillon installed in the tower of the Broodhuis on the Market Square, and organized a competitive carillonneur exam on 22 July. Among the large group of listeners was Aalst city carillonneur Karel De Mette. The official participants were unimpressive, after which De Mette was encouraged by his friends to try his luck. He stepped from the audience, climbed the tower and obliged with a spontaneous performance of a fantasy from *La fille du régiment* by Donizetti. The audience on the Market Square burst into cheers and triumphantly carried De Mette around the square. The jury then unanimously appointed him as carillonneur of the Broodhuis. De Mette would not be able to enjoy the new carillon much, because the light instrument by Causard from Tellin in the Belgian province of Luxembourg sounded so thin and out of tune that it became the object of ridicule and was dismantled after two years.[146]

The out-of-tune sounds of the Brussels carillon awaken us from the world of the romantic imagination and place us again in audible reality. In the following chapter, we will learn whether the 19th century carillons sounded as melodious and soothing as they did in the imagination of the poet.

CHAPTER 13

In search of the sound of the past

In the nineteenth century, fascination for the past and unwavering confidence in the future went hand in hand. It was not only the time of ruins and nostalgia, but also the age of railways and steam engines, of mass production and grand World Exhibitions where the latest accomplishments of the human race were on display. The progressive minds of the nineteenth century also focused their attention on carillon construction. The results, however, were not always in proportion to the efforts made.

Bell-founding in the 19th century

In the 19th century, bell casting was not doing well. The industrial revolution had led to a strong decrease in the number of bell-founders. Previously, bronzesmiths worked in most cities who produced, in addition to bells, also artillery, sculptures and diverse tools and utensils. Thanks to better mining and casting techniques, iron and steel were used increasingly as raw material for domestic, industrial and military goods, so that the market for bronzesmiths became limited to bells and sculptures.

The Netherlands had suffered little from the confiscation of bells by the French, which meant that there was little demand for new bells. Almost all existing demand was handled by two bell-founders. No bell-founder of significance was active in the center of the country. In 1821, the once famous Amsterdam city bell-foundry was closed and its contents auctioned. In the north of the Netherlands, the company Van Bergen was active in the small village of Heiligerlee in the province of Groningen. The market in the southern part of the country was dominated by the company Petit & Fritsen. During the course of the 18th century, the traveling Lorraine bell-founders Petit had settled in the Peel region east of Eindhoven. Thanks to good, heavy clay ground, the region was a suitable destination for a nomadic bell-founder in search of a place to settle. In 1815, the last bell-founder with the name Petit, Henricus Petit, was succeeded by his cousin Henricus Fritsen, who continued the company in Aarle-Rixtel, and out of respect for the family history, retained the name Petit in the company name. The companies Petit & Fritsen and Van Bergen successfully cast swinging bells, but seldom produced carillons. And when such an instrument was built, the result was unsatisfactory. In 1867, Petit & Fritsen delivered a carillon for the Eindhoven town hall that sounded so out of tune that it ultimately was taken out of use. The cause of this failure was self-evident: with the death of Jan Albert de Grave in 1729, the skill of bell tuning was lost in the North, and the 19th century bell-founders delivered their bells in an untuned state. They camouflaged this ignorance with a romantic alibi. Fully in the spirit of the time, they viewed the bell as an artistic creation that was complete at the moment it was released from the mold. Afterwards it could be cleaned and polished, but turning it would damage its integrity and artistic perfection.

The plight of bell-founders in the region that had become Belgium in 1830 was more favorable since there was an extensive replacement market for the many bells that had disappeared at the time of the French occupation. Here again, however, the number of bell-founders was drastically reduced, and only André Louis Vanden Gheyn remained as important bell maker. When he returned from Nivelles to Leuven in 1792, he continued the foundry of his father. He cast no carillons, because most church and abbey carillons that had disappeared at the time of the French domination were not replaced. André Louis Vanden Gheyn had no male descendants and thus was the last bell-founder to bear the famous family name. He did, however, ensure the survival of the foundry on Tiensestraat. He had trained his oldest grandson, André Louis Jean Van Aerschodt, in the art of bell casting.[147] After his death in 1833, his grandson took over the business, without fully abandoning the Vanden Gheyn name. He signed his bells:

ALJ VAN AERSCHODT SUCCESSOR MAJOR AL VANDEN GHEYN ME FUDIT.
ALJ Van Aerschodt, the eldest successor of AL Vanden Gheyn, cast me

His younger brother Séverin, who was trained as sculptor, initially worked together with him, but in 1851, began to cast bells in his own name. He too saw himself as part of the Vanden Gheyn tradition. On his letterhead, under his name, was the description *petit-fils d'A.L. Van den Gheyn*, and in his prospectuses, he called himself the heir to the family tradition of the Vanden Gheyns who, from the 16th century, were at the basis of the fame of the Belgian bell. Both Van Aerschodts added to their products, abundantly but tastefully, the typical ornaments of Neo-Baroque and the Gothic Revival: garlands, flowers, pointed arches and coats of arms. They were children of the Catholic revival of the 19th century, and consequently, their bells contained numerous likenesses of Mary and saints.

Interior of a bell-foundry, probably in Leuven, by Albert Geudens

In contrast to their Dutch colleagues, the Van Aerschodts tuned their bells. Séverin claimed in his prospectuses that he could cast bells with a minor third harmonic *and* with a major third harmonic, according to the preference of the client. Despite these promising claim, it appears that – like his older brother – Séverin had not mastered the tuning technique of the Hemonys or of their own great-grandfather Andreas Jozef Vanden Gheyn. The attractiveness of the Aerschodt bells thus lies primarily in their rich sound, which was the result of their thick profile and careful casting. This deep, mystical sonority was realized among others in *Salvator*, the heaviest swinging and carillon bell of St. Rumbold's in Mechelen, which André Louis cast in 1844 with the help of the young Séverin. This eight-ton bell would be the heaviest bell in Belgium for more than a century. The Van Aerschodts were not alone in their pursuit of impressive sonority. In the second half of the 19th century, other European countries also received mammoth swinging bells, in service of both religious zeal and national pride. The heaviest were the 27-ton Kaiserglocke in the Cologne Cathedral, the 17-ton Great Paul for St. Paul's Cathedral in London, and the 19-ton Savoyarde in the Basilica of Montmartre in Paris.

The Van Aerschodt brothers dominated the Belgian market and also tried their hand at carillon construction. They cast small bells to expand existing carillons and delivered new instruments. André Louis sold carillons to Herentals, Namur, Aalst, Dunkirk, Broekburg, 's-Hertogenbosch and Boston in England. Séverin cast instruments for Wingene, Roeselare, Kortrijk and Antoing. He also received orders from countries not traditionally associated with the carillon, and delivered carillons to Hamburg, Rome (Church of St. Paul Within the Walls), Eaton Hall, Cattistock and Aberdeen. In 1883, he sold a carillon to Holy Trinity Church in Philadelphia. While the instrument with its limited size of 25 bells was not important musically, it subsequently would receive important historical significance. It was the first carillon with a baton keyboard in the New World.

The carillons of the Van Aerschodts were highly praised in their time. In practice, it appears that they alternated well-tuned bells with inaccurately tuned bells, which gave their carillons a heterogeneous sound. In the French market, the Van Aerschodts received competition from two French bell-founders who had begun to cast carillons. Paccard from Annecy-le-Vieux did so without tuning, but father and son Amédée and Ernest Bollée from Le Mans, who were also automobile pioneers, tuned their bells and did so no less ably than their competitors from Leuven. The sonorous and visually attractive bells of the nineteenth-century bell-founders were especially good as swinging bells. Their carillons, however, could not measure up to the best bell-founders of earlier centuries, since the skill of producing pure sounding bells had disappeared in the mists of time.

Innovations in keyboard construction

The decline in carillon casting stood in glaring contrast to the progress that had been made in the meantime in the construction of other musical instruments. Throughout Europe, instrument makers were developing systems to make creating music easier. Natural horns and trumpets received valves; wooden wind instruments were equipped with keys and valves; the humble pianoforte of Mozart's time was perfected into a piano with a sophisticated key action; in organs, the traditional mechanical tracker action was replaced by pneumatic or electric action. And new instruments were created, such as the saxophone family, developed around 1840 by Belgian Adolphe Sax. In addition to increased playing comfort, the new or revamped instruments were given a broader spectrum of volume differences, so that they could meet the expressive demands of the new music.

Around 1860, instrument makers discovered the carillon.[148] They saw the ponderous efforts of carillonneurs on the primitive baton keyboards, heard the resulting

Picture from an advertising brochure for the carillon system of Frederik Smulders

thin sound, and decided to make the life of the carillonneurs more pleasant. Ghent organ builder Leo Lovaert presented a pneumatic *Carillon piano*. According to his prospectus, the instrument could also be played by persons who did not excel in physical strength. What's more, the keyboard could be placed on the ground floor, so that the performer no longer had to climb to the bells. The carillon piano was equipped with two pedals that were connected to bellows. By operating the pedals, the carillonneur forced air through fine tubes to the bells themselves. Pressing a key caused a lever to pull the clapper. The Roeselare city government decided in 1864 to equip its new Van Aerschodt carillon with a Carillon piano. The system never worked well, which led to a legal dispute between the city of Roeselare and the successors of Lovaert, who had died in 1872.

Maastricht piano builder Smulders also developed a keyboard with two harmonium pedals. They activated a rotating cylinder to which teeth were attached. When a key was pressed, a sort of clamp was raised that collided against one of the rotating teeth, causing a clapper to be catapulted against the bell wall. Smulders' advertising brochure featured a young woman playing a carillon, which must have been an unusual image at the time. Henceforth, the most masculine of all musical instruments could also be played by elegant women. Smulders' invention won a prize in Amsterdam in 1875, and the following year it was installed on the two carillons in Maastricht. A year later, a commission from Antwerp came to Maastricht to evaluate the result. The commission approved the new system, after which the baton keyboard and the wire connections of the city carillon in the Antwerp Cathedral tower were replaced by a Smulders keyboard. In 1880, Smulders delivered a keyboard for the new Van Aerschodt carillon in Kortrijk, and the Hemony carillons in Hamburg and Copenhagen were also equipped with keyboards from his hand.

At the same time, so-called *machines à carillonner* were developed in France. New systems were developed by Paris clockmaker Armand-François Collin, Canon Maisonnave, bell-founders Ernest and Amédée Bollée and others. Most were variants on the flywheel technology used in the Smulders keyboard. The general public became acquainted with the machine à carillonner during the Paris World's Fair of 1878, which attracted thirteen million visitors. A carillon by Ernest Bollée was installed on the Champs de Mars and was played with a piano keyboard. The periodical *Le magasin picturesque* contained an article that praised the Bollée system. It allowed music to be played that was more varied than the monotonous carillon drum, which – while well-regarded by the residents of North France – annoyed foreigners due to its repetition. And in contrast to the old baton keyboards, which were very fatiguing for the carillonneur, the new piano keyboard could easily be played by girls ten to twelve years of age.

After the initial enthusiasm, it was noted that the new piano keyboards had a number of disadvantages. They were strongly affected by the unfavorable climatic conditions in carillon towers. Moreover, they were incapable of producing nuances in volume. The clapper was activated by pneumatic or amplified mechanical energy, so that it always struck the bell wall with equal force. Consequently, it was impossible to play music properly. It was indeed odd that the producers of piano keyboards strove only for easy playability of the carillon and not for the greater expressiveness that had become so important in romantic music. At the beginning of the 20th century, clock and carillon installer Eijsbouts in the Dutch city of Asten attempted to combine the best of both worlds. He retained the carillon's traditional wire system, but connected the wires to a keyboard with large piano keys. This system would allow expressive carillon playing without the carillonneur needing to use his fists. Eijsbouts installed his system in the carillons of Maastricht, Enkhuizen, Eindhoven, Goes, Middelburg, Sint-Truiden, Bourgh, Rouen and Montpellier. The keys had a travel and width of approximately 1.5 inches. The giant keyboard was not comfortable to play: classical piano technique with one finger per key resulted in pain in the fingertips, so the only feasible playing technique involved using the index finger and middle finger together, similar to the way preschoolers approach a piano.

None of the clever inventions of the 19th and beginning of the 20th century withstood the test of time. The inventors wrongly assumed that there was something wrong with the *concept* of the baton keyboard. In fact, the problem lay with the concrete implementation and with how well the baton keyboard was maintained. And of course the carillonneur's skill also played an important role. The Englishman Haweis reached this insight after one of his visits to Belgium.

Hughes Reginald Haweis was a striking figure in many respects. He had weak health and the posture of a dwarf, which did not prevent him from excelling at the violin. After his studies in Cambridge, he traveled to Italy and joined the troops of freedom fighter Garibaldi. Back in England, he became a successful vicar who succeeded in filling his East-London church with his theatrical preaching. In the meantime, he continued to travel around the world, and wrote books and articles on diverse subjects. His greatest bestseller was a collection of contemplative texts on music that appeared in 1871 with the title *Music and Morals*, which in the meantime has been reprinted more than 50 times. In this book, Haweis focused extensively on bells and carillons, and was not afraid of making controversial statements. He, for example, was very critical of the sound of London's Big Ben and its four forestroke bells. According to him, the bells should have been banned because they sounded so out of tune that they damaged the hearing of the audience. To his dismay, the writer heard boys on the street whistling the forestroke music, the so-called *Westminster Chimes*, out of tune, and he found it a disgrace that the MPs in the House of Parliament just under the tower were untroubled by the terrible sounding bells. The writer was certain that such dissonance would not be tolerated in Belgium. Then his thoughts drifted to Belgium, where music was played in the towers eight times an hour. Haweis wrote lovingly of the carillon, the instrument that spread music which blended with the imagination of the listeners and evoked varying memories in them: 'to return from a town like Mechlin to chimeless and gong-like England, is like coming from a festival to a funeral.' However, when Haweis was confronted with the crude baton keyboards used by carillonneurs, he concluded that the golden age of the carillon was over. None of the living carillonneurs were still able to play the famous preludes of Matthias Vanden Gheyn. Consequently, he concluded, somewhat sadly: 'The age of carillons is past, the art of playing them is rapidly becoming a lost art, and the love and the popular passion that once was lavished upon them had died out, and left but a pale flame in the breasts of the worthy citizens who are still proud of their traditions, but vastly prefer the mechanical performance of the tambour to the skill of any carillonneur now living.' Haweis saw a solution in the new piano keyboards of the time. He knew that the company Gillett and Bland in Croydon close to London had developed a new mechanism that allowed hammers to fall against the bells using a piano keyboard. This new system made it possible for women to easily play the carillon, and carillonneurs would no longer have to undress in order to wrestle with a series of uncooperative keyboard batons. Haweis thus envisioned the return of the golden age of the carillon, and advised his readers: 'We should order our bells in Belgium, and get them fitted with clavecin and carillon machinery in England.'

Six years later, Haweis changed his mind. When he again visited Mechelen, he had the opportunity to attend a carillon concert by city carillonneur Adolf Denyn.[149] On the street, he heard how Denyn played a brief prelude that began on the small bells and expanded to include the heavy bass bells. When the carillonneur began to play his repertoire, Haweis entered the tower. Arriving in the playing cabin, he saw Denyn bathed in sweat, with each muscle in his body strained to the maximum due to the speed with which he played the keyboard. The carillonneur played Beethoven's *Adelaide* and Bellini's aria *Casta Diva* in a 'grand legato style', as if he was playing a piano score. He then astonished his listener with a bravura performance: he played a melody in the pedal board to a bubbling accompaniment of 32nd notes on the small bells. After a few swishing arpeggios, Denyn began a solemn piece that made Haweis think of Chopin's Funeral March. When the carillonneur was in the middle of a fantasy on *La dame blanche*, the mechanical drum began to turn. Denyn stopped playing briefly and, just as Franz Liszt would seize on a mistake as an opportunity to demonstrate his improvisatory talent, immediately after the programmed music, Denyn played an adapted improvisation intended to give the people on the market the illusion that the mechanical drum had gone crazy. While playing, Denyn demonstrated to Haweis his perfect mastery of the pianos and the fortes, striking keys sometimes lightly and sometimes with force. In honor of his English visitor, he concluded with *God Save the Queen*. Haweis was dumbfounded: 'I must say that I never, on piano or violin, heard more admirable and expressive phrasing, whilst the vigor and fire of the virtuoso reminded me of one of Rubinstein's finest performances.' He decided that the carillon had found its Liszt in Adolf Denyn. All that was needed was a Beethoven to one day write sonatas for the instrument.

After his second Mechelen experience, Haweis understood that expressive and smooth carillon playing was perfectly possible on a good baton keyboard played by a great musician. He had witnessed a precursor to a renaissance that a short time later would again lift carillon playing in Belgium to high artistic level. At approximately the same time, the art of bell tuning would be rediscovered in England. If Haweis had been aware of both revolutions, he would have given his readers the opposite advice: install a perfected baton keyboard from Belgium and purchase your bells in England.

Rediscovery of the art of bell tuning

It may seem surprising that the art of tuning as developed by Hemony and Vanden Gheyn was rediscovered in a country without a carillon tradition. England nevertheless had an intimate relationship with bells, which could be seen among others from the fact that George Frideric Handel called it the 'ringing isle'. *Change ringing* was for England what the carillon was for the Low Countries and the zvon was for Russia. This tolling technique developed in the 17th century from ordinary church tolling and was executed with a series of five to twelve bells that formed a diatonic major tone sequence, i.e. a series without sharps or flats. In the start position, the bells are hanging upside down. When the bell-ringer pulls the bell rope, the bell rotates 360 degrees and sounds once. A change ringing *Exercise* consists of a large number of tone patterns executed quickly, with a tight tempo. For each series, all the bells are used once, but always in a different order and according to specific rules. The ringing patterns bear colorful names such as *Cambridge Surprise Maximum* and *Double Norwich Court Bob Major*. Change ringing is as English as afternoon tea and the bowler hat: today in England, tens of thousands bell-ringers still ring their changes each Sunday, creating a festive mood in the English villages and cities. Practising is done with handbells in the church, or – better still – in the pub. A new bell instrument has even developed from this training tool: the handbell choir. Handbell choirs were especially popular in North America from the 19th century. A handbell choir of course no longer performs the classical serial change ringing, but rather plays classical music and religious hymns, with two handbells per man or woman.

One of these enthusiastic change ringers was Canon Arthur Simpson, the rector of a church in Fittleworth in the county of Sussex in the south of England. Like Vicar Haweis, he was bothered by the poor tuning of the bells on the *ringing isle*. Simpson listened to numerous bells, looked for the causes of the annoying tuning, and proposed solutions. In 1895 and 1896, he published two short articles in the cultural periodical *Nash's Pall Mall Magazine*, both titled 'On Bells Tones'.[150] In the first, he sketches the problem. He claims that it was likely that no bell was to be found in all of England that was 'in tune with itself', and no change-ringing peal with bells 'in tune with each other'. Simpson says that a bell is only correctly tuned when the three most important partial notes – fundamental, prime and octave – are a perfect octave from each other. After many years of observations, he noticed that the fundamental is usually too high, the prime usually too low, and the octave usually somewhere in between. As a result, the three tones, which produce *almost* the same note (albeit an octave higher or lower) fight for mastery and leave the listener in the dark concerning the bell's precise tone. This melodic vagueness is unacceptable, certainly in the interplay of a change ringing peal or a carillon. Simpson closes his article with an appeal to

The Toning of the Bell. Engraving after an oil painting by Walter Shirlaw from 1874. This scene from a bell-foundry in Bavaria suggests a perfection of tone that was not achieved in that time.

the reader to place greater demands on bell-founders and bell-tuners with respect to tone purity; they after all wouldn't do so of their own accord.

In the second article, Simpson proposes concrete solutions. He declares his openness with the argument that he is not a bell-founder and consequently has no interest in keeping his discovery to himself: 'let bell-founders take it or leave it as they may think best'. Then the Canon describes at what height the inside of the bell must be turned in order to lower or raise the prime and the octave, and thus bring the two partial notes into harmony with each other. He then indicates with which segments of the clock profile the three other important partial notes can be tuned: the third, which strongly determines the character of the bell's sound, the less audible fifth, and the fundamental, which due to its long decay time is strongly audible especially in heavy bells. These last three partial notes can only be lowered in tone. Simpson does not say what led to his discovery. He is also vague concerning the method he uses to make each of the bell's partial tones separately audible, so that they can be tuned. He, however, promises to help all who wish to become proficient in the art of tuning. A letter to Fittleworth Rectory, Sussex, was all that was required.

Only one bell-founder accepted Canon Simpson's offer: John William Taylor, a bell-founder from Loughborough in the county of Leicestershire.[151] Taylor descended from a family that had been casting bells since 1784. Like the other 19th century bell-founders, he was proud that he could deliver bells as *maiden bells*, thus without tuning afterwards. While he and his son John William II were on holidays in Belgium, they were introduced to the Belgian carillons: from then on, their goal was to equal the art of the Hemonys and the Vanden Gheyns. The bell-founders had been in contact with Simpson already before the publication of his groundbreaking articles. On 10 August 1895, father Taylor ordered a tuning machine. When the 15-ton machine arrived at the foundry in March of the following year, the great work could begin. Just like the encounter 250 years earlier between Jacob van Eyck and the Hemony brothers had led to the first precisely tuned bells in history, the collaboration between the priest-scientist Simpson and the bell-founder Taylor would result in the first precisely tuned bells of the modern age.

The first purely tuned bell series was a change ringing peal of eight bells for the church of Norton close to Sheffield. Subsequently Taylor found it difficult to give full credit to the merits of Simpson, and their collaboration weakened. The Taylor family was determined to keep the discovered technique secret. Outsiders were refused access to the tuning shop of the foundry, and the news that other bell-founders were going to study the tuned Taylor bells in church towers was viewed with suspicion. Son John William II was clear on the intentions of the foundry concerning the tuning process: 'we have not published any account of our process of tuning church bells as now carried out by us and probably shall not do so.'

The rector of the small church in Fittleworth died in 1900. He would not witness the casting in 1904 by the Taylor Bell Foundry of the first properly tuned carillon since the death of Andreas Jozef Vanden Gheyn. It was a demonstration instrument that was hung in a tower of the foundry. Two years later, Taylor received his first order for a carillon from chocolate manufacturer and philanthropist George Cadbury. Cadbury had built a new factory in the vicinity of Birmingham, with a model village where his workers and their families lived. The entrepreneur was concerned about the well-being of his workers. Thus, the new village of Bournville had all the needed utilities and social services. After hearing the carillon in Bruges, Cadbury decided to install a carillon in the tower of the village school. He considered music a part of the utilities to be provided to his personnel.

The first purely tuned carillon on the European mainland followed in 1911. Taylor sold a carillon for St. Nicholas Church in Appingedam, a city in the northern part of the Netherlands. The instrument was financed by the proceeds from unclaimed customer assets at the local savings bank of the *Oud-Diakengezelschap der Nederlandsche hervormden* (Old Dutch Reformed Church). This lightweight carillon of only 25 bells was a milestone in carillon history. For the first time in more than a century, a carillon was installed in the Low Countries with pure sounding bells. The time was ripe for new carillons: at the beginning of the 20th century, the carillon indeed had begun a spectacular revival. This revival came about not due to social or cultural developments, but thanks to the talent and the insights of one man. The backdrop of the new carillon art was Mechelen, the old capital of the Low Countries where the first carillons were made in the 16th century.

CHAPTER 14

A soul in peace, among the stars

A carillonneur with an interest in technique

19th century Mechelen was a sleepy provincial town, geographically hemmed in between the administrative capital of Brussels, the commercial metropolis of Antwerp and the intellectual center of Leuven. The city was a soul mate of Bruges, the other city that relished in nostalgia for a once-glorious past. Romantic souls could dream among the numerous old buildings, the bumpy streets and the brooks that crisscrossed it all. Like Bruges, the historical center became almost literally overshadowed by a mammoth tower from which music emanated. The St. Rumbold's Tower should have been 167 meters high, but never made it past 97 meters. According to tradition, the building material for the stone steeple was taken during the Eighty Years' War by insurgents from the North, who used it to build the fortified city of Willemstad on the Scheldt. Numerous authors are of the opinion that the tower's unfinished state makes it more impressive than it would have been with its intended steeple.

Unlike Bruges, Mechelen provincialism had a certain grandeur. The city not only had been the political capital of the Low Countries, it was an archiepiscopal residence for three hundred years. Under the protection of the archdiocese, churches and monasteries flourished in Mechelen, and in 1879, the Interdiocesan School for Religious Music was founded by Nicolas Lemmens. A second difference with Bruges was the means with which Mechelen had escaped its lethargic existence at the end of the nineteenth century. Where Bruges had found new life with the port of Zeebrugge, Mechelen was awakened by the sounds of the carillon.[152]

The seeds of a revival were already present in Mechelen at the second half of the nineteenth century. Witnesses to this fact include the texts of Vicar Haweis, who considered city carillonneur Adolf Denyn among the greatest of living carillonneurs. Denyn's eyesight deteriorated around 1880. His son Jef was responsible for providing the livelihood, which consisted of a trade in tobacco and liqueurs, and as a result was unable to begin his planned engineering studies. For his carillon concerts, father Denyn increasingly had to be replaced by his students. When on Easter Day 1881 his apprentice Edward Steenackers was scheduled to play the carillon of St. James on

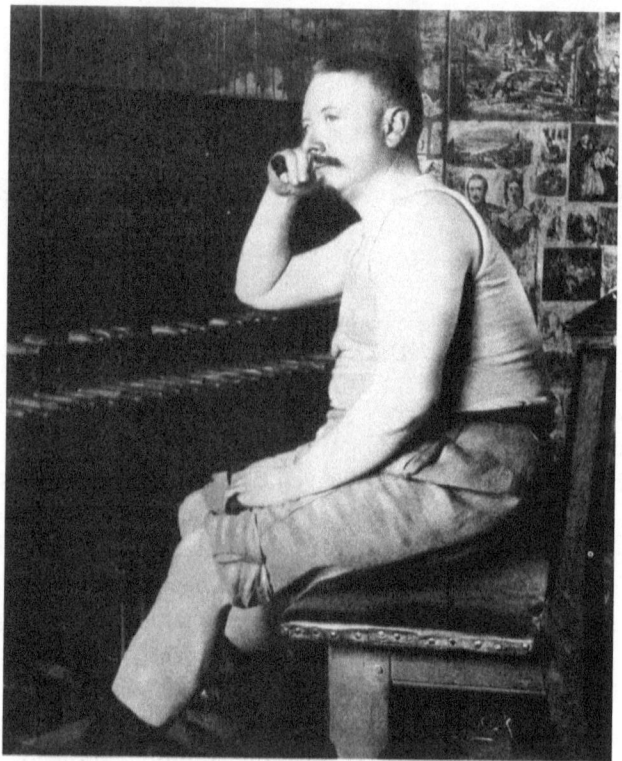

Jef Denyn in 1912 at the keyboard of St. Rumbold's.
Note the finger protectors and the light clothes.

Coudenberg at Brussels, Adolf sent nineteen-year old Jef into St. Rumbold's Tower. He only knew three songs and filled the hour by playing the series three times with long breaks in between. Jef was immediately attracted to carillon playing, and under the supervision of his father, his playing progressed quickly. On 1 January 1887, he was appointed as Mechelen's 23rd city carillonneur.

Jef Denyn had a practical mind, and from the beginning he strove for better playability of the carillon. He sought the solution not in the then fashionable piano keyboards, but rather in an improvement of the baton keyboard and the wire connections between keys and clappers. He aimed not so much for lighter playability, but for full control of the clapper by the player. Denyn judged that the historical system of the schering, the hingeless system of the three wires that converged in a single ring, was too elastic. It allowed the clapper too much freedom, which resulted in unstable carillon playing. Denyn's preferred system was a variation on the other historical system, which made use of tumblers or levers in the form of a bracket to convert the vertical keyboard wires into horizontal clapper wires. The heart of Denyn's system was the so-called tumbler rack that consisted of a series of horizontal, hinged tubes installed on top of one another. Perpendicular to each tube was a horizontal tumbler arm that received the keyboard wire from the baton key and a vertical tumbler arm from which the clapper wire departed to the bell located opposite it. Denyn equipped the clappers for the smaller bells with springs at the back in order to increase their resistance. Thus the clappers were clenched between the pulling force of the carillonneur and the opposing force of the springs. The tumbler axis system required the bells to be hung in straight rows next to and above each other. Denyn connected the clappers of adjoining bells to one another by chains. When a clapper was drawn, the chains tightened so that the clappers could not swing sideways.

Denyn preferred relatively short keyboard batons, which did not result so much in light carillon action, but in direct contact with the clapper that made nuanced carillon playing possible. The keyboard batons contained turnbuckles with which the carillonneur was able to change the length of the keyboard wire. Thus the distance from the clapper to the bell was always optimum, regardless of changes in temperature: after the key was pushed, the clapper did not 'stick' to the bell wall but still hung close enough to strike it with a gentle push of the key. The carillonneur obtained full mastery over the clappers: he could quickly execute passages with the required rhythmic regularity, and he was able to produce unlimited dynamic variations by changing the pressure of his fist on the keyboard batons. The player was no longer subject to the cumbersomeness of his instrument: he was now boss of the carillon. Denyn wished to bring an end to the motley collection of keyboard sizes that were to be found everywhere, and proposed the measurements of his keyboard at St. Rumbold's as the sole standard. He was assisted in his technical improvements by Mechelen tower clockmaker and carillon installer Désiré Somers, with whom he had been a business associate for a number of years.

Jef Denyn was not the inventor of the tumbler system, despite the fact that it sometimes is called the Denyn system or Mechelen system. It possibly had been used earlier in a number of carillons. Moreover, the system of tumbler axes was only a variation on the separate tumblers that were present especially in historical carillons of the Southern Netherlands. In 1892, Denyn had improvements made to the St. Rumbold's Tower carillon, but the details of this work are unknown.[153] It is possible that the tumbler axes were already present at that moment, because there are reasons to believe that also father Adolf Denyn had already worked on the St. Rumbold's Tower carillon. Jef Denyn never called himself the inventor of the tumbler system, and always mentioned his father as co-author of the improvements to the Mechelen carillon. Father Denyn had already been making recommendations for carillon design elsewhere in the country, and if we remember the description of his carillon playing by Vicar Haweis, we cannot avoid the conclusion that Adolf Denyn also must have had access to a sophisticated playing mechanism. Otherwise he could never have played 32nd notes and virtuoso arpeggios, nor had perfect mastery of piano and forte that he was so happy to demonstrate to his English visitor. He also would not have been capable of applying the *grand legato style*, as Haweis called it, to opera melodies. This technique can have been nothing other than tremolo playing that could only be successfully executed on a perfectly adjusted instrument with tumbler system, return springs behind the clappers and turnbuckles to adjust the length of the wires.

Tremolo playing offered a solution to one of the musical limitations of the bell: its inability to expressively reproduce sustained notes. Its decay time after all has a fixed pattern over which the player has no more control after the moment of striking. Bells produce a strong but very short strike note that is followed by a quite long but relatively soft decay. This gives the carillon the character of a plucked or staccato instrument, which is a limitation compared to most other musical instruments. On the piano, staccato playing can be alternated with connected or legato playing by keeping the keys depressed. Strings, wind instruments and singers can even add expression to a sustained note by first allowing it to swell and then letting it subtly fade away; and strings and singers can give a sustained note extra color by applying small variations in pitch: so-called vibrato. In the 17th and 18th centuries, the one-sided staccato character of the carillon was not an impediment, since Baroque music did not rely strongly on the expressive effect of sustained notes. The bel canto pages and vocal and instrumental romances of the 19th century, however, required an expressive eloquence that the carillon could not provide – until carillonneurs began using the tremolo technique.

In tremolo playing, two to four notes are repeated in quick succession. The carillonneur could now cause the sound to swell or decay as he wished, and the listeners receive the acoustic illusion of an expressively played sustained note that stops only when the carillonneur finishes his tremolo. Thanks to the quickly repeating notes in tremolo playing, particularly the short decay time of the small bells is camouflaged, so that they sound fuller. The tremolo technique is not unique to carillon playing: it is a common technique used on the xylophone, the mandolin and the cimbalom, the stringed instrument used among others in gypsy orchestras and klezmer ensembles. Refined tremolo playing on the carillon demands not only a finely adjusted keyboard and wires, but also a closed tower. A closed bell chamber contains relatively more wall surface than window space, for example in a ratio of 70/30. The sounds echo against the walls and as a result decay less quickly such that the sounds blend better and create the illusion of sustained notes. Moreover, the collisions with the wall space weaken the higher overtones, allowing the lower harmonics to dominate: thus possible impurities in the tuning are filtered out and the carillon receives a fuller timbre.

An ideal closed sound chamber was present in the St. Rumbold's Tower in Mechelen. Because of the high vault, Jef Denyn – or his father – had a zinc sounding board installed at the top of the belfry that directed the sound of the small bells downward. The wooden floor was covered with cloth.[154] Thanks to the sound chamber created by the closed tower and to the tumbler connections, Jef Denyn was able to play romantic melodies such as *La voix des chênes* or the romance of Nadir from Bizet's *Les pêcheurs de perles* in tremolo, with all the nuances and emotive power required by the music. Denyn made the carillon sing, and the *gebonden zang*, as Denyn called tremolo playing, became a trademark of the Mechelen carillon movement.

Enchanting Monday evenings

Several Mechelen residents began to realize that Jef Denyn was a major artist and in 1891, Alderman for the Fine Arts Theodoor De Coster asked the carillonneur to replace his afternoon concerts on Saturday and Monday with concerts on Monday evening during the months of June, August and September. There would be no concerts in July due to noise from the annual fair. Alderman De Coster believed that carillon music would receive more attention from the public during the quiet evening hour. He defended his proposal to the city council with the argument that soon the English and the Americans would come to Mechelen to listen to the carillon. The simple idea of Alderman De Coster meant a radical shift in thinking about the carillon. For centuries the instrument had only produced decorative music that brightened up the marketplace, added splendor to municipal events and animated this or that political cause. Henceforth, the carillon would be listened to on its own merits.

On Monday 1 August 1892 at 7 p.m., Jef Denyn played the first full-fledged concert in the history of the carillon. In the early years, public interest was very weak. Each Monday evening a dozen or so people would stand in the *Straatje zonder Einde* along the Melaan to listen to the carillon, and the choir master of St. Rumbold's Alois De Smet would invite friends into his garden on the Wolmarkt square to listen to the carillon concerts. After a few years, a private initiative was undertaken to provide printed programs. Response on the part of the general public remained cool and Alderman De Coster was mockingly asked by colleagues how many Americans had already visited.

Despite the initial indifference of the Mechelen public, the quality of Denyn's concerts and his clear opinions on the carillon mechanism attracted attention beyond Mechelen. In 1891, the city administrators of Scottish Aberdeen crossed the Channel to ask Denyn to install their new Van Aerschodt carillon. In 1892, Vicar Van Horenbeeck, a Mechelen childhood friend of Denyn, asked him to make improvements to his Vanden Gheyn carillon in St. Gertrude's church in Leuven. Denyn and Désiré Somers installed a system with tumbler axes and a keyboard with the dimensions of the St. Rumbold's carillon. In 1893, Denyn and Somers dismantled Lovaert's dilapidated *Carillon piano* in Roeselare and replaced it with a tumbler system. In 1894, their services were requested in Oudenaarde, and on the advice of Denyn, the entire carillon was moved from the open town hall tower to the tower at St. Walburga Church, which better met the acoustic ideal of a closed tower. In the succeeding years, more Flemish and Walloon carillons followed. In 1898, Denyn and Somers installed a Van Aerschodt carillon at Cattistock in England. All instruments were set up according to the model of the St. Rumbold's carillon, which was presented by Denyn as the standard in carillons.

Around the turn of the century, attention for Denyn's Monday summer concerts at St. Rumbold's began to increase. In 1902, the city printed its first program booklets, and in 1906, the spark would ignite that would make the Monday concerts in Mechelen a mass phenomenon. In August of that year, the Language and Literary Congress – which was held alternately in the Netherlands and Flanders – took place in Brussels. At the invitation of the Mechelen branch of the *Algemeen Nederlands Verbond* (General Dutch Association), on 29 August, the congress participants came to Mechelen to attend a carillon concert given by Jef Denyn. The concert made a huge impression, and enthusiastic reviews appeared in Dutch newspapers. The articles contained the elements that would also be used later by dozens of writers, poets and journalists to convey to their readers the atmosphere of a Denyn concert: the magic of the colossal St. Rumbold's Tower in the twilight, the hypnotic power of Denyn's carillon playing, and the incomprehensible paradox between the enormous work on the part of the carillonneur and the refined sounds that he elicited from the huge instrument. From this moment on, the Monday concerts by Jef Denyn enjoyed international fame. Under the impetus of teacher Edward De Keyser, the association *Mechelen-aantrekkelijkheden* (Attractions of Mechelen) had leaflets printed and distributed these in trains, boats, travel agencies and at domestic and foreign hotels. The central geographic location of Mechelen also turned out to be an important asset. The city was the hub of the Belgian railway, and the Belgian parliament decided that the Monday evening audience could travel by train to Mechelen at half price. And late trains to Brussels and Antwerp were put into service to give listeners the opportunity to get home after the concerts. Carillon enthusiasts came to Mechelen in droves, and each Monday evening an anthill of thousands of admirers formed around the singing tower. Prominent personalities such as Maurice Maeterlinck, Emile Verhaeren and Camille Huysmans came to hear Denyn, and their impressions of the carillon were eagerly cited and used as publicity. The program booklets bulged with ads for the most suitable terraces from which to listen, the best carillon drinks, and products ranging from shock absorbers to aspirin. While tourists on the terraces sipped their Cinzano, 'real' fans, including the people

The *Straatje zonder einde* during a carillon concert by Jef Denyn.
Drawing by Alfred Ost (August 1910).

of Mechelen, stood packed together in the legendary *Straatje zonder Einde* along the Melaan, eagerly awaiting the voice from the tower.

The commercial exploitation did not prevent the concerts of Jef Denyn from continuing to arouse strong emotions. For many, they had a mystical character. On Monday evening, the robust St. Rumbold's Tower, which as it were overshadowed the entire city center, became a totem that from Mechelen allowed its divine voice to be heard by humanity. In 1908, the program booklets proclaimed that 'Mechelen must become the holy place of pilgrimage for the carillon', and the city was referred to as the 'Mecca' and the 'Bayreuth' of the carillon. Centuries after pilgrims came to Mechelen to worship the relics of St. Rumbold, the worshipers of the carillon came to the city to attend the high mass of the carillon. On 21 and 22 August 1910, 30,000 attended the international carillonneurs' competition, and two years later, just as many admirers celebrated the silver jubilee of Denyn as city carillonneur.

The collective enchantment was the greatest when Denyn played his *Prelude in D minor*. The work in fact was based on an improvisation that the master often played as finale at his concerts. At the time, it was designated as a *postlude* in the program. Edward De Keyser recounts: 'And when the final sounds had died away and the concert ended, listeners continued to wait, hoping that the master would play an encore and – yes – play the wonderful prelude that he had lovingly composed to allow his most beautiful bells to sing, which he had christened "the soul of bells".' The prelude was written down only after Denyn's death based on extant recordings. Until today, however, it is known as the *Unwritten Prelude* and is handed down by memory from master to student at the Mechelen carillon school. The unwritten prelude is the prototype of the Mechelen compositional style for carillon. The piece begins with a theatrical introduction of massive chords and rapid runs in various tonalities. Then follows a soft and hesitating rubato that announces the most important part of the piece: the lyrical tremolo melody on the small bells. This scheme has been followed many times in the carillon music of the Mechelen school. At the beginning of the piece, the silence of the evening is broken by a massive entree in which the listener can hear a drum roll, kettledrums and brass bands. As soon as the listener's attention has been aroused, the mood changes. An invisible curtain opens and the Mechelen miracle is revealed to the audience: the tremolo melody on the high bells, often floating above the sonorous foundation of the eight-ton Salvator bell. It is striking that a number of the tremolo melodies of Denyn's students Staf Nees, Jef Rottiers and Eugeen Uten are quite faithful variants of the melody of the Unwritten Prelude. They are as it were a reflection of the Platonic 'ideal' melody of the master. In Mechelen, the ancient link between bells and magic had been restored.

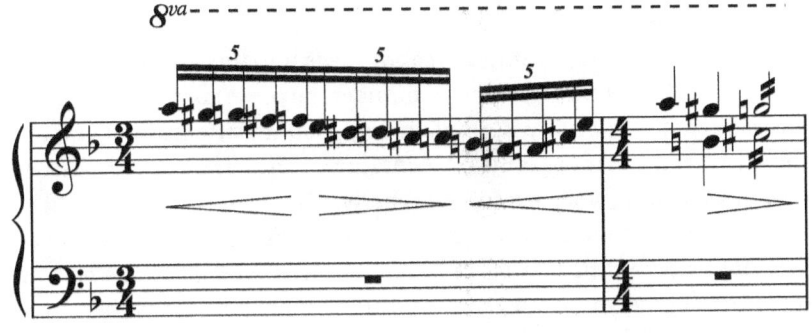

Tremolo melody in Jef Denyn's *Unwritten Prelude* (notation Arthur Bigelow)

The vision of the master

Jef Denyn as person did not have the air of an etheric demigod. He came from a family of merchants, and with his wife he ran a lace shop along IJzerenleen. With his small form, potbelly, glasses and beard, he looked like an average citizen. He was fluent in the Mechelen dialect and spoke perfect French, and he liked to drink his beer in the cafes *De Kamers* or *Le cheval d'or*. Denyn never hid the secret to his success: in various lectures, he clearly explained his views on carillon construction, its repertoire and his manner of playing.[155] Denyn attached much importance to a concert's development. 'The habit of the carillonneur to start on time helps the listening crowd to immediately become silent and attentive. As soon as the final stroke of the hour has sounded, I play a few chromatic runs as precursors and run through the scales, develop a theme, modulate, produce a few contrasts from the smallest and large bells. Often it's a pleasure to already begin very softly, while the hour is still sounding; each stroke of the hour of course serves as bass note.' Denyn often improvised between the pieces, a practice he acquired from his father. 'The carillonneur (...) will arrange his concert such that he evokes a mood, maintains it and allows it to linger.' According to Denyn, a concert consists of four parts. As initial number, he prescribes a prelude, fantasia or etude: the requisite virtuosity will immediately grab the attention of and charm the audience. The second part, as contrast, contains a series of simple songs, music the audience enjoys hearing when executed properly. The classical work should be placed half way through the concert: a sonata, rondo or minuet; in short, music that adds refreshing diversity and that satisfies the musically developed listener. The fourth and last part of the concert again contains a number of stately melodies, but of a different character than the songs in part two. 'The sequence will always give the pieces greater emotional impact toward the end. The player thus increasingly moves the audience, in order to leave the most lasting impression.' Denyn mentions as possible closing numbers among others the *Ave Maria* by Schubert, *Träumerei* by Schumann and *Solveig's song* by Grieg, as well as old Flemish songs: 'songs that require a very delicate interpretation.' Denyn ended his concerts not with a virtuoso closing number, but with an emotional climax. Each summer, he even concluded his last concert with Chopin's *Funeral March*, as a sign of remorse that the summer season had again come to an end. Denyn advised the apprentice carillonneur to play from memory: 'reading music distracts from the keyboard and prevents him from focusing on mastering the keys in freedom.' He said that he memorizes the texts of the songs that he performs beforehand. Freedom of execution is essential for him: 'I have often said of myself, with all humility, that I am a vagabond on the carillon. This means that I do not consider myself bound by clear-cut rules, but rather take the freedom that appears desirable and comfortable at the moment to serve the music's beauty.' Denyn's tremolo playing is heard most clearly in the tension created between the sound of the large and small bells: 'On large carillons with four octaves and deep basses, the most intense effect is obtained via the contrast at the ends of the tonal space – without the middle. The singing harmony of a good tremolo of small bells with crystalline timbre above simple bourdon accompaniment is truly pleasant.' However, in 1938, at an advanced age, Denyn warns of abusing tremolo playing: 'I continuously warn against clumsily using tremolo at poorly chosen places in the music. It is a nuance in the performance that depends on skill and in the first place on taste.'

In 1912, Denyn was at the high point of his glory and some around him were worried about the future. Denyn was now 50, and there was a concern that upon his death, the *Mechelen miracle* would also disappear. In the meantime, Henry De Coster had appeared on the scene. He was the son of Alderman Theodoor, who in 1891 had convinced Denyn of the idea of the Monday concerts. De Coster proposed that Denyn establish a school in Mechelen for carillonneurs and be its director.[156] Since Denyn had no official music diploma, he hesitated for a time before accepting the proposal.

In 1913, Edward De Keyser and Henry De Coster published a provisional prospectus containing the curriculum of the future school. The carillon school would be a carillon university with, in addition to carillon instruction, also general formative courses focused on educating 'developed men prepared to contribute to the flourishing of this profound national art'. The Catholic city government of Mechelen was not enthusiastic about an independent institution, and via Canon Francis Dessain, brother of the mayor and secretary to Cardinal Mercier, undertook discrete attempts to convince Denyn and De Coster to integrate the new initiative in the existing – then French-speaking – Interdiocesan Church Music School. De Coster answered that carillonneurs did not belong in a denominational school. In contrast to organists, they depended on a government and for this reason, they were free to profess various creeds or even none. The Canon did not insist. At approximately the same time, Denyn received an attractive proposal from the Antwerp city government to establish a carillon school there. De Coster, however, continued to insist that Mechelen be the location for the school, and on 14 August 1913, the Chamber of Representatives approved a subsidy of 4,500 Belgian francs that the school would receive after it had effectively begun operations. Much private money was still needed for the start-up, and De Coster focused, as he himself writes, 'on luring rich people to Mechelen and then slaughtering them via his begging for the school.' He picked out benefactors from the crowds around the tower whom he could use for his purposes. In 1912, the prediction of father De Coster came true. In the audience was the American couple William Gorham Rice and Harriet Langdon Pruyn.

An American much interested in carillons

William Gorham Rice lived in Albany, the capital of New York State.[157] He worked in the state administration as Civil Service Commissioner and was secretary to the governor. His wife Harriet Langdon Pruyn was the daughter of the chancellor of the State University of New York and had founded in Albany a public library in memory of her father. The Rices received numerous visitors in their home, including the later President Franklin D. Roosevelt. By marrying Harriet, William in a certain sense also married her ancestors. In 1660, they emigrated from Antwerp to Albany, which was then a Dutch settlement with the name Beverwijck. Harriet was proud of her family's roots and the couple often crossed the ocean to visit cities in Flanders and the Netherlands. William dutifully followed his twelve year younger wife – but not with the same enthusiasm – during her visits to monuments, galleries, family and friends.

In the summer of 1912, William and Harriet visited Bruges, Middelburg, Veere and The Hague.[158] William felt that these four cities, however much they differed

William Gorham Rice in 1912

from each other, had 'something' that united them. Upon hearing the carillon in the large church in The Hague, residence of the royal family, he understood: 'In this reflective mood, again my ear caught the sound of the bells. They answered the question. It was the tower melodies which united these places, individual as they were in other respects.' And thus a passion was kindled in the 56 year-old Rice that would never leave him. He devised a plan to write a publication containing tourist carillon routes, a book in which foreigners could read information that could be found nowhere else about carillons. From the De Oude Doelen hotel in The Hague, Rice wrote dozens of postcards with *paid reply* – 'the most convenient of messengers' – to Dutch and Flemish carillonneurs with as only address the salutation *Den Heer Klokkenist* ('To Mr. Carillonneur'), followed by the name of the city. The hotel porter helped him translate the messages into Dutch. Two days later he came to Rice with a dozen postcards held against his ear: 'Hush, I hear carillons ringing all through the land.'

The Rices traveled via land and water to discover the carillons of the Netherlands and Flanders and to meet their players. For many carillonneurs, attention from America was a pleasant surprise, and the couple received a warm welcome everywhere. Several local newspapers even reported their arrival. Rice diligently took notes wherever he went. When a friend from Antwerp informed them of the concerts by Jef Denyn in Mechelen, they went there to hear the master carillonneur. William and Harriet would continue to visit Mechelen. One of their most memorable memories was Denyn's concert on 18 August 1913, about which Rice writes: 'Indeed, the tower seemed a living being, opening its lips in the mysterious night to pour out a great and noble message of song to all mankind.' After the concert, when the congratulations of the audience were finished, Denyn and Rice exchanged ideas in the pub about the societal power and the educational value of music that could be played for an audience of thousands. Rice was convinced that carillon music could promote a sense of community and foster true patriotism. An intense and prolonged friendship emerged between the American and the Mechelen city carillonneur. Years later, Rice would describe the music-making Denyn as 'a soul in peace, among the stars'.

William Gorham Rice continued his investigation into the carillon and found scant information in libraries in Antwerp, Brussels, The Hague, Amsterdam, Paris and the United States. When the assistant librarian of the British Museum wrote him that he knew of no book on the carillon, Rice's conclusion was clear: 'there was need of another book in the world.'[159] The American continued his research, with a book in view. Denyn recommended that he consult Prosper Verheyden, a resident of Antwerp born in Mechelen and an enthusiastic carillon historian. On 6 August 1913, Rice sent Verheyden a postcard from Paris with the opening sentence: 'I am an American much interested in carillons ...'. Verheyden agreed to Rice's request and helped him with his research. Rice completed his book in August 1914. In that same month, war broke out in Europe.

CHAPTER 15

The broken bells of Flanders

War rages over Belgium

The conflict that later would be called the Great War was not unexpected. After the assassination of the Habsburg heir to the throne Franz Ferdinand and his wife Sophie in Sarajevo on 28 June 1914, the cataclysm predicted by all and desired by many approached quickly. Belgium and the Netherlands were neutral and hoped to stay out of the war.

At the middle of July, the Great Triumphant in the Ghent belfry cracked. The swinging system had been automated shortly before, and this proved fatal to the bell when announcing the Ghent Festival. Hundreds came to examine the crack in the mythical bell Roland, curious and also uneasy that this might be an ominous sign. It was feared that Germany would not respect Belgium's neutrality and King Albert announced a general mobilization. During the night of 31 July and 1 August, Carolus in the Antwerp Tower of Our Lady tolled and with it, hundreds of other bells in the Belgian cities and villages. For the last time in history, they heralded a storm over Belgium. Men crawled from their bed and received a summons from the constable: they were to join their corps before twelve noon.[160]

On 2 August, Germany requested free passage through Belgium in the event that it would be attacked by France. King Albert stood by the absolute neutrality of the country and refused the requested passage. The Belgian public responded enthusiastically and the entire country, as if in a daze, rallied behind its government and its monarch. On 4 August, German troops crossed the Belgian border close to Liège. The Liège forts resisted stubbornly. On 9 August, a soldier was buried in Aalst who had been killed in defense of the forts. Eyewitness Petrus Van Nuffel writes: 'The flags of the allies were hoisted on the facade of the town hall; the carillonneur played a vigorous *Vlaamse Leeuw*, and the enraptured people cheered along: *The army troops are slain, but a people will not perish!*' The last Liège fort fell on 16 August, and the Belgian army retreated in the direction of Antwerp. The next day, at his Monday concert, Denyn played a series of patriotic songs for a mixed group of citizens and soldiers. American poet Henry Van Dyke, then minister of the USA in the Netherlands and Luxembourg, was there and wrote a review of the concert in verses, whose title included the French name for Mechelen *The Bells of Malines*:

> (...)
> O brave bell-music of Malines,
> In this dark hour how much you mean!
> The dreadful night of blood and tears
> Sweeps down on Belgium, but she hears
> Deep in her heart the melody
> Of songs she learned when she was free.
> She will not falter, faint, nor fail,
> But fight until her rights prevail
> And all her ancient belfries ring
> "The Flemish Lion," "God Save the King!"[161]

This would be Denyn's last full concert in Mechelen for four years: on the following Monday, 24 August, he interrupted his concert because the Germans were approaching the city.

In the same week, patriotic enthusiasm would give way to horror and terror. After heavy fighting, French troops were forced to abandon the city of Dinant. On Sunday 23 August, the city was plundered and destroyed by German troops. More than 600 residents were shot. The Church of our Lady and its carillon were destroyed in the city fire. Two days later, Leuven suffered a similar fate. The Belgian army had launched a counterattack from Antwerp and had repelled the German field army to just outside Leuven, which had already been occupied for six days. At eight o'clock in the evening, shots were heard in the city center. In the confusion, German soldiers had begun shooting each other. The commanders ruled, however, that Leuven citizens had shot the soldiers, and ordered revenge, *das Strafgericht über Löwen*. Soldiers went from home to home with phosphorus tablets and set the city center ablaze. Residents were taken from their houses and shot. More than one thousand homes were totally destroyed, two hundred residents were killed and numerous citizens were captured and deported. Bell-founder Félix Van Aerschodt, son and successor of Séverin, was taken as hostage to Antwerp. Along the way, he and his companions were subjected to a mock execution three times. In the meantime, his bell-foundry on Leopoldstraat burned to the ground. The gothic town hall was spared since it was the headquarters of the occupying power, but the Collegiate St. Peter's Church on the opposite side of the Market Square went up in flames. The crossing tower was transformed into a burning torch and the magnificent carillon of Claes Noorden and Albert de Grave – which the city of Leuven had received from the monks of Park Abbey in exchange a century earlier – was consumed by fire. Shortly before midnight, the historical university library on the Old Market was set on fire. Thousands of manuscripts and three hundred thousand printed books disappeared in the inferno.

The boundless German violence was fueled by a bugaboo drilled into the German soldiers during their training. In the Belgian cities, citizens hiding behind each window would flout the law of war and shoot at the passing regular troops. Bad-intentioned Catholic priests were said to have been the driving force behind this *franc-tireurs* movement. In fact, the German terror in Belgian cities was a conscious strategy to force passage through Belgium into France with as little opposition as possible. The Teutonic Fury, as the German violence was called at the time, cost the lives of more than 5,000 Belgian citizens in the August and September days of 1914. In Dinant, Visé, Tamines and Andenne, the occupying forces were even more ruthless than in Leuven, if the level of cruelty may be measured by the number of lives lost. However, the burned books of Leuven, whose charred pages fluttered about the streets of the city for days, appealed most to the indignation of the Western intelligentsia. Leuven – *the Oxford of Belgium* – became the capital of the Belgian martyr cities and the *Flames of Louvain* became a household word in global public opinion. The Flemish city became the foundation on which Western countries built a theory of good and evil, with on the one side Western *civilization*, and on the other, German *Kultur*. By destroying the Leuven University, the invaders from the East in fact had revealed their true barbaric face. In the face of global indignation, German scholars frenetically sought justification for the Leuven fury in the franc-tireurs doctrine.

While the Western world expressed sympathy with small Belgium, the poorly organized Belgian army stubbornly obstructed the German army's progress. French troops tried to cut off access to Northern France, and British soldiers flocked to West Flanders. In September, Belgians and Germans fought for a month for the fortified city of Dendermonde. The Belgians had recaptured the city from the Germans on 18 September, after which the belfry was fired upon. Around 5 p.m., a German mortar shell struck the wooden steeple, which caught fire and fell to the Market Square, taking with it the 40 bells of the Vanden Gheyn carillon. The city was completely destroyed.

Antwerp fell on 10 October. To celebrate this important conquest, the bells were sounded in Germany, which could be read among others in the *Kölnischer Zeitung*. The French newspaper *Le Matin* misinterpreted the report and wrote that the Antwerp clergy had been forced to ring their own bells. In response to which *The Times* reported that Belgian priests who refused to ring their bells were removed from their office. The *Corriere della Sera* fanned the flames further and announced that the unfortunate priests were sentenced to hard labor. Reacting to this, *Le Matin* – no longer recognizing its own information – wrote that the occupying forces had punished the unfortunate priests by hanging them by their feet in the bells as live clappers.[162]

A bell from the carillon of Dendermonde, with German soldiers,
from *L'actualité illustrée* of 11 December 1914

The atmosphere of confusion and terror thus fed the wildest fantasies, up to and including the surreal fantasy of the human clapper.

After the fall of Antwerp, the front moved to the west, and on 13 October, Belgian, French and English troops assembled behind the Yser River and the Ieperlee Canal. At the mouth of the Yser lay Nieuwpoort. On 17 October, Belgian troops blew up the tower of the Church of Our Lady to prevent it being used as a target by the Germans. Only a few of the bells of the carillon of Brother Peter Vanden Gheyn were removed intact from under the rubble. The bronze shards from the rest were filed into rings by Belgian soldiers, a new application of bell bronze. At the end of October, Diksmuide was attacked, being defended by French and Belgians. The city was reduced to rubble, and the St. Nicholas Church and its carillon were destroyed. The Germans finally occupied the city, but were able to progress no further, because in the meantime, Belgian commanders had the plain around the Yser flooded. In November, Ypres – being defended by the British – was attacked. On 22 November, the city suffered heavy German bombing. Around 9 a.m., the cloth hall and the belfry came under fire. Fire bombs set the building ablaze and at 11 a.m., the bells of two carillons fell to the ground. Five years earlier, at the advice of Jef Denyn, a new carillon by Felix Van Aerschodt had been installed in the body of the tower. The old carillon continued to hang in the tower lantern. Ypres would be further ravaged in the coming months, until it was no longer a city. The Germans, however, would never capture it.

While the allied soldiers, from trenches, continued to defend the small piece of the fatherland behind the flooded Yser Plain, one million Belgians crossed the border into the Netherlands, which had been able to maintain its neutrality and avoid hostilities. Hundreds of thousands of refugees crossed the Channel and received shelter in England. Among them was bell-founder Félix Van Aerschodt, who became managing director of the recently established *Foundry & Munition Works* in London. The factory was located in the buildings of the Warner bell-foundry – another example of the macabre relationship between bells and artillery.

In Mechelen, the occupying forces wanted Denyn to continue to play the carillon in the St. Rumbold's Tower. However, the carillonneur had fled after the shelling of the city, which also had hit his home. The Denyn family was given shelter in Tunbridge Wells in the County of Kent with bell expert William Wooding Starmer. In the bombing of Mechelen, St. Rumbold's Tower was also hit, but the carillon suffered no damage. One night the tower watchman removed all the pins from the drum, so that the carillon would not have to continue to play the same traditional music in these circumstances. The carillons were also silenced in most other cities. Bruges city carillonneur Toon Nauwelaerts sent his wife and child to England, and went to the Yser Front. His Antwerp colleague Gustaaf Brees gave the keys of the Church of our Lady Tower to the mayor. Each time the Germans asked for the carillonneur to wind up the drum, they were told that he had left. In many cities, the Germans banned the ringing of bells, especially in the evening. But the residents of the occupied territory also had no need of swinging bells. In Mechelen, the 8-ton bourdon Salvator was even removed from its yoke by the residents to prevent it being rung by the occupying forces. The Belgian cities fell silent.

The voice of fallen carillons

The reality of the destroyed and disused bells and carillons was given a poetic interpretation. For the poets, the bells were in mourning and were awaiting the moment at which they would celebrate the country's liberation and victory over the barbarians.[163] Much poetry was written during the war years, especially in England. Already on 18 October, when the carillons of Diksmuide and Ypres had not yet fallen, Thomas Hardy, author of *Tess of the d'Urbervilles*, picked up his pen. In the sonnet *On the Belgian*

Expatriation, the poet dreams that one morning Belgians would come to England to fill the towers with musical carillons. But he awakes and sees only a group of ragged refugees from Bruges, Antwerp and Ostend. They come with empty hands, because the carillons of their city have been shot to pieces. Fortunately, this was poetic exaggeration, because the only carillon to be destroyed was that of Ostend, and this only in 1918.

> *I dreamt that people from the Land of Chimes*
> *Arrived one autumn morning with their bells,*
> *To hoist them on the towers and citadels*
> *Of my own country, that the musical rhymes*
> *Rung by them into space at meted times*
> *Amid the market's daily stir and stress,*
> *And the night's empty star-lit silentness,*
> *Might solace souls of this and kindred climes.*
> *Then I awoke; and lo, before me stood*
> *The visioned ones, but pale and full of fear;*
> *From Bruges they came, and Antwerp, and Ostend,*
> *No carillons in their train. Foes of mad mood*
> *Had shattered these to shards amid the gear*
> *Of ravaged roof, and smouldering gable-end.*

Hardy's poem was included in *King Albert's Book*, which was published in London around Christmas 1914. The book was published by *The Daily Telegraph* and was intended to demonstrate to the world the martyrdom of the Belgian people, and the heroism of the king-knight Albert and the caring nurse-queen Elisabeth. The initiative was not only inspired by sincere sympathy for the fate of the Belgian people, but also by the desire to keep neutral Belgium and its king strongly in the allied camp. *King Albert's Book* contains 238 poems, sayings, compositions and graphic works by the great of the earth. Page 147, for example, contains a *Berceuse Héroïque* for piano by Claude Debussy. The great impressionist had allowed himself to be enticed into composing a lullaby on the theme of the Brabançonne, the Belgian national anthem. On page 113, art potter, tile designer and writer William De Morgan recalled a childhood memory from Leuven. Once, when passing through the city, he stayed at a hotel close to the town hall. It was hot and he slept with the windows open. Every fifteen minutes the carillon played its tune, allowing the Englishman little sleep that night. The following day he used his best French on the young female innkeeper:

> 'Je ne poovay par dormir parceque du song des cloches. Ils songt assez pour éveiller les morts.'
> 'Plaît-il? Dites-le-moi encore une fois. Ze bell weck you up? Ees that ride?'
> I felt my forces demoralised, and merely answered: 'We!'
> (...)
> 'ici on entend la <sic> carillon dès sa naissance – jusqu'à la mort. Je suis née dans la maison, moi; grand'mère aussi. S'il n'y avait plus carillon, il n'y aurait plus sommeil, ni pour elle, ni pour moi.'

The writer concluded his article as follows:

> And Marie – after 50 year he still remembers her name – may be turned of seventy if... Well! – if German Culture has spared her. But neither she nor any other Louvainoise will ever sleep the better now for the music of the bells, nor any guest of hers be kept awake an hour. For the old hostelry, I take it, is a heap of ashes, and the sound of the carillon is ended for ever.

Page 84 to page 91 contained a contribution by Edward Elgar, a piano adaptation of his composition *Carillon*. He had the work written for orchestra and speaking voice to a poem by Belgian writer Emile Cammaerts. The work, which lasts only seven minutes, is based on a descending bell motif that reminds one more of English change ringing than of Belgian carillon music. The music is alternately exuberant and lyrical, fully in agreement with the spirit of the time. The spoken text looks ahead to the final victory of the Belgian people, who in the end will penetrate to Berlin. Nowhere in the text is there talk of a carillon. The symbolic value of the Belgian carillons was so strong in those days that the word *carillon* by itself already evoked the desired emotions. On 7 December 1914, the work premiered at Queen's Hall. The performance was an immense success, after which the production, under the direction of Elgar himself, made a triumphant tour through a number of English cities. The profits were for the benefit of the ailing Belgian people. The declamation was initially performed by Tita Brand, wife of the lyricist, and later by Lala Speyer, wife of the Belgian socialist leader Emile Vandervelde. According to some sources, she entered the stage fully draped in a Belgian tricolor flag.[164]

Reports of the destroyed Belgian carillons also reached the United States of America. The carillon book by William Gorham Rice was published in December 1914. He had found a publisher whom he was able to convince – with some difficulty – that the topic had not yet been treated in book form. *Carillons of Belgium and Holland* became a major success. The somewhat idealized picture that Rice sketched of the peaceful prewar *carillon region* struck a chord with the American public, especially in light of

French image of the silent bells of Leuven

the catastrophe that had hit Belgium. The book would be reprinted three times in the coming years. Strengthened by the success of his first book, Rice published *The Carillon in Literature* in 1915, an anthology of old and new texts on the carillon, with attention given to the recent war poetry.

Fantasy increasingly replaced reality. In 1916, the book *Vanished Towers and Chimes of Flanders* was published in Philadelphia, written by George Wharton Edwards. Edwards had studied art among others in Paris and Antwerp, and was a celebrated impressionistic painter in the States. In 1911, he had written a romantic tourist guide titled *Some Old Flemish Towns*. In his new book, he contrasted the idyllic Flanders that he had visited before the war with the situation as he imagined it in 1916. He offered his readers a dramatic fresco of a Flanders in which virtually all carillons had been destroyed, including the instrument in Mechelen: '... those bells which now lie broken among the ashes of the tower in the Grand' Place of the ruined town of Malines'.[165]

In 1917, the successful American author Robert Chambers published *Barbarians*, a novel with Maryette Courtray as heroine. She was the young female carillonneur of Sainte Lesse, an imaginary, small Northern French village close to the front line. Maryette is called *Carillonnette* in the village, and she consoles the villagers in the evening with her carillon playing, which includes performances of music by Jef Denyn:

> *All the people who remained in Sainte Lesse and in Alincourt brought out their chairs and their knitting in the calm, fragrant evening air and remained silent, sadly enraptured while the unseen player at her keyboard aloft in the belfry above set her carillon music adrift under the summer stars – golden harmonies that seemed born in the heavens from which they floated; clear, exquisitely sweet miracles of melody filling the world of darkness with magic messages of hope.*
>
> *Those widowed or childless among her listeners for miles around in the darkness wept quiet tears, less bitter and less hopeless for the divine promise of the sky music which filled the night as subtly as the scent of flowers saturates the dusk.*

When the neighboring town of Nivelle is threatened with occupation by the Germans, she devises a plan together with Jim, an American soldier who came to Europe to fight the Germans despite the military neutrality of the USA. At night, they creep into the town's carillon tower. There, Carillonnette falls prey to melancholy:

> '... there are few carillons left. The Huns are battering them down. Towers of the ancient ages are falling everywhere in Flanders and in France under their shell fire. Very soon there will be no more of the old carillons left; no more bell-music in the world.'

When the sun rises, it's time for action. German soldiers have penetrated the town to launch a gas attack on the French from the trench under the tower. Soldier Jim attacks them from the tower with several bombs and calls out to Carillonnette to play the Brabançonne. The Belgian folk song was the agreed symbol for the counterattack by the French.

> 'Ring out your Brabançonne !' he cried. 'Let the Huns hear the war song of the land they've trampled! Now! Little bell-mistress arm your white hands with your wooden gloves and make this old carillon speak in brass and iron!'
> (...)
> The bells above her crashed out into the battle-song of Flanders, filling sky and earth with its splendid defiance of the Hun.
> The airman, bomb in hand, stood at the head of the stone stairs; the ancient tower rocked with the fiercely magnificent anthem of revolt – the war cry of a devastated land – the land that died to save the world – the martyr, Belgium, still prone in the deathly trance awaiting her certain resurrection.

And thus the Germans were chased from a French battlefield by the sounds of the Belgian national anthem. No fantasy was too great to demonstrate to the world the heroism of the Belgian people. *The Broken Bells of Flanders* – to cite a poem by Scottish-Canadian poet James Lewis Milligan – became a powerful metaphor for evoking the destruction of the small country and the enslavement of its people. It is striking that French Flanders, which lost many more carillons in the Great War than Belgium, remained virtually unmentioned in the romanticism surrounding the war.

International solidarity for *Brave Little Belgium* was not limited to words. The ruins of the Leuven library were still smoldering when the first initiatives emerged to donate new books to the university. In addition to burned books and destroyed carillons, there was the daily reality of famine. This was caused by the hard occupation regime and the British sea blockade that obstructed the transport of food to Germany. To help the starving Belgian population, in the United States the *Commission for Relief in Belgium* was set up under the leadership of Herbert Hoover, mining engineer and later president of the USA. The food aid for Belgium was the first large-scale humanitarian relief operation in history. The commission set up massive solidarity campaigns in the homeland and organized transport by ship to Belgium with a monthly budget of 20 million dollars. From 1915 until the American declaration of war in 1917, the Belgian people were provided with more than 3 million tons of beans, bacon, flour, rice, cornstarch and other foodstuffs.

Carillon war in the Netherlands

In 1915, a small carillon war broke out in neutral Netherlands: less cruel but just as bitter as the Great War that raged in the surrounding countries.[166] To learn the causes of the fight, we need to go back several decades in time. At the end of the 19th century, interest in the carillon had also increased in the Netherlands. The instrument was

Jacob Vincent, the carillonneur of the palace, at the keyboard

primarily approached as a monument, a shining example of the Dutch Golden Age, with the Hemony carillons as sonorous reminders. The repertoire was largely inspired by the music of the people: traditional psalm settings, 17th century Geuzen songs – named after those who opposed Spanish rule in the Netherlands – from the collection *Nederlandtsche gedenck-clanck* by Dutch poet and composer Adrianus Valerius, and 19th century songs with historical topics such as *De Zilvervloot* (The Silver Fleet). Most carillons were equipped with the traditional wire schering, which was now called the *broek system*. Since Jef Denyn's celebrated concert for the 1906 Language and Literary Congress, the fame of the Mechelen carillon movement had also penetrated to the Netherlands. Not only journalists, but also carillonneurs such as Marius Brandts Buys, who played the oldest Hemony carillon at Zutphen, praised the enchanting effects of the Mechelen carillon style. The fact that Dutch carillonneurs could not achieve the Mechelen expressivity on their broek systems was painfully revealed during the 1910 Mechelen carillon competition, with the six Dutch participants finishing in the sixth last places.

The best known Dutch carillonneur was Jacob Vincent. He played the Hemony carillon in the Amsterdam town hall, which in 1815 was converted into a royal palace. Hence, he was the personal carillonneur of Queen Wilhelmina. The chief royal concern in the first years of the 20th century was the queen's fertility problem. Wilhelmina had already had four miscarriages, and many feared that the Orange Dynasty would die out with her. It was even possible that due to dynastic blood ties, the Netherlands would receive a German monarch. In 1908, however, Wilhelmina was again with child, and the entire country was in joyful expectation of a prince or princess who would continue the dynasty. Vincent had agreed with the press that he would play the palace carillon when news of the birth became known. When on 30 April 1909, he played the Hemony bells in the palace dome to announce the joyful event to the world, the Dam Square in front of the palace was packed with people. His fame was immediate. As 'carillonneur of the palace', Vincent became a national symbol, and a cigar brand even marketed a cigar *De carillonneur J. Vincent*. Shortly before the war, acceptance of the carillon in the Netherlands received broader support. Thus the National Association for the Folk Song called upon all carillonneurs in the country to add splendor to the celebration on 18 July 1913 of the one hundredth anniversary of the expulsion of Napoleon's troops from the Netherlands with a carillon concert.

In the same year, Jef Denyn appeared in the Netherlands for the first time. He had been invited by Marius Brandts Buys to inspect the carillon in the Winery Tower at Zutphen, with a view toward renovating it according to the Mechelen model. When Denyn was traveling through Arnhem, he had visited the Hemony carillon in the Eusebius Tower and given advice on its renovation. Since the bells were hanging in rows, and there already was a tumbler rack present, it would cost little for him to modify the carillon to make legato playing possible. The outbreak of the war hindered these plans. In Arnhem, however, Denyn was not forgotten. When in 1915, the congress of the National Association of Tourism was being organized, the Arnhem branch wished to invite the Mechelen carillonneur to give a concert at the congress. Since the Arnhem tourist office did not know where Denyn lived, it made a guess and sent the letter of invitation to London. The letter arrived too late in Tunbridge Wells, so that Denyn could not be present at the congress. On 5 September, the last day of the congress, a letter from Denyn was read aloud in which he stated that he was prepared to make the crossing to the Netherlands, but that he did not want to commit himself to giving concerts, since the Dutch carillons were not equipped for artistic carillon playing. The Arnhem tourist office, however, wanted definitive advice on its carillon, so that it too would now have the Mechelen sound and attract large numbers of tourists. Denyn crossed the Channel, and on 8 October was honored by the tourist office and the city government of Arnhem. The mayor saw great possibilities for the city, and addressed the famous carillonneur as follows: 'I thank Mr. Denyn for his arrival during these sad times, and I am proud to state that Arnhem will be at the forefront of improvements to carillons in the Netherlands, because the master carillonneur has proposed to educate the Dutch people in this beautiful art.' On the same day, the tourist office sent a circular to the approximately fifty Dutch towns that possessed a carillon. It wrote that the new carillon art of Jef Denyn in the Flemish cities had already generated much new revenue thanks to the rise in tourism. A proposal was made to the municipalities that they have Denyn equip their carillon according to the Mechelen model, so that they also would enjoy the greater tourist interest that undoubtedly would come to the Netherlands after the war ended. If Denyn were to receive a sufficiently large number of orders, he was even prepared to settle in Arnhem to guide from there the renovation of the Dutch carillons.

In the days that followed, Denyn received invitations from fifteen municipalities to inspect their carillon, after which he traveled for three weeks through the Netherlands. At some places, such as Amersfoort and Schoonhoven, he guaranteed that he could obtain a good result since the bell-chamber had sufficient room to hang the bells in rows and install tumbler axes. At other places, such as Alkmaar and Haarlem, he was faced with open lantern towers and could not guarantee an optimum result. While he had not been invited to Amsterdam, he visited the Dutch capital anyway and was there during the weekend of 16 and 17 October as a guest of Jacob Vincent. As expected, he advised removing the bells in the palace dome from the openings and hanging them inside the tower. To compensate for the visual impoverishment of the lantern tower, he advised hanging imitation zinc bells in the openings. The prince of carillonneurs arrived home empty handed, because except for Arnhem, only the municipality of Nijkerk had expressed interest in having its tower instrument rebuilt according to the Mechelen model. In Schoonhoven, the mayor was a proponent of the proposed renovation, but the city council voted him down six to votes to three. In November, the municipal authorities received a letter from Bonaventura Eijsbouts, who proposed a revision with Mechelen keyboard but retaining the broek system. He argued that he could do the same work as Denyn had proposed, and that Dutch industry would still be supported. He was given the order.

After Denyn's return to England, the controversy in the Netherlands spread and became grimmer. In January 1916, the *Bond Heemschut*, a heritage society which championed the preservation of historical monuments, sent a circular to all carillon owners in the country and warned about the innovations being proposed by Denyn. The owners were urged to leave the carillons in the state in which they were. Especially the re-hanging of the bells from the lantern openings to the interior of the tower was rejected, as was the hanging of pseudo bells to restore the visual effect. The strongest reaction came from Utrecht. When the Utrecht city government received the circular from Arnhem in October, it presented it to the local tourist office. It considered itself incompetent to express an opinion on Denyn's proposed renovations, and appointed a nine-member committee of experts that included among others Jacob Vincent and Utrecht city carillonneur Johan Wagenaar. The commission submitted its conclusions only at the middle of 1916. It ruled that the improvements of Jef Denyn were unnecessary since they were only important for tremolo playing. This musical technique, however, was rejected in principle since it did not correspond to the nature of the bell and thus violated the original character of the carillon. They favored the old Dutch playing style, in which the flat hand was used to play psalm melodies and other simple melodies, and which gives the bells time to decay. Most of the committee members, however, had never heard tremolo playing, and given the war situation in Belgium, this would also not have been possible. The negative opinion was perhaps partially inspired by a certain need for revenge, because local carillonneur Johan Wagenaar was one of the Dutch participants who did poorly in the Mechelen carillon competition in 1910. For the rest of his life, Jacob Vincent retained a suspicious attitude to the innovations of Denyn, whom he called 'that cloth merchant from Mechelen'. Over time, the dispute became personal, and the tourist office of Arnhem was accused of wanting to provide a needy Belgian with a source of income. The Belgian 'Burgundian' playing style with closed fist was rejected, the effect of tremolo playing was compared with the sound of village station bells, and tremolo playing itself was scornfully referred to as the milking of cows.

Despite conservative resistance, it was the followers of Denyn who impressed the general public. In the spring of 1916, the first of two Dutch-speaking books on the carillon was published. Amsterdam journalist Adriaan Loosjes – the only member of the Utrecht committee to support Denyn – published the richly illustrated work *De torenmuziek in de Nederlanden* (Tower Music in the Low Countries), which in addition to a historic overview, contained a description of all the carillons in the Netherlands. Next to the title page was a full-page photo of Jef Denyn. Loosjes distanced himself from what he called 'the deadly embrace of several antiquarians', and expressed his standpoint very clearly: 'No, the carillon is not a monument, and all changes that can improve its task were not only justified in the past, but are also justified in the present.' At approximately the same time, the pocket book *De torens zingen!* (The towers sing!) by young Arnhem folklore specialist Dirk Jan van der Ven was published. The exclamation point in the title is significant, because the treatise was a pro-Mechelen pamphlet that meticulously chronicled the polemic that was taking place during these months in the Netherlands. Van der Ven attempted to convince his compatriots – 'a critical folk so difficult to excite' – of the great value of Denyn's approach and to put them at ease. This was not a type of 'foreigner worship', as could be read in the press. In the 17th century, had not the Dutch made no objection to the French Hemony brothers who, like Denyn, had fled a war, and cast imperfect forestrokes into tuned bells? Van der Ven argued further that the interventions of Denyn could always be undone if they did not achieve the desired effect in Arnhem. Moreover, the changes could always be limited to those towers that would suffer no aesthetic damage due to a rearrangement of the bells. Finally, Dutch craftsmen could do the work. The writer looked forward to

30 April 1916, the day on which Denyn would officially inaugurate the renovated carillon in Arnhem. The renovation and the concert, however, did not happen. German U boats were now active in the Channel, and Denyn remained in England, awaiting the war's end.

Bells of victory

The war took longer than everyone had expected. In 1917, a revolution broke out in Russia, and the Bolsheviks wished to make peace with Germany to save their revolution. In March 1918, the war on the Eastern Front came to an end. That year, Lenin had two revolutionary songs programmed on the mechanical drum of the Kremlin, including *The Internationale* – and thus music by Fleming Pierre De Geyter was heard on a carillon in Moscow.[167] The war continued in the West, and Germany used up its metal stocks. On 1 March 1917, a regulation was promulgated that made the bells in Germany and the occupied territories available to the war industry. In Germany, 70,000 bells were taken from the towers. No symbols were spared: On 20 June 1918, the largest of all German bells, the Kaiserglocke in the Cologne Cathedral, was removed from the tower for military purposes.

Germany also requisitioned metal in the occupied territories. Breweries lost their kettles and brass bands were required to hand in their musical instruments. On 8 February 1918, Governor General Ludwig von Falkenhausen announced that he soon would requisition Belgian bells and organ pipes. Cardinal Mercier responded with the pastoral letter *La saisie des cloches et des orgues en Belgique occupée*, in which he condemned the possible requisitioning as a violation of The Hague Conventions. The Belgian church leader called on the population to resist a possible requisition. Little came of the bell requisition in Belgium, and Mercier acquired world fame due to his unyielding stand. After the war, Rice called him *the savior of carillons*. Only in the Etappengebiet in the west of the country, which was under military rule, did the Germans dare lay a hand on the bells. On 7 September 1917, those living close to the St. Hilonius Tower in Izegem were startled at night by the sound of bells, a sound that hadn't been heard for three years. The carillon was being disassembled by six German soldiers, assisted by three Flemings. The church organist succeeding in hiding the three smallest bells. The carillons in Ostend, Roeselare and Torhout also disappeared into the smelting furnace. Two more Flemish carillons were lost during the final allied offensive. On 18 October 1918 in the small city of Wingene, the retreating German army destroyed the St. Amand's Tower and its carillon, which throughout the war had continued to play *De Vlaamse Leeuw*, the official anthem of Flanders. Two weeks later, the Vanden Gheyn carillon in the St. Walburga Tower at Oudenaarde was destroyed.

'Easter of liberation', from *Les Annales* of 20 April 1919

On 11 November 1918, as predicted in the war poetry, enthusiastic tolling in all cities and municipalities announced to the population that the war was over. In Mechelen, the bourdon Salvator rang only at 3 in the afternoon, after residents had again hung the 8 ton-bell on its yoke. Everywhere, carillonneurs prepared their instruments to play patriotic songs. The tolling and playing of the bells, after more than four years of occupation, must have contributed strongly to the revelry of the Belgian population.

In 1918, the number of carillons worldwide had dropped to an historic low of approximately 120. The Great War had accomplished its destructive work in Belgium and Northern France, before the carillons had even had a chance to recover from the requisitions during French domination. On the other hand, the romance surrounding the war had raised the image of the carillon to an unprecedented level. Four days after the armistice, Anna Thorne, wife of the mayor of Cape Town, called upon her fellow female citizens to create in the tower of the town hall a memorial carillon to the soldiers of the Great War.[168] And thus began a period of spectacular expansion of carillon culture.

CHAPTER 16

Memorial bells

A school for carillonneurs

When the cannons fell silent and the sound of the victory bells had faded, the winners and losers of the Great War gathered in Versailles to once again redraw the map of Europe. During the course of the war, relations between Belgium and the Netherlands had soured for other – more important – reasons than the smear campaign around the carillon. Belgian Minister of Foreign Affairs Paul Hymans claimed Dutch Limburg and Zeelandic Flanders as Belgian territory. In 1919, however, the image of *Brave Little Belgium* was no longer as strong as it was during the war, and the moral credit that Belgium had accumulated in the previous years could not be capitalized on at the political negotiating table. In addition to German reparations in kind to the Leuven university library, the great powers allowed Belgium only the Middle African mandate Rwanda-Urundi and a piece of western Germany now called the East Cantons. In the meantime, the Dutch army was in a state of alert, should a preventive attack on its overconfident southern neighbor be needed.

Emotions also continued to run high in carillon circles after the war. The conservative Utrecht advisory committee, the Dutch Bells and Organ Council (*Nederlandsche Klokken- en Orgelraad*), was formed in 1917. It was an uncompromising organization that advised on carillon construction with as goal, safeguarding carillons as Dutch patrimony. The General Carillon Association (*Algemeene Klokkenspel-Vereeniging*) was founded at Arnhem in 1919 as countermovement. This association wished to promote the carillon as a contemporary instrument typical to both Low Countries. For this reason, the association would consist of a Northern Netherlands and Southern Netherlands – read Belgium – branch. The Northern Netherlands branch was led by the enthusiastic propagandist Adriaan Loosjes, and Emiel Hullebroeck was chosen as president of the Southern branch. This popular composer of Flemish songs and operettas gained fame in the Netherlands during the war thanks to the numerous song evenings he organized there for the Belgian refugees. The idea of one large association for both the Northern and Southern Netherlands was unpopular with a number of Belgian politicians, and Hullebroeck was accused of subversive activities by the

Chamber of Representatives. The carillon movement threatened to become enmeshed in a Flemish nationalistic or even a Greater Dutch ideology, which was problematic in post-war Belgium with its growing tensions between the language communities. The wrangling around the carillon also threatened to become an obstacle to the yet to be established Mechelen carillon school. The way was only cleared when Hullebroeck, in 1921, gave up his co-presidency of the General Dutch Carillon Association and became president of *Onze beiaarden - Nos carillons*, a linguistically neutral association that operated out of Brussels. Several years later, the northern branch of the General Carillon Association would abandon the South and limit its activity to Dutch territory under the name *Nederlandse Klokkenspel-Vereeniging* (Dutch Carillon Association).

When the neutral association *Onze beiaarden - Nos carillons* formally requested the founding of a carillon school in Mechelen, Minister of Arts and Sciences Jules Destrée promised financial support as soon as the school was up and running. Resistance to the school continued, however, even after this ministerial commitment. The news that the creation of the school was imminent prompted Gustaaf Brees, Antoon Nauwelaerts, Karel De Mette and Theo Vandeplas, city carillonneurs of Antwerp, Bruges, Aalst and Diest respectively, to write a letter of protest that was published in *Het Laatste Nieuws* on 5 October 1921. The carillonneurs distanced themselves from the Mechelen carillon movement and from the school initiative. On 2 February 1922, the Walloon newspaper *Le Soir* published a letter to the editor with as title 'Un carillonneur activisant [An Activist Carilloneur]', in which Denyn was accused of Flemish nationalist sympathies. In Mechelen, he had been heard playing militant songs by Jef van Hoof, the Flemish composer who was convicted of activism during the war. *Le Soir* was attacked by the Flemish media and lost a court battle over the issue. In the end, the polemics in the press were only rearguard actions. The die had been cast, and the formation of the first carillon school in history was imminent.[169]

The entire carillon community gathered in Mechelen from 12 to 15 August 1922 to attend a triple event: the celebration of Jef Denyn's 35th year as carillonneur, the first carillon congress, and the establishment of a carillon school. The program was lavish. A procession of Mechelen associations marched through the streets of the city, Jef Denyn was presented with a jubilee bell to complete his carillon, two cantatas were performed in his honor, there was a large carillon exhibition, there were lectures and of course many carillon concerts with the 'colored lighting' of the St. Rumbold's Tower. One of the most remarkable lectures was that of William Gorham Rice. The American reported on his activities of recent years. His first book was in its fourth edition; in various American cities he gave a total of 35 lectures, illustrated with slides and a recording of the Bournville carillon, the only recording of carillon music that was then available; he had articles published in magazines; he spoke on radio programs and presented exhibition material at various places. He proudly communi-

Participants of the 1922 carillon congress at the archi-episcopal palace in Mechelen. In the middle are standing Jef Denyn, cardinal Mercier and William Gorham Rice.

cated to the audience that his efforts had borne fruit: for several months now, carillon music could be heard on the North American continent. The year 1922 was indeed historic in a number of respects. Not only was the carillon renaissance in the Low Countries sealed by the establishment of the Mechelen carillon school; in the same year, the musical instrument of the Low Countries also set foot in the New World. North America had embraced the carillon, and it would play an important role in its further development.[170]

Carillon sounds across the Atlantic

There had already been a modest import of European carillons to North America in the 19th century.[171] In 1856, French bell-founder Bollée delivered a forestroke of 23 bells for Notre Dame University, and in 1870, he sold an instrument with 43 bells connected to a pneumatic system to St. Joseph's Cathedral in Buffalo. In 1883, Séverin Van Aerschodt delivered a series of 25 bells that were playable with a baton keyboard for Holy Trinity Episcopal Church in Philadelphia. Finally, in 1900, St. Vincent's Seminary in Philadelphia received a series of 26 bells by Paccard with a piano keyboard and a flywheel drive. Thus, only the Van Aerschodt instrument was a traditional carillon.

The instruments were poorly tuned, if tuned at all, and did not contribute to the local popularity of the carillon in the USA. America for that matter had its own bell tradition.

Chiming had been practiced in North America from the beginning of the 19th century. The appearance and musical possibilities of an American chime strongly resembled the primitive carillons of the Low Countries in the 16th century. A chime stand consisted of 8 to 18 bells ordered as a diatonic series, thus without the black notes of the piano. The keyboard batons were in the shape of handles that were pressed downward with the open hand. The player stood upright and thus could play only one note at a time with the pedals – if pedals were present at all. Chime bells were cast by American bell-founders and were poorly tuned at best. Most instruments hung in protestant church towers and were used for playing church hymns in a simple setting. Today some 650 chiming installations still hang in American towers. The term chime is derived from a term we encountered above: *cymbala*. Because a chime bears a superficial resemblance to a carillon, American authors often incorrectly use it when writing about the carillons of the Low Countries.

After the Great War, however, the time was ripe in the States for a successful introduction to the real thing: Belgian carillon culture. The romance surrounding the war had given Belgian carillons an aura of heroism and melancholy, and William Gorham Rice developed an attractive and consistent ideology around the instrument. For him, the carillon was a collective medium, a bearer of democratic feelings and a means to a sense of community, important values in American society. Moreover, of crucial importance was what Rice called the *memorial idea*, the power to keep people and events alive in the memory of the following generations.[172] This concept found fertile ground in one of the deepest characteristics of the American psyche: the desire to be remembered after death. The fear of being forgotten was one of the driving forces behind American charity, just as charity was stimulated in the European Middle Ages by the fear of hell and purgatory. The human toll of the Great War had made the memorial idea still more relevant, and the Americans discovered that the carillon, more than any other monument, could be a memorial with immense emotional value. Music after all has the power to invoke the memory of a benefactor or loved one to the generations to come. Last but not least, the ambitions and the financial resources were present in post-war America to realize grand projects. A carillon after all costs more than a commemorative stone in a wall or a copper plate on a bench.

The first appeal for an American memorial carillon appeared two weeks after the armistice.[173] The artist James Marion Shull published an article in various magazines calling for the construction of 'Peace Carillons' in the capital cities of all allied countries, with bells that would be cast in bronze obtained from German cannons. A new tower with carillon in Washington would keep alive the memory of the heroes of the Great War, and in addition, be a 'business asset', since thousands of music lovers would come to the American capital to listen to the bells. Washington would become the mecca of an art that was already known elsewhere in the world, but that was still new to America. The artist closed his article with a visionary review of the future opening concert. Prior to the concert, the audience would be introduced to the monument, containing stones from Reims, Verdun, Leuven and other destroyed European cities. When the concert started, the audience would be surprised by the sounds that swelled and ebbed like the waves of the swirling sea and that would overwhelm them like 'a veritable Niagara of sound'.

> *The concert closes with the National Air, as is our wont, but played as never had it been played before on our own soil, the clear, pure tones dropping from high aloft as shaken from the very folds of our bright emblem there, each scintilant note a star, flung off in ecstasy, to bear a message to the ears of men, of peace on earth, but peace with freedom still.*

Shull convinced the Art Club in Washington of his idea, and a carillon committee was founded to implement the concept of the National Peace Carillon. The American architect of French origin Paul Cret designed a tower more than 300 feet high, and Taylor designed a 154,000-pound carillon that would be the heaviest such instrument in the world by far. It would have 54 bells, one for each of the then 48 American States and one for each of the six territories: the Philippines, Alaska, Hawaii, Cuba, Puerto Rico and the District of Columbia. The state that had lost the most lives in the Great War would receive the largest bell, the following state the second bell, and so on. The carillon would be erected on the National Mall, right next to the White House. It would be a new wonder of the world that would attract tens of thousands of music lovers from throughout world, just as Jef Denyn had done with his carillon in the St. Rumbold's Tower. The visions of Shull and the Art Club, however, were never realized, and the New World had to wait until 1922 to hear the sounds of the carillon.

The first actual order for a carillon came from the Church of Our Lady of Good Voyage in Gloucester, Massachusetts.[174] The town was located on the Atlantic Ocean and was inhabited primarily by fishermen of Portuguese origin. The ocean was treacherous near Gloucester, and in the 350 year history of the town, more than 10,000 fishermen had died at sea – reason enough for a musical memorial in the newly constructed church. One of the town's leading residents, Piatt Andrew, had traveled in Europe and had become acquainted there with the carillon. Andrew came in contact with Rice, who supported the project, and after a fundraising campaign, a 25-bell carillon was ordered from Taylor. When the bells arrived in Boston in February 1922, they were promptly subjected to the standard import tax of 40% on musical instruments.

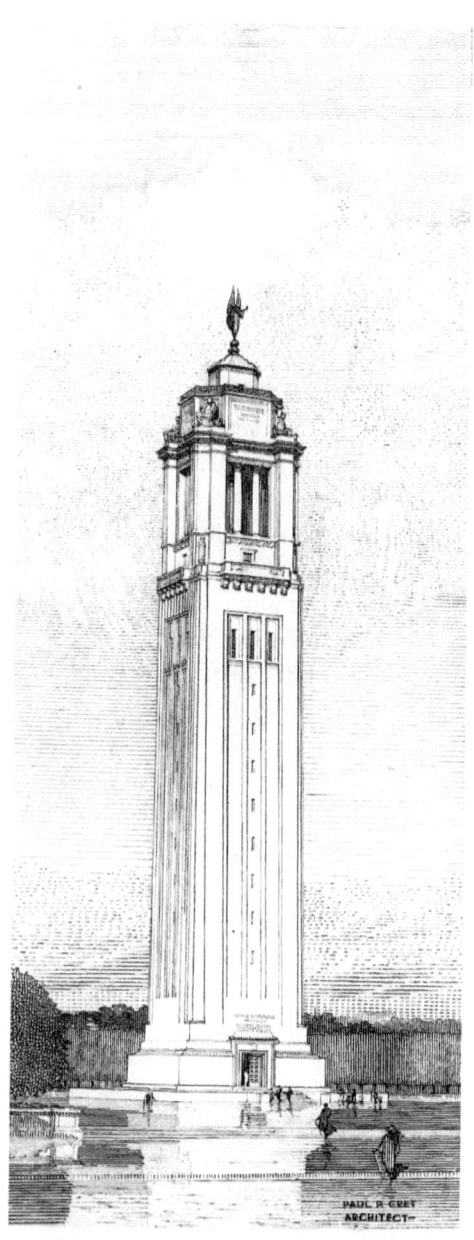

Design of the proposed tower of the
National Peace Carillon in Washington DC, by Paul Cret

This led Piatt Andrew, as he was a member of Congress, to submit a bill to qualify a carillon as a work of art, which guaranteed tax-free import. The law was passed by the congress and signed by President Harding, so that on 23 July 1922, the carillon could be officially inaugurated by organist George B. Stevens, who became the first official player of the instrument. For Taylor, the bells were a splendid calling card for the promising American carillon market. The foundry had undergone difficult years during the war. It had to suspend its bell production in favor of the production of shells, and John William Taylor Jr. had lost three sons at the front. After his death in 1919, the business was continued by his brothers Pryce and Denison, and better times were on the way.

The delay for tax reasons of the first carillon for the USA meant that the first North American carillon sounded on Canadian soil. Entrepreneur and benefactor Chester Massey donated a 23-bell carillon to the Metropolitan Methodist Church in Toronto in memory of his wife, who had died the year before. The instrument was inaugurated on 2 April 1922 by Englishman Harry Withers. The local organist asked one of his students, Frank P. Price, to play the new instrument. The young Price was familiar with carillons: during a tour of the European mainland in 1920, Antoon Nauwelaerts had showed him the Bruges carillon. Frank Percival Price became the first North American carillonneur and would become the founding father of American carillon culture.

The Toronto carillon was not cast by Taylor, but by a new player on the market: Gillett & Johnston, a bell-foundry in Croydon, close to London. Gillett & Johnston was established in 1877, when clockmaker William Gillett and bell-founder Arthur Johnston joined forces. In contrast to rival Taylor, Arthur Johnston was not interested in the innovative ideas of Canon Simpson. He did not tune his bells, or rather did so maximally by chipping out the inside, to the joy of his daughter Nora who collected the bronze chips and hung them in the Christmas tree, and to the chagrin of his son Cyril, who had been working at the foundry since he was 18. Cyril had read the groundbreaking articles of Arthur Simpson in 1906, and wished to try the technique. His father refused to purchase a tuning machine, so Cyril purchased one with his own money. Without the help of Simpson, who had died six years earlier, Cyril succeeded in tuning bells accurately. A surprising side-effect of the purely tuned bell appeared to be its ability to be heard at greater distances. When the English coast guard wished to purchase new bell buoys, Cyril Johnston conducted an experiment. Together with directors of the coast guard, he went to sea in order to hear two buoys from a distance. The buoy that was equipped with a standard bell could be heard at a distance of one mile, and the one with a bell that was tuned according to the *Five-Tone Simpson Principle* could carry twice the distance. After this experiment, the English navy always used Johnston bells as standard.

This new development was not only interesting for the audibility of buoys. For the first time in history, two competitors were simultaneously capable of producing pure sounding carillons. From now on, potential buyers would be in a stronger position when negotiating with carillon makers than in the time of the Hemony brothers and Andreas Jozef Vanden Gheyn, who each in their time had a de facto monopoly on pure sounding carillons. Cyril Johnston and Denison Taylor went at it head to head to capture the promising American carillon market. Taylor neglected to patent several of his developments because it was too expensive, which gave Johnston the opportunity to quickly close his technological gap. Attempts at price-fixing between Taylor, Johnston and the London foundry Whitechapel failed because Cyril Johnston broke the agreement on a regular basis. The somewhat enigmatic Denison Taylor attempted to maintain a fixed price, assuming that the quality of his products would persuade the consumer. He, however, was forced to watch how Cyril Johnston, from more centrally located Croydon, had easier access to London and the world. Johnston also invested strongly in public relations. Each inspection of a new carillon became a celebration. When an order was complete, the foundry was converted into a concert hall, and the bells were hung in order to be inspected and played by the best carillonneurs of the time. Jef Denyn regularly traveled to Croydon to play foundry concerts for an audience of dignitaries. On these occasions, another part of the foundry was converted to an ad hoc restaurant where Cyril's mother and his sister Nora entertained the guests.

Rockefeller and his Belgian carillonneurs

The carillons of Gloucester and Toronto attracted the attention of the richest man on the planet, John D. Rockefeller Jr. Rockefeller was heir to the Standard Oil empire that had been built by his father, John D. Rockefeller Sr. Rockefeller Jr. did not focus on the further expansion of the empire that, given its monopoly position, had already grown as large as it could, but he primarily focused on charity and large public projects, of which the Rockefeller Center skyscraper complex in the center of New York remains the most visible result. Rockefeller was strongly religious and had a church built close to his New York home at the intersection of 64th Street and Park Avenue: Park Avenue Baptist Church. He decided to equip the tower with a chime, and his staff advised him to use as reference the 12-bell chime at West Point Military Academy, which was viewed as one of the best chimes in the USA. Contact was made with West Point, and in January 1922, Rockefeller concluded an agreement with local organist Frederick Mayer to assist him in purchasing a chime. After an offer arrived from American bell-foundry Meneely, Mayer learned that European carillons had been installed in Gloucester and Toronto. He visited the Toronto instrument and wrote to

Rockefeller that he was immediately convinced of the musical superiority of a carillon over an American chime. On 26 July, Rockefeller sailed with his yacht to Gloucester to hear the new carillon at the Portuguese church. He was elated, and presented a 500-dollar check for the purchase of two additional bass bells, on the condition that the gift would remain anonymous.[175] The oil magnate was now convinced that only a carillon would be good enough for his church, and he requested a price from two English bell-founders for an instrument with 35 bells. Cyril Johnston probably saw better than his rival Denison Taylor the immense commercial potential of an order by Rockefeller. He in any case bid the lowest price, and on 26 October 1922 signed a contract for 42 bells, built around a 10,000-lb. bass bell sounding A-flat.

In July 1923, Rockefeller himself traveled to English Loughborough, Taylor's home port. Several days earlier the Loughborough War Memorial had opened, a new tower with a Taylor carillon that was dedicated to the 478 residents of the city who were killed in the Great War. The people of Loughborough wished to commemorate their dead with a carillon, since they were buried on Flemish ground. The names of the three Taylor brothers who were killed in action were cast on the largest bell. On 22 July, Jef Denyn inaugurated the instrument before an audience of 100,000. His program included *Memorial Chimes*, a composition written by Edward Elgar especially for the occasion. Five days later, Denyn played for Rockefeller, who was thoroughly impressed with what he heard. A day later, the oil magnate wrote to Denison Taylor:

> Dear Mr. Taylor,
>
> *I want you to know how much we all appreciated your courtesy in arranging a special carillon Recital for us yesterday noon. Your bells are wonderful. They open quite a new field to me, for, of course, I had never heard anything approaching them, and really did not know what carillon playing was. Again I congratulate you on so splendid an achievement as this carillon. It was a rare privilege to hear Mons. Denyn play, and his great skill and artistic temperament combined with your wonderful carillon, produced a result that was extraordinarily beautiful. (...)*

In the meantime, Rockefeller had committed himself to Gillett & Johnston. In December 1923 the contract was even expanded: the carillon would now have 53 bells, with a 10-ton bass bell that sounded low E. Rockefeller wanted more bells than the carillon of Ghent, which with 52 bells was the largest at the time, and heavier bells than the carillon of Mechelen that had as bass bell, the eight-ton F sharp Salvator. The instrument would be a memorial to Rockefeller's mother Laura Spelman.

In anticipation of the installation, Rockefeller and Mayer went in search of a suitable carillonneur. At that moment there still were no well-known American carillonneurs, and the best carillonneurs were found in Belgium. In the meantime, Jef Denyn was too old to relocate, but the son of Antwerp city carillonneur Gustaaf Brees appeared to be a suitable candidate.[176] 27 year old Anton Brees played the poorly tuned carillon of Borgerhout. He initially had taken lessons in Mechelen, but quickly went his own way. On 12 March 1924, he left Antwerp and boarded for New York to sign a contract with Rockefeller. In the meantime, he had close contact with Taylor, and inaugurated several of his new American carillons. At the home front, Denyn was unhappy because he had to learn the news from the newspaper, and neither Brees nor Taylor had informed him of the inaugurations.

In the meantime, the installation of the Rockefeller carillon was not going smoothly. The elegant neo-gothic tower was designed to house a chime stand, and was too small for what was intended to be the largest carillon in the world. Out of necessity, the heaviest eight bells were installed next to the tower on the roof of the church. When the carillon was ready at the end of 1925, the result was disappointing. The sound of the bells mercilessly reverberated through the high apartment buildings surrounding the church, with musical chaos as the result. Residents complained bitterly, including mothers no longer able to put their children to sleep. To make matters worse, the relationship between Anton Brees and his employer soured. The young carillonneur was not happy with the configuration of the carillon, and complained about the noisy environment. Thus he demanded that traffic on Park Avenue be stopped during concerts. The church council answered that this was not realistic, and in turn requested a more American repertoire, which Brees refused. When Brees requested an apartment with a personal bath, he was summoned to Rockefeller. The benefactor pointed out to his carillonneur that he was earning five times more than in Belgium and then asked him: 'Did you have a bath in Antwerp?', a question that Brees was forced to answer in the negative. Rockefeller ordered lunch for both in his office, and the discussion continued for a time, without result. A short time later Brees invited a member of the church council – some sources say Rockefeller himself – to have a martini at a speakeasy. This was the time of the great prohibition, and this daring gesture did not sit well with teetotaler Rockefeller. Anton Brees was dismissed and replaced by Frank Percival Price, who in the meantime was building up a good reputation. After this, Brees attempted to develop a business association with Taylor.[177] In April 1926 he offered his services to Denison Taylor as official 'Technical Advisor and Carillonneur to the Taylor Bellfoundry, Loughborough'. 'I'll make publicity for your firm. You push my name so that I become a moral factor (some kind of authority on carillons).' Denison responded politely but hesitatingly, and the deal did not go through. On 12 October, Brees inaugurated the new carillon at Mercersburg

Academy in Pennsylvania, a Gillett & Johnston instrument with high commemorative value. The bell bronze contained metal collected worldwide by alumni and friends of the school: shrapnel gathered from French battlefields of the Great War, a bronze splinter of the Liberty Bell and material that came from the HMS Victory, Admiral Nelson's flagship during the Battle of Trafalgar. Brees was appointed as carillonneur.

A second Flemish carillonneur landed in North America a few months after Anton Brees. Kamiel Lefévere was from Mechelen and together with Staf Nees was assistant teacher at the Mechelen carillon school, where he was awarded his diploma in 1924. That year he played several concerts in England, upon which Cyril Johnston asked him to inaugurate the new carillon at St. Stephen's Episcopal Church in Cohasset. The 23-bell instrument was donated by Jane W. Bancroft as a memorial to her mother Jessie M. Barron. Her stepfather Clarence W. Barron was one of the leading figures of the financial world in the USA. After the death of Charles Dow, he became owner of Dow Jones & Company in 1903, and from this position he controlled the *Wall Street Journal*. On 21 September 1924, Lefévere inaugurated the new carillon before an audience of thousands. From 1925, Lefévere returned to Cohasset each summer to give concerts that met with great success. He became friends with the Bancrofts and was introduced to the upper class in Cohasset and Boston. Interest in the concerts increased noticeably in Cohasset. During the first Tuesday concert on 25 May, 1925, Jane's husband Hugh Bancroft counted 225 cars in the parking lot. During the closing concert on 25 August he counted, no doubt with a bit of help, 4,317 cars. Assuming each car held five passengers, and including all the listeners who came by train, plus the residents of Cohasset who came on foot with their guests, Bancroft estimated the total audience at 25,000. In 1925, the carillon was expanded to 43 bells, and in 1928 to 51. In the 1920s, the small town of Cohasset was briefly the Mechelen of the New World. When Clarence Barron died in 1928, he was succeeded as head of his financial empire by his son-in-law Hugh Bancroft. One year later, Wall Street crashed, and in the aftermath, Bancroft committed suicide in 1933. The glory days of the carillon in Cohasset were quickly over.[178]

Kamiel Lefévere (1888-1972), illuminated by the light of the New World

The race for bigger and heavier

The new large carillons succeeded one another quickly and a race developed for heavier and bulkier instruments, similar to what happened four centuries earlier in the Low Countries. On 1 July 1927, the 60th anniversary of Canada as an independent country, a new carillon was inaugurated at the Peace Tower of the Parliament building in Ottawa. The instrument was cast by Gillett & Johnston and commemorated the Canadians who were killed during the Great War. Like Rockefeller's carillon, this instrument had 53 bells tuned to the same notes, but the bells had a heavier profile, so that with its 54 tons of bell bronze, it was the heaviest carillon in the world. The inauguration concert was attended by the Prince of Wales and was broadcast during the first Canadian coast-to-coast radio broadcast. The carillonneur was Frank Percival Price. The festivities received an unexpected tragic twist.[179] Charles Lindbergh was expected as guest of honor on 2 July. All were eagerly awaiting the arrival of the young pilot, who several weeks earlier had successfully completed the first solo flight across the Atlantic Ocean. Lindbergh flew with the Spirit of St. Louis into Ottawa, escorted by a squadron of twelve aircraft. Shortly before the landing, two of the aircraft collided. First Lieutenant John Thad Johnson attempted to open his parachute, but plunged to his death. The festivities were canceled immediately and replaced by a state funeral for the American pilot. At the ceremony, Kamiel Lefévere made a deep impression with his performance of Chopin's *Funeral March* and the Dead March from Handel's oratorio *Saul* on the Peace Tower carillon. Frank Percival Price became the instrument's permanent performer, and he left his post in New York to become Dominion Carillonneur of Canada. In the meantime, his name had been changed to Percival Price. William Gorham Rice reportedly had advised Price, for reasons of publicity, to drop his first name in favor of only his middle name. The Canadian was succeeded in New York by Kamiel Lefévere.

On 18 September 1927, a Taylor carillon was inaugurated in the Albany town hall tower,[180] the fulfillment of a long cherished dream of William Gorham Rice. He had been campaigning for this instrument for years and had collected donations from thousands of Albany residents. It was the first city carillon in the New World and thus perfectly fit Rice's ideals of good citizenship and urban community life. The American was able to persuade his good friend Denyn, at the age of 65, to cross the Atlantic for the first time to play the inauguration concert. Denyn knew the instrument, because he had inspected it at Taylor's facilities in England. The concert was attended by an estimated 50,000 people, listening in streets and parks, from the steps of public buildings, in the open windows of the capitol building and the hospital, and from cars on the bridge over the Hudson River. While Denyn played, Rice burned a red lamp from the bell-chamber as a sign that the police should block the traffic between the New York State Capitol and the river. During the intermissions, Rice swung a green lamp as sign that the traffic could proceed. A day later, Denyn gave a second concert, after which he went on a six-concert tour that included Ottawa, New York and Cohasset. He was accompanied by Prosper Verheyden, who gave lectures with light images. Out of respect for the local authority of Rice, Verheyden did not speak about the carillon, but about other aspects of Flemish history: the Flemish béguinages and the cities of Mechelen and Antwerp. It was Denyn's only tour of the United States.

On 1 February 1929, American President Calvin Coolidge inaugurated the most beautiful carillon project in history: Mountain Lake Sanctuary in Lake Wales, Florida, a creation of Edward William Bok. Bok came from Den Helder in the Netherlands, and had moved to Brooklyn with his parents at the age of six. Edward Bok has realized the *American Dream*: he started his career as stenographer and ended it as press tycoon and philanthropist. After his move to Philadelphia, he published the progressive *Ladies Home Journal,* the first periodical in the world with a circulation of 1 million copies. He won the Pulitzer Prize in 1921 for his autobiography *The Americanization of Edward Bok: the Autobiography of a Dutch Boy Fifty Years Later.* His motto was: 'Make you the world a bit better or more beautiful because you have lived in it' and he put this saying into practice. He purchased a piece of sandy ground on one of the highest hills in Florida and had a park designed by landscape architect Frederick Law Olmsted Jr., the son of the designer of Central Park in New York. Olmsted had fertile ground, trees, plants and birds brought in, and created a subtropical park as a sanctuary for birds and plants on the barren hilltop. During the work, Bok found that his park was missing a focal point, and he decided to add a carillon tower. He asked architect Milton B. Medary to design a bell tower that would be as beautiful as St. Rumbold's Tower in Mechelen, but adapted to Florida's sunny climate. Medary designed a neo-gothic tower with decorations in art deco style. The tower was covered with pink and grey marble from Georgia and shell stone from Florida. The sculpture contains plant motifs as well as pelicans, swans and flamingos. The copper entrance gate is divided into scenes that depict the six episodes of the creation story. The tower is surrounded by a moat and is reflected in a mirror pond. Thus nature, architecture and music blend seamlessly at the Mountain Lake Sanctuary. The carillon was ordered from Taylor and – like the instruments at New York and Ottawa – contained 53 bells. With its 10.5-ton bass bell, it was a half tone lower than the two preceding record holders.

The inauguration concert was given by Anton Brees, who was appointed as full-time carillonneur. During the same year, a collaboration developed with the Curtis Institute of Music in Philadelphia, a school for top musicians that was founded in 1924 by Bok's wife Marie Louise Curtis Bok, and that remains one of the leading music schools in the USA today. Each winter, several talented students from the Curtis Institute came to Florida to learn campanology from Brees. This collaboration

Shipping of the bourdon for Riverside Church in New York City lasted only to 1933, but did result in interesting carillon work by students who later would become famous composers: Samuel Barber, Gian Carlo Menotti and Nino Rota. Brees remained carillonneur at the Mountain Lake Sanctuary until his death in 1967. After recovering from a severe illness, he revised his relationship to the carillon: henceforth the instrument would be a means of giving his audience a spiritual experience. He renounced the virtuoso repertoire of his youth and limited himself to simple melodies, which he often played from the original song or piano score. The concerts by Brees were not thrilling, but undoubtedly the bells sounded in unison with the peaceful nature surrounding them. Like Edward Bok would have wanted. The founder died a year after the completion of what he called *America's Taj Mahal*.

In the meantime, John D. Rockefeller Jr. was busy in New York with a new grand plan.[181] His church on Park Avenue turned out to be too small due to the popularity of its minister Harry E. Fosdick, a progressive and inspired speaker. In addition, the flow of people to the church hampered the through traffic in the surrounding streets. Rockefeller's church was especially visited by the well-off – in New York it was called the Millionaires' Church – but the benefactor did not want a church with an elite image. So he sold it to the Central Presbyterian Church and built a new church on the banks of the Hudson River, at the edge of Harlem. Riverside Church became an interdenominational church: all Christians were welcome, regardless of belief. Riverside Church was a spacious neo-gothic church, inspired by Chartres Cathedral. The tower was 120 meters high and was able to house a larger instrument than the carillon of Park Avenue Baptist Church. Gillett & Johnston received the order to expand the carillon in height and depth, resulting in a 72-bell instrument that sounded two notes lower than the previous carillon. It was a huge instrument: sounding two notes lower required a doubling of the weight of the bells. This is the result of the principle of dynamic similarity that we encountered while discussing the small bells of Hemony. The new bass bell with pitch C would weigh 20 tons, and the complete carillon no less than one hundred tons.

Cyril Johnston cast the new bass bell for Riverside on 2 December 1927. Since this would be the heaviest carillon bell ever cast, he had a picture postcard of it printed and invited numerous visitors to visit it in his foundry. Six months later Frederick Mayer, who also advised Rockefeller in this project, rejected the bell because it exhibited a metal fourth. The metal fourth or secondary strike note is a loud note that sounds a fourth above the main strike note. It is a defect that often occurs in bells of more than six tons and it results in the listener perceiving the bell sounding higher than intended – a frustrating discovery for bell-founders who try their hand at heavy bells. Mayer thought that a heavier profile would solve the problem since there would be a greater margin for tuning. The second bell, however, was no better and Johnston then cast a third bell weighing 22 tons. In the end, the first bell was chosen. Riverside is the heaviest carillon in history and will remain so for eternity, not only because of the excessive cost, but especially since this instrument exceeded the boundary of what was musically and technically desirable. The largest bells had such heavy clappers that electric assistance was needed to get them moving, and the melodic quality of the bass bells was lacking due to their prominent overtones and audible metal fourths. In addition, the carillon was difficult to hear: it was no longer too loud, as it had been at its previous location, but on the contrary was insufficiently audible from the street due to the extreme height of the bell-chamber. Kamiel Lefévere played the instrument at the time of the move to Riverside, and would remain the Riverside carillonneur until his retirement in 1960.

After Riverside, Rockefeller ordered a carillon from Cyril Johnston for the tower of Rockefeller Chapel, the central building of the University of Chicago. He also dedicated this instrument to the memory of his mother. The second Laura Spelman Memorial Carillon had 72 bells like its sister in New York, but since it sounded a half tone higher, its bass bell weighed 'only' 17.3 tons. This instrument too came about after many disputes between Mayer and Johnston concerning metal fourths and other problems. On Thanksgiving Day 1932, the carillon was inaugurated by Kamiel Lefévere. The American Frederick L. Marriott, who would obtain his diploma from the Mechelen carillon school in 1936, was appointed as official carillonneur. With the instruments in New York and Chicago, John D. Rockefeller Jr. had built the two heaviest carillons ever, and thus surpassed his namesake King John of Portugal, who 200 years earlier had purchased two large instruments from the Low Countries for Mafra. One had achieved this with gold ore from Brazil, the other with the liquid gold of Standard Oil.

Contours of a new carillon culture

In 1932, scarcely ten years after the arrival of the first carillons in North America, there were already forty carillons sounding in the New World. The economic depression in the years following the crash did not mark an end point, but at most a temporary cooling in the rate at which new American carillons were installed. As a musical instrument with a message, the carillon, from the beginning, had planted deep roots in American soil. Gradually the pattern of a new carillon culture became visible. North American cities seldom erected a carillon, as was customary in Europe. The experience of the New York carillon had shown that the typical American cities with their checkerboard layout, busy traffic flows and high buildings were less suited to a carillon than the European cities, which had grown organically from a central marketplace. Thus, the carillon had developed differently than William Gorham Rice had imagined: it was not so much the musical expression of good citizenship and democracy in an urban context, but rather an expression of piety and the pursuit of beauty in a spiritual or intellectual setting. Most carillons were the result of a personal initiative or collective fundraising, and they were installed in church towers, university bell towers and new towers in public parks. The carillon received an interesting biotope especially at a number of universities. Musical experience was traditionally an important part of American campus life due to the way it enhanced the identity of the campus and stimulated camaraderie among students. A number of universities installed a carillon based on this campus ideal. For Americans, the European instrument was a source of fascination due to its ambiguity: it had something old-fashioned due to the use of bells, and something modern due to its playing mechanism and its originality.[182]

Almost all of the new carillons in the USA were cast by the English foundries Taylor and Gillett & Johnston. The English bells were appealing not only thanks to their good tuning, but also due to their pleasing, sensuous timbre, which was unknown in Europe. Taylor and Johnston carillons were above all praised for the rich sound of the bells in the bass and middle registers. The treble bells, however, were weak, and due to their lack of sonority, sounded shrill compared to the heavier bells. Taylor and Johnston did not thicken the walls of small bells like Andreas Jozef Vanden Gheyn had done in the 18th century to reinforce their sound. Taylor attempted to reinforce the descant of his carillons by doubling the bells of the high register, similar to the way the higher notes of a piano are produced by two or three strings. Thus the carillons in Albany and Lake Wales respectively had 13 and 18 more bells than notes. The experiments with the double descant, however, would prove to be a failure: they resulted in a sluggish attack, and from the moment that the double bells differed in pitch by a fraction, disruptive beats could be heard.

Cyril Johnston gave his carillons a distinct 'sound' by tuning the minor thirds of his bells slightly higher than prescribed by equal temperament tuning. He strove for the so-called pure minor third, whose frequency was related to the melody note at a ratio of 6/5. By doing so, Johnston clearly opted for the beautiful sound of each bell separately, to the detriment of the harmony created by the different bells together. The slightly high thirds of the bells clashed with the purely tuned strike tones and primes of the bells that sounded a minor third higher, which resulted in beating during some passages. Johnston continued to experiment with his bells. He gradually began to tune his small bells a bit higher than prescribed by the theory. This deliberate deviation was intended to undo an auditory illusion. In the region of the high notes, human hearing perceives purely tuned notes as slightly too low. This can be offset by tuning these notes slightly higher, a technique that is often used by piano tuners. As years progressed, Johnston went increasingly further in stretching the tuning.

Cyril Johnston is the first bell-founder in history whose life we are able to view in detail.[183] This is thanks to his daughter Jill, who was born of a secret relationship her father had with the American nurse Olive Marjorie Crowe, who was seventeen years younger. Olive and Cyril met in June of 1927 on a voyage from Southampton to Boston. Cyril was going to the States for carillon business; Olive was a nurse at the American hospital in Paris and was accompanying a patient on the crossing to the USA. At the time, transatlantic voyages presented more opportunity to make friends than do the fast flights of today, and a relationship developed between the bell-founder and the nurse from which daughter Jill was born two years later. Mother and daughter settled in New York; Cyril married in England and fathered two children. After the death of the bell-founder in 1950, Jill went in search of her unknown father and his work, which in 2008 resulted in a biography. Here, Jill Johnston reconstructed the life of the bell-founder, with his high ambitions, resounding successes and bitter disappointments. The title of the book, *England's Child*, is a double entendre. It refers to American carillon culture that received its own identity thanks to the grand English carillons, but obviously also to her own family history.

The English bell-founders were not only innovative with their bells. Also new was the fact that they produced and delivered complete carillons, including keyboard and connections. Previously a bell-founder would usually supply the bells, and the installation was handled by a local artisan or a specialized tower clockmaker. For the connections, the English bell-founders took over the tumbler system advocated by Denyn, but they deviated from the Mechelen standard in their keyboards. The first American carillons were very heterogeneous in weight and especially in size, since they varied from 23 to 72 bells. Consequently there were continuous experiments with the action and keyboard sizes, and there was no standardization during these first years. Nevertheless, a clear trend could be seen, principally in the construction of the pedal board. Where the Mechelen pedal board covered only one and a half octaves, American pedals extended to two and a half octaves. Organ building no doubt was an important source of inspiration here. Rockefeller's adviser Frederick Mayer was after all an organist. To keep the entire pedal board accessible to the feet, the furthest pedal keys were made higher and longer. The American keyboards would gradually converge toward a new standard that would deviate strongly from that of Mechelen. In addition to a baton keyboard, the carillons delivered by both Taylor and Gillett & Johnston regularly included as additional playing devices a piano keyboard and a roll for automatic playing. In practice these extra components were seldom or never used.

The number of North American carillons increased so quickly that there was a lack of skilled carillonneurs. In the beginning, the carillon scene in North America was dominated by only three musicians: two from Flanders and one from Canada. They handled virtually all of the new carillon inaugurations, and traveled the continent giving guest concerts. In southern Lake Wales, the previously so restless Anton Brees found his final destination. He kept far from the budding American carillon movement, but continued to exert influence by inaugurating all new Taylor instruments and through his teaching activities. Kamiel Lefévere was the leading figure in central United States. On the large instrument at Riverside Church, he continued to play in the virtuoso Mechelen style Jef Denyn had taught him – something that undoubtedly was necessary to make the music audible at ground level. Lefévere had a talent for diplomacy and public relations. He promoted the carillon in articles, lectures and radio talks in which he especially emphasized the Belgian origin of the instrument. Percival Price – ambitious, eager to learn and headstrong – played in northern Ottawa.[184] While still playing for Rockefeller in 1926, he had gone to Mechelen and studied with Jef Denyn at his employer's expense. In 1927, he was the first non-European to obtain his diploma, albeit only *cum fructu*. Price was uncomfortable with the Flemish nationalistic path that he felt the carillon school – at least in its repertoire – had taken. He was the first carillonneur to openly state that the busy-sounding Mechelen repertoire did not take advantage of all the musical possibilities of the sonorous American carillons. Out of this insight, a new carillon movement would be born in North America after the next war.

New carillons in other parts of the world

The memorial idea, the powerful motor behind the flowering of the carillon in the United States, would also result in impressive new instruments elsewhere in the world. We already mentioned the War Memorial Carillon in English Loughborough and the Peace Tower carillon in Ottawa. Singing memorials would also appear in other countries of the Commonwealth. In 1925, the 1918 appeal by Anna Thorne was realized and the Cape Town city tower received its peace carillon: a Taylor carillon with 39 bells. The bells contain the names of battlefields in Flanders, France and elsewhere, and pacifist notions and proverbs such as

> RING OUT THE THOUSAND WARS OF OLD
> RING IN THE THOUSAND YEARS OF PEACE

On 30 April 1925, Anton Brees played the inaugural concert in the presence of the Prince of Wales, the later Edward VIII.

The University of Sydney received its War Memorial Carillon in 1928. It was dedicated to keeping alive the memory of the 197 students and staff of the university who died in the Great War. The carillon was cast by Taylor and had 62 bells, including

Students of the University of Sydney welcome their new carillon.

13 doubled treble bells. The English carillonneur Bryan Barker inaugurated the new carillon on Anzac Day, 25 April 1925. Anzac Day – a national holiday in Australia and New Zealand – was the anniversary of the landing in Gallipoli in 1915.

New Zealand received its memorial carillon in 1932. Shortly after the war, the government had decided to build a large national monument in Wellington to commemorate the 16,697 New Zealand soldiers killed in the Great War. The idea arose in private circles to equip the monument with a carillon to gather the living in order to commemorate the dead. The government found the plan too expensive and opted for a 'silent symbolic monument'. The proponents united in the Wellington War Memorial Carillon Society and conducted a large-scale media campaign in which the 49 required bells were symbolically offered for sale to associations, companies and individuals who wished to honor their fallen soldiers. This strategy worked, and in no time the required funds had been raised, allowing the order to be placed with Gillett & Johnston for casting the carillon. The financing of the monument itself went less smoothly, and there was still no tower when the bells were ready. So, the carillon was temporarily installed at an exhibition in Newcastle-upon-Tyne, where it was played for thousands of listeners. When construction of the tower continued to drag on, the bells were installed in London at the initiative of the newspapers *Daily Sketch* and *Sunday Graphic*.[185] A temporary tower was installed in Hyde Park that passers-by initially associated with a water tower or a lighthouse. On Christmas Eve 1929, New Zealander Gladys Watkins gave the initial concert on the half completed instrument. Shoppers halted their activity, thousands flocked to Hyde Park, and motorists stopped to listen to the carillon, causing major traffic congestion. On 1 January 1930, Clifford Ball, the Bournville carillonneur, gave the official inauguration concert. The concerts in Hyde Park attracted large crowds. The local media regularly counted 100,000 to 150,000 listeners who gathered around the temporary carillon, often listening in the rain under their umbrellas. It is estimated that in nine months' time, 10 million Londoners listened to the Wellington bells. Never before in history had a carillon received so much attention. Before the carillon was dismantled in October 1930 to be shipped to New Zealand, Gladys Watkins made a number of recordings on the instrument. Watkins had presumably come in contact with the carillon via her relationship with Ernest Edward Muir, editor-in-chief of *The Evening Post* and secretary of the Wellington War Memorial Carillon Society. Without a concrete prospect of an appointment, she traveled to Mechelen in 1929 to study under Jef Denyn. She progressed quickly, and on 27 July 1930 – at the age of 46 – obtained her carillon diploma. In the meantime, New Zealand had looked into whether Kamiel Lefévere might want to become its national carillonneur. Lefévere politely declined the offer and mentioned this to Denyn, who in 1930 successfully recommended his New Zealand student. In the meantime, the financing needed for the monument itself had been found in Wellington, and construction of a sober and impressive art-deco tower was begun at one of highest points of the city. In the meantime, His Master's Voice capitalized on the New Zealand audience's impatience to hear the carillon and launched a record of Watkins' London recording with the slogan 'At last you can hear Wellington's Carillon'. On Anzac Day 1932, Gladys Watkins and Clifford Ball inaugurated the carillon amid great public interest. Watkins' career, however, was short. There was insufficient funding for the concerts and her health declined. She gave her last concert in 1935, and four years later she died from the effects of pleurisy.

The Wellington carillon was immortalized in a special way by William Longstaff, one of the war painters who portrayed scenes of war and peace at that time. The monumental oil painting *Carillon* evoked the Belgian coast: a calm sea beneath a cloudy night sky. On the moonlit beach stands a group of blueish shadows: soldiers from New Zealand who are buried on Flemish soil. They are listening to the new carillon that was installed in their homeland, making music for them from across the ocean. The allegorical presentation made a huge impression on the audience, reproductions were hung in New Zealand classrooms and the work entered the country's collective consciousness. Like Elgar's composition *Carillon* says nothing of the carillon, the painting of the same name depicts no bells. The work makes a reciprocal connection between Flanders and New Zealand. Men from New Zealand came to Flanders and found there a final resting place, while the musical instrument that originated in Flanders penetrated to New Zealand and reached a geographic end point there.

We will now return to the carillon's homeland to see whether the high expectations that arose during the Great War were realized.

CHAPTER 17

New carillon construction in the Old Country

Belgian and English influence in the Netherlands

After the Great War, the renewal-minded in the Netherlands awaited with impatience the return of Jef Denyn, the man who would make the Dutch carillon towers sing, and bring about the long-expected revival of Dutch carillon culture. Denyn set up the action of the carillons at Nijkerk and Arnhem according to his insights, but the promised result did not materialize: in neither tower did the tremolo playing melt into a unity of sound. The large church tower at Nijkerk was an open lantern and consequently did not approach the acoustic ideal of the closed tower. Denyn had reverb plates installed in front of the bells, but due to the short distance between the bells and the reverb plates, the desired echo effect was not created. The tower at Arnhem also proved to be too open for an optimum echo effect. Despite this less favorable start, carillonneurs and listeners in the Netherlands began to appreciate the added value of the tumbler system, because it made possible more stable playing and did not necessarily lead to excessive tremolo playing as claimed by its opponents. Hence, more and more instruments were set up according to the Denyn system.

The Dutch also demonstrated that they would finally opt for quality above local sentiment and national interest in the choice of new carillon bells. Both the conservative Dutch Bells and Organ Council and the innovation-oriented Dutch Carillon Association advised public authorities to purchase English bells instead of products from national bell-founders Van Bergen and Petit & Fritsen, who continued to deliver untuned bells. Taylor had already proved what he could do in Appingedam in 1911, and he would deliver another ten carillons in the Netherlands in partnership with the company Addicks from Amsterdam. The most important of these instruments was the carillon at the new Rotterdam town hall from 1920. Gillett & Johnston approached the Dutch market in partnership with clockmaker Bonaventura Eijsbouts from Asten. In 1925, he delivered his first two carillons outside North America in the Netherlands. They were installed in St. Gregory's Tower in Almelo and St. John's Tower in 's-Hertogenbosch. Especially the latter instrument was the subject of much attention. It was purchased to replace an out-of-tune instrument made by André L.J. Van Aerschodt and was handed over by the carillon committee to the city during the Second Carillon Congress that took place in 's-Hertogenbosch. On 14 August, Jef Denyn played the inauguration concert for the congress participants, which he started with the old Wilhelmus. Enthusiasm for the congress and the new carillon was great. Dr. J. Casparie of 's-Hertogenbosch, a neurologist and the dynamic chairman of the Dutch Carillon Association, predicted in his speech that 's-Hertogenbosch would be the starting point of a new golden age of the carillon in the Netherlands. Gillett & Johnston would cast a total of ten carillons for Dutch towers. The success of the two English bell-founders shook the faith of both Dutch bell-founders in the untuned bell, and in the 1930s they conducted their first tuning experiments. Van Bergen delivered his first reasonably tuned carillon in 1932 for the Cunera Tower in Rhenen, and Petit & Fritsen cast an acceptable test carillon in 1939. The foundry was assisted in this by skilled bell expert Jan Arts, alias Brother Getulius.

The Dutch carillons were played more frequently than previously, and summer concerts were organized according to the Belgian model. Especially Staf Nees was an often-heard guest performer. Local carillon associations were founded in various cities, and from 1927, the Dutch Carillon Association organized national carillon competitions. Initially the participants could choose whether they would compete in the broek system category or in the tumbler system category, and consequently the contests always took place in two different cities. Starting with the Zwolle contest in 1935, only the tumbler system was used, indicating that at that moment the Mechelen system had definitively won the argument. The intense carillon activity raised the bar for carillonneurs, and the most important carillonneurs went to Mechelen to study with Jef Denyn and Staf Nees. In 1925, Rotterdam city carillonneur Ferdinand Timmermans was the first from the Netherlands to study in Mechelen. He was a strong advocate of the southern playing style, and in 1944, he wrote the very readable book *Luidklokken en beiaarden in Nederland* ['Swinging bells and carillons in the Netherlands']. Until the Second World War, another ten carillonneurs from the Netherlands would obtain a diploma in Mechelen. In the meantime, Jacob Vincent – champion of 'authentic' sober Dutch carillon playing – was a lone figure in uncompromisingly continuing to play as before. He, however, was innovative in one way. In 1935 and 1936, at the request of the Philips Company, he recorded ten records from the palace carillon in Amsterdam and the Deventer carillon.[186] Philips sold the recordings together with a sound system to public authorities that lacked the financial resources to install a carillon. Philips evidently encountered little opposition in carillon circles, because for a number of years, the program for the Mechelen Monday evening concerts contained an advertisement for the *carillon sans cloches Philips*. Vincent himself justified his surprising actions with the sober argument: 'if I would have refused, Philips would certainly have approached someone else, and the "imitation carillon" would have come about anyway...' Another example of Dutch common sense.

Protectionist reflexes in Belgium

In Belgium, the wartime poetic prophecies materialized, and most of the twelve carillons that were destroyed in the Great War were succeeded in the 1920s by new carillons. The Mechelen carillon school played a central role in the reconstruction movement, among others by organizing benefit activities for rebuilding the carillons at Oudenaarde, Dinant, Wingene and St. Quentin in North France. In the absence of advisory bodies like those in the Netherlands, Jef Denyn often acted as adviser. The resurrected carillons did not sound as festive as the war poets had dreamed: while most Belgian bell-founders tuned their bells, they had not yet fully mastered the art of tuning. Moreover, the Belgian market remained closed to the English bell-founders. The cause of this was principally economic in nature. Four years of painful war conditions had left its mark on Belgium, which led to protectionist reflexes. In addition, the Belgian franc had dropped to one fourth of its pre-war value, making imports from England unaffordable. The board of directors of the Mechelen carillon school saw the seriousness of the situation and contemplated sending a letter to the government. In their report of 30 December 1923, they complained about the protectionism of the Belgian municipalities, and stated clearly that in the 19th and 20th century, no Belgian, French, Dutch or German bell-founder had succeeded in delivering a high-quality carillon, and that the tuning of their bells was below standard. They argued for ordering bells from England, and thus paying a higher price, as long as the situation did not improve.[187]

The English bell-founders of course were interested in the Belgian market and both were regular advertisers in the program booklets for the Mechelen Monday evening concerts. Especially Cyril Johnston actively sought new market opportunities. He was in Belgium in the autumn of 1923 to inspect bells and listen to carillon concerts. The young Anton Brees brought him to the Vanden Gheyn carillon in Turnhout, where he took measurements and molds of the bells.[188] While doing this, he encountered a bell that was cracked and that had already been recast three times by a Belgian bell-founder without a satisfactory result. He smelled an opportunity and proposed to the city government that he would replace it with a new one, free of charge and without further obligation. The gift was accepted, and Johnston cast an excellent bell with as inscription:

GIVEN TO THE TOWN OF TURNHOUT
BY CYRIL F. JOHNSTON
TO REPLACE ONE THAT WAS NOT TRUE
JANUARY 1924

During the same trip, he learned that the municipal authorities of Nieuwpoort were planning to replace the Vanden Gheyn carillon destroyed in the war.[189] Several weeks later, the mayor of Nieuwpoort received a friendly letter from the bell-founder. He wrote that he understood that the municipal authorities might prefer a Belgian bell-founder, for patriotic reasons as well as for reasons of cost. However, he wanted to deliver a first carillon in Belgium: 'we are most anxious to install an example of our modern work in your country – as we know that this will lead to further orders, after our bells had been heard by others also interested in such installations.' Johnston stated that he was prepared to offer a very low price. He would be happy to pay the travel and hotel expenses of two members of the city government to visit the foundry and satisfy themselves concerning the quality of the bells and carillons that were destined for the USA, Canada and England. Moreover, Johnston would also accept the judgment of an expert appointed by the municipal authorities. The municipality, however, did not deem the time right for a new carillon, and postponed the purchase. The sales efforts of Cyril Johnston did not go unnoticed in Belgium and were a source of concern. On 30 January 1925, the directors of *Onze beiaarden – Nos carillons* issued a circular to the municipal governments in which it was reported that a short time before, a foreign bell-founder had copied the bells of one of the best Flemish carillons. The directors warned that foreign bell-founders were attempting in this way to steal the secrets of the famous Flemish art of bell casting. On 28 February, Antwerp carillonneur Staf Gebruers published an opinion piece in which he interpreted Cyril Johnston's generosity in Turnhout as a distraction allowing him to make molds of the Vanden Gheyn bells. The author also criticized the recent American interest in the carillon. American support for the Mechelen carillon school would not have been prompted by true interest in the instrument and its culture, but rather by typical American self-interest. Thus Flemish cities were being deprived of one of their most beautiful characteristics.

It was no accident that the only carillon that Cyril Johnston was able to supply in Belgium was an American project.[190] In the aftermath of the Great War, more than three hundred American universities and other institutions had raised funds to present a new library building to the ravaged Leuven University. The committee engaged Whitney Warren, an American architect who had made a name for himself with the design of large New York hotels and Grand Central Terminal in Manhattan, at the time the largest *railway cathedral* in the world. Warren designed a library in Neo-

Renaissance style. The building was rife with reminders of the Great War: portraits of the royal family above the entrance and of Cardinal Mercier on the side wall, grim allied animal symbols on the roofs, and in the middle, a helmeted and armored Our Lady of Victory who imperturbably pierces a screeching German eagle. American eagles and Belgian lions can be found at various locations, and the four clock faces on the tower include stars that refer to the then 48 American states. Warren wanted an inscription placed on the seventy meter long balustrade with the text *Furore Teutonico diruta, dono Americano restituta* ('Destroyed by German fury, restored by American generosity'). Rector Paulin Ladeuze refused the placement of this aggressive message on his library, after which a bitter polemic broke out that poisoned the mood in political Belgium. The inscription was carved, but did not make it to the balustrade. In addition to the political vicissitudes, there were equally great concerns of a financial nature, and the building could only be completed thanks to a major contribution from what remained of the Herbert Hoover's Belgian relief fund. A carillon had been foreseen for the belfry tower from the beginning. During the laying of the foundation stone for the building on 28 July 1921, Cardinal Mercier had predicted: 'The voice of the carillon shall proclaim the eternal principles for which Belgium has made sacrifices: honor, rights, humanity.' But the financial problems led to the removal of the carillon from the budget. In 1927, Edward Dean Adams, engineer and chairman of the Niagara Falls Power Company, visited the site of the nearly completed building. When he noticed the empty carillon tower, he decided to provide a carillon as a memorial to the American engineers who were killed during the war. Under his impulse, sixteen American engineering associations raised the needed funds within a short period of time. Initially a carillon with 35 bells was considered, but Kamiel Lefévere judged that this was not enough. He invited the carillon committee to a concert on the Princeton University carillon, which had 35 bells, and to a concert on his own 53-bell carillon in Park Avenue Baptist Church. After the two concerts, the committee was convinced of the benefits of additional bells, and in December 1927, Gillett & Johnston received an order for a carillon with the symbolic number of 48 bells. The carillon was set up by Rockefeller's consultant Frederick Mayer and looked very American. The keyboard was constructed in neo-gothic style and was equipped with a radial pedal board. To make it easier to play, the lowest six pedal notes were equipped with electro-pneumatic assistance pistons. There were twelve extra keyboard batons on the right side, so that the carillon could later be expanded to 60 bells. The 7-ton bourdon received the name *Liberty Bell of Louvain*, after the famous Liberty Bell of Philadelphia. According to the inauguration brochure, the carillon – with a total weight of nearly 32 tons – was the largest 'in the eastern hemisphere'. It was in the same key as the Mechelen carillon, but was slightly heavier and had three more bells (the writer of the brochure omitted the heavier carillons of Mafra in his statistics).

The bass bells of the university carillon of Leuven

The new carillon did not have a programmable drum – this was not part of the American carillon culture – but only a small drum with fixed pins. Warren had wanted the national songs of Belgium, France, England and the USA to be played every quarter hour, but in the end, this political message was rejected in favor of four variations on the Flemish bell song Reuzegom in an adaptation by Jef Denyn. Gillett & Johnston completed the assignment in record speed, so that the *American Engineers' Memorial Carillon and Clock* could be inaugurated on the Fourth of July 1928 together with the building. Jef Denyn played a program that was adapted to the mixed audience with, among others, the *Rubens March* and *My Old Kentucky Home*. The engineering associations also presented the library a small Liberty Bell that was hung in the hall and that is still rung today fifteen minutes before closing time to warn library visitors that it is time to leave. The ever-cordial Cyril Johnston presented Rector Ladeuze with a copper inkwell in the form of the Liberty Bell. With the donation of the Leuven university carillon, the American engineers planted a piece of American carillon culture on European soil and created the most beautiful Belgian carillon of the interwar period. Even after this magnificent achievement, Cyril Johnston received no further access to the Belgian market. His only other order was for fourteen bells for St. John's Church in Liège in 1930. His rival Taylor never delivered a bell to Belgium.

Malaise among the Belgian bell-founders

In the 1920s, there were five bell-founders active in Belgium who claimed to cast pure carillons. After his return from England, Félix Van Aerschodt of Leuven resumed bell casting. He cast two more carillons after the war: one for St. Gertrude's Church in Nivelles in 1926, and an instrument for Santa Monica, California in 1928. In the meantime, he was facing stiff competition in Leuven. His nephew Constant Sergeys was initially active in Chênée near Liège, but he moved back to Leuven in 1926 where he focused on casting swinging bells. In addition, there was Omer Michaux, who had succeeded Alphonse Beullens, an uncle of Félix Van Aerschodt. Michaux was quite successful in the 1920s. He not only installed a new carillon in Halle, but also cast new instruments to replace the carillons of Wingene, Oudenaarde and Dendermonde that had disappeared during the war. The committee that arrived in 1925 to inspect the Dendermonde bells was warmly received by Michaux in his Leuven foundry. The inspection started only after the requisite drinks, and took place in an extremely positive atmosphere, except for the fact that the city carillonneur was drunk and fell from the bench during the test playing. The inspection report, already prepared beforehand by the bell-founder, was then promptly signed.[191] After Denyn had officially inaugurated the instrument, he gave the mayor of Dendermonde his honest advice: 'These are not bells, but kettles, Mr. Mayor!'

In addition to the three Leuven bell-founders, there was also Marcel Michiels from Mechelen, a son of clockmaker Edward Michiels. He had learned bell casting from Van Aerschodt, and in 1886 settled in the former Drouot bell-foundry in Tournai. In 1924, he cast an instrument to replace the carillon at Izegem that was requisitioned in the war. The new carillon was unsatisfactory. Michiels died in the same year and was succeeded by his 26-year son Marcel Jr. Finally, in the Province of Luxembourg, bell-foundry Slegers-Causard was active in Tellin. In 1925, it cast a new carillon for the Ostend town hall.[192] The names of the Belgian kings and queens, the members of the city government, the Martyr Cities, and victories of the Great War were inscribed on the forty bells. The bells were inspected, with some being rejected by Denyn. Nevertheless, the instrument was installed and inaugurated on 31 May 1925 amid great public interest. For the occasion, Benoit's Rubenscantate was accompanied by a choir and Theban trumpets. Denyn, however, refused to play the instrument. Journalists used descriptions such as 'pots and pans', 'a haunting campanological cacophony' and 'a hellish carillon'. Nevertheless, the contraption continued to play for years – with every half hour the piano work *Flirt des marionettes* by famous painter James Ensor – until it was permanently silenced in 1940 by a merciful German bombing.

The ongoing malaise in Belgian carillon construction was a great concern for Jef Denyn. The director of the carillon school knew the quality of the English carillons that he had approved and played regularly in their workshops. These instruments found their way to all parts of the world except Belgium, the carillon land par excellence. At the age of 64, he was close to achieving his last great dream: the creation of a single, large Belgian bell-foundry that could compete with the English bell-founders.[193] This of course would have to be located in Mechelen, the city where bell-founders Waghevens and Van den Ghein cast the first musical bell series in the 16th century. The aim was for the new carillons in the Mechelen foundry to be played by the students of the carillon school, so that afterwards they would promote the foundry's products in their countries of origin. On 20 March 1926, Félix Van Aerschodt, Marcel Michiels Jr., Omer Michaux and Constant Sergeys convened in the carillon school. All signed a declaration of intent drawn up by Jef Denyn to establish a public limited company under the name *Fonderie Nationale de cloches et de carillons à Malines*. The bell-founders agreed to transfer their material to Mechelen and dismantle their own foundries. The new bells would be formed based on the profiles of Van Aerschodt, who was the only one authorized to continue to cast sculptures in his own name. Pending the start-up of the new foundry, the four bell-founders would meet at least once per week in all discretion to make pricing agreements concerning their interim production. In the end, the deal did not go through. In 1928, a brief association was created between Michiels and the ageing Van Aerschodt, who had no successor. Around the same time, Michaux stopped casting bells to become a sales representative for his two former competitors. Sergeys continued to work independently. His most important work since then was a new carillon for St. Peter's Church in Leuven to replace the carillon of Noorden and De Grave that was destroyed by fire in 1914.

Jef Denyn now resolutely came out in favor of the young Marcel Michiels. He had initially taken carillon lessons from Denyn, and was looking for ways to make his bells sound more in tune than his father's work. Denyn supported him in word and deed, and saw in the progress of the young bell-founder the long-awaited Belgian answer to the products of the English bell-founders. The carillon that Michiels delivered in 1929 for the Abbey of Grimbergen, while far from perfect, was the first reasonably tuned carillon by a Belgian bell-founder since the death of Andreas Jozef Vanden Gheyn.[194] From then on, almost all orders for new Belgian carillons went to the bell-founder from Tournai. Instruments were installed in Ronse, Ypres, Diksmuide and Charleroi. Michiels did not penetrate the Dutch market, but did produce an instrument for Ottawa and three carillons for the United States.

Marcel Michiels tests the partial notes of a bell.

Marcel Michiels later told how he had discovered the technique for tuning bells by accident.[195] After five years of fruitless experimentation, in 1927 he asked his bell tuner to tune three bells in his absence, and he wrote down the instructions for this. The next day, the tuner admitted that he had interchanged the bells when tuning. Michiels wanted to discard the bells, but listened to the sound of the largest of the three anyway. It produced a perfect fifth without the tuning having shifted the fundamental. Thanks to the tuner's mistake, Marcel Michiels Jr. is said to have discovered the secret of bell tuning. It is not clear where the truth stops and the myth begins in this story.

Belgian carillons in the United States

All three of Michiels' American carillons are exceptional, not so much for their intrinsic qualities but due to the anecdotes that surround them.

The first American customer of Marcel Michiels was one of the most talked-about Americans of the time: media tycoon William Randolph Hearst.[196] His turbulent professional and private life inspired Orson Welles to produce and direct the film *Citizen Kane* in 1941, according to many the best movie of all times. Welles had his main character spend the last years of his life in Xanadu, a private palace on a hill in Florida. The Xanadu of the real William Randolph Hearst was located on the other side of the United States, half way between San Francisco and Los Angeles. Starting in 1919, he had a house built for himself and his mistress, the actress Marion Davies, in San Simeon on a hill overlooking the Pacific Ocean. He named the place *La Cuesta Encantada* or the enchanted hill, and together with architect Julia Morgan, he created a utopia in which he gave a suitable place to thousands of works of art from Europe that he had collected during his life. The main building was called the *Casa Grande* and looked like a southern style church, fully in line with the architecture of the historical missions in California. The complex housed 56 bedrooms, 61 bathrooms, 19 living rooms, an indoor and outdoor swimming pool in antique style, a zoo with 300 species of animals, and an airport for his political and artistic jet-set guests. A carillon was also added.

Architect Julia Morgan contacted Jef Denyn in 1921, since Hearst wanted to install a Belgian style carillon in the two towers of the Casa Grande. For the bells, Denyn referred her to Marcel Michiels Sr. He advised hanging the bells in rows, at a central location in one of the towers, but Morgan and Hearst wanted to distribute the bells across the two towers and hang them visibly in the lantern openings, as was the custom for Spanish swinging bells. Denyn responded by proposing that all the bells be brought together in one tower and imitation bells be hung in the window openings of the second tower to achieve a visual balance. If this wasn't possible, as an alternative, he could purchase two carillons, one for manual playing and another for automatic playing. And should the buyer also not accept this proposal, it might be possible to hang the eight heaviest bells in one tower and the other bells together with the keyboard and the mechanical drum in the other tower. Hearst's construction project proceeded so slowly, however, that he lost his chance to acquire the first carillon in North America. When the two towers were completed in 1924, Hearst found them too severe and had them torn down and replaced by two more elegant towers that also provided space for more bedrooms and for the *celestial suite*, a luxury suite for the most important guests. After the death of father Michiels, Marcel Jr. took over the carillon assignment. The 36 bells were cast in 1929 and installed in 1932. They were evenly distributed between the two towers, visible in the window openings, and struck with hammers that were connected to an electric motor. They could be played manually or with a roll from a piano keyboard that was located in a passageway on the ground floor, where the bells were scarcely audible. It's possible that the only time carillon music was heard on the enchanted hill was when one of the guests happened to pluck a few notes on the way from the movie room to the game room. Hearst Castle was used as film decor for among others *Spartacus* and *The Godfather*, and is a National Landmark that is visited by hundreds of thousands of tourists each year. Carillon music, however, is heard there no more.

A piece of European culture was also exported to the new world at Alfred University.[197] In 1937, the alumni of Alfred University in New York State conceived the plan to donate a carillon to their former rector Booth Colwell Davis and his wife as a *living memorial*: both in fact were still alive and well at that moment. The donors were given a golden opportunity: former bell-founder Omer Michaux offered them a historical carillon composed of 16 bells cast by Joris Dumery, mainly from 1737, a bell by Andreas Jozef Vanden Gheyn from 1781, and no less than 18 bells by Pieter Hemony from 1674. Michaux stated that the bells had found their way to bell-founder Marcel Michiels Jr. in various ways. With these bells, Alfred University would not only own the only historical carillon on American soil, but it would save a unique piece of heritage from imminent destruction since a new war threatened in Europe. The historical instrument was purchased and installed on the campus in an open wooden construction that resembled an oil derrick. Kamiel Lefévere inaugurated the instrument on 12 June 1938. Because Michaux and Michiels told vague and conflicting stories on the origin of the bells, some observers doubted the authenticity of the bells. The full truth came to light only in 2003, after campanologist André Lehr consulted the archives of the Michiels foundry. A number of the Dumery bells came from the Harelbeke carillon that was restored by Marcel Michiels in 1932. Michiels, however, had cast several copies himself according to the Dumery model. He had also cast a series of 18 imitation Hemonys and an imitation Vanden Gheyn bell based on molds of the bells at St. Rumbold's. The Mechelen city government had these made during the First World War when the bells were threatened with requisition by the German occupying forces. The unsuspecting city government had loaned the molds to Michiels. The forged carillon earned Michaux and Michiels 90,000 Belgian francs, twice the price of a new instrument.

The third Michiels carillon in the USA arrived in California via a stopover in New York.[198] A World's Fair took place in the city in 1939 and 1940. The Belgian pavilion was designed by famous architect Henry Van de Velde and had a tower with a Michiels carillon containing 35 bells. Kamiel Lefévere inaugurated the instrument on 1 May 1939 and regularly gave concerts for the 6 million people who visited the Belgian pavilion this first year. The mechanical drum alternated between Flemish and Walloon songs. At the inauguration, Herbert Hoover was honored for the benefits he had bestowed on Belgium during and after the Great War. Two weeks later, Hoover wrote a letter to the rector of Stanford University with the request to purchase the Belgian world's fair carillon for Hoover Tower, a copy of the cathedral tower of Salamanca on the Stanford campus. This tower would house his library with documentation on war and peace. The archives and storerooms would be located in the lower floors and a reading room was foreseen for the top floor with a splendid view of San Francisco Bay. After hearing Hoovers desire for a carillon, architect Arthur Brown Jr. changed the plan for the tower. He moved the reading room to the ground floor and designed a bell-chamber for the top floor. The carillon was purchased from the Belgian government by the Belgian American Educational Foundation, the organization that until today continues to manage the assets of Hoover's previous relief fund for Belgium.

Kamiel Lefévere dismantled the Michiels carillon in New York with the help of an assistant and replaced the Belgian songs on the mechanical drum with music such as *Hail Stanford, Hail* and *America the Beautiful*. He later accompanied bells, keyboard and mechanical drum on their voyage to California and installed the instrument in the Hoover Tower. With its standard programmable drum and its Mechelen keyboard, the Hoover Carillon represented a piece of old carillon culture in California. Tower and carillon were inaugurated on 20 June 1941 on the occasion of the fiftieth anniversary of Stanford University. Lefévere played the bells, and Herbert Hoover dedicated his library, *The Hoover Institute and Library on War, Revolution and Peace*, to the pursuit of peace. Six months later, the American fleet at Pearl Harbor was destroyed and the United States was caught in the maelstrom of war.

The Mechelen carillon school during the interwar period

The young Mechelen carillon school experienced eventful years during the period between the wars.[199] As mentioned above, the school's creation was clouded by the growing communal disputes in Belgium just after the First World War. The carillon – as Flemish musical instrument – received a place in the Flemish nationalist discourse. Despite this, however, the Belgian royal family continued to value Denyn as the innovator of what King Albert in 1922 called 'an essentially Belgian art form'. Queen Elisabeth sometimes came to listen to Denyn's concerts in Mechelen, and the old master received the royal family for the last time in 1938 when King Leopold visited the carillon exhibition in Mechelen with his children Baudouin and Josephine-Charlotte. Jef Denyn achieved a balance between loyalty to the Belgian State and solidarity with the Flemish cause. Gradually he played more Flemish songs than previously, but for ceremonies, he adroitly combined Belgian and Flemish folk songs. When speaking, Denyn also stayed clear of the ideological danger zone. In interviews and lectures, he did not allow himself to be seduced into making pronouncements on people and politics, but limited himself to musical aspects such as carillon technique, repertoire and keyboard construction. Thus the Mechelen carillonneur remained an unassailable figure, standing above the ideological fray. Nevertheless the magic of the Monday evening concerts began to wane, and the enormous numbers of visitors of the pre-war period were no longer obtained. Denyn turned 70 in 1932, and he allowed himself to be succeeded as city carillonneur by Staf Nees. He, however, did remain director of the school.

The overall appreciation for the carillon school did not prevent the financing of the school's operations in the interbellum from being uncertain and strongly dependent on support from America. The school would not have survived its first twenty years without the many years of efforts by William Gorham Rice. When it was founded in 1922, the Belgian government provided funding only after Hoover's Belgian American Educational Foundation, at the insistence of Rice, had issued a check for 200 dollars to the school. Rice also convinced Rockefeller to make a gesture. On 8 February 1926, Jef Denyn received a check from New York with a friendly letter in which Rockefeller recalled fond memories of their meeting at the inauguration concert of the Loughborough carillon. He justified his gesture with the charming sentence:

> *Because I am so much interested in carillons, because I have such high regard for you as the greatest living carillonneur, because I am so fully in sympathy with the purposes of your school, to which you are giving yourself so generously and unselfishly, I hope you will allow me to have a little part in its support, through the enclosed contribution.*

Denyn answered with a word of appreciation for the magnificent bells of the New York carillon that he had approved a year earlier at Gillett & Johnston. Rockefeller would later lend a helping hand a number of times, usually after the mediation of his carillonneur Kamiel Lefévere. Lefévere proved himself a loyal ally of the school and raised funds via his contacts in Cohasset, New York and elsewhere. He also gave lessons to aspiring American carillonneurs, so that they later could obtain their degree in Mechelen more quickly. In 1930, Rice established the *Carillon League*, an international organization of friends of the carillon for which he was the treasurer. One of the most important goals of the League was financial support of the Mechelen carillon school. Until well into the 1930s, two thirds of the financing for the school would come from the United States. The economic malaise of the 1930s brought the school to the brink of failure: the subsidy from the Belgian government was decreased by 55% and the devaluation of the dollar diluted support from the United States. Out of necessity, the salaries of the director and teachers were temporarily reduced by 40% in 1935. In addition to its vulnerable financial situation, the school also suffered from a housing problem. The city of Mechelen met this need, but due to competition with other urban needs, the school was forced to move to a different building a number of times.

Despite the practical and business worries, the school did what was expected of it. Insofar as the financial resources allowed, it issued annual reports with historical articles and published new carillon music, including pieces by harmony teacher Jef van Hoof. Thanks to his five works for carillon, he was the first composer of name to write a carillon oeuvre. The school's curriculum was seriously biased toward the Mechelen playing tradition. The students of Jef Denyn learned to play as he did, with an emphasis on the contrast between virtuosity and lyricism, and with tremolo playing as an essential style element. The theoretical lessons assumed that the Mechelen carillon was the model for all carillons in the world. The theoretical exam contained the same four questions each year: describe the Mechelen carillon keyboard, its wire connections, its bells and its mechanical drum. Thus the illusion was created that those who knew how the Mechelen carillon was constructed, also knew carillon culture. Despite this one-sided approach, the Mechelen carillon school was recognized as the global center for knowledge about the carillon. In the 1920s and 1930s, fifty Belgian and foreign students received their diploma and several of the Flemish students would enjoy a remarkable career abroad. In addition to 'Americans' Lefévere and Brees mentioned above – the latter only followed a few lessons in Mechelen – there was Staf Gebruers.

Gebruers started his career as assistant city carillonneur of Antwerp and carillonneur of the small Van Aerschodt carillon in Antwerp-Kiel. In 1924, he was offered the position of carillonneur in the southern port city Cobh in Ireland. A new cathedral had been built there in 1919 with a Taylor carillon in the tower. The instrument was installed under the impulse of the nephew of the resident bishop who had become acquainted with the carillon during travels to Belgium. Cobh is located on a hill that emerges from the Atlantic Ocean and forms a natural harbor. The streets of the city center run around the neo-gothic granite cathedral like a natural amphitheater. The cathedral tower is a landmark for approaching ships and the last connection with the country for those departing. Small Cobh was a location with many memories. In the 19th century, hundreds of thousands of Irish left here for North America in search of a better life. On 11 April 1912, the Titanic moored here to board the last 123 passengers before departing on its fatal voyage. And in the cemetery lie a number of dead from the Lusitania which sank off the coast of Cobh on 7 May 1915. Something of all this must have appealed to Staf Gebruers, because he did not complete his carillon studies in Mechelen and in 1924 became carillonneur and organist in the Irish town. He walked in the footsteps of other Flemish musicians who made a name for themselves as church musicians in Catholic Ireland, and in addition to his work at the cathedral, he developed numerous activities in Cobh and beyond. He taught, composed and arranged, directed choirs and staged opera and operetta productions. He wrote articles on his new fatherland for the *Gazet van Antwerpen*, and was sales representative for publishers and producers of religious objects. Gebruers experienced his moment of glory on 9 September 1953, when the comic duo Laurel and Hardy came ashore in Cobh. The duo's best years were behind them, and Cobh was the first stop on a new promotional tour through Europe. Stan Laurel tells the story:

> *Our last good pictures were made in the thirties, and you'd think people would forget, but they don't. The love and affection we found that day at Cobh was simply unbelievable. There were hundreds of boats blowing whistles and mobs and mobs of people screaming on the docks. We just couldn't understand what it was all about. And then something happened that I can never forget. All the church bells in Cobh started to ring out our theme song, and Babe looked at me, and we cried. Maybe people loved us and our pictures because we put so much love in them. I don't know. I'll never forget that day. Never.*[200]

Only after they had recovered from their emotions and wanted to congratulate the bell-ringers did Stan Laurel and Oliver 'Babe' Hardy learn that all the bells were played by only one musician. Staf Gebruers had made splendid use of a golden opportunity and was assisted in this by his experience accompanying silent films during his early years in Antwerp. Today the Cobh carillon is the only such instrument in Ireland. It is presently played by Staf's son Adrian Patrick.

Theo Adriaens of Mechelen went to Mafra.[201] In 1927, at the age of 23, he obtained his carillon diploma with great distinction and was Denyn's most promising young apprentice. In November 1927, Denyn stayed for two weeks in Mafra to inspect the carillons with a view toward their restoration. The Witlockx carillon was restored by Désiré Somers, and in 1929 Theo Adriaens was appointed as carillonneur of the royal palace. In a letter to his friend and colleague-carillonneur Jef Rottiers, he sketched the mood of his new place of work. The inauguration concert of 16 May was magnificent: he had played for an audience of 30,000 and was photographed 20 or 30 times. In addition to the local audience, the Sunday concerts attracted 500 listeners from Lisbon, and this number would double when the road from Lisbon to Mafra was repaired. He worked hard to prepare for the approaching summer season, because each program had to contain Portuguese music, and he had none in his repertoire. The young carillonneur was given a friendly and hospitable welcome wherever he went, but on the street, he saw primarily old women, soldiers and apes. He also confided that he often went to Mass because this was the only place he was able to see attractive young girls. Theo Adriaens played the summer concerts in Mafra in 1929 and 1930. He was forced to interrupt the series in 1931 when he came down with TB. He returned to Mechelen and was replaced by Maurice Lannoy, carillonneur from St. Amand-les-Eaux and alumnus of the carillon school. Theo Adriaens died in Mechelen in 1935 at the age of 30.

In addition to Flemish students, the carillon school was visited in these years by two Walloon students who would make a name for themselves: Léon Henry from Nivelles and Géo Clément from Tournai. For the rest, there were starting and established carillonneurs from the Netherlands, France, England, the USA, Canada and New Zealand. We already met Ferdinand Timmermans from Rotterdam, Percival Price from Toronto and Gladys Watkins from Wellington. One of the most striking students was Nora Johnston, sister of the bell-founder. We know her better than most of the other students thanks to her memoirs.[202]

Nora Violet Johnston began as actress and divided her time between the London theater scene and the foundry of her brother Cyril, where she and her mother welcomed the numerous guests. In 1923 or 1924, she and her brother visited Mechelen to attend a concert by Jef Denyn. Impressed by this concert, she decided to take lessons from him. Nora sketches a romantic and sometimes exalted picture of 'cobblestoned' Mechelen, which had retained its 17th century appearance. She describes her first and only sleepless night amid the sounds of the Mechelen carillon, her sore little fingers after the first lesson, her clumsy attempts to speak Dutch, the fantastic Belgian mussels, pastries and coffee, and the terrible tasting escargots. We get to know the antics of the students of the carillon school, the fatherly concern of Denyn and the prudishness of assistant teacher Staf Nees with respect to carillon-playing ladies in shorts.

Nora enjoyed her long stay in Mechelen and obtained her diploma with passing marks only in 1933. A short time later, she and Victor Van Geyseghem, who was an assistant teacher at the carillon school, would play the inauguration concert for the carillon in Jerusalem, the first carillon in Asia. The international ecumenical youth movement YMCA, with financial support of American philanthropist James Newbegin Jarvie, had built a new building in the middle of the city. Arthur Loomis Harmon, the architect of the Empire State Building, had drafted a design that combined Neo-Byzantine, Art Deco and Islamic stylistic features. The complex consisted of three parts that symbolized the central YMCA concepts body, mind and spirit. The building was equipped with a library, auditorium, restaurant, swimming pool and

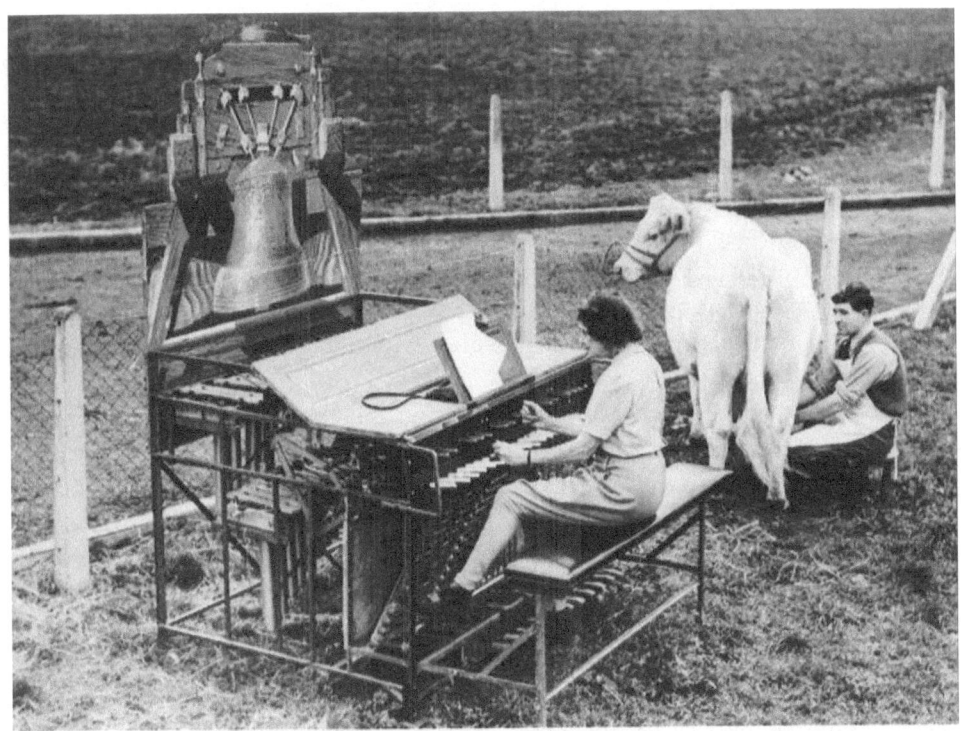

Nora Johnston plays her mobile carillon during an agricultural experiment.

football field, all focused on interfaith relations and the development of body, mind and spirit. A 35-bell Gillett & Johnston carillon was installed in the Jesus Tower. The instrument was donated by Amelia Jarvie, a niece of the founder. The inauguration of the building on 18 April 1933 was attended by YMCA leaders from throughout the world and was led by Lord Allenby, the British field marshal who had captured Jerusalem from the Ottoman Empire in 1917. Above the heads of the dignitaries, Nora Johnston played on the bells made by her brother Cyril. The intent was that she would remain in Jerusalem for a time to play concerts and to teach, but she was forced to return to England early at the beginning of May. Cyril had been notified that his sister was behaving unacceptably due to excessive alcohol use, and in consultation with the secretary of the YMCA, he arranged an early return. Thus his sister would no longer be inaugurating new carillons.

Since the few carillons in England already had a permanent player, Nora's career as carillonneur was threatened with an early end. So she ordered a portable carillon, a type of practice keyboard that she used as concert instrument. After patient experimentation, she was able to develop an instrument with sounding bars and resonators, and a silent keyboard. She crossed the Atlantic Ocean with her instrument twice in 1938 to tour the United States. She often combined a concert with a lecture titled *The Romance of Bells*. In America, she played for documentary radio programs and commercials, played concerts with an orchestra, and was received at the White House by Eleanor Roosevelt. A third tour had to be canceled due to the threat of war. After the war, Nora took her career in a new direction. She had her carillon towed onto the meadow and played for cows while they were being milked. She wanted to show that the music played on her portable carillon would stimulate cows to produce more. It was perhaps no accident that she was staying at an alcohol rehabilitation center during the same period. Nora Johnston died in 1952, but her idea of a traveling carillon would live on.

A second apprentice who would be responsible for an extraordinary piece of carillon history was Arthur Lynds Bigelow.[203] In March 1930, Jef Denyn received a letter from a young American engineer from Massachusetts with the request to attend his classes. The young man had become acquainted with the carillon during his studies at the University of Pittsburgh, and this experience had given him a mission in life. Bigelow wrote to the old master with a combination of admiration and self-confidence: 'If I am privileged to study under you, I will devote my whole time to the bells, and try to carry in America that which you have so well done in Europe.' Bigelow began his studies in Mechelen in October 1930 and obtained his degree in 1932. Shortly thereafter the engineer-carillonneur moved to Leuven to follow courses at the university in Romance and Germanic philology, in addition to a number of historical and artistic courses. The inquisitive American also found in Leuven what he was seeking with respect to the carillon. In addition to the Vanden Gheyn carillon in St. Gertrude's Church, a large carillon hung in the library tower – paid for by the American engineers – that had no permanent carillonneur. Bigelow became the player of the American Engineers' Memorial Carillon, even though he was never officially appointed as carillonneur. At the time of Bigelow's arrival in Leuven, work on the new Sergeys carillon for St. Peter's Church was already in an advanced stage. Bigelow advised on the construction of the instrument and submitted his candidacy for city carillonneur. Since there were no other certified carillonneurs living in Leuven at that moment, the city government accepted his application and, effective 15 December 1934, appointed him as city carillonneur for a probationary period with a mandate of two recitals per week. Afterwards his contract was tacitly renewed. Citizens of Leuven who saw him play, describe him as a carillonneur of the 'grand gesture'. Bigelow indeed played with much outward panache, in the best Mechelen tradition. His repertoire primarily contained Flemish folk songs.

Bigelow was accepted by the citizens of Leuven as one of their own. He spoke the Leuven dialect perfectly as well as proper Dutch. Bigelow had friends sympathetic to the Flemish cause and he himself became an activist in the Flemish movement. He traveled to give lectures on the carillon for Flemish cultural associations. He illustrated his argument musically with a self-made salon carillon that he transported in two crates. The instrument consisted of 42 light bells that he struck with two felt-coated hammers. A young American who traveled throughout Flanders to familiarize people with their carillon culture in their own language: it captured the imagination and Bigelow became a popular figure. Bigelow met his wife in Leuven, the Belgian Johanna Canivez. When the war broke out, the couple fled on bicycle and settled in the South of France, where they married. When safety could no longer be assured there, they traveled further to Portugal, and in the winter of 1941-1942, took the last boat to the USA. Arthur Bigelow left the old continent and its rich history with much reluctance. When a quarter of a century later he wrote down the unwritten prelude of Jef Denyn based on a recording of the old master, he justified the choice for this 'old-fashioned' piece to his young colleagues as follows:

> *Romantic? Perhaps. But it was a romantic time. It was the end of the truly romantic period in music. And the sound of this great prelude coming down from the high belfry, from that most beautiful tower of all, played by our teacher who was, to us, more than a legend, it seemed a perfect piece of music in a perfect setting, and it fulfilled all our needs. We were so much in love with everything.*[204]

A new war would bring a brutal end to two wondrous decades in the development of the carillon culture. Where in the preceding war, bells and carillons were symbols of freedom and heroism, in the coming cataclysm, singing bronze would become raw material for the industry of death.

CHAPTER 18

'The bells fight with us'

Nazi bells

The Nazis were fond of bells. The sound of heavy swinging bells supported their efforts to feed the German population ideas of magnificence and destiny. Durable bronze was perhaps even a good metaphor for the immortality of the Thousand-Year Reich that would soon begin. Already in the early 1920s, Dietrich Eckart, the poet to whom Hitler dedicated *Mein Kampf*, wrote a popular poem titled *Deutschland erwache*. It opens with the following words:

> *Sturm, Sturm, Sturm, Sturm, Sturm, Sturm!*
> *Läutet die Glocken von Turm zu Turm!*
>
> [Storm! Storm! Storm! Storm! Storm! Storm!
> Ring the bells from tower to tower!]

On 4 March 1933, the eve of what would become historical elections, Joseph Goebbels directed a speech by Hitler in Königsberg that would be broadcast over national radio. He announced that the bells of the cathedral and all the bells in East Prussia would toll in the prospect of the freedom regained. The Church authorities refused to participate, and the nazis were forced to embellish the speech with the sound of recorded bells. On 21 March, President Hindenburg and newly elected Chancellor Adolf Hitler shook hands in front of the garrison church in Potsdam. This symbolic site was chosen to consecrate National Socialism as the continuation of the Prussian monarchy. All the bells of Potsdam tolled, and the carillon in the tower of the garrison church was programmed to play, as always, the Prussian song *Üb' immer Treu' und Redlichkeit*. Two months later, a new bell was consecrated in the seminary of Maulbronn that bore the name of the Führer. The local newspaper spoke with pride of the first Hitler bell in Germany. It was proof that the Führer was taking the Church under his protection, in contrast to Stalin, who had the churches destroyed and the bells melted into imple-

The Olympic Bell is escorted to the Olympic stadium in Berlin, 1936.

ments for agriculture.[205] In the same year 1933, Edwin Espy, an American priest then living in Germany, saw a photo of a bell on which an image of the Führer had been cast 'so that every time it would ring, it would ring the call of the new Messiah to the chosen people.'[206]

In 1936, Nazi Germany organized the Olympics and the regime wanted to promote its ideas to the world. A hall was built in the Olympic stadium in Berlin to commemorate the Battle of Langemark in West Flanders, where numerous young German soldiers had died on 10 November 1914. On top of the Langemarckhalle was a 77-meter high bell tower in which a 9-ton bell in cast steel was hung: the *Olympiaglocke*. On its waist were the five Olympic rings, clenched in the claws of the Prussian eagle. Below these were two swastikas with in between the inscription 'Ich rufe die Jugend der Welt' [I call the youth of the world]. The bell announced the games and was its logo. In subsequent years all the bells in Germany were regularly tolled, among others on Hitler's 50th birthday in 1939 and out of gratitude for the failure of a bomb attack against the Führer in the same year. The few German carillons were also put into the service of the New Order. Talented carillonneur Wilhelm Bender played National Socialist songs on the Jan Albert de Grave carillon in the Parochialkirche in Berlin, among others on Hitler's birthday.

Gradually, military needs shifted Nazi attention from the sound of the bells to the material they were made of. The military buildup after all required large amounts of metal. Bronze cannons were a thing of the past, but copper was required among others for ammunition and motor parts, and tin was used in packaging material and electric appliances. German soil contained little copper and no tin, and the largest supplies were in the hands of unfriendly countries. Consequently, on 15 March 1940, Chancellor Hermann Göring, who was responsible for the metal supplies, promulgated a law confiscating all bells for military purposes. Enforcement of the law was suspended because shortly afterwards Germany was granted a credit for the delivery of copper and tin from Russia, which had concluded a non-aggression pact with Germany. The German people breathed a sigh of relief and acknowledged: 'Stalin saved our bells.' The war machine could continue without the use of sacred metal, and the bells were further used to celebrate the military victories of the Reich.

Carillon music in occupied territory

As was the case in the previous war, the Netherlands and Belgium had a neutral status. This, however, would not keep both countries out of the war. On 10 May 1940 *Fall Gelb* began, the German invasion of the Low Countries. Bombing destroyed a number of carillons. On 14 May, the Walloon city of Nivelles was bombed. City carillonneur and composer Léon Henry lost his residence, including almost all of his scores. The Collegiate Church of St. Gertrude went up in flames, but the fall of the Van Aerschodt bells was broken: they came to rest on the vault of the choir. On the same day, Rotterdam was the victim of a destructive bombing raid. Literally nothing remained of the Hemony instrument at the Old Stock Exchange. St. Lawrence Church was also destroyed, but a recently poured concrete floor in the tower prevented the flames from reaching the Hemony bells. The Dutch army surrendered a day later, but in Zeeland, Dutch and French troops continued to resist the German attack. To break the morale of the resistance, German bombers razed the Zeeland capital Middelburg on 17 May. The abbey tower, known to the people as the *Lange Jan*, was destroyed together with the carillon of Noorden and De Grave. On the same day, British and German troops battled in Leuven. The American university library was shelled and caught fire. Almost all the books collected after the previous war, including numerous manuscripts and books from German libraries, went up in flames. The tower remained standing, and thanks to the concrete intermediate floors, the Gillett & Johnston carillon was undamaged. The Germans and English blamed each other for the second Leuven library fire, and minister of propaganda Joseph Goebbels personally came to Leuven to ascertain the crime of the English. On 23 May, Belgian troops in Harelbeke blew up the St. Salvator Tower. Most of the Michiels bells survived and were safely stored away. Ostend was bombed during the night of 27/28 May. The town hall and its carillon were destroyed, bringing to an end the pre-war controversy concerning the out-of-tune bells of Slegers-Causard. A few hours later, King Leopold surrendered the Belgian army. The allied defense quickly collapsed, and at the end of May, more than 300,000 French and English soldiers were trapped around Dunkirk in northern France. The city was destroyed by the Luftwaffe, and on 27 May, belfry and carillon succumbed to the bombs. On the same day, the operation began that Churchill later would call *the Miracle of Dunkirk*: in nine days, the allied troops crossed into England in hundreds of large and small boats, thus narrowly escaping the superior German forces.

The Netherlands was treated differently by the Nazis than Belgium. Given the cultural affinity between the Dutch and the Germans, the Netherlands received a civilian government as preparation for its full integration in the greater German Reich. Austrian national socialist Arthur Seyss-Inquart became Reich Commissioner for the occupied Dutch territory and was given the task of gradually winning the people over to the National Socialist ideology. Hitler had not yet taken a decision on the future fate of Belgium and for this reason temporarily placed the country under military rule. Belgium and Northern France came under the authority of General Baron Alexander von Falkenhausen, the nephew of Ludwig von Falkenhausen, who had administered Belgium during the previous war. In contrast to Seyss-Inquart, who reported directly to Hitler, Von Falkenhausen reported to the central army command. General Eggert Reeder was responsible for domestic security and administration, and at the instructions of Berlin, initiated a *Flamenpolitik*, a policy of favoring the racially-related Flemish over the Walloon population. In general, Belgium enjoyed a substantially more favorable occupation regime than the Netherlands, and the carillon would also benefit from this.

The occupying forces appeared to appreciate Belgian carillon music. This began already at the start with the occupation in Steenokkerzeel. Upon their arrival in the center of this small Brabant town, to their surprise, German soldiers heard the carillon in St. Rumbold's Church playing the German folk song:

> *Deutschland, Deutschland über alles,*
> *Über alles in der Welt...*

The familiar melody of Haydn, however, was not meant as a welcome. It had been programmed on the carillon in its status as Habsburg-Austrian hymn:

> *Gott erhalte, Gott beschütze*
> *Unsern Kaiser, unser Land!*

The Vanden Gheyn bells were paying tribute to the best known resident of Steenokkerzeel, the Habsburg Empress Zita. Since 1929, the empress with her eight children had been living in exile in the nearby castle of Ham, and regularly attended mass at St. Rumbold's Church. When the Germans arrived, she had already fled to France with her family and entourage.

On 10 August 1940, the *Brüsseler Zeitung* dedicated a long article to Mechelen. The newspaper spoke highly of the city where the forefathers of Beethoven had lived and where the art of carillon playing was so intensely practiced. The writer of the article pointed to the similarity in sound between the word *beiaard* ('carillon') and the verb *beiern*, which referred to the long-standing Rhineland tradition of chiming on bells. He saw in this proof of the racial affinity between the residents of the Low Countries and those of the Rhineland. On the bells, Staf Nees played for the journalist music by Bach and Handel, and at his request, also a piece by Beethoven. The ageing Jef Denyn, like many other Flemish artists, allowed himself to be seduced by the cultural collaboration. In April 1941, he was a member of the honorary committee for the Mechelen Culture Days organized by the occupying forces and dedicated to folk art after 1830. Moreover, he was nominated for the Rembrandt Prize for 1942.[207] This was a German prize that had been awarded already in the 1930s, but since the war was used by Joseph Goebbels to strengthen cultural ties between Germany and the Low Countries. We will never know whether Denyn would have accepted this possible recognition, because he died on 2 October 1941 after a fall in the street. His body lay in state for three full days in the Mechelen town hall, while his students kept watch over the casket. During the funeral, Denyn was honored by Flemish nationalistic circles as a folk artist who had breathed new life into an old Middle Dutch art form. After Denyn's death, the carillon school continued to function in muted fashion, since only Belgian students were registered. City carillonneur Staf Nees was the obvious candidate to lead the school, but his official appointment would have to wait due to the war. He succeeded in keeping the carillon school outside the political risk zone. Once he was reprimanded by the occupying forces for playing a work by Felix Mendelssohn-Bartholdy on the carillon. After that incident, he resolved the issue by omitting the names of Jewish composers on his programs.[208] The cities that had been organizing summer concerts, suspended these, but in contrast to the previous war, most Belgian carillonneurs continued to play their instruments. They had a special reason for doing so, but more about this later.

The Germans were sometimes mistaken concerning the significance of carillon melodies in the Netherlands as well.[209] When on 15 May 1940 the occupation forces marched into Amsterdam, they were unintentionally greeted by the palace carillon playing the chorale melody well known in Prussia *Nun danket alle Gott*. On the half hour, however, the Dutch patriotic song *Al is ons prinsje nog zoo klein* [Though our little *prince is still so small]* was played. Only when members of the collaborationist party NSB drew the Germans' attention to the improper content of the latter song, did the melody have to be removed. Palace carillonneur Jacob Vincent programmed a new song to play on the hour: Psalm 42, a plea to God to release the people from the tyranny of the enemy. Vincent proved himself to be just as uncompromisingly opposed to the new political order as to the Flemish carillon movement in the preceding years. When the Germans wanted to use the palace carillon for their major events, Vincent refused to participate. On 11 June 1941, a special concert was organized with German music, with as title *Glocken singen für Soldaten [Bells sing for soldiers]*. Due to the unavailability of Vincent, Berlin carillonneur Wilhelm Bender was sent to Amsterdam. A choir and a brass band were assembled on the Dam Square, and the entire event was broadcast via radio. However, the microphone was too far away from the bells and the music was drowned out by the street noise. The next day, a new attempt was made with only the carillonneur. The microphone was placed closer to the bells, but this recording must also have failed, since it never made the radio. Vincent was also the carillonneur at St. Lawrence Tower in Weesp, but was dismissed when he refused to play for the installation of a mayor from the collaborationist NSB party.

In the occupied Netherlands, especially music from the bundle *Valerius Gedenck Clanck* was given special significance. The prominent melodies of *Merck toch hoe sterck [See how strong]*, *Gelukkig is het land [Fortunate is the land]* and other songs from the Eighty Years' War supported the Dutch population's national identity and sense of community. The poorly tuned Van den Ghein instrument in Arnemuiden that continued to play the old Wilhelmus hymn during the French period, again played a political role.[210] Since 1902, it had been hanging as musical museum exhibit in one of the towers of the Amsterdam Rijksmuseum, to the annoyance of nearby residents, who had even requested the minister to silence the forestroke. In the sad days of the occupation, however, the false sounding carillon was music to the ears of the hundreds of Jews and resistance fighters awaiting an uncertain fate in the prison along the Weteringschans across from the museum. It very recognizably played the Valerius song *O Heer, die daer des hemels tente spreyt [O Lord, who has unfurled a tent in heaven]* and thus presented a message of consolation. Protestant minister and resistance fighter Jan Buskes testifies: '...when the night came and Amsterdam, Amsterdam ravaged by the Germans, restlessly slept, we – my Catholic comrade who later went to Germany and never returned and I – kept each other awake listening to the sounds that entered the cell window like so many encouragements. And our restless hearts were filled with peace.' Among the prisoners along the Weteringschans was also the Frank family.

Before her arrest, from her hiding place Anne Frank had a comforting companion in the Hemony carillon of the Westertoren.[211] On 11 July 1942, the sixth day of her stay in the secret annex along the Prinsengracht, she wrote to her fictitious girlfriend Kitty:

> *Dear Kitty,*
> *Father, mother and Margot are still unable to adapt to the sound of the Westertoren bell, which sounds the time every quarter of an hour. I, however, immediately took a liking to it, and it is something familiar, especially at night.*

The uncompromising regularity of the automatic carillon playing was for Anne and her companions one of the few signals from outside and thus sufficient to offer them consolation. That became clear when the forestroke no longer played at the beginning of August 1943:

> *For a week we have all been somewhat confused about the time, since our dear and cherished Westertoren bell evidently has been removed for use in a factory, and we do not know exactly what time it is, day or night. I still hope that they will find something that reminds the neighborhood of the bell, for example a tin, copper or whatever object.*

The carillon was also a source of consolation outside of Amsterdam. At the time, poet Ida Gerhardt lived in Kampen and must have listened to the local Hemony bells playing the Valerius song *O Heer, die daer des hemels tente spreyt*. She cites a verse from the song in the war poem *Het carillon*. The poem describes how people dejectedly walk the streets, until in the bell tower the carillonneur begins a song by Valerius. The poet listens together with many nameless people to the song that sings of her violated country and concludes with the thought 'Never have I felt such a bitter, bitter love for what has been taken from us'. The poem appeared in various resistance newspapers and left a great impression on the people. To this day *Het carillon* remains one of the most read poems in Dutch literature.

The occupying forces were surprisingly tolerant of the subtle musical protest emanating from the Dutch carillons. Only occasionally was there an incident. One day, Leen 't Hart, the city carillonneur of Delft, was called to the Gestapo. A letter had arrived there stating that 't Hart had played songs by a certain Valerius that were hostile to Germany. 't Hart answered that songs by Valerius were also sung in Germany, such as *Wir treten zum beten*. The Valerius song *Wilt heden nu treden* in fact was often sung during Nazi mass rallies, giving them a pseudo-religious grandeur. The opening verse *Wir treten zum Beten vor Gott, den Gerechten* indeed suggests the mission of the Thousand Year Reich as the legitimate successor to the Holy Roman Empire. Thus it was not surprising that the Gestapo member in Delft knew the song. When 't Hart told him that Valerius had written many other beautiful songs, he tore up the informant's letter and let the carillonneur go.[212]

Several Dutch carillonneurs sympathized with the occupier. The most prominent of these was Jacques Vermaak.[213] Vermaak was named after his father Isaak, but had his first name changed to Jacques in 1931. He had obtained his carillon diploma on 3 August 1940 in Mechelen and was appointed as city carillonneur of Haarlem. He was the only carillonneur invited by the German administration to the Department of Arts in The Hague to exchange ideas on a thorough reorganization of musical life in the Netherlands. Vermaak drew up a plan with a number of clear stipulations. Carillonneurs with a diploma from Mechelen could play three carillons and be paid a fair price for this. They had to train young people who would be sufficiently remunerated for their recitals, so that they would receive the resources needed to later study at the Mechelen carillon school. Carillonneurs who had studied in Mechelen but were unable to finish their studies due to the war, could play one carillon. Non-certified carillonneurs older than 55, for whom according to Vermaak carillon playing was a secondary activity and who had limited interest, would be forced to retire. Municipal governments would be required to organize summer evening concerts with program booklets. In March 1941, Vermaak wrote to his master Jef Denyn that great things were about to happen in the Netherlands concerning the carillon and that everything that had to do with carillons would be done according to the Mechelen model. Vermaak occasionally played the Amsterdam palace carillon for pro-German events such as Rembrandt Day on 15 July 1944. The great painter from the Golden Age had indeed been exploited by the Nazi regime as an example of the Germanic spirit. Vermaak was never able to realize his plans for the carillon. It was thwarted by a larger program: the confiscation of bells in Europe.

The confiscation of bells in Europe

On 22 June 1941, Hitler gave the order to launch Operation Barbarossa, the full-out attack on Russia. As a result, the supply of metal from the Soviet Union disappeared and the Nazi regime was obliged to obtain the required metals by recycling bells and other objects.[214] The Nazis began at home. They organized the confiscation of bells with the same administrative efficiency that they applied to the persecution of people. First, all the bells in Germany were inventoried and subdivided in four classes:

A: the least valuable bells, usually cast after 1918
B: bells of greater value

C: bells of still greater value
D: the most important historical bells, i.e. bells from the Middle Ages and the three historical carillons of Berlin, Potsdam and Darmstadt

Bells in the first three categories had to be disassembled. The A bells were immediately transported for processing, and the B and C bells were placed in warehouses pending the evolving needs. The owners of the seized bells would be compensated for the value of the metal after the war, but only in the case of a victory. Only the D bells, representing 20% of the total weight of the bronze, were definitively exempted and allowed to remain in the towers. Photos were taken of this last category, among others for art lover Göring. The *Reich Office for Iron and Metals* initially set up seven factories to process the bells. From July 1942, production was concentrated in two refineries in the vicinity of Hamburg: the Deutsche Zinnwerke in Wilhelmsburg and the Norddeutsche Affinerie in Hamburg. The first bells were removed from German towers on 8 November 1941. Initially, the intent was to mitigate negative emotions on the part of the German population by removing bells from the towers in the occupied territories first, but this plan was not carried out. After Germany came Poland, Czechoslovakia, Belgium, the Netherlands and a part of France. The collaborationist Vichy regime of Marshal Pétain was able to save the bells in southern France by offering statues in their place. No confiscation of bells took place in Luxembourg, Denmark and Norway. In Italy, the fascists had concluded an agreement with the Vatican that half of the total weight in bells would be made available to the war industry. The bells in Italy were chopped into pieces and sent to Hamburg for processing. Afterwards, the separate metals would return to Italy for further processing. In reality, only part of the copper was returned to the sender.

On 23 July 1942, a regulation was issued in occupied Dutch territory requisitioning diverse metal objects, including church bells. Archbishop De Jong immediately sent a letter of protest to Reich Commissioner Seyss-Inquart. The archbishop stated that the Dutch Church had forbidden its subordinates from declaring the bells, but that they would not resist if the occupier acted with force. Seyss-Inquart was not impressed. Three months later in a speech, he called it self-evident that the Dutch would spontaneously offer copper to the German soldiers in order to keep Bolshevism from their borders. The contracting firm P.J. Meulenberg from Heerlen was appointed as *General contractor of the special bureau for metal mobilization*. Meulenberg was able to start the dirty chore immediately, because in the Netherlands, a bell inventory was already available. Shortly before the war, the Dutch Ministry of Defense had ordered the Art Protection Inspectorate, in consultation with the Dutch Bells and Organ Council, to designate the most important bells as monument. These represented a maximum of 15% of the total bell weight in the country. The government in fact had already considered the possibility that it itself would need to requisition bells in the case of war, and they wanted to designate the bells that should never be used. The protected bells were painted with the letter M and warning signs in four languages were installed next to them. Since the quota for valuable bells in the Netherlands was lower than the norm the Germans had determined for their own bells, negotiations were conducted with the occupier, which resulted in an exemption for 25% of the bell weight. This concerned 570 swinging bells that usually were from before 1600, and 52 carillons. By flattering Seyss-Inquart, in fact all historical carillons and several important modern instruments were preserved as examples of *Niederdeutsche Kultur*. Like elsewhere in Europe, the unprotected bells received the code A, B or C.

On 22 September 1942, Meulenberg removed a 'test bell' from the Roman Catholic Church in Hoensbroek. When no appreciable resistance resulted, the systematic confiscation of bells started. In less than one year, several hundreds of workers in various teams removed 6,700 A, B and C bells from towers in the Netherlands. Municipalities without protected M bells were allowed to keep a small C bell as alarm bell in the case of bombing raids, or they received a protected bell that came from elsewhere. From the spring of 1943, protected M bells and carillons were also removed from the towers in the buffer zone in the west of the country, not to requisition them, but allegedly to keep them out of allied hands in the case of a possible allied invasion of the Dutch coast. Seldom was there physical resistance to the removal of bells, but bells were regularly buried or hidden in ditches and ponds. In the empty towers, the bells were replaced by gramophone records or substitutes such as steam boilers and the like. The residents of Bergen-op-Zoom told the occupier that their new Van Bergen carillon was cast by Hemony.[215] The instrument was left alone, but would be destroyed by German bombs in October 1944.

The removed Dutch bells were transported to 24 warehouses where they were registered and weighed. The first bells were placed on the train to Germany in March 1943. The Germans initially wanted to send all A, B and C bells to Germany where two Dutch experts would assess their artistic and historical value. J.W. Janzen, adjunct inspector with the Art Protection Inspectorate, was able to persuade the Germans to have the bells assessed in the Netherlands by a German expert. To facilitate their work, a pre-selection would be made in the meantime. The bells to be assessed were marked with the letter P, for *Prüfung* or inspection, and received a temporary protected status. With these delaying tactics, Janzen succeeded in slowing the transport of the removed bells to Germany. In the meantime, the Art Protection Inspectorate mobilized volunteers throughout the country to describe the bells while they were still on Dutch soil. Molds or rubbings were made of markings and decorations. Thus steps were taken to ensure that the endangered patrimony remained more than just a

Making a rubbing in the warehouse of Hilversum

memory. In addition, the descriptions could be of value after the war to identify bells that might be recovered.

In September 1943, Bell Peter, as Meulenberg was popularly known, had completed the work. All the bells in the Netherlands eligible for disassembly were on the ground or had already been sent to one of the processing camps in Hamburg. As a tangible reminder of its contribution to the expansion of the German empire, Meulenberg was given a bell with the inscription:

1942-1943
METALLMOBILISERING
GLOCKEN KÄMPFEN MIT FÜR EIN NEUES EUROPA

1942-1943
Metal mobilization
Bells joining the fight for a new Europe

Confiscation of the bells in Belgium only really began after the disassembly work was complete in the Netherlands. This had to do with both the nature of the occupation regime in Belgium and the firm stance taken by the Archdiocese of Mechelen. As stated, Hitler had not yet taken a decision on the future fate of Belgium. Only the East Cantons, which had become Belgian territory after the previous war, were already 'liberated' and absorbed into the Reich. They had to hand in their bells immediately. Pending political clarity, the rest of Belgium remained under military rule. General Alexander von Falkenhausen was not 100% sympathetic toward the Nazis and he implemented a policy of the lesser evil. To this end, he developed the best possible relations with the ecclesiastical authorities in Belgium. When on 1 November 1941 the decree was issued requisitioning the bells in Belgium, Quartermaster General Franz Thedieck sent Cardinal Van Roey the reassuring message that execution of the decree would not take place immediately. The church leader was also assured that a possible operation would not be performed by Belgian workmen. Moreover, all carillons would be exempt from the requisitioning. On 1 July 1942, the start of the requisitioning was announced. Cardinal Van Roey protested to Von Falkenhausen and wrote a letter to the Pope, who in turn wrote to Berlin. There was again a postponement. In February 1943, the military government in Belgium was ordered by Berlin to urgently execute the requisitioning, since this work was largely complete in the rest of the Reich and in the occupied territories. Three administrators of the carillon school under the leadership of its president Henry De Coster went to the office of Dr. Köhn of the Art Protectorate in Brussels to request that all carillons in the country, including new ones, would be exempt from requisitioning.[216] This was permitted on the condition that the carillons would also be played. This commitment was only a repetition of the earlier pledge by Franz Thedieck to Cardinal Van Roey, but De Coster judged that it was the result of the prestige – also in the eyes of the occupier – enjoyed by Jef Denyn and the carillon school.

The church for its part hardened its resistance. On 21 March, a letter from the Belgian bishops was read aloud in all churches in which the bell requisition was condemned in stinging words. According to the bishops, the requisitioning of the bells violates article 46 of the Hague Convention, which obliges an occupying power to respect freedom of religion; and article 52, which limits requisitions of goods in kind to the immediate needs of the occupying power; and article 56, which grants full immunity to places of worship in time of war. The bishops condemned any cooperation with the confiscation of bells as a severe crime against conscience, and called upon priests and believers to assume a peaceful and passive attitude.[217] In response to this, the military government dropped its pledge that the removal of the bells would be done by German workers, and on 14 April, a contract was signed with the company Nicolas Van Campenhout in Machelen for disassembly of the bells. Since a list of bells was not yet available, the ministry of education put together a commission with as task to inventory all the bells in the country. The *Commission pour la sauvegarde des cloches en Belgique* [commission for the protection of bells in Belgium] was placed under the chairmanship of Jozef De Beer, the curator of the Sterckshof Museum in Deurne close to Antwerp. They worked together with the occupier but, like the Art Protection Inspectorate in the Netherlands, attempted to save the bells as much as possible. All non-carillon bells received the standard codes, with the following meaning:

A: swinging bells, cast after 1850
B: swinging bells, cast between 1790 and 1850
C: swinging bells, cast between 1700 and 1790
D: swinging bells, cast before 1700

In addition to the carillon bells, all D bells could remain in the towers. Due to the requirement that all carillons be played, the Leuven university carillon was endangered, since it was no longer accessible after the fire in the library. The librarian told the Germans that the bells must have melted in the fire, which was probably not verified. Things went less well for the new carillon in Dinant. Slegers-Causard had cast a new instrument in 1940 to replace the carillon that was destroyed in 1914. The carillon sounded so out of tune that the municipality refused to pay for it. Slegers-Causard lost the court case, and the municipality sent the bells to Leuven by train to be recast by Félix Van Aerschodt. In Leuven, they were intercepted by the Germans and sent to Hamburg. Separate carillon bells on a train were not considered as a carillon.

The immunity granted to the Belgian carillons also offered a possibility to protect other bells. In various carillon towers, swinging bells were connected to the baton keyboard to make them appear as carillon bells. A traveling keyboard was even available for towers without a carillon. Especially former bell-founder Omer Michaux, who was also administrator of the carillon school at the time, was active in falsifying for a good cause. When the four swinging bells at St. Gertrude's Church in Leuven were endangered, he connected them to the keyboard. Just to be sure, Jef Van Stappen of Mechelen gave recitals on the expanded Vanden Gheyn carillon. In St. Leonard's Church in Zoutleeuw, Michaux connected the swinging bells in the west tower with the carillon keyboard in the crossing tower thirty meters away. Player on duty was Tienen city carillonneur Jan Wauters. In the Abbey of Maredsous, Michaux with the help of the monks constructed a new carillon based on a hodgepodge of nine bells, including the seven-ton Elisabeth and the bell from the cloister. When the monks were visited by three German officers on 2 January 1944, Brother Irénée demonstrated the carillon with the song *Ich hatte einen Kamerad*. The effort was in vain, because on 24 February, a team of thirty workmen arrived to remove the nine bells. The giant bell

Elisabeth was crushed on location since it would not fit through the gate.[218] The city government of the municipality of Essen in the north of Belgium also engaged in preventive tinkering with bells. The five swinging bells were assembled into a carillon on which could be played the Marian hymn *The Lourdes Ave Maria*. Professor Rosemann of the Art Protectorate initially allowed the carillon to remain despite the fact that, according to the official standard, a carillon must have at least eight bells. The standard was increased shortly thereafter, and only carillons with more than 27 bells were spared. Thus, on 9 March 1944, four of the five bells were removed from the tower.[219] The most colorful rescue story took place in Ath. The residents had assembled in St. Julian's Church a number of swinging bells from neighboring churches and connected them to a keyboard made available by the municipal authorities of Braine-le-Comte. The keyboard was available because the municipality had removed its Michaux bells before the war, after which they were taken by the Germans. The residents of Ath demonstrated the presence of a carillon in the St. Julian's Tower with an old brochure that still mentioned the Witlockx carillon that had disappeared years ago. As ultimate proof of the presence of a carillon, a record with carillon music was played regularly in the tower. The bells survived the war. Once a carillon was deliberately given to the occupier: in Leuven, the new Sergeys instrument in St. Peter's Church was sacrificed in exchange for the Van Aerschodt swinging bells in St. Quentin's Church and Keizersberg Abbey. Swinging bells that could not be camouflaged as carillon bells were sometimes hidden or thrown from a train.

Despite the major and minor successes of the commission, the directors of the carillon school and local residents, most of the Belgian bells were shipped to Hamburg. The departing bells were tolled one more time – sometimes recordings were made – and once they were on the ground, they were adorned with wreaths. With the help of volunteers, the commission registered and photographed the bells as best they could before the bells departed. A number of bells were in a sorry state: in addition to their original cast inscription, they bore the letter code that indicated their category and thus had determined their fate, a Roman numeral for the province of origin, and sometimes initials indicating that they had already been registered by a volunteer. Occasionally a protest slogan was painted on a bell. The most popular protest rhymes were:

> *Wie met klokken schiet*
> *Wint de oorlog niet*
> *[Whoever shoots with bells*
> *Will lose the war]*

and

> *Klokken uit de toren*
> *Oorlog verloren*
> [*Bells from the tower*
> *War lost*]

In September 1943, the inventory was expanded to include organs since there were indications that the German government would begin requisitioning organ pipes to fill the growing need for tin. With a view toward this new inventory, the *Commission pour la sauvegarde des cloches en Belgique* was reinforced with Dom Joseph Kreps, organ specialist and monk of Benedictine Abbey of Keizersberg in Leuven. On 17 March 1944, the feared decree was issued that made possible the requisitioning of the organ pipes in the Reich. The war's end would prevent the execution of this decree.

6,500 Dutch and 5,000 Belgian bells were transported by boat or train to the two Hamburg bell warehouses. They were processed in three steps. First, the bells that were still intact were reduced to bronze shards. Three methods were used for this. The simplest was smashing a bell with hammers. When this failed, the bell was lifted thirty to sixty feet in the air and then dropped on another bell. If this too failed, a heavy weight was dropped on the bell. After that, the pieces of the bells were melted. The third and final phase was separating the liquid bronze into tin, copper and other metals via electrolysis.

Liberation

While many bells disappeared to the East, a friendly bell from the West brought a message of hope. Several times per day the forestroke and hour chime of London's Big Ben sounded in living rooms in the occupied territories during the banned – but nevertheless very popular –news broadcasts of Radio London. The constancy of the hour bell that continued to strike the hour despite the clearly audible sound of the flying bombs above London increased the feeling of solidarity of free England with the occupied continent. Only after June 1944, when the terrorization of London by flying bombs increased, was the direct reproduction of Big Ben temporarily replaced by an audio recording. This prevented the sound of the numerous strikes from becoming a tactical advantage for the enemy. The recording caused a number of listeners to mistakenly believe that the London bell had been destroyed.[220] Bells from the United States also provided help and consolation. The *Office of War Information* in Washington asked Kamiel Lefévere to record European Christmas carols on the Riverside carillon. Lefévere noted the songs that he heard from European immigrants in the streets of New York, and recorded them. The Voice of America broadcast the recording to the occupied territories.[221]

In the meantime, the fortunes of war had turned and allied bombing on the continent increased in intensity. In July 1943, bombs hit the melting chamber of the Norddeutsche Affinerie, taking it partially out of service. Occasionally, bombing resulted in collateral damage to carillons in occupied territory. On 22 February 1944, St. Stephen's Tower in Nijmegen was hit by an American bomb. The bells survived the blow and were brought to safety. In May, the center of Leuven suffered repeated heavy hits by poorly targeted allied bombing. On 12 May, a bomb blew a hole in the St. Gertrude's Tower, shattering a carillon bell. The bass bell fell thirty feet and landed, undamaged, on an oak beam. The allied bombing reached as far as Berlin. On 24 May, an allied fire bomb hit the Parochialkirche. Only two bells of the magnificent Jan Albert de Grave carillon survived the inferno. Carillonneur Wilhelm Bender did not witness the demise of his carillon. He had died in an airplane crash in the Balkans shortly before.[222] The city of Cologne was often in the line of fire and was largely destroyed in various bombings. The Germans threatened to destroy the carillon at St. Rumbold's if the Cologne Cathedral and its bells were destroyed.[223] The cathedral was repeatedly hit, but remained standing among the ruins of the German city.

On 6 June 1944, allied troops set foot on the beaches of Normandy. Initially they met heavy resistance, but starting with the liberation of Paris on 25 August, things went quickly, albeit with occasional damage to bells. In Avesnes in Northern France, for example, the Vanden Gheyn carillon in St. Nicholas Church was destroyed during the liberation of the city on 2 September. On Sunday 3 September, British troops liberated Brussels. The next day in Mechelen, Staf Nees followed the troop movements between Brussels and Mechelen on the radio. He climbed St. Rumbold's Tower, from where he could hear the approaching army. When the British entered the city and the Germans were chased from the Market Square, a triumphant *Brabançonne* was heard throughout liberated Mechelen.[224] Antwerp was liberated the same day.

The rapid advance of the allies through Belgium created impatient expectations in the Netherlands, and when British radio broadcast the erroneous message that the Dutch border city Breda had been liberated, unjustified festivities broke out in numerous Dutch municipalities. That 5th of September full of confusion and dramas entered history as *Dolle Dinsdag* or Mad Tuesday. Leen 't Hart climbed the tower of the new church in Delft and played patriotic songs for an hour before he realized that he'd best make a quick exit. It became clear too late that the allies had liberated only a narrow corridor in the middle of Belgium to quickly reach Antwerp. The advance was temporarily halted to consolidate the positions and wait for reinforcements. On 8 September, Polish and German soldiers were still fighting one another in the West-Flemish town of Tielt. Battles raged on each street, and the belfry was riddled with bullets. The keyboard and the wiring were destroyed, but the historical Dumery bells remained unharmed. In the meantime, the allied bombing above Germany continued. In the night of 11 to 12 September, 200 RAF bombers flattened the Darmstadt city center. 12,000 residents lost their lives, and the carillon of Pieter Hemony in the castle was permanently silenced. This brought an end to a conflict between the carillonneur, who had continued to program religious melodies on the drum, and the government, which had fired him and had the bells play Nazi songs.

The allied army command wished to take advantage of the chaotic German retreat to quickly penetrate into the north. Operation Market Garden began on 17 September. In a first phase, airborne troops captured the bridges on the Meuse and the Rhine, so that ground troops from Belgium could advance to Arnhem. From there, the allies would isolate the German troops in West Netherlands who were firing V2 bombs into London, and then advance into the heart of the German war industry in the Ruhr Area. The result is described in the book *A Bridge too Far* and the movie of the same name. British airborne forces captured the rail and traffic bridge above Arnhem, but were quickly forced to relinquish it due to stubborn German resistance and the absence of the needed ground troops. St. Eusebius Church in Arnhem was in the line of fire. Debris fell on the swinging bells, which eerily began to ring. The heat caused the mechanical drum to start. The Hemony carillon of Arnhem, once the bridgehead of Belgian carillon culture in the Netherlands, made itself heard one last time before perishing. Operation Market Garden was abandoned on 26 September, and the front became fixed along the major Dutch rivers. The subsequent cold winter and a German food blockade caused a dramatic famine in the northern part of the Netherlands and it would be another seven months before all Dutch territory was liberated.

In the final weeks of the war, the last of the three historical German carillons fell. The final major allied bombing was intended for Potsdam, the former residence of the Prussian monarchs. British bombers appeared above the city at 8 p.m. on 14 April, as the bells of Jan Albert de Grave in the garrison church were playing the Prussian song *Üb' immer Treu' und Redlichkeit*. The bombing was brief and fierce, but when the aircraft had disappeared, the garrison church appeared not to have been hit. While the rest of the city burned, the carillon continued to play its familiar melodies. The imperial stables next to the church were on fire, however, and during the course of the night ignited the church and tower. The fire department was unable to reach the fire due to low water pressure, and the tower burned down slowly, from top to bottom. The bells played until they fell – one by one – 250 feet below. Thus the last remaining carillon of Jan Albert de Grave, heir to the Hemonys, disappeared.

When the carillon at Potsdam fell, Hitler's days were numbered. In his bunker in Berlin, the Führer lost touch with the hopeless reality, and while Russian bombs reduced Berlin to rubble, he sometimes stared for hours at the scale model of the new

Bells in the destroyed St. Eusebius Church in Arnhem

Linz, the city that was chosen by him to become the cultural capital of the Thousand Year Reich and the place where he would spend his old age. A mausoleum would be built for his parents on the banks of the Danube. The dome-shaped building was inspired by the Pantheon in Rome and would be crowned with a 550-feet tall bell tower. The Führer told his architect Hermann Giesler that he wanted a carillon in the tower.[225] It would not sound every day. Rather, on specific days it would play a motif from Bruckner's fourth symphony, a melody that touched the Führer deeply and that he believed was suitable for bells. Sketches dating several days before his suicide on 30 April show a sarcophagus above a monumental staircase. This reinforces the suspicion that in his last days, the dictator no longer thought of Munich as a site for his mausoleum, but of Linz, the city of his youth. While his empire was collapsing around him, Hitler continued to believe in a grand end and a grave in the highest bell tower in the world. The Nazis were fond of bells.

After the surrender of Nazi Germany, the war continued to rage in the Far East. On 6 August, the American atomic bomb fell on Hiroshima. When Japan refused to capitulate, the bomb on Nagasaki followed on 9 August. Found in the ruins of Urakami Cathedral was the Angelus bell. It rang for the first time again on Christmas Eve 1945.[226] The bell of Nagasaki was a *signum*, a sign of hope in a nuclear wasteland.

CHAPTER 19

Dutch manufacture versus Carillon Americana

The return of the bells

As was the case after the previous war, the carillons contributed to the festivities in liberated Belgium. However, the celebrations were less noisy than those of 1918, because more than half of the bells had been requisitioned and no one knew their fate.[227] On 30 September, the Belgian government returning from London decided to expand the task of the commission for the protection of bells in Belgium to include tracing and returning the missing bells. Since almost all the requisitioned bells had been sent to Hamburg, the commission could only begin its work after Germany had been conquered by the allies. The two bell warehouses in Hamburg came under the control of the British, who scornfully called them the *Belsen of Bells*. In July 1945, a message came from Hamburg that some 600 Belgian bells had been found undamaged. On 1 September, commission chairman Jozef De Beer traveled to Hamburg. He found 718 undamaged bells in the Zinnwerke facility. This high number was thanks to the bombing by the RAF that had halted production already in September 1944. The British had seized the bells, as was usual in the unwritten law of war. However, they respected the prescriptions of the Hague Convention and gave their management to the *Office of Monuments, Fine Arts, and Archives*. The Belgian bells were quickly released, and on 8 October they arrived in the Port of Antwerp on board the Belgian steamer *Lys*. Cardinal Van Roey and numerous dignitaries watched from the grandstand. With the help of the commission, the bells were identified and returned to their legitimate owners. D bells that had temporarily served as alarm bells elsewhere were again sent to their original home. In the vicinity of Antwerp, towers that remained without bell were temporarily given Hemony bells from the dismantled church carillon of the cathedral.

In the Netherlands, missing bells could be sought as that country was gradually liberated. This initially went more quickly than in Belgium, because thanks to the delaying tactics of the Art Protection Inspectorate, a large number of bells had

Bells in one of the German bell cemeteries

remained behind in Dutch warehouses. Moreover, in July 1945, 148 carillon bells and 107 valuable M bells were fished out of the IJsselmeer close to the municipality of Urk. Against the agreement with the Dutch, the Germans had transported them on board the vessel *Hoop op zegen*. The owner of the ship had refused to accompany the transport, and his replacement had the vessel run aground in the IJsselmeer, presumably out of patriotism rather than incompetence. Most of the bells from the carillons of Appingedam, Brielle, Goes, Sint-Maartensdijk, Tholen and Zierikzee were saved in this way. J.W. Janzen of the Art Protection Inspectorate traveled to Hamburg, where he found 300 bells. On 19 November 1945, four Dutch coastal vessels brought them to the Netherlands.

Around the middle of 1946, a second Belgian delegation, this time under the leadership of Fr. Kreps, traveled to Hamburg. The delegation found sixty bells from the East Cantons in the Norddeutsche Affinerie as well as a 6,623-ton pile of bell shards. Even after a bombing had damaged the melting chamber in 1943, demolition of the bells had continued. These fragments of rare bronze would be valuable for casting new bells, and six countries were interested in the shards. The British proposed dividing of everything based on the total bell weight confiscated per country. According to this rule, Germany would receive 60% of the weight and Belgium 12%. Fr. Kreps made a counter proposal to identify the bell fragments and return them to the country where they originated. Identification was possible, because the fragments were stacked in layers according to their arrival, and the transport and production data from the occupier were available. In addition, there was the registration information of the commission itself and information that Kreps had gathered in a long conversation with Nicolas Van Campenhout in the prison of Huy. The English accepted the proposal. When the identification work was complete, Belgium received 40% of the bronze and Germany only 12%, since most of the German bells had been requisitioned and processed before those of the occupied territories. The fragments of 3,180 Belgian bells were identified, from which Kreps concluded that only 132 Belgian bells had been fully processed into material for the war. The bronze remnants arrived in Antwerp on 1 December 1947. They became property of the government. Germany received back its few intact bells only after all the allied countries had received back their surviving bells. German church governments who had sought information from the British concerning their bells received a standard answer that left nothing to the imagination: the German church is said to have participated in the bell requisitioning, in contrast to the churches in the allied countries, which had tried to hide bells; the request to receive back bells when so many other stolen bells had yet to be returned, testified to an arrogance that only a German would be capable of; the German demand for transport for bells in a period in which even food was unable to properly reach its destination, again testified to an insensitivity that one could find only in Germans; and finally, forcing their own church towers to remain silent would be a suitable reminder of the personal guilt of the church government.

In both the Netherlands and Belgium, approximately half of the prewar bells were lost, and thus the demand for bells was great. During the war, Petit & Fritsen had sent a circular to the churches in which it offered them the possibility to reserve their bells in the meantime.[228] In 1945, the foundry restarted production with 300 tons of fragments from Hamburg. The waiting lists were long, and it would be ten years before supply would meet demand.[229] In Catholic areas, the numerous blessings of bells were a final expression of the rich Roman Catholic liturgical life before the Second Vatican Council simplified the Church liturgy in the 1960s. The new bells were decorated and – according to the ancient ritual – blessed in the presence of their godfather and godmother and the entire parish community. Those present received a baptism card as remembrance.

While almost all Belgian carillons and most Dutch carillons had survived the war, the confiscation of bells had important ramifications for the study of the carillon. Following the armistice, some 12,000 intact bells were at easily accessible locations, ready to be inspected close up. Percival Price, who at that time was carillonneur and professor at the University of Michigan in Ann Arbor, had seen a photo of one of the German bell cemeteries and saw in this a unique opportunity. He was able to travel to Europe with a grant from the university. In addition, he received from the Canadian government the grade of lieutenant colonel and the availability of a car with driver, so that he was able to travel through West and Central Europe unhindered. In 1946, he lived for a year in Europe, noted down stories from various countries, took photos of the bells in the Hamburg workshops, collected statistics, and examined the decorations and sound properties of hundreds of bells. In his research, he worked together with a research commission from the German Evangelical Lutheran Church. Together with the German researchers, Price tested a number of bells at the Norddeutsche Affinerie and in the laboratory of the Northwest German Broadcasting organization in Hamburg. The bells were hung and their sound recorded. The partial notes were no longer measured with tuning forks, but using an oscillator. This is an electric measuring instrument with a pen that can be caused to vibrate. First the oscillator was placed on the lip of the bell and caused to vibrate at various frequencies until a partial note in the bell began to sympathetically vibrate. This made possible the measurement of the frequency and decay time of this partial note. Then the device was placed slightly higher, and the process repeated until the top of the bell was reached. The systematic measurements identified at which frequency the bell responded best to the various partial notes and what their properties were. The oscillator made it easier to quantify the pitch than was the case with traditional adjustable tuning forks, and thus purity of tone became objectively measurable. In 1948, Price published the report of his sabbatical in *Campanology, Europe 1945-1947*, a unique document with figures and stories on the largest confiscation of bells in history. According to Price's study, in all of Europe, more than 175,000 bells were taken from their towers, and more than 150,000 of these were destroyed. Germany was the worst off, with a loss of 90,000 bells. Belgium and the Netherlands each lost more than 4,000 bells. The total loss in bronze was estimated at 100 million pounds.

Reconstruction in the Low Countries

While Price was active especially in northern Germany, engineer Engelbert 'Bert' van Heuven was conducting research on bells that had remained in the Netherlands.[230] He examined among others the carillon bells that were taken from the IJsselmeer and used an oscillator to test them for partial notes and decay time. His study was financed by the Dutch government. The government in fact was hoping that the study might lead to the discovery of suitable bell metal that was cheaper than bronze. Van Heuven was unable to offer the Dutch government an alternative, because he came to the conclusion that steel is not equivalent to bronze and that only lead at a temperature of -70°C[231] had the same properties as bronze. His study was followed with interest by Tuur Eijsbouts of Asten, a manufacturer of tower clocks and a carillon assembler.[232] The high demand for new bells had given him the ambition to grow by casting bells himself instead of assembling other people's products in towers. Eijsbouts began casting bells in 1947 and delivered a test bell for Van Heuven's measurements. Van Heuven succeeded in producing graphs that reflected the behavior of the most important partial notes when the bell wall was turned at various heights. He thus went a step further than Canon Arthur Simpson, who had only shown the locations where each partial note could best be tuned. Based on an example, Van Heuven demonstrated that it was best for the bell tuner not to try to tune all partial notes simultaneously, but that the so-called cascade method was a better technique. He first selected the two partial notes that required the least work to be tuned, and with the help of the graphs, he determined the best place in the bell wall to do this. Once the first partial note had been tuned, he measured the result and tuned the following partial note at the location where the other partial notes do not react. Van Heuven's tuning graphs were a practical and infallible recipe for the bell tuner. On 21 December 1949, the young researcher obtained a doctorate from the Delft Institute of Technology with the thesis *Acoustical Measurement on Church-bells and Carillons*. This was a historical day, because Van Heuven's thesis stripped the technique of bell tuning of its aura of mystery, and gave campanology a scientific foundation that could be consulted by all. Bert van Heuven contracted MS, however, and thus was unable to continue to use the

Eijsbouts' traveling carillon leaving for Belgium (18 March 1950)

knowledge he had built up to guide the construction of new carillons. He died in 1976 at the age of 58.

On 1 January 1949, Tuur Eijsbouts hired nineteen-year-old André Lehr as bell tuner. As newcomers to bell-founding, Eijsbouts and Lehr were not hampered by the burden of tradition, and they experimented with new techniques. In order to work more quickly, they no longer constructed the bell forms with clay, but with various compositions based on cement and, like Van Heuven, they verified the tone purity of their bells using the new oscillator. During the initial years, the casting of bells of more than 650 lbs was done in the Lips propeller factory in Drunen. They produced their first carillon in 1949. Tuur Eijsbouts told his employees that it was an order for Wervershuizen, a small town in North Holland. Wervershuizen, however, could not to be found on any map, and Eijsbouts firstborn was in fact a factory carillon that would serve as a reference with a view toward future orders. Following the example of the mobile carillon with which Nora Johnston had traveled before the war, it became a traveling carillon, but this time with real bells. André Lehr used bell profiles that were copied from Hemony bells. He tuned the small bells on a lathe on which shell cases had been turned during the First World War, and the larger ones on a lathe that was purchased from Petit & Fritsen. The traveling carillon toured throughout the

Netherlands and promoted the carillon in general and its maker in particular. This was 1949, and the first orders for traditional tower carillons followed in the same year.

The carillon was taken up in the reconstruction movement: the general mood of optimism and patriotism that dominated post-war Netherlands. The Dutch government stimulated domestic carillon construction with financial incentives, and a number of local governments used the damage compensation for lost church bells to purchase a carillon. English bell-founders were not allowed to participate in this growth market, because the scarce foreign currency the Dutch government had was reserved for goods more urgently needed than carillons. Moreover, the Netherlands now had three foundries capable of tuning bells.

Due to the closure of the Dutch carillon market, Taylor again focused on North America. After the war, Gillett & Johnston cast practically no more carillons. This was a result of the difficult financial situation Cyril Johnston found himself in due to a decline in the number of orders in the 1930s. After appealing in vain for a loan to his old friend Rockefeller, the English bell-founder accepted two London investors as majority shareholder in 1935. In addition, for three years he was forced to train the mediocre son of one of the new partners in the technique of casting and tuning bells. In 1948, the sick bell-founder was dismissed. In 1949, he intensified contacts with his former Dutch installation company Eijsbouts, and followed with great interest the development of the traveling carillon. Cyril Johnston died on 30 March 1950, and shortly thereafter Gillett & Johnston would return to the production of tower clocks. The Dutch carillon world did not mourn the demise of the English foundry for long, because the Dutch art of bell casting, the art of Van Wou and the Hemonys, was back. The 23 carillons that were lost or damaged in the war were quickly repaired or replaced by new instruments, and a large number of towers received a manually playable carillon for the first time. In the Netherlands, 50 new carillons were installed between 1946 and 1960, and this pace would increase still further in the 1960s.

While the Dutch carillon movement was borne only by a limited number of enthusiastic culture lovers between the two world wars, the instrument had now reached the general public. The young novelist Harry Mulisch chose carillonneur Maurits Akelei as the main character for his novel *Het zwarte licht* (The Black Light). Mulisch tells that on 20 August 1953, the day on which the world was predicted to end, Akelei gave the ultimate carillon recital. All in the city stopped their activities and looked upward, spellbound. Mulisch's prize winning short novel became required reading at school, increased knowledge of the carillon among the general public, and undoubtedly aroused among some carillonneurs the bold dream to one day play the ultimate tower recital themselves. In his writing, Mulisch was not inspired by an existing carillonneur. As background, he had climbed the tower of St. Bavo Church in his hometown of Haarlem in order to view the Hemony bells and the playing mechanism.[233]

In view of the renewed flourishing of the carillon, it was not logical that the Dutch should still have to go to Belgium to learn the profession of carillonneur. The Dutch Carillon Association, after a short interruption during the war, had resumed its activities and campaigned for the introduction of accredited national examinations for carillonneurs, but without result. The local carillon association of Amersfoort then proposed the idea of establishing a carillon school in the city. The city government further developed the idea, and the Dutch carillon school opened its doors on 24 October 1953. Leen 't Hart, who had studied in Mechelen under Staf Nees, was appointed as lecturer and director. 't Hart developed a virtuoso playing style, and composed and arranged many pieces for the tower instrument. His compositions were influenced by organ playing, have a strong structure and contain new tone colors, among others due to the use of ancient modal tonalities. In addition to the carillon school, the Dutch Carillon Association, under the impetus of its dynamic president Romke de Waard, played an important role in promoting the carillon.

In Belgium, the evolution was calmer. In 1945, Staf Nees was honored in Mechelen for his 25 years of carillon playing, and officially appointed as director of the carillon school. The people of Mechelen gave him a new keyboard to replace the keyboard on which Jef Denyn had once celebrated his major triumphs. Nees taught at the church music school Lemmens Institute, was organist and choir director, and in addition to choir music, he composed some fifty pieces for the carillon. He continued the tradition of Denyn, but gave it greater musical depth. In his fantasias, dances and variations, rhapsodic passages full of vitality alternate with lilting tremolo music. Under his influence, Benoit Franssen, Jos Lerinckx, Jef Rottiers, Gaston Feremans and others wrote authentic carillon music with a traditional romantic bias. The carillon work of Arthur Meulemans was more innovative due to its percussion effects, new tonalities and almost Dionysian exuberance. Much of this work was written for composition contests at the carillon school and was published later by the school. The carillon school moved to the building *Het schip*, and a light practice carillon by Marcel Michiels was installed in 1954 in the tower of the nearby Court of Busleyden. In the same year, a carillon organization was founded under the name *Oudleerlingenbond van de Mechelse Beiaardschool* (Alumni Association of the Mechelen Carillon School). Its first president was Antwerp city carillonneur John Gebruers.

Belgian carillons had scarcely suffered during the war and consequently fewer instruments were ordered than in the Netherlands. During the 1950s, some twenty carillons were produced in Belgium, usually from the workshop of Marcel Michiels Jr. The first post-war carillon was ordered from Michiels in 1947 by the monks of the Norbertine Abbey of Postel. In 1952, the city of Nieuwpoort purchased a carillon in Tournai that would attempt to do the impossible: combine bells in 'pure' Pythagorean tuning with an unlimited choice of tonal keys. To achieve this musical ideal, the bells for the chromatic keys were doubled, so that for example in addition to an F sharp bell, a G flat bell was also available. The manual had not two, but three rows of batons stacked one above the other, and depending on the tonality, the carillonneur could choose which of the two 'black keys' he would play. It goes without saying that this playing style was technically very difficult, and the Nieuwpoort carillon experiment was never repeated. Michiels' bells were well made and reasonably tuned. They were better than Belgian products made during the interwar period, but with respect to sonority, they were not the equal of the products made in the Netherlands. However, northern bell-founders did not immediately penetrate the Belgian market. The greatest obstacle to exporting was the rationing of still scarce bronze. Both in the Netherlands and in Belgium, copper and tin were allocated by the government to the bell-foundries based on concrete projects. The reconstruction of bells and carillons in the home country were given priority, hence bronze was difficult to obtain for foreign projects. To gain access to the Belgian market, Eijsbouts established a bell-foundry in Lokeren around 1952 called Horacantus. In 1952, this branch of Eijsbouts delivered a small carillon in Herzele, and in 1956, a large carillon for the St. Lawrence Tower in Lokeren. The Belgian branch would remain active until 1969. Petit & Fritsen delivered its first Belgian carillon in 1959 for the Church of St. Peter in Chains in Nederbrakel. At the end of the 1950s, both bell-founders were ready for a breakthrough in Belgium, and Petit & Fritsen already had a foot in the door in the United States. On the other side of the Atlantic Ocean, however, there was a new enemy that threatened the existence of the traditional carillon. It was called *Carillon Americana*, and in Europe was known as 'the electronic threat'.[234]

A carillon without bells

Like modern Dutch bell casting, its electronic opponent emerged from the ruins of the Second World War. The shortage of bell bronze inspired various companies to develop systems that electronically imitated the sounds of bells. This was not unusual, because the Hammond organ had been developed already before the war as an inexpensive alternative to the pipe organ. Electronically simulated bells had a number of advantages over their bronze counterparts: they were cheaper, occupied less space, and placed less demands on the construction of the tower. After the Second World War, belief in progress reigned supreme, and electronic bells and carillons were promoted as products that reconciled tradition with innovation. The Paris company Vox Campanae framed its advertising in the mood of post-war reconstruction. It addressed pastors with the slogan 'Ring your bells even before your bell tower is rebuilt', and its brochure displayed the ruins of a church. The firm guaranteed that its system conformed to liturgical prescriptions. The company Martin from Versailles designed speakers in the form of bells and claimed that their sound would carry 6 miles. The Brussels company SBR resolutely opted for innovation. It distributed advertising brochures with a drawing of two exhausted bell-ringers crying out: 'Oh! If only we had an electronic carillon.' The company glossed over the fact that bell-ringers had already disappeared for the most part from the towers, since almost all such bells featured motorized swinging.

The United States had faced a shortage of bronze already during the war, and consequently was also familiar with companies promoting electronic bells and carillons. The Los Angeles based company Maas-Rowe, for example, marketed a *Symphonic Carillon* with a unique feature: for each note, you could choose whether its sound was a minor-third or a major-third bell sound. The new bell makers did a good business, but did not disrupt the market for traditional carillons. This changed when George Schulmerich appeared on the scene.

In 1935, Schulmerich had founded an electronic 'carillon' company in Sellersville, Pennsylvania. Its flagship product was the *Carillon Americana*. The sounds of the instrument were produced by narrow metal rods that were tapped by hammers. The soft sound of the rods was picked up by microphones, amplified and emitted by four speakers located in the window openings of a tower. With the help of regulators, several sound parameters – including volume – could be adjusted to one degree or another. The customer could choose between different 'registers' of rods that generated diverse tone colors. The most popular registers were *Flemish Bells*, which had a heroic character and on which all harmonies could be played, *English Bells*, which were not suitable for all harmonies, or 'softlike' *Harp Bells*, which were especially suited to accompaniment. Customers could expand their instruments by combining registers. The largest Schulmerich carillon – called 'the largest carillon in the world' by its maker – contained almost 1500 rods or *carillonic bells*. The Carillon Americana was played from a keyboard with classic keys located on the ground floor of the tower or even in a different building. It produced a sweetish sound, and ultimately the carillonic bells of Schulmerich were only a pale reflection of singing bronze. Yet there was a market for the instrument. Just after the war, George Schulmerich launched a new and daring marketing strategy. He would infiltrate the traditional carillon milieu and hire famous carillonneurs to play and promote his products. Around 1946, he contacted a carillonneur living in the region of Sellersville: Arthur Bigelow.

After their flight from Europe, the Bigelows had moved to Princeton in 1941. Their only daughter Marianne was born there, and Arthur became a professor at the university and *bell master* for the Gillett & Johnston carillon in the Cleveland Tower located on campus. He wanted to expand his new carillon from 35 to 49 bells in order to have as many bells as his former carillon in Leuven, where for that matter he was still the official city carillonneur. Since European bells could not be obtained due to the war, he decided to cast the missing bells himself. He assembled bronze, among others with material from a discarded locomotive bell, made 14 bell forms, had the bells cast in an industrial bronze foundry, polished the raw bronze and tuned the bells on the Princeton campus. The carillonneur cum bell-founder: it was a romantic idea that fit the passionate and idealistic personality of Bigelow. Hence, it is surprising that several years later, Arthur Bigelow accepted the offer of George Schulmerich to promote the Carillon Americana. The carillonneur organized courses on how to play the instrument, and in 1949 wrote a textbook at the request of Schulmerich: *English Type Carillonic Bells: Their History and Music*. At the same time, he continued to actively advise with respect to traditional carillons. For Bigelow, the carillon and the Carillon Americana were two different musical instruments that could exist side by side in perfect harmony. He found the electronic bells only acceptable if a tower was too small for bronze bells or if an institution did not have the financial resources to purchase a traditional carillon. Most American carillonneurs, however, experienced the imitation-instrument as a threat to the pure experience of the carillon, and for years, Bigelow was persona non grata within the Guild of Carillonneurs in North America. He, however, was not alone in working for Schulmerich: during the 1950s and 1960s, other carillonneurs would also play the Carillon Americana.

Schulmerich had a different vision of the role and the future of his products than Bigelow. This is illustrated by a tragicomic series of events that took place at the Ward-Belmont School for Women in Nashville.[235] On the campus stood a 19th century water tower that was converted into a carillon tower in 1929. The alumnae of the school donated a Gillett & Johnston carillon with 23 bells as a memorial to the Americans killed in Flanders during the Great War. Amid great interest, Percival Price played an inauguration concert, which was broadcast via the radio. In 1951, the school was taken over by the Tennessee Baptist Convention, and it became a religiously inspired institution with the name Belmont College. Shortly thereafter, the school board received an offer from Schulmerich for an electronic carillon for the price of 10,000 dollars. The manufacturer argued that the religious character that the school had recently been given could be enhanced with daily carillon playing. Thus for example, the beginning and the end of lessons could be announced with hymns from the Baptist Church. And a Schulmerich carillon was best suited to this, because it was better adapted to automatic playing than was a traditional carillon. If the school was prepared to give its 23 Gillett & Johnston bells to Schulmerich, it could even have the electronic carillon free of charge. The bells would receive a place in the bell museum that Schulmerich was developing next to his company. The deal went through, and Belmont received carillonic bells in exchange for its bronze bells. The latter were hung, ready to play, in an open tower next to Schulmerich's workplace. The Carillon Americana at the school fell into disrepair after only a few years. In 1982, the college wanted its previous bells back, and it began negotiations with Schulmerich. Schulmerich's price was too high, so, in order to again have a real carillon, Belmont College was forced to purchase a new instrument from Petit & Fritsen.

In 1957, Schulmerich won what probably was his most important victory on American soil. In that year, an electronic carillon was installed in Bok Tower, the carillon tower par excellence. A Schulmerich advertising brochure justified this as follows: 'To bell tones of traditional majesty, the Singing Tower at Lake Wales now adds the enchanting voices of the plucked harp and silvery celesta!'

Carillon battle in the Vatican pavilion

1956 presented a golden opportunity to introduce the entire world to the wonder of the electronic carillon: the World's Fair that would take place in Brussels in 1958.[236] The expectations of the world were high, since there had been no global exposition since the 1939 World's Fair in New York. The event would be dedicated to the progress and the infinite possibilities of technology. On 14 June 1956, extensive documentation on the Carillon Americana arrived at the Commissioner General of the Holy See in Brussels. Schulmerich proposed providing an electronic carillon free of charge to Civitas Dei, the Vatican pavilion at the Expo. Paul Heymans, former Belgian minister and commissioner general of the Vatican pavilion, rejected the offer. According to the pavilion records, his rejection was dictated by 'respect and esteem for the time-honored bells and an almost innate aversion to any electro-mechanical invention that would replace the venerable and symbolically rich bronze bells.' In August, Heymans received a visit from J.P. Goemaere, the sales representative for Schulmerich in Belgium. He expressed his surprise at the fact that his product was not given a chance to be installed in the Holy See's pavilion, despite the fact that Schulmerich was prepared to pay for the installation costs and the fees of the carillonneurs. He explained that the sound of the Carillon Americana was not an electronic recording, but live music produced by a hammer striking a bronze rod, which was then electronically amplified. This removed any liturgical objections. Goemaere also had with him the recommendations of four American cardinals, and an album with photos of cardinals and bishops blessing Americana instruments. 5,000 Schulmerich instruments had already been installed in the USA, and in Europe, Americanas could be heard at Montmartre in Paris and in the North American College in Rome.

Heymans presented this new information to the management committee, which could no longer refuse the offer. He justified his change of mind with the argu-

Cardinal McIntyre blesses a Schulmerich Carillon Americana
at the Great Seminary of Los Angeles

ment that the modern works of art and technologies that would be on display in the pavilion did not imply a rejection of the old masterpieces that were exhibited next them. The fact that the bell tower would house a traditional and a modern carillon was an ideal opportunity to experience the difference between them. Schulmerich was given permission to install his product and proposed delivering the two latest variants, the harp bells and the celesta bells. The Commissioner General also received offers from the traditional carillon milieu. At the end of 1956, Marcel Michiels offered free delivery of a carillon for the temporary bell tower. In March 1957, the Alumni Association of the Mechelen Carillon School offered to have concerts played regularly on the Michiels carillon by its members. The management committee decided to leave the coordination of the carillon concerts to Staf Nees, and advised the carillonneurs to contact him for further arrangements.

In the meantime, Schulmerich was also making contacts elsewhere in Belgium and the Netherlands with a view toward installing demonstration instruments. The Alumni Association of the Mechelen carillon school received wind of the threat from

America and under the impetus of chairman John Gebruers, the Belgian carillonneurs were called upon to boycott the new instrument. On 15 June 1957, the Alumni Association and the Dutch Carillon Association met in Amersfoort to formulate a common position with respect to the electronic threat. The front was quickly formed, and the chairman of the Dutch Carillon Association, Romke de Waard, called for a boycott of the intruder and for the protection of Dutch bell casting, which finally was flourishing again. He called it a case of immense national importance. In the meantime, a Carillon Americana had been installed in the gothic steeple of the Brussels town hall. On 20 October, the instrument was played by the carillonneur from Cobh, Staf Gebruers, which undoubtedly was an uncomfortable experience for his brother John, who was leading Belgian opposition to the Carillon Americana.

A new initiative by Schulmerich suddenly focused all attention on the future Vatican pavilion. To emphasize that his carillon was a full-fledged musical instrument and not simply a recording of carillon music, the company announced that it would have several carillonneurs from the USA brought over to play the instrument at the Expo. At the same time, it offered all certified carillonneurs the opportunity to play the Carillon Americana for pay. The directors of the Alumni Association and the Mechelen Carillon School then decided to send a form to all Belgian and foreign members of the Alumni Association to be signed by them stating that they would never play the Carillon Americana, even if it were to be demonstrated at the upcoming Brussels World's Fair. A great majority of members returned the form signed. The same thing happened in the Netherlands and France.

On 20 February 1958, the management committee for the Vatican pavilion received a telephone call from the Michiels company with the message that it was withdrawing its offer of making a carillon available to the pavilion free of charge. Thus less than two months before the start of Expo, the committee had only one electronic carillon. The problem appeared to be unsolvable until it was remembered that two years ago, Petit & Fritsen – 'the oldest Catholic bell-foundry in the world' – had submitted a request to install several bells at an exhibition in the pavilion. The committee contacted the North Brabant foundry. It had already promised a carillon for the Dutch pavilion, but still had carillon bells available that were destined for the city of Hulst. The Hulst city council was asked to postpone the inauguration of its new carillon for four months. The council members considered it an honor to be able to assist the Vatican pavilion. Petit & Fritsen made the bells available to Civitas Dei for 100,000 Belgian francs, transport and installation included.

In the meantime, Mechelen alumni who were carillonneurs in Canada had passed on to the Belgian carillonneurs a brochure in which Schulmerich claimed that the Carillon Americana had been chosen as official carillon of the World's Fair. As a result, the Belgian carillonneurs hardened their position and now also refused to play the traditional carillon of the Vatican, unless they were paid a fee. Staf Nees attempted in vain to mediate by pointing out to his colleagues the difficult financial situation faced by the Vatican pavilion. Again, the solution came from the Netherlands. When bell-founder Fritsen heard of the conflict via the press, he proposed that the traditional carillon be played by Dutch carillonneurs. Since they would have already traveled to Brussels and were being paid to play the carillon in the Dutch pavilion, perhaps they might be prepared to play the traditional carillon at the Vatican pavilion for free. The Dutch Carillon Association approved the arrangement, and the Vatican had only to cover the lodging for the carillonneurs and their spouses. As might be expected, the Belgian carillonneurs were not very pleased with the pragmatic attitude of their Dutch colleagues. On the 15th of April, two days before the start of the Expo, they made a final proposal. They now were also prepared to play on the Petit & Fritsen carillon free of charge on the condition that the Carillon Americana would not be used for the full duration of the exhibition. The Civitas Dei management committee rejected this proposal. Staf Nees was trapped between the interests of the Vatican and those of his colleague carillonneurs. He himself played the concert at the pavilion's opening.

Much carillon music could be heard at the Expo. In addition to the two Vatican carillons and the Dutch pavilion carillon, an Eijsbouts carillon could be heard in the folkloric imitation village *Vrolijk België - Belgique Joyeuse*, and in the dome of the French pavilion, a carillon played *Auprès de ma blonde* every hour. With all of the carillons sounding together unabashedly, it quickly became clear that agreements needed to be made to coordinate the sounds emanating from the various pavilions. In the Vatican pavilion, the carillonneurs were annoyed that the speakers for the Carillon Americana were placed in the open tower just above the bells of the traditional carillon, giving many visitors the impression that the electronic sound came from the bells of Petit & Fritsen. In the end, things did not turn out as badly as feared: 16 Belgian carillonneurs were prepared to play the Petit & Fritsen carillon at the Civitas Dei pavilion free of charge and without conditions. They alternated with 21 Dutch colleagues. The concert programs required prior approval by the pavilion managers. For the concerts on the Carillon Americana, Schulmerich brought in among others Anton Brees and Kamiel Lefévere, the two Belgian pioneers of carillon culture in the USA. Their reunion with their Belgian colleagues was no doubt not a warm one. In addition to the daily concerts, the Carillon Americana tolled the Angelus and every half hour it played a fragment from the papal hymn *Viva Pio dodicesimo, Padre nostro e Papa*. Presumably it did not play this for the full duration of the Expo, because Pius XII died ten days before its end. The 12 million visitors to Civitas Dei probably noticed nothing of the conflict that had torn apart the carillon world for months. It appeared that the Carillon Americana had won this battle.

The Vatican pavilion at Expo '58, with the loudspeakers of the
Carillon Americana above the bells of the traditional carillon

At the time of the Expo, Schulmerich was close to a breakthrough in Ostend.[237] On 1 August 1958, a demonstration instrument was hung in the Culture and Festival Palace located on Ostend's main square, the Wapenplein. The new complex was built on the site of the town hall that had been bombed in 1940. Ostend had many problems before the war with the false sounding carillon bells of Slegers-Causard and it now expected something better. The Schulmerich instrument was played by Géo Clément and Ephrem Delmotte. This was despite the fact that both had signed the Alumni Association's form promising fidelity to the traditional carillon. Clément was one of the leaders of carillon culture in Wallonia. He was the city carillonneur of Tournai and Mons, where he had also established a carillon class. Moreover, he was an esteemed composer of carillon music. His works *Suite archaïque* and *Campanella* are still played today. Delmotte was a known figure from Ronse, where he was city carillonneur and had founded the popular Bommelsfeesten, a sort of winter carnival. Schulmerich paid the carillonneurs a generous fee of 1,500 Belgian francs per concert. The first concerts provoked diverse reviews in the press. The articles in the newspaper *De Zeewacht* were very enthusiastic, but turned out to be written by Delmotte himself under a pseudonym. Initially a trial period of two weeks was foreseen, but this period was extended.

A number of Ostend residents thought the new instrument sounded more pure than the carillon they remembered from before the war; opponents launched rumors concerning a conflict of interest on the part of the city government. To refute the insinuations, the city government held a press conference on 4 September. There the masks came off: J.P. Goemaere, Schulmerich's sales representative, spoke clearly for the first time. He showed compassion for the carillonneurs, whom he called the most miserable of musicians. They were poorly paid to sweatily play until their fingers became callused. He accused the Flemish of clinging too strongly to the past. Carillon culture, however, was in its death throes and the only way to save it was by replacing bronze bells with electronic ones. Progress couldn't be stopped: was not the ox finally replaced by the tractor, and the pen by the typewriter? Goemaere continued: Schulmerich was planning to set up installation and perhaps even production facilities in Belgium and preferably in Flanders, the cradle of carillon playing. The city of Ostend, however, did not take the bait, and in February 1959, the Carillon Americana was removed to continue its campaign of conquest in Norway. Dissidents Géo Clément and Ephrem Delmotte were expelled from the Alumni Association. Several years later, Delmotte offered his services to the city of Ostend free of charge to play its new carillon with traditional Paccard bells. He then entertained visitors to the outdoor cafes with romantic melodies and light pop songs, at the time giving the Ostend carillon the nickname *jukebox on bells*.

The Carillon Americana and its ilk never made a breakthrough in Europe. In North America, a number of towers contain electronic bells, but they did not replace the traditional carillon. In the 1950s, North America in fact developed a carillon culture which was so innovative that according to some, the musical instrument of the Low Countries only reached full maturity on the other side of the Atlantic Ocean.[238]

CHAPTER 20

Innovations in the Old and the New World

American Beauty

The broad American public got to know the carillon in 1953. In that year, *Niagara* appeared in the movie theaters, a *film noir* by Henry Hathaway with Marilyn Monroe in the leading role and the carillon in an important supporting role. Marilyn plays Rose Loomis, an attractive woman who – with the help of her lover – wants to get rid of her husband George. The carillon of the Rainbow Tower at Niagara Falls is a partner in crime, because after the elimination of her husband, her lover would post a pre-agreed song as a request in the mailbox under the tower. When the music of the song *Kiss* enters Rose's room via the open window, she slowly awakens and a blissful smile comes across her lips as she realizes that the carillon is playing the desired song. The request, however, turns out to be a misunderstanding, because her lover is killed in the fight. Rose is pursued by her husband and flees into the Rainbow Tower. She climbs higher and higher, passes the keyboard and enters the bell-chamber, where her husband strangles her in the shadow of the silent carillon bells.

The Rainbow Tower carillon was cast by Taylor in 1946. Taylor continued to cast a number of magnificent instruments after the war, usually under the supervision of his regular carillon fitter Frank Godfrey. Godfrey paid much attention to the playability of the instruments and made a number of technical improvements to the keyboard, the action and the placing of the bells. The most important Taylor carillon of this time was the instrument at the University of Kansas from 1951. The campanile with carillon was established as a memorial to the Americans killed in World War II. An impressive carillon for Washington National Cathedral followed in 1963, and in 1966, Yale University expanded a chime of 10 bells into a carillon with 54 bells. In 1951, a year following the death of Cyril Johnston, Gillett & Johnston delivered its last carillon to Culver Military Academy in Indiana.

A new name on the American carillon scene was Alfred Paccard. Shortly before the war, the French bell-founder succeeded in accurately tuning his bells, and entered the North American market via the mediation of Arthur Bigelow.[239] Bigelow and Paccard met one another at the end of the 1940s and a lasting friendship developed.

Marilyn Monroe and Joseph Cotten in the carillon tower of Niagara Falls

The carillonneur was especially charmed by the clear sound of the Paccard bells, which sounded crisp and bright thanks to a strong prime and a less prominent minor third. In 1950, the American department of finance ordered 55 Paccard bells via Bigelow. They were not carillon bells, but life-size replicas of the Liberty Bell. The bells were given to the states and territories to promote the issuance of government bonds, with the slogan 'Save for Your Independence'. Bigelow and Paccard installed some fifteen melodious carillons in the United States, among others at the University of the South in Sewanee (1958) and at the National Shrine of the Immaculate Conception in Washington D.C., the largest Catholic church in North America (1963). In the meantime, Bigelow had stopped working with George Schulmerich. One of the points of contention that caused the two to separate was an incident in Pittsburgh. Bigelow had drafted a plan for a traditional carillon for the East Liberty Presbyterian Church, a church with a tower that was very well suited to a carillon. Due to technical problems during installation, the foreseen budget was exceeded, and Schulmerich used the opportunity to sell the church a cheaper Americana. After this, Bigelow concentrated on consulting work for traditional carillons, and conducted experiments on small bells in partnership with colleague engineers at the School of Engineering in Princeton. In 1961, this research resulted in the comprehensive study *The Acoustically Balanced Carillon: Graphics and the Design of Carillons and Carillon Bells*, in which he advised improving the sonority of the smallest carillon bells by strongly reinforcing their walls and striking them with a heavier clapper.

Until the Second World War, North America was familiar with European carillon culture only through English carillons and Belgian carillonneurs. After the war, it also got to know Dutch carillon culture. The most important Dutch project of the 1950s was the Netherlands Carillon, a gift of the Dutch people to the American nation in gratitude for American support during and after the war. A new carillon was intended to be a shining example of the friendship between the two countries. The initiative was enthusiastically received by the Dutch people, and in April 1952, Queen Juliana visited Washington to symbolically hand over a first bell to President Truman. Since the instrument was intended to be an example of Dutch craftsmanship, the order for the 49 bells was given to the three Dutch bell-founders, which each separately would cast a number of bells according to the Hemony profile. The bells were given the names of the Dutch provinces and the social groups that had contributed to financing the instrument. The carillon was hung in a temporary tower in West Potomac Park in 1954, and in 1960, it received a permanent home in an open tower at one of the most symbolic places in the USA: Arlington Cemetery. 300,000 dead from many wars lie next to a number of famous Americans, including the Kennedy brothers. The politically inspired decision to distribute the order among three bell-founders had unpleasant musical consequences, so that the Netherlands Carillon did not represent the best of Dutch bell casting. Only after a thorough restoration and retuning of the bells in 1995 were the dead at Arlington granted harmony and peace.

From the beginning of the 1950s, instruments by Van Bergen and Petit & Fritsen had found their way to the United States. Petit & Fritsen delivered its most important carillons in 1960. It installed an instrument with 77 bells in Kirk in the Hills, a church in Bloomfield Hills, Michigan, which became the most extensive carillon in the world. In Springfield, Illinois, Petit & Fritsen installed a carillon in a new tower at Washington Park, a perfect environment for listening to carillon recitals and concerts. The tower and carillon were installed according to the last will and testament of newspaper publisher Thomas Rees who died in 1933. Emigrated Flemish organist Raymond Keldermans became the instrument's carillonneur and a yearly carillon festival was launched. Eijsbouts would deliver his first American carillon only at the end of the 1960s.

Many North American carillons functioned in religious and educational settings, and as a result included a spiritual dimension that did not exist or had disappeared in Europe. The instruments found a congenial environment in parks and university

The participants of the congress in Ottawa where the Guild of Carillonneurs in North America was founded on 3 September 1936. Percival Price is sitting second right.

campuses, which usually were located outside the busier parts of the city. Most carillons were a pleasure to listen to: their tuning was pure and they had a long decay that could best be appreciated in a quiet listening environment. American carillonneurs realized the pure beauty of this new musical instrument, and an American carillon movement emerged.

The American carillon movement

The roots of the American carillon movement go back to the 1930s. On the 3rd and 4th of October 1934, eleven carillonneurs and twenty family members and supporters gathered at Trinity College in Hartford, Connecticut.[240] Carillonneurs who lived hundreds of miles apart got to know one another and for the first time debated the type of music that was best played on the carillon. Two years later, the Guild of Carillonneurs in North America was founded in Ottawa, Canada.[241] At the time, American carillonneurs still teetered between the urge to renew, and respect for the Mechelen tradition to which most of them were indebted. After the Second World War, the balance resolutely shifted in favor of innovation. With the death of Jef Denyn in 1941 and his great admirer William Gorham Rice in 1945, two icons of the Mechelen tradition disappeared, and the self-awareness of the American carillonneurs grew. The major driving force behind the American carillon movement was Percival Price, who held the first campanology chair in history at the University of Michigan.

In 1947, Price wrote the article 'The Elements of Carillon Music' in the *Bulletin of the Guild of Carillonneurs in North America*. He stated that it was possible to discover the qualities of a carillon only if you were aware of its disadvantages – *like bringing out the beauty of a woman*, he added. And he considered himself and his colleague carillonneurs lucky, because contrary to the players of instruments for which an extensive repertoire had already been written, they played a new instrument whose musical abilities were yet to be fully explored.[242] Price himself would not make full use of these possibilities. His compositions focused on simplicity, transparency and the avoidance of dissonances, and thus indicated only one possible direction in writing music for the carillon. The carillon world needed a composer who dared to take the offensive in order to make the very best of the bell's rich sound palette, including the mood-inducing power of their dissonances. This would have to wait for an encounter between a composer with a sense for adventure and a carillonneur who was able to show him the way. This encounter took place on the campus of the University of Kansas in Lawrence.

In 1951, 24-year old Ronald Barnes was appointed as the university's carillonneur. As carillonneur, Barnes was largely self-taught, but given his daily playing duties at the university, he quickly expanded his repertoire. A year after Barnes' appointment, Roy Hamlin Johnson arrived at the campus as piano teacher. The two musicians got to know one another, and Johnson became fascinated by the sound possibilities of the Taylor bells that sounded so lavishly throughout the campus. In 1956, Johnson composed *Summer Fanfares* for his colleague. Barnes played it at the congress of the Guild of Carillonneurs in North America which was held at his university later that same year. Carillon music like none heard before sounded throughout the campus. The piece

began very softly with a motif of thick chords that calmly moved up and down, creating a cloud of sound. Suddenly vivid fanfare motifs appeared, like ink stains on a plain canvas. The new motif increased in frequency and announced an approaching marching band. The fanfare motif was repeated at an increasing rate, first softly in the smaller bells, then louder in the middle register, always accompanied by the swaying starting motif, which could now be heard in the bass bells. Seven heavy clusters in the bass bells announced the departure of the marching band. The starting motif returned in the middle register and the music dissolved as it were into thin air. *Summer Fanfares* made a huge impression on the congress participants. The piece contained almost all the elements on which the great American carillon repertoire of the last decades has been built. Repetitions of simple motifs are framed in the minimalist and repetitive music trends of the time, but also recall the obsessive repetition of swinging bells; chords and melodies include intervals of minor thirds in order to achieve maximum overlap of the partial notes and thus maximum consonance; sharp dissonances are often composed of superimposed minor thirds, so that they sound surprisingly harmonious; soft dissonant harmonies on the other hand provide an impressionistic effect; extreme changes in volume create a dramatic mood and hold the listeners' attention; and the long decay of the heavy English bells immerses the music in a soothing bath of sounds. Johnson would later expand his style with transparent polyphony. He would also use the melodiousness of the bass bells in stately pedal melodies under a fast-paced accompaniment in the smaller bells. His most important later works are *Sonata for Carillon*, *Fantasy for Carillon* and *Carillon Book for the Liturgical Year*. Johnson and several other composers who worked in Kansas, including John Pozdro and Gary White, often wrote their melodies using the octatonic scale. This consists of a sequence of whole and half tones, which produces many harmonies of one and one-half tones and thus maximum consonance with the minor-third partial note of the bells.

The new American music was the antithesis of the music heard in Mechelen and other Flemish cities. While many Mechelen pieces began with a rhetorical, toccata-like opening movement in order to grab the attention of the audience for the tremolo playing that followed, American carillon music often emerged from silence, and only swelled to full power during the course of the piece. It was no accident that many American carillon works bear impressionistic titles such as *Landscape* (John Pozdro), *Image* (Emilien Allard), *Emanations* (Gary White), *Pastel in Bronze* (Albert Gerken), *Reflection* (Robert Byrnes) and variants on these. The Americans avoided tremolo playing for the same reason as the conservative Dutch carillonneurs at the beginning of the 20th century, i.e. in order to do justice to the natural sound of the bell. The American carillonneurs, however, had better reasons for doing so than their earlier Dutch colleagues: the long decay of heavy modern bells worked well in a quiet listening environment and did not need to be filled in with tremolo playing. American carillon music, perhaps unknowingly, borrows several stylistic elements from the carillon music of the 17th and 18th centuries. In many American hymn arrangements, the original melody is initially presented in its simplicity, just as two centuries earlier in Danzig, Joachim Eggert began his arrangements of Lutheran chorales with the monophonic, unembellished melody. The rapid harmonious figures in the small bells as accompaniment to pedal motifs in turn were similar to the virtuoso passages in the carillon preludes by Matthias Vanden Gheyn.

Ronald Barnes not only caused others to start composing. He himself composed an extensive oeuvre that was both of high quality and accessible, and that forms the backbone of the American carillon repertoire until today. Barnes explored all styles, felt equally at home in Neo-Baroque and Impressionism, and often used the traditional suite or serenade form as a recognizable model. With his imaginative approach, he transformed folk songs and religious melodies into genuine carillon music. Barnes had a keen interest in history, and published studies on the carillon music of Theodoor de Sany, Matthias Vanden Gheyn and André Dupont. After his stay at the University of Kansas, he was appointed carillonneur at Washington National Cathedral and then at the University of California at Berkeley. He took over the role of ageing Percival Price as godfather of the American carillon. Barnes advocated a lyrical playing style that contrasted with the toccata technique of many European carillonneurs. Despite his interest in and appreciation for the European roots of his instrument, he became the driving force behind a self-assured American carillon movement that considered the carillon as a pure concert instrument and that gave artistic integrity absolute priority over easy success by the masses. The forestroke did not fit this artistic approach and thus the new American concert carillons did not have them. American carillonneurs distanced themselves from the European carillon tradition that still bore the marks of the social circumstances in which they developed and that often had to do with the less homogeneous carillons that emerged over a period of several centuries.

The prototype American concert carillonneur was Daniel Robins, a student of Ronald Barnes. After exploring monastic life and the army, Robins opted in the end for a career as carillonneur. In 1960, he was the first American to be awarded a diploma at the Dutch carillon school in Amersfoort. In the same year, he was appointed full-time carillonneur for the Rockefeller carillon at the University of Chicago. Robins presented himself to the 1961 congress of the Guild of Carillonneurs in North America held in Culver, Indiana. In the pouring rain, he astonished his colleagues with a performance of Bach's *Chaconne for Solo Violin* and an extremely difficult composition of his own with the misleading title *Five Short Pieces*. Robins took his task as performing musician very seriously, and saw himself as the 'Segovia of the carillon'. Just as the Spanish guitar virtuoso had lifted the guitar from the context of folklore, he would elevate the carillon to a full-fledged concert instrument. He reacted against the European concept that the carillon was a folk instrument ('the only true folk instrument in the twentieth century is television') and he was opposed to the programming of popular music on the carillon ('we must select music which will dignify the instrument, rather than trying to dignify trivia with its performance on the carillon').[243] Robins studied hard, reportedly until his hands bled, performed concerts in a tuxedo, and introduced innovations such as carillon music combined with fireworks, and carillon in concert with brass and percussion instruments. However, he was unable to keep his artistic ambitions alive and eventually lost his way. He was dismissed by the university in 1969, and took his life a year later.

The congresses organized each year by the Guild of Carillonneurs in North America played an important role in establishing the North American carillon movement. Since American carillonneurs lived throughout the continent, they had less contact with each other than their European colleagues. Hence, the congresses were the ideal occasions to listen to each other's concerts and exchange experiences with colleague-carillonneurs, composers and carillon makers. During the congress at the University of Michigan in 1962, Percival Price and Arthur Bigelow were asked to develop a North American standard for carillon keyboards. At the congress held at Princeton in 1966, a standard was established that most closely resembled the views of Price. The most important characteristics of the standard were an expanded pedal board of 2.5 octaves that did not begin with B flat or C as was the case in Europe, but with low G. The keys of the manual were slightly farther apart than those in Europe, their key travel was less, and the position between manual and pedal board was different. With this, the differences in playing style between American and European carillonneurs also became visible in the keyboard: American carillonneurs leaned backward in front of their keyboard, as if sitting in a chair; their European colleagues bent forward over the keyboard, ready to assault it and become one with the instrument.

Details of the American standard were fine-tuned in the following years, and the standard was updated in 1970 and in 1981.

Belgian influence across the Atlantic Ocean decreased further as the generation of North American carillonneurs educated in Mechelen became smaller. Bigelow had died, and Lefévere settled back in Belgium after his retirement from Riverside. Robert Donnell (Peace Tower, Ottawa), Frederick Marriott (Kirk in the Hills), Wendell Westcott (Michigan State University) and James Lawson (New York) remained faithful to the musical legacy of their masters Denyn and Nees, but the tone was set by a new generation of carillonneurs that was educated by American colleagues. The most important of these were Albert Gerken, the successor to Barnes at the University of Kansas, and Milford Myhre, who succeeded Anton Brees at Lake Wales in 1967.

Acid rain in Europe

The accomplishments of the young American carillon culture did not penetrate to Belgium, where the influence of the Mechelen carillon school continued to hold sway. In 1961, the Mechelen carillon movement experienced a last great moment with the performance of *Het Bronzen Hart*, an oratorio for soloists, choir, orchestra and carillon by Gaston Feremans. Het Bronzen Hart or The Bronze Heart is a musical glorification of St. Rumbold's Tower, its carillon and its carillonneur. Folk life at the base of St. Rumbold's Tower is depicted in eight colorful scenes. The seventh scene is an impressive fugue for carillon and orchestra based on the name 'Staf Nees'. The oratorio premiered at the Mechelen vegetable market hall under the direction of Staf Nees, and several months later the composer himself directed a triumphant performance in the Palace for Fine Arts in Brussels on the occasion of the hundredth anniversary of the birth of Jef Denyn.

Feremans' grand ode to the carillon of St. Rumbold's Tower could not hide the reality that the glory of the instrument as the best carillon in the world had faded considerably. Outside Belgium, the short decay time and out-of-tune bells of the famous carillon were openly written about. In 1944, Rotterdam city carillonneur Ferdinand Timmermans ascribed the instrument's enchantment to especially the magic of his former teacher Jef Denyn: 'And the wonder is that, as soon as the carillon was played by Mr. Denyn, you forgot you were listening to bells that were out-of-tune; they no longer mattered, since you were completely taken up in the very distinct and unique mood of carillon music.'[244] And in 1949, Percival Price wrote somewhat ironically that the bells of the Mechelen carillon made him think of old women who each had their own personality. They suffered from shortness of breath, a defect that could be resolved by tremolo style playing. He concluded that the venerable carillon was best used for the music for which it was best suited: you wouldn't ask your old grandmother to play a game of baseball, would you?[245]

In Belgium, the taboo concerning the Mechelen carillon was only broken on 15 May 1964, when the newspaper *De Standaard* headlined: 'Grimbergen gets purest sounding carillon in Europe' and 'Mechelen carillon is out of tune...'. It all started with the announced inauguration of a new carillon by Horacantus in the abbey tower of Grimbergen on 24 May to replace the Michiels carillon from 1929. The bells of the new instrument reportedly were so accurately tuned that for the first time, bells had been created that were completely free of beating. In the article, Fr. Jan Feyen, Grimbergen carillonneur and former student of Staf Nees, called the Mechelen carillon completely out of tune and predicted that from now on, carillon lovers would no longer go to Mechelen, but to Grimbergen. And as proof, he added that Staf Nees had made the carillon recording of the fugue from *Het Bronzen Hart* not on his own St. Rumbold's carillon, but on the modern carillon at Lokeren. Staf Nees was not pleased with the story and initially refused to play at the inauguration in Grimbergen. Two days after the inauguration, *De Standaard* published an interview with the Mechelen city carillonneur. He explained that each historical carillon could lose at most one thirtieth of a tone of its purity, a difference that could scarcely be heard by the naked ear, and that it was much more important how and by whom a carillon was played. Fr. Feyen attended the interview and contritely agreed with the words of the master.

Fr. Feyen was the first who dared say out loud what many felt. The weaknesses of the St. Rumbold's carillon had been camouflaged for years by the inspired playing of Denyn and Nees, who knew the qualities and weaknesses of the Mechelen carillon well and adapted their interpretations to them. Objectively, however, the famous instrument was indeed out of tune, and the confrontation with the ever more numerous purely tuned carillons by Dutch makers made this all too clear. There were various reasons for the failures of the famous instrument. The St. Rumbold's carillon was made up of bells from twelve bell-founders cast over a period of 450 years, and thus it did not sound homogeneous. The 27 bells by Pieter Hemony, which made up the heart of the bell series, did not sound optimum and presumably were not the best that Hemony had ever cast. The continuous dripping of water from the hammers on the surface of the bells had made cavities in many of them, which resulted in the sound having numerous beats. And there was yet another cause that was discovered in the Netherlands.

There had been concern in the Netherlands since the 1950s about the historical carillons of the Hemonys. Disruptive impurities were heard, chiefly in the smallest bells. Moreover, the overall sound of some Hemony instruments tended to be dull. Was the genius of the Stradivarii of the carillon rated too highly and did this only become clear when confronted with the pure and rich sounding modern carillons? Or was something else going on? The answer came from André Lehr.[246] At the beginning of the 1950s he had analyzed the tuning of the Hemony carillons at 's-Hertogenbosch and Amersfoort with a view toward their restoration by Eijsbouts. He proposed the hypothesis that the detunings had occurred recently and that they were caused by acid rain. Acid rain is the result of the intensive use of fossil fuels such as petroleum and especially coal. When incinerated, the sulfur present in fuels is converted to sulfur dioxide or SO_2. When this is released into the atmosphere and mixed with oxygen, sulfur trioxide or SO_3 is produced. In a moist climate such as that of the Low Countries, sulfur trioxide quickly binds with water, producing sulfuric acid or H_2SO_4. Together with precipitation, sulfuric acid returns to earth in the form of what is usually called acid rain. A high concentration of sulfuric acid has disastrous consequences for bell bronze. In a first phase, a patina forms on the bell wall that inhibits the free vibration of the bronze and makes the bell sound shorter and duller. While the patina layer protects the bronze from further corrosion, as the patina becomes thicker, it tends to flake off. The erosion process is put in motion by the constant vibrations that occur when the bell is tolled or played. The bronze skin becomes thinner, the pitch of the bell lowers and it also becomes out of tune with itself since the separate partial notes do not lower in pitch at the same rate. Lehr called his hypothesis the *corrosion theory* and based it on three observations. In the first place, the damage to the bells was clearly visible to the naked eye. Light green spots could be seen on the bronze and flaking occurred at a number of places. For that matter, the same phenomenon could clearly be seen on bronze statues. The corrosion theory also explained why the smallest bells dropped the farthest in pitch. With a constant level of contamination in absolute units over an entire carillon, percentually, the small bells are affected the worst. In extreme cases, the pitch of small bells dropped up to one fourth of a tone. Finally, sound analyses by André Lehr pointed out that not all historical carillons had suffered equally. The Hemony carillons at Amersfoort, Kampen and Utrecht still sounded relatively pure, while the Amsterdam instruments were strongly affected by the big city's pollution.

The commission set up to guide the restoration of Hemony carillons in Amsterdam did not believe in the corrosion theory. According to it, the bells were still in the condition that Hemony had intended, thus any attempt to correct the pitch was out of the question. Retuning by turning would result in further damage to the valuable Hemony bells. If there was a desire to eliminate the impurities in tone, the commission even preferred replacing the smaller bells in Hemony carillons with new ones, so that the large bells would be saved without being retuned. The smaller bells could then serve as museum pieces. This vision was followed in the early Hemony carillon restorations. In 1959, the bells of the Munt, West and South Towers were cleaned, so that they regained their previous lively sound, but they were not retuned. In the West Tower, the Hemony bells most in need of tuning were replaced by new bells, leaving only 14 Hemony bells hanging in the carillon. In 1964 and 1965, most of the Hemony bells in the Palace and the Old Church were replaced, so that respectively only 9 and 14 Hemony bells remained. An important side effect of these measures was that the weak sounding high bells of Hemony were replaced by powerfully sounding bells with a heavy profile. Only around 1970 did the insights of the government and advisory commissions change, and was the retuning of historical bells considered an acceptable method of restoration. The further turning of the bells indeed resulted in an additional thinning of the walls and an overall decrease in the carillon's pitch, but the technique did restore the original mean tone temperament of the Hemony bells and thus returned them to their full glory. This new principle was applied to the restoration of the city carillon in Antwerp in 1972, where Eijsbouts under the direction of André Lehr retuned the carillon, while retaining all 36 Hemony bells.

Acid rain formed a new threat to the carillon. Bronze appeared not to be as indestructible as previously thought, and corroded bronze – brought to vibration by the playing of music – threatened to become ever thinner. Consequently, in the long term, the carillonneurs in the polluted cities of the Low Countries would literally play their bells to death. Out-of-tune bells could not continually be retuned since each retuning would further thin the bell wall. And adding bronze to increase the pitch was not technically feasible. Fortunately, the quality of the atmosphere improved significantly after 1965, especially due to the replacement of coal by natural gas as raw material for heating, and due to stricter standards concerning the amount of sulfur allowed in petroleum products. Moreover, if needed, bells could be protected by a regular treatment with an anti-corrosion product.

Using the computer

Along with the restoration work, the number of new carillons in the Netherlands increased. And even after the war damage had been repaired, the market continued to be an attractive one for the Dutch bell-founders. Van Bergen was unable to keep up with the increased activity of his two competitors, and the foundry was converted into a bell museum in 1980. Petit & Fritsen combined the craftsmanship built up over generations with the accurate tuning of its bells and delivered reliable quality. It was the most successful exporter of Dutch carillons in the 1950s and 1960s. Under the impetus of his bell expert André Lehr, Eijsbouts experimented regularly with the tuning and action of carillons, and specialized in restoration projects. During these restorations, old bells, keyboards and mechanical drums were given by their owners to the bell-founder. Old bells were no longer simply thrown into the bell-founder's furnace, and Eijsbouts acquired a collection of historical objects that formed the basis of a national carillon museum that

Restoration project of the carillon of the Royal Palace in Amsterdam opened in Asten in 1969. André Lehr became the museum's curator and wrote important articles and books on diverse aspects of bells, carillons and clocks.

Starting in the 1960s, things went less well for the Belgian bell-founders. The post-war demand for new bells had been met, and the Dutch bell-founders had established themselves in the Belgian market. Overwhelmed by financial and private problems, Marcel Michiels attempted suicide in 1962 and died a short while later. Eijsbouts and Petit & Fritsen purchased the foundry with the aim of jointly continuing its activities under the name *M. Michiels Successeurs*. This undertaking failed, and Eijsbouts sold his share to Petit & Fritsen in 1963, which halted casting activities in Tournai a short time later. The foundry's archives were moved to the Municipal Archives in Helmond. After the demise of the once successful Michiels foundry, only the Leuven-based company of François Sergeys and his son Jacques remained in Belgium. Sergeys primarily cast swinging bells, but after the death of Michiels, the company also produced or restored a number of carillons. The copper, tin and beeswax for finishing the false bells were imported from Congo, and many finished bells returned to Congo, where their sound aided in the spread of the Catholic faith in the rain forest. In the end, the Sergeys foundry would also not survive the competition with the more efficient Dutch bell-founders. The closure by Jacques Sergeys of his foundry in 1980 marked the end of the craft of bell casting in Belgium. It also marked the end of one of the most impressive artisanal dynasties in history. For nearly five centuries, descendants of Willem Van den Ghein – under the names Vanden Gheyn, Van Aerschodt and Sergeys – had written bell and carillon history in Flanders and beyond. Fortunately, many of their carillons continue to play, such as the old and headstrong Van den Ghein instrument in Arnemuiden that we encountered several times in this book. After the war, its false sounds again began to annoy the local residents of the Amsterdam Rijksmuseum. In 1963, it was replaced by a new Petit & Fritsen instrument and moved back to its original location. Since then, the sounds of former times again float over the small Zeeland city of Arnemuiden.

In Mechelen, the realization grew that the sound of former times that came from St. Rumbold's was hurting the reputation of the City on the Dijle as world center for the carillon, and the problem was openly discussed for the first time under new director Piet van den Broek. The Mechelen city government decided not to retune the carillon on which Jef Denyn had celebrated his triumphs, and that a new instrument would be installed above the existing carillon. Initially a medium-sized carillon was contemplated, but in the end the choice was made for a 40-ton carillon based on F, thus a half tone lower than its predecessor. This would become the heaviest carillon in Europe – except for the instruments in Mafra – and the St. Rumbold's Tower would house a total of 75 tons of bronze. A new Eijsbouts instrument was installed in the bell-chamber at the top. The old carillon was installed – ready to play – one floor lower, and received the status of museum exhibit. A tower with two carillons was unique in the modern age, and during the inauguration on 17 September 1981, Belgian King Baudouin and Queen Fabiola climbed the 440 steps to try a couple of notes on the new instrument. After an interruption of more than twenty years, the automatic mechanism was put back into service and the new carillon again accompanied the passage of time, day and night. The twenty-year period of silence, however, had left its marks on the population and numerous complaints reached town hall concerning the noise at night. Under pressure from the *vox populi*, the city government limited to daytime the music played every 15 minutes. In most other cities, for that matter, nighttime carillon playing had already been eliminated, often at the insistence of hotel owners who received complaints from their guests. Surprisingly enough, not everyone in Mechelen was thrilled with the new bells. Some residents could not or would not adapt to the pure but somewhat neutral timbre of the new carillon. There was nostalgia for the colorful old sounds that had long been a part of the city's history. The charm of imperfection was cherished, and it was even alleged that the new carillon was tuned 'too precisely' and that it was a soulless product of the computer. The reactions of the Mechelen residents in the face of their new carillon illustrates the – difficult to understand for outsiders – attachment of a population to the imperfect but safe sounds with which they grew up and were familiar.

The allegation that carillons were designed by computer was not totally unfounded. Since the 1970s, researchers at the Eindhoven University of Technology had been working with André Lehr to design bell profiles using the computer. The aim was a concrete bell profile that allowed for the perfect sound. In 1985, Lehr and engineer Bert Schoofs had advanced far enough to realize a long-cherished dream: a major-third bell.[247] As described earlier, the bell's third partial note is normally a minor third. This partial gives bells a somewhat melancholic character, even when playing cheerful music. This was one of the obstacles to musicians accepting the carillon as a 'classical' musical instrument. All other musical instruments in fact could produce a major third, albeit only as the fifth partial. It was expected that major-third bells would not only sound more cheerful, they would also better lend themselves to playing together with other instruments.

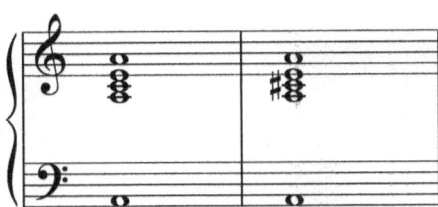

Lowest five partial notes of a minor-third bell   Lowest five partial notes of a major-third bell

A major-third bell of the first generation

In order to replace the melancholic minor third by a bright-sounding major third, the third partial note had to be raised by a half note, without this disrupting the other partial notes. This was easier said than done, because the minor third was, as it were, built into the elegant bell shape that we have known since the late Middle Ages. Thus it was only logical that it was a part of the ideal series of partial notes that nobleman Jacob van Eyck had established for the Hemonys in 1644. In the 19th century, bell-founders in Germany, England and Belgium had attempted to cast bells with a major third, but the result was always at the expense of the purity of the other partial notes. Computer technology, however, opened up new possibilities. Lehr and Schoofs were convinced that if a pure major-third bell was possible, its design would come from the computer. Before the computer was allowed to do its work, research was done concerning how the public would react to a major-third bell. The Institute for Perception Research of the Eindhoven University of Technology set up a test environment with simulated major and minor-third bells. A song in a major-third scale was played with traditional minor-third bells and with major-third bells. This was repeated using a melody written in a minor-third scale. As expected, the test group of carillonneurs reacted conservatively: they preferred the traditional bells for both melodies. The judgment of professional musicians who were not carillonneurs followed musical logic: they preferred minor-third bells for the melody in a minor-third scale, and vice versa. The non-musical public liked the major-third bells better for both melodies. This was reason enough for André Lehr and Eijsbouts to proceed with the development of the revolutionary bell. Perhaps the search for the ideal bell had now reached its terminus and the carillon could definitively take its place in the pantheon of classical musical instruments. In March 1985, the computer performed its calculations, and on the screen appeared a bell with a shape never before seen: a pronounced bulge could be seen at the middle of its waist. Eijsbouts first produced a mobile carillon as demonstration instrument. The instrument was heard for the first time by the carillon public from 5 to 8 July 1986 during the World Carillon Congress at the University of Michigan. The reactions were predominantly negative. Carillonneurs and carillon lovers, who for all of their lives had listened to the typical sound of the minor-third bell, heard all sorts of strange harmonies in the new type of bell. The bells had a shorter decay time due probably to their more complex shape, and the larger versions reminded people of electronic bells due to their less prominent strike note. Their case was also not helped by their shape: the public spoke scornfully of Coca-Cola bells. Undoubtedly, in addition to the visible and audible elements, a built in conservatism also played a role in the rejection of the new bell: i.e., a possible breakthrough by a major-third bell would make all carillons with traditional bells old-fashioned and unattractive. Consequently, the commercial success of the new bell was limited, and Eijsbouts sold his first major-third carillon to the city of Deinze only in 1988. A second order followed in 1990 from California. In Garden Grove, not far from Los Angeles, stood Crystal Cathedral, a church with glass exterior walls and a tower of tubes in stainless steel that reflected the sunlight like a prism. Crystal Cathedral was established by televangelist Robert H. Schuller. For the tower, Schuller purchased a carillon that he called the Arvella Schuller carillon in honor of his wife. The bells with the optimistic major thirds no doubt were in harmony with the messages of positive thinking preached to visitors of Crystal Cathedral.

André Lehr and Bert Schoofs were not discouraged by the negative reactions to their major-third bell. In a following research phase, they limited the freedom of the computer, requiring it to perform its optimizations within the straitjacket of the traditional bell profile. This worked well, and in 1990 a major-third bell without a bulge in its waist emerged from the mold. It also demonstrated a greater audible similarity with the minor-third bell. However, commercial success again did not follow, and only the University of Groningen allowed itself to be seduced into purchasing a second generation major-third carillon in 1996. Thus the major-third bell did not become the new standard, but the experiment cannot be labeled a failure. It indeed showed that the computer could be an important tool in designing bell profiles. More than ever, carillon buyers could be offered customization, and in recent years – thanks to the computer – bell series were deliberately created with partial notes that deviated somewhat from the ideal of the beat-free carillon. Light, slow beating was again accepted as a tasteful embellishment that gave the sound of the bell extra character. For the first time, impure tuning was the result not of ignorance, but of a deliberate sound ideal.

In the meantime, the computer has also been put to use in the automatic carillon. Since the 1950s, the expensive mechanical drums in the towers have been succeeded by less bulky means of storing musical data. First, experiments were conducted with metal plates containing small pins. This system was quickly abandoned, among others because the music could only be changed by replacing the plates. Then systems with punched tapes were used for a time. Instead of inserting pins on a drum, the carillonneur programmed the musical information by punching holes in a plastic tape. When the forestroke was required to play, the punched tape turned, and each time a hole passed an electric contact, an electrical circuit was closed. An electromagnet was charged and pulled the handle of a hammer, which catapulted it in the direction of the bell. The punched tape system was very efficient for the carillonneur: all that was needed to change the music was to switch punched tapes, and once the carillonneur had enough pre-programmed tapes available, he could simply reuse existing programs. However, the system was not well suited to the damp conditions present in carillon towers. Presently carillons are played automatically using a memory card and electronic clock. The carillonneur enters the music in MIDI format using a PC

The first carillon keyboard according to the North European standard
(University Library Leuven, 1983)

application or a keyboard, and the hammers accurately respond to the programmed commands. Compared to the falling hammers of the old carillon drums, the forestrokes with electromagnetic hammers generally sound hard and aggressive. To remedy this, experiments are presently being conducted with touch-sensitive hammers or with pneumatic applications driven by the baton keyboard.

The keyboards and mechanisms also evolved. In the Netherlands, the distance between manual and pedal board grew to accommodate the increasingly larger carillonneurs. In Belgium the Mechelen measurements – tailored to the small stature of Jef Denyn – were retained for a time. Nevertheless, the need for standardization increased, and on 7 October 1983 members of the Belgian Carillon Guild and the Dutch Carillon Association met in Leuven to sign the protocol for a North European keyboard standard. The keyboard of the restored Leuven university carillon was the first application of the new standard. Later Denmark and France also joined in accepting the North European keyboard standard.

There was a high degree of uniformity in the carillon action: all new carillons used the tumbler system. When the bells hung in rows next to each other, the tumbler axes advocated by Denyn were installed, and when the bells were distributed throughout the bell-chamber, use was made of separate tumblers oriented to the bells. In 1972, however, a Dutch carillon was again equipped with the – then so controversial – broek system. This was not an attempt to blow new life into the old Dutch system at the expense of the tumbler system. Rather, in line with the increasing interest in performing old music on authentic instruments, a reconstruction was made of a 17th century carillon in the Bakenesser Tower in Haarlem. A Hemony carillon had once hung there that was sold by the city government for scrap in 1795. When 24 Hemony bells from the restoration of the carillon at St. Bavo Church came free in 1972, these were hung in the Bakenesser Tower and connected with a broek system to a copy of a 17th century keyboard. There was little interest in the experiment: the carillon world was not yet ripe for the new trend of performing old music on authentic instruments.

In 1995, a more interesting reconstruction took place in Amsterdam. The Hemony carillon in the Amsterdam South Tower was equipped with a broek system and a copy of the extant original keyboard. The intervention was controversial, but on the other hand could be justified in the context of Amsterdam's five Hemony carillons, four of which had a smooth, modern action. The South Tower carillon was also the only Amsterdam instrument that had retained nearly all of its Hemony bells. The project showed that keyboard batons with a long travel and a broek system required a very different playing technique than carillons equipped with the modern tumbler system. The player's fists must remain in almost continual contact with the keyboard batons in order to control the swinging wires and remain master of the musical result.[248]

The most ambitious restoration project of recent years took place between 1996 and 2000 in Amersfoort, the city where the Dutch carillon school is located.[249] The twelve treble bells that were added to the Hemony carillon in the Tower of Our Lady in 1953 were removed, reducing the number of its bells to 35, a common number for Hemony's time. The bells were equipped with wrought-iron clappers according to the weight series typical for Baroque carillons. A reconstruction of a 17th century keyboard was used and the connections were made using the broek system. To give students of the carillon school the opportunity to also play a modern carillon, a new instrument with 58 bells was ordered from Eijsbouts. This too was a special carillon, because the bells were reconstructions of bells by Cyril Johnston, considered by some as the greatest bell-founder of the 20th century. The new bells were cast based on information from Johnston's tuning manuals, and exhibit typical Johnston characteristics such as pure minor thirds and octave stretching in the small bells. They were equipped with heavy clappers with the same weight series that, after much research, was used in the carillon of Berkeley. The result was a carillon with a mild and somewhat sluggish character, a typically 'American' instrument that contrasted strongly with the lively and immediately sounding Hemony's in the same bell-chamber.

As finishing touch for the project, the German bell-founder Rincker cast seven swinging bells. These were not allowed to have the pure partial series of carillon bells, but were given a prime that was a full tone below the 'pure' prime, after the example of the greatest founder of swinging bells in history, Geert van Wou. Following the time-honored tradition, Rincker cast the bells to be in tune right out of the mold. Only two of the bells required slight retuning. The bells were sounded with the hand, but could also be chimed the old-fashioned way. Thus the Amersfoort Tower of Our Lady brought together three milestones of Western bell culture: a reconstruction of Van Wou swinging bells, a Hemony carillon in original condition, and a reconstruction of a heavy English carillon from the beginning of the 20th century. The Amersfoort tower now contains exactly 100 bells, or two more than St. Rumbold's Tower in Mechelen. It is the provisional last word in a rivalry between North and South across 500 years of carillon history, a battle that perhaps took place more in the perception of historians than in the field.

Carillon music in the East

Outside the historical heartland of the Low Countries, carillon installation has been more striking in the East than in the West in the most recent 30 years. In 1984, the instrument gained a foothold in Japan when the Flemish government donated a traveling Sergeys carillon to the Flanders Center in Osaka.[250] This Flemish cultural center was established by Flemish musicologist Robert Vliegen, who taught aspiring Japanese carillonneurs under the auspices of the Mechelen carillon school. The second carillon hangs in Itami, a suburb of Osaka and a sister city to the Flemish City of Hasselt. To seal their friendship, the two cities exchanged gifts: Hasselt received a landscaped Japanese garden and Itami received a carillon. The *furandoru no kane* or Flemish carillon is played only once per year. On the evening of 15 August, the bells pray for peace during the annual commemoration of the armistice following the Second World War.

The third Japanese carillon is located in the mountainous region of Shiga. A sanctuary is located in the pine forests of Misono that was designed by Minoru Yamasaki, the architect of the former WTC Towers in New York. The sanctuary is the headquarters of Shinji Shumeikai, a religious movement with branches throughout the world. It attaches great importance to the beauty of art and nature, and has as goal the creation of heaven on earth. And the heavenly music of a carillon fits this aspiration. The carillon tower was designed by I.M. Pei, the Chinese-American architect of the Louvre Pyramid. It is 60 meters high and constructed of white granite from Vermont. Its shape is inspired by the bachi, the plectrum with which Japanese plucked instruments are played. The followers of Shinji Shumeikai call the carillon *Joy of*

Pei's carillon tower in Misono

Angels. This attractive Eijsbouts instrument automatically plays every day at 12 noon, but for the rest is seldom used. We encounter a different Japan in the vicinity of Nagasaki. Huis ten Bosch opened a theme park there in 1992 containing reconstructions of a number of Dutch buildings, including an almost life-size replica of the Dom Tower of Utrecht. It houses a bell museum, and a mobile carillon resembling a barrel organ travels throughout the park. In addition to bells and a baton keyboard, the instrument contains two jaquemarts, a light organ and a synthesizer. In recent years carillon culture didn't expand further in Japan, and only several automatic bell instruments have found their way to the Land of the Rising Sun. In any case, the Japanese are charmed by the sound of the Western bell, which can be heard among others in its lighter music. Pop groups sometimes use a light bell series that is played with a keyboard.

Russia is also on the carillon map again, partly due to a linguistic misunderstanding. The Russian word for carillon is *malinovji zvon*, which literally means 'sweet sound' or 'pleasant sound'. The term has existed since the 16th century as a synonym for the *trezvon*, a joyous sound pattern used in the Russian Orthodox Church.[251] In Mechelen, however, the word was translated as 'Sound of Mechelen'. *Si non è vero, è bene trovato*, and a certain affinity grew between Mechelen and Russia that was encouraged by Mechelen carillon school director Jo Haazen, who speaks fluent Russian. In the 1990s, Haazen took the initiative to reinstate carillon culture in Russia. The Western carillon culture of 18th century Russia had disappeared, and only the discarded carillon of Nicolaes Derck in the Peter and Paul Cathedral still testifies to the short golden age of the carillon in the Russian tsarist empire. Haazen found hundreds of Flemish companies, institutions and individuals who were prepared to contribute financially to a new carillon for the cathedral where the tsars were buried, and in 2001 a *Flamandskii kariljon* or Flemish carillon, cast by Petit & Fritsen, was inaugurated. In 2005 a second instrument by Petit & Fritsen was inaugurated at Peterhof, the summer palace of Peter the Great. All are curious whether these instruments will mark the beginning of a wider spread of the Western carillon in this enormous country where the sound of the zvon is rooted so deeply in the local culture. A new center of carillon activity emerged not so far from St. Petersburg on the Baltic Sea: the Polish city of Gdańsk, formerly Danzig. Between 1998 and 2000, St. Catherine's Church and the city hall tower each received an Eijsbouts carillon to replace the instruments that disappeared in 1945 when the city was destroyed by the Red Army.

Since 2002, the largest carillon in the world is located in South Korea.[252] In that year, Petit & Fritsen delivered an American style memorial carillon to Hyechon College in Daejon, a city of one and a half million residents. The instrument was an initiative of Byung-I Lee, a textile manufacturer who had become acquainted with the carillon while living in the United States. He presented the school with a tower that is an enlarged copy of Hoover Tower at Stanford University, and a carillon in remembrance of his deceased mother. His mother died when she was 78 and her age became the basis for both the height of the tower and the number of carillon bells. With this number of bells, the new instrument dethroned the carillon at Kirk in the Hills as the largest carillon in the world. However, because the heaviest bell is not connected to the keyboard and only sounds the hour, the record is not undisputed. The future will tell whether the carillon will find a fertile breeding ground in West-leaning South Korea.

Let us conclude this story with an overview of the current state of carillon culture five hundred years after Jan Van Spiere first connected nine bells to a keyboard in Oudenaarde.

CHAPTER 21

Panorama of the new carillon art

The carillons of the world

Today there are approximately 640 carillons worldwide. This is five times more than in 1918, the moment in carillon history at which its number had fallen to a historic low. It is remarkable that the strongest growth has been in the last sixty years, the same period in which new music devices such as the radio, CD and mobile music players should have made the carillon superfluous. The spectacular growth of the carillon, however, occurred across a geographically limited area. Of the 29 countries where carillons can be found, only 10 possess more than four instruments, and the three 'great' carillon countries – the Netherlands, the United States and Belgium – are responsible for almost 70% of all carillons worldwide. Until now, outside its territory of origin, the carillon was only able to take root in North America. And even the popularity of the carillon in the United States must be seen in the right perspective: Lithuania, with only two carillons on its territory, in fact has more carillons per resident than the United States. If we correlate the number of carillons per country to its population or its surface area, the Netherlands and Belgium stand alone at the top of the list, with Denmark – surprisingly – in third place. The imbalance in geographical distribution becomes most clear when we conduct the following thought experiment. If we were to extrapolate the number of carillons per resident in the Netherlands and Flanders to the world's population, the number of carillons in the world would increase to 60,000, one hundred times the present number. And if we were to fill our planet with carillons at a density per mi equal to the Low Countries, we would need no less than 600,000 instruments. Thus it quickly becomes clear that after 500 years, the carillon remains an ethnic instrument that has a significant distribution only in the Netherlands and Flanders, and is still a rarity in the rest of the world. In most carillon countries, we see only small islands of intense and passionate carillon activity, without the virus spreading to other cities or regions.

The carillon has an opportunity to evolve from an ethnic instrument into a world instrument. However, its repertoire and perhaps even bell series will then need to adapt to local musical traditions.[253] It would then follow in the footsteps of that other musical instrument of Belgian origin, the saxophone. The invention by Adolphe Sax did not remain in its original context of brass bands and symphonic orchestras, but quickly received new forms of expression in jazz, klezmer music and many other genres, and it made the transition from white to black culture. Until today, the carillon landscape has remained a white phenomenon, although a project at Virginia Union University in Richmond might change this. The university was founded on the location where Lumpkin's Slave Jail once stood, an infamous holding area and place of discipline for black slaves. The historically black university is presently engaged in the project *Bells of Peace* to collect funding for the acquisition of a carillon. The institution in fact owns the Belgian carillon tower from the New York Expo in which the carillon that is now in Stanford once hung. A carillon in the middle of a black community would be a small but significant step in the further development of the instrument from the Low Countries. While the carillon developed during its first 400 years in a social context that was specific to the Low Countries, it is capable of speaking many musical languages.

Almost all carillons in the world date from the last hundred years. Only some fifty historical carillons from the 18th century or earlier still play. Belgium has twenty, and the Netherlands – which suffered fewer bell requisitions than Belgium – has approximately thirty, on the understanding that some Hemony carillons contain only a few of the original bells. Outside the Low Countries, only the Witlockx carillon of Mafra is an historic instrument playable with a baton keyboard. Only eight Belgian carillons use a programmable drum that is still in service. The Netherlands is doing much better on this point: instruments are still traditionally programmed by the carillonneur in some forty-five towers.[254]

The global carillon population is very heterogeneous concerning total weight of the bells, with as extremes the 100 ton carillon of Riverside Church in New York and several light 1-ton carillons. Most instruments weigh between five and seventeen tons. The number of bells also varies considerably. To be officially called a carillon, the minimum series with baton keyboard is 23 bells, but 45 to 50 bells are needed to play most of the carillon repertoire. The difference in weight between carillons means that the same music can be heard in very diverse keys. In recent years in North America, an increasing number of instruments have been installed in concert pitch. These have a standard bell series of approximately 30 tons, with a C on the keyboard connected to a bell with this same absolute pitch. This standardization finds its context in the American aspiration to upgrade the carillon to a full-fledged concert instrument. This facilitates the quality of concerts by guest carillonneurs since they are no longer surprised by the different pitches of unfamiliar carillons. On the other hand, this could result in a more monotone carillon landscape than is the case in the Old Country, which is a motley patchwork of the most diverse instruments in the

Carillon tower of Berlin-Tiergarten, that was given to the city by Daimler-Benz. The tower is composed of four pillars, a reminiscence to the origin of the word carillon.

most diverse towers. The newest important carillon development is the world standard for carillon keyboards. In 2000, the American carillonneur and carillon builder Richard Strauss presented a keyboard that was a compromise between the European and the American: it had the arched and radial pedal board and the shorter key travel of the American keyboard, and the smaller lateral distance between the keys of the European keyboard. At the carillon congress held in Groningen in 2008, the design of Strauss was adopted as a third standard alongside the existing European and American standards. In the meantime, Strauss keyboards were being installed on both sides of the Atlantic, generally to the great satisfaction of the local carillonneurs.

Today a few dozen bell-founders are still active worldwide. Bell-founders that cast tuned carillon bells, however, can almost be counted on one hand. The two Dutch bell-founders Eijsbouts and Petit & Fritsen are responsible for the lion's share of the market. In 2014, the two foundries merged and the production was concentrated in Asten. In France, Paccard has a strong position, and in England, the carillon tradition is upheld by the firms Taylor and Whitechapel. Olsen-Nauen of Norway casts carillons, and Meeks & Watson in the USA also casts tuned bells. In addition to the bell-founders, installation firms are active in several countries. In recent years, restoration work has expanded to include 20th-century carillons. After the Second World War, bell and keyboard frames, tumblers and wires were usually made of iron, which quickly resulted in corrosion and mechanical problems such as a heavy touch. Many of these instruments have been fully restored in the meantime using more durable materials such as wood, stainless steel, aluminum and PVC. In a number of carillons, the original small bells – the Achilles heel of many earlier bell-founders – have been replaced by more sonorous bells.

Carillon organizations

The community of carillonneurs is united in the World Carillon Federation. The idea for a global carillon organization took shape during the 1974 World Carillon Congress in Douai and was formalized four years later at the Congress in Amersfoort. In a certain sense, the WCF is the successor of the Carillon League founded by William Gorham Rice in the 1930s. The WCF, however, has broader support since it is a federation of the – presently thirteen – active national or regional carillon associations. The two oldest associations, the Dutch Carillon Association and the Guild of Carillonneurs in North America, have been mentioned earlier in this book. When the World Carillon Federation was created, the Alumni Association of the Mechelen carillon school transformed itself into the Belgian Carillonneurs' Guild and, in the wake of the Belgian state reform, split into two autonomous associations: the Vlaamse Beiaardvereniging and the Association Campanaire Wallonne. For the rest, there are certified national or regional carillon associations in France, Germany, England and Ireland, Australia and New Zealand, Scandinavia, Switzerland, Lithuania, Poland and Catalonia. The World Carillon Federation organizes an International Carillon Congress in one of its member countries or regions every three years. The programs include concerts, lectures, committee meetings as well as social and tourist activities. Most associations publish a periodical that presents an up-to-date picture of the carillon culture per region. In addition, there are a number of associations active at city level that support the carillonneur in the logistics and promotion of concerts and that develop a local network around the carillon.

There are various museums and documentation centers on the carillon located throughout the world. The largest carillon museum in the world is the Klok & Peel Museum in Asten, the Netherlands. In addition to an extensive collection of bells, chimes, clocks, keyboards and the like, it contains an extensive library, a photo archive and the archives of the Dutch Carillon Association. The Mechelen carillon school houses an extensive library and a collection of carillon-related objects. The school's archives are located in the Mechelen city archives. The Bok Tower in Lake Wales houses the Anton Brees Carillon Library, a large library that also contains the archives of the American Carillon Guild. The personal archives of Anton Brees, Arthur Bigelow, Ronald Barnes and other American carillonneurs are also preserved in Bok Tower.

Training as carillonneur can be obtained in a number of places. The Royal Carillon School 'Jef Denyn' in Mechelen remains the most sought after carillon program in the world. The carillon school has local branches in several cities. In addition, the LUCA School of Arts in Leuven, the former Lemmensinstituut, offers a master's program in the carillon. The Dutch carillon school in Amersfoort is now part of the Utrecht School of the Arts. Elsewhere in Europe there are official carillon programs in Douai, France and at the Church Music School in Løgumkloster, Denmark. In addition, local institutions or carillonneurs organize less formal training initiatives. In the United States, ten universities offer a carillon program within their academic curriculum. In 2012, the North American Carillon School was founded in Centralia, Illinois, an organization with regional offices that works closely with the Mechelen carillon school. The Guild of Carillonneurs in North America organizes a carillon examination during its annual congresses. Carillonneurs who pass, are certified as carillonneur-member of the guild. Some schools or institutes offer master classes or summer courses, and the time-honored method of individual instruction from master to apprentice is still used in some places. Carillon contests are held regularly. The most important is the Queen Fabiola International Carillon Competition in Mechelen, which began in 1987 and takes place every five years. The Dutch Carillon Association hosts a yearly competition in different Dutch cities. There are also regular one-off competitions on the occasion of jubilees and other events.

Carillonneurs and their audience

Outsiders often see the carillon as an old-fashioned instrument that requires considerable physical strength. Hence they assume that a carillonneur must be an older, somewhat tough and corpulent man. This image is seldom debunked, since carillonneurs perform their task invisibly in a tower. Mobile carillons and social media, however, allow for a more correct and nuanced view of the carillonneur. In reality, there are as many types of carillonneurs as there are types of people. The only characteristic that carillonneurs share is a layer of calloused skin on their little fingers. Since today's carillon keyboards are no longer the stiff instruments of torture they used to be, the carillon has lost much of its 'masculine' image and an increasing number of women are successfully playing the largest musical instrument in the world. In this regard, the USA is a clear trendsetter. The impressive glove-like protectors of yesteryear are no longer used, and most carillonneurs wear only a felt or leather tube on their little fingers, or play without protectors. Playing a carillon no longer requires heavy physical effort, and carillonneurs break out into a sweat only on hot summer days.

Since no entrance fee can be asked for carillon recitals and concerts, carillon events in a city depend heavily on public financing. The budgetary burden for the carillon-owner is quite limited: once it has a sufficiently-maintained instrument at its disposal, it is set for centuries and it only needs one employee to provide a large part of the city with music. The situation of carillon players varies widely. On one side of the spectrum are the pure idealists, who maintain a neglected instrument by playing it regularly, without remuneration. On the other side, there are full-time musicians with professional music training who, in addition to playing as organist or pianist, are also carillonneurs, sometimes as employee of the city, sometimes self-employed. In cities with a long carillon tradition, the present carillonneur is approximately thirtieth in a line of carillon players. Only a limited number of carillonneurs in the world earn a living only from playing the carillon. Several American carillons include a full-time carillonneur, usually financed with the interest on the fund with which the instrument was built. In Belgium and the Netherlands, a limited number of carillonneurs are able to build a full-time career by combining multiple instruments. Combining multiple carillon jobs means that carillonneurs can focus full time on arranging and practicing new carillon music, which benefits the quality of the carillon playing. On the other hand, carillonneurs working in multiple cities find it more difficult to develop the social network at all of their workplaces needed to promote the instrument. A few places have a carillonneurs' collective. At Yale University, for example, students come together under the auspices of the Yale University Guild of Carillonneurs and educate one another in the art of carillon playing.

Carillon performances are of two types: recitals and concerts. Recitals usually last an hour and continue the tradition of the performances that have been held for five centuries on fixed days of the week. They take place during the weekly market, during special evenings when the stores are open, or at a time that suits the schedule of the carillonneur. In most cities, the carillonneur plays one or two recitals per week, significantly less than during the *ancien regime*. Some locations have playing schedules that differ from the norm. At UC Berkeley, for example, the carillonneur and his assistants perform three short ten-minute recitals every day. During the recitals, the carillonneur is playing for an invisible audience of passers-by in the city or on campus. They in turn experience the music consciously or unconsciously, whistle along, are pleased or annoyed, and from time to time make their appreciation known via a note under the tower door or an e-mail message.

In addition to their regular recitals, many places organize a series of summer concerts in the tradition started by Jef Denyn in 1892. A program is usually available, and the audience is able to assemble in a quiet location to listen. Some places further pamper their audiences with a live video display of the carillon playing, a local presenter who provides commentary on the program, a lecture, or a free tour of the tower. Of course the concert is also free of charge. Yet seldom are the audiences attending a special summer concert large, and a concert attended by one hundred people is considered to be a major success. The time of Denyn is long gone. Occasionally, however, charismatic and virtuoso carillonneurs appear who revive the spirit of Denyn. In the 1960s and 1970s, Jaap van der Ende assembled an extensive circle of friends around the Eijsbouts carillon of the Church of Our Lady in Dordrecht. He was a pioneer among others in the programming of complete suites of Bach, piano music by Chopin and organ work by Max Reger. In the same period, young virtuoso Jo Haazen attracted the attention of the citizens of Antwerp with refreshing and sparkling carillon playing on the Hemony carillon of the Antwerp Cathedral. The Antwerp Monday evening concerts became a mass phenomenon, and thousands listened in silence to the music emanating from the gothic tower. Over time, the listening experience became secondary to the social happening around the concerts, and in the end, the concerts suffocated under the weight of their own success. While it is often difficult to find a location in Europe where it is possible to fully enjoy the music, many American carillons are blessed with spacious lawns or parks around the tower. Hence, carillon concerts attract hundreds of listeners at various locations. They take up their places in lawn chairs or on blankets, while soft drinks and ice cream keep the children happy. The most important carillon festival takes place each year in June in Springfield, Illinois.

The mediocre interest by the public in traditional carillon concerts has caused carillonneurs to engage in musical experiments, referred to with the collective term *Carillon Plus*. Since most concert carillons have four or more octaves, the carillon can be used for duets. In various countries, duos are exploring the possibilities of the carillon for duet playing, and gradually a repertoire is developing for this combination. Duet carillon playing makes the carillon sound fuller, and extends the range of music that can be played, since some pieces such as symphonic works and complex polyphonic music cannot be played by a single carillonneur. Some carillonneurs go even further with ensemble playing and combine the carillon with one or more other instruments. This phenomenon is not new: the carillon was widely used to accompany large singing groups already in the 19th century. At the beginning of the 20th century, Jacob Vincent played concerts with brass instruments, and in the 1930s, Jef Denyn accompanied the vocalist Edmond Verlinden, better known as the tower singer Verlini. The possibilities for ensemble playing are now explored more intensely, due in part to the availability of mobile carillons, the proper tuning of modern carillons and the capabilities of sound reproduction technology. There are combination concerts with concert bands, brass bands or hunting horns, with choir, guitar, accordion, keyboard, to mention but a few. They are performed on both mobile and tower carillons. In student cities such as Leuven, the carillon is regularly used to accompany mass activities such as student singing or a folk dance festival. Sometimes the carillon plays together with a larger totality of bells. Spanish composer Llorenç Barber organized *Conciertos de Ciudades* in various cities, in which carillon, swinging bells and other sounds play together for the entire city. New York composer Charlemagne Palestine also regularly does original things with carillon and other bell instruments. Some alternative formulas reach a very wide audience. In 2006, Maastricht carillonneur Frank Steijns playing a chamber carillon made a successful world tour with André Rieu's Johann Strauss Orchestra.

The American man in the street got to know the instrument from the Low Countries via the carillon show *Cast in Bronze* by Frank DellaPenna, who plays a mobile carillon in combination with other instruments or a recording. In his show, the carillonneur is presented as the *Spirit of the Bells*: he is dressed in a black suit and wears a golden mask in the form of a phoenix. The musician has a mission: his disguise refers to the invisible carillonneur in the historical European carillons, and he crisscrosses the States to promote and preserve the endangered instrument for future generations.

Of course there are a large number of CDs today containing carillon music. Recording carillon music is a nightmare for recording engineers and an agony for nearby residents, because a carillon cannot be confined to a recording studio. Each extraneous sound that is easily overlooked during a live recital or that provides a

Frank DellaPenna, alias *The Spirit of the Bells*

charming touch to the performance, remains an aggravating blot on a recording. For this reason, microphones are placed as closely as possible to the bells, which exaggerates the individual sound of each bell to the exclusion of the total sound, while the natural filtering of the overtones due to the distance is unable to do its work. And mixing is difficult since the decay of the bells hampers clean cut-and-paste work. A recording of course lacks the urban environment that is an integral part of appreciating the carillon. You could compare it to the less than impressive effect of fireworks on TV.

Summer concerts, Carillon Plus performances and recordings have the major advantage that they create a new and broader audience for the carillon. However, they cannot exist without the support of the weekly recitals for people on the street that remain the backbone of carillon music. There after all is still the magic of the moment, of that instant in the city when you realize that the tower is singing. The sounds mix with the conversations on the street; as you walk further, the music's intensity changes, like a game of light and shadows; the notes bend to the swell of the wind or are given extra brilliance by the silence of the evening; and you search in vain for the name of that song hidden deep inside your memory.

The diversity of carillon music

The repertoire of music especially written for the carillon increases each year. Innovative carillon work has been written in recent decades by composers who have discovered the carillon as an interesting and inspiring medium. In Belgium, among others Frans Geysen, Frédéric Devreese and Kurt Bikkembergs have written works with many repetitive elements. Carillonneur-composer Geert D'hollander continues to skillfully enrich the carillon repertoire with new work, inspired by the typical sound of bells. In the Netherlands, well known composer Henk Badings has written nine melodious and often virtuoso works. Later, composers such as Louis Andriessen and Daan Manneke surprised the carillon world with sounds never heard before. Dutch carillonneurs such as Sjef van Balkom and Jacques Maassen have also written innovative carillon music. In the United States, in addition to Ronald Barnes, carillonneurs such as Albert Gerken, John Courter, Robert Byrnes and Frank DellaPenna have made a name for themselves with captivating bell music: sometimes light and melodious, sometimes powerful, in order to demonstrate the sound of the heavier bells. Of the great composers, until now only Mauricio Kagel has written carillon music, or – to be more precise – music for the mechanical drum of the Utrecht Dom carillon. *Music for Carillon #1 to #4* by musical icon John Cage are seldom performed. It is not always clear for that matter for what type of 'carillon' this music was written. In composing *Music for Carillon #4*, Cage created the score by placing a lined transparent overlay on a star atlas.

Despite the growing amount of good music composed specifically for the carillon, 'covers' or arrangements of existing music remain the core of the repertoire. A simple rule of thumb is that music that can be easily adapted to piano or other instruments also sounds good on bells. In the classical repertoire, Baroque music is an inexhaustible source of appealing carillon music. Bach is a favorite: the performance of his *Toccata and fugue in D minor* or one of his cello suites by a skillful carillonneur guarantees a great listening experience. Viennese classical music can also be used, on the understanding that the chromatic twists and sprightly alternations between staccato and legato playing by Mozart will sound less crisp than the original on heavy bells. Romantic Lieder and simple piano works by Schubert, Schumann, Mendelssohn and Grieg are perfect for the carillon. On the other hand, the finesse of Chopin is more difficult to reproduce on bells, while some of his waltzes and mazurkas do work well. The melodious qualities of Tchaikovsky and the Russian pathos of Mussorgsky lend themselves perfectly to bells. The massive sound of late Romantic works by Wagner, Mahler and Richard Strauss in turn are to be avoided, since the bell's long decay time results in confusion. Orff's Carmina Burana on the other hand, with its percussion effects and primitivism, appears to have been written especially for bells, and American repetitive music of the 1950s and later provides interesting bell material. Thus for example, the music of Philip Glass has already been successfully arranged for bells. Hundreds of songs from more popular genres have been successfully adapted to the carillon. Film music, melodious pop songs, Latin rhythms, jazz, folk dances, eastern music, French chanson: all music with a predictable melodic character sounds good to magnificent on bells, given a good arrangement. Rock and heavy metal are less suitable, although songs by Metallica and Lady Gaga have already been convincingly played from towers.

The secret to good carillon music lies in achieving a balance between simplicity and complexity. On one hand, it must be transparent without becoming boring; and on the other hand, it must have something to say, but preferably not all at once. This balance differs for lighter and heavier carillons. The character of light carillons is similar to that of harpsichords or fortepianos. The succession of clear strike tones with only a thin decay in between, yields a pronounced plucking character. Carillonneurs who play light instruments must fill the empty space between the sounds, like decorators embellishing large surfaces with diverse ornaments. Thus they can indulge in quick and virtuoso carillon playing. Melodies are accompanied by a smooth bass line that follows the meter of the music, and often they are augmented with a fast middle voice that keeps the listener on the right rhythmic path. Light instruments are well suited to compositions from the Baroque and the Vienna classical repertoire that combine speed with a clear structure. Lively folk songs also sound wonderful on light carillons. Music for guitar, lute and harp is also especially well suited. These plucked instruments have a strong 'attack' and gentle decay, which gives them a special affinity with light carillons. Light carillons, however, often do not do justice to slow music due to the void between the notes. Tremolo playing can solve this problem in some cases. The dynamic range of light carillons is limited, which in romantic music is an obstacle to expressivity and the creation of contrasts.

Heavy carillons have a long decay and are somewhat similar to sonorous concert grand pianos with the sustain pedal always depressed. The music is wreathed in a halo of sound made up of the history of the notes just played. The melody delineates itself within this cloud of sound. When composing music for large carillons, the harmonies must be chosen such that this halo sounds harmonious and there are as few dissonances as possible in the sound texture. Heavy carillons are well suited to romantic and impressionist music, and slow, stately melodies. Arrangements of fast music must be written somewhat 'thinner' than is the case for light carillons. Otherwise the music will become blurred and confusing, and the listener will be confronted with too many notes. The ideal tempos are often slightly slower than those of light carillons.

A standard rule that applies to both light and heavy carillons is that thick chords should be avoided in order to prevent partial notes located together from colliding and clashing. Four-note chords can often be thinned out to two notes in order to make the harmonies more transparent. The same result can be obtained by arpeggiating the chords: the notes are then played in quick succession, with the top note played last. The chord can also be unraveled into several notes that are played one after the other in a regular rhythm. The sounds are then spread out in time and a continuous web of sound is created similar to guitar accompaniment. In the musical jargon this is called *diminution*. The diminution technique is well suited to the carillon: the carillonneur alternates high and low notes and changes fists, without the one needing to cross the other.

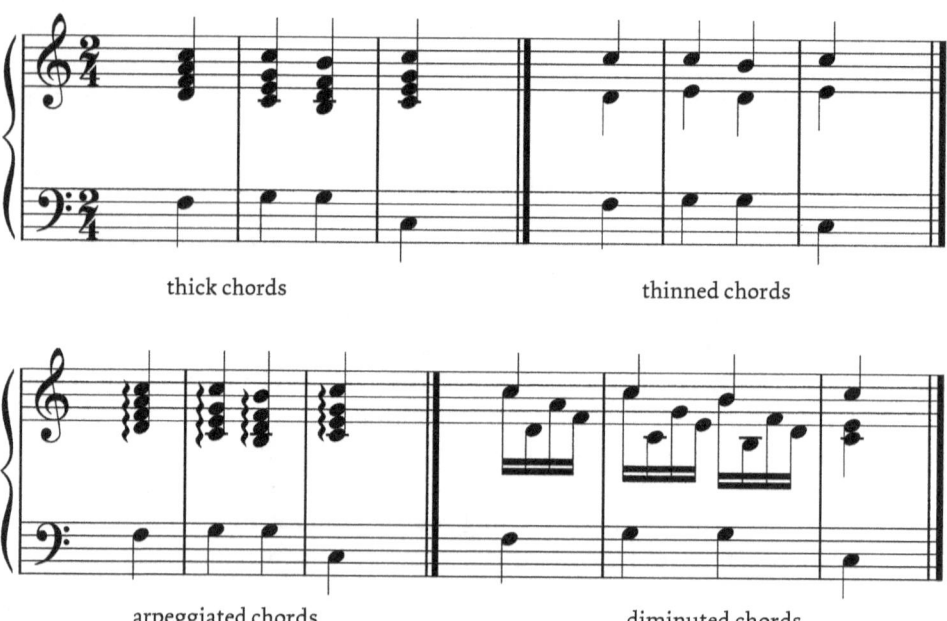

thick chords   thinned chords

arpeggiated chords   diminuted chords

There of course are exceptions to the rule on thick chords. Softly played chords can create a very special mood, and loud clusters or unpredictable changes in tonality can attract the listener's attention due to the collision of sounds they create.

When arranging, a carillonneur often is required to deviate creatively from his source score in order to give the arrangement the same *feel* as the original. He often will write short notes an octave higher since small bells better reproduce staccato effects. Smooth legato lines in turn are better played by heavier bells. The arranger or player must be aware that it is not the sound heard in the bell-chamber that is important, but rather its effect on the audience on the ground. The atmosphere indeed filters away a number of annoying overtones. What's more, the effect is different for each carillon: it depends on the instrument, on the character and height of the bell-chamber, and on the listening environment.

A future for the carillon

Much more difficult than the technical question concerning which music sounds good on the carillon is the fundamental question of which music *ought* to be played on the carillon. This question is not relevant to musical instruments played in a closed space. They after all only reach an audience that has deliberately chosen to listen to the repertoire being played. The carillon, however, is an instrument of the public space. The carillonneur is playing for a heterogeneous and unknown audience that has no say in the music being played and usually has not even chosen to listen to the carillon at that moment. Consequently, the question concerning a 'suitable' repertoire for the carillon is as old as the instrument itself, and until today results in lively and occasionally heated debates among carillonneurs and listeners. With this respect, there are three major movements among carillonneurs. Some musicians consider the carillon as a concert instrument and play primarily classical music and original carillon music. They especially see the carillon as a means of educating the public and cultivating taste: a nice, but somewhat outdated ideal in a society that is less open than previously to paternalistic impulses and that is familiar with a wide variety of music channels other than the carillon. Others have as goal a revival of the sound of the golden age of the carillon, and consequently they especially draw from the carillon repertoire of the 18th century. This group takes no account of the fact that at any moment in its history, the carillon played the music that was popular at the time. A final group sees the carillon primarily as a folk instrument for playing music that appeals to the masses. These carillonneurs opt for pop numbers, popular tunes and light classical music. For them, carillon music is a type of musical wallpaper with a recognizability that is intended to make people feel good. In practice, we see the various points of view expressed, depending on the situation: during a summer concert, players like to display their virtuosity and ability to interpret via the great carillon repertoire, while when playing for a market audience, they can indulge themselves in Music for the Millions, perhaps accompanied by improvisation to brighten up the presentation.

The carillon is a public medium and thus can be seen as a reflection of the preferences and feelings of a local community. For this reason, it could be argued that the carillon functions well as a collective musical memory. It can play a meaningful role by presenting music that has already survived past musical trends, and that continues to have a special meaning for today's audiences. Possible bearers of meaning are known works from the classical repertoire, songs from lists of the 'Top 100 music of all time' and music from Oscar-winning movies. The concept 'meaningful' also has a local and situational dimension. For this reason, it is beneficial to also play local songs, and music that fits the occasion of a local sports club winning the title or the death of a public figure. In this way, a carillonneur can present him or herself as a local bard.

For carillonneurs to remain true to their vocation, they must be aware that their audiences are continually evolving. Today, many carillonneurs work in locations where various cultural groups live together. Logically then the carillon repertoire also needs to reflect this cultural diversity. Thus carillonneurs should be in dialogue with immigrant groups in order to determine together with them which music is meaningful and playable on the carillon. For some passersby, it no doubt would be a shocking experience if African rhythms or Indonesian motifs were suddenly heard from the bell tower, but in any case the intercultural debate must be had, also with respect to carillon music.

The carillon has always been a musical reflection of society, and it will only survive if it is able to continue to bring people together in the future. It is precisely this social dimension that makes the instrument so unique. Bell music creates a collective listening experience and in this way plays a binding role in society, like monuments, parks, squares and public buildings. Carillon music is decorative in two meanings of the word: it belongs to the decor and it adds to the aesthetic quality of the surroundings. It immerses its audience in a bath of recognizable sounds that touch the emotions and evoke associations and memories. Carillon music also connects the generations. It is an element of continuity in an urban environment that is continually changing, and it provides an unconscious but very real feeling of certainty and safety. Weekly recitals can be considered a fixed musical ritual, and over the years, the musical forestroke becomes a sort of mantra that reinforces a city's identity. All of this is summarized in the term *mood*, that is often used by listeners when speaking of carillon music. While the experience of listening to carillon music often takes place at an unconscious level, carillon music appears to be highly regarded by many. The few studies conducted in this regard confirm this.[255]

Thus, carillon music can contribute to the quality of life in the city of the future. This city, however, is no longer that in which the carillon emerged five centuries ago. No tower instrument is still capable of serving the entire population of a city, and consequently the concept 'city carillon' is also outdated. This is one of the reasons why the campus carillon has originated in North America. In the future, it would make sense to also foresee towns and smaller residential areas in cities with carillon music. These are often ideal places for carillon music to flourish: they have a strong social fabric, traffic is limited, and there is a square with greenery, benches and a church tower that is strong enough to house a light carillon.

In this book, I wished to describe the close link between carillon music and society. The carillon for that matter is a suitable metaphor for our complex society. When it plays, dozens of bells of diverse weights interact, and their many partial notes and eternal decay cause them to collide. However, thanks to the carillonneur, they are able to transcend their individuality and evolve from chaos into harmony and beauty. The carillonneur transforms multiplicity into unity. Which perhaps is a good reason to hope that the tradition of carillon music will continue in the world for generations to come.

Sources and acknowledgements

This book is a revised and translated edition of *Zingend brons*, which was published by Uitgeverij Davidsfonds in 2010. With a view toward the English translation, the original text was shortened, principally in parts 1 and 2. The structure of the chapters was also adapted in places, and some new information was added.

Singing Bronze is written for readers without previous knowledge of bells or carillons. Consequently a choice was made to keep the storyline simple and to be selective in mentioning specific carillons and persons. Detailed information on carillons, carillonneurs, associations, schools and concert programs can be found on the websites of the World Carillon Federation (www.carillon.org) and the national carillon associations, as well as on other websites. The journals of the Guild of Carillonneurs in North America, the Dutch Carillon Association and the Flemish Carillon Association are also a good source of in-depth information. A number of articles from these journals are mentioned in the bibliography. For readers wishing a more detailed treatment of carillon and bell culture in general, *Bells and Man* by Percival Price and *The Art of the Carillon in the Low Countries* by André Lehr et al. are recommended. Like almost every book on carillons, this publication is indebted to the research and publications of André Lehr. Lehr is responsible for important and sometimes groundbreaking publications on all conceivable aspects of carillon culture. As is evident in this book, he himself has also become a part of the carillon's history.

I owe much to my partner An, who volunteered to share me with this book. I am grateful to Leuven University Press for its willingness to publish my book *Zingend brons* in English and to the translation agency Communicationwise for its high-quality work and flexible approach. I thank the Flemish Government and the Guild of Carillonneurs in North America, which provided funds for the extensive translation effort. The support of the latter organization originates from the endowment left to the guild by the late Sally Slade Warner (1932-2009). Sally was carillonneur at St. Stephen's Church in Cohasset, MA and at the Phillips Academy in Andover, MA.

It is my sincere hope that this book will make a modest contribution to the cause to which she devoted herself during her lifetime: a greater appreciation of the art of making music on bells.

Questions, suggestions and comments are welcome at beiaard@kuleuven.be.

Notes

1. Lehr (1996), p. 145-146.
2. General information about the Chinese art of bell casting in among others Lehr (1985a); Id. (1997); Shen.
3. General information in among others Schaepkens; Schatkin.
4. General information in among others Baudot; Schaepkens.
5. *Ut parati sint monachi semper et, facto signo absque mora surgentes, festinent invicem se prævenire ad opus Dei, cum omni tamen gravitate et modestia* (Regula S.P.N. Benedicti, Caput 22).
6. Bearda, Sergeys and Teugels, p. 19-35.
7. Koldeweij, p. 165-173.
8. Among others Price (1983), p. 146; Patart, p. 170-177.
9. Lehr (2002b), p. 126-139.
10. Haakma Wagenaar.
11. *Divina Commedia, Paradiso, Canto X*, verse 143.
12. *Vir erat robustus, fortis, westphalus, et opere mechanicus. Officium sacriste post fratrem Gerlacum custodiendum suscepit: cymbalum septem notarum, cum malleis suis et rota ferrea hos duos versus: Sancti Spiritus adsit nobis gratia qua corda nostra sibi faciat habitaculum, circum eundo decantans, pro suscitatione fratrum, fundens, fabricans et coaptans, super gradum dormitorii ante cellam custodis apte satis composuit.* (Gilliodts-Van Severen, p. 8).
13. Smits van Waesberghe; Van Schaik.
14. Lehr (1981a).
15. On social unrest with respect to the work bell: Landes, p. 53-82, 191-200.
16. General information on jaquemarts: Rombouts (1998); Van Immerseel.
17. Janssens (1973).
18. Rottiers, p. 117.
19. Rombouts: (1990a), p. 12 and 18.
20. Van der Straeten, part 5, p. 380-382.
21. Deinze, p. 91.

22　Verheyden (1926), p.113 ff. The *Excellente Chronycke* was published in 1531; the part until 1482 is by De Roovere, who died in that year; the fragment is on page cc. Original text: *In desen tijt woonde een Ionckman te Duynkercke, ende was daer clocluydere, ghenaemt Ian van Bevere, dye welcke op syne clocken speilde alle maniere van ghestelde liedekins, ende alle Hymnen, ende Sequencien, Kyrieleyson, ende alle kerckelicke sangen. Twelcke men daer te voren noeyt gehoort end hadde, ende was een grote nyeuwigheyt ter eeren van gode.*

23　Verheyden (1926), p. 170. Original text:
Het beyaerden met tant(werp)en eerst vernam
Dwelck door eenen sot van aelst eerst op quam.

24　Rombouts (1995), p. 29.

25　Fischer, p. 2.

26　*Jan de bayaerdere van Aelst in hoofscheden omme dat hij Cornelis Praet bayerdere van dese stede gheinduseert ende onderwijst heeft van dien / een couslake ende XXd gro* (Brand, p. 64-65).

27　Verheyden (1926), p. 115-116.
En int selve Iaer begonst men te spelen op clocken
tAntwerpen alder donde tyecken die seel wel soecken.
The second verse is corrupt and was reconstructed by Prosper Verheyden as follows:
tAntwerpen aldaer doende trecken die seel met stocken.

28　Verheyden (1925), p. 170.

29　Steurs, p. 42.

30　Lehr (1981b), p. 163.

31　Van der Straeten, part 5, p. 383. Original text: *Ter causen van ix clepels in de weckers van der orloge xlviij sch. / van riemen, metgaders van gespen daer de clepels an hangen ix sch. / Van xxvi pont loots in den steen van de weckers, xxxi sch. / Een clavier in torrekin om te beyaerdene.*

32　*Ende trac hem uut dat eene dinc / Dat tusschen sine been hinc / In die burse al sonder naet / Daermen dien beyaert mede slaet* (Verses 1266 ff.)

33　On the etymology of the word carillon, see among others Bets; Fagot (1958).

34　Van Even, p. 348.

35　Debrabandere and Deleu, p. 141.

36　Huybens (1982), p. 33.

37　Stins, p. 9.

38　Roggen, p. 10.

39　Bruges: Vander Straeten, part 5, p. 18; Antwerp: Verheyden (1925), p. 171; Mechelen: Van Doorslaer (1893), p. 14-15.

40　Friedrich, p. 29; Lehr (1964); Rice (1925), p. 113; Id (1927), p. 67.

41　Cosaert (1995); Van Bets and De Coster; Van Doorslaer (1908); Id. (1910).

42　Jacob delivered forestrokes and carillons in Aalst, Alkmaar, Amsterdam, Mons, Bruges, Tournai, Ghent, Ypres, Mechelen and Oudenaarde. Medard delivered among others bell series for Aalst, Diest, Middelburg, Schoonhoven, Tienen, Tongerlo and Zoutleeuw.

43 Lehr (1999).
44 Between 1540 and 1615, these three generations cast instruments for Aalst, Arnemuiden, Brussels, Diest, Edam, Lier, Mechelen, Monnikendam, Oudenburg, Rosendaal near Mechelen, Sint-Maartensdijk, Veere and Zierikzee.
45 Patart, p. 121-133.
46 Lehr (1981b), p. 176.
47 Verheyden (1925), p. 170-171.
48 Lehr (1987a), p. 24-27.
49 *Aedium sacrarum splendore ac magnificentia, Campanarum quas vocant magnitudine ac pulcherrimo sonitu reliquos Belgas longe praecellunt. Modulantur illis tintinnabulis non secus atque cytharis variarum cantilenarum genera* (Flandricarum Rerum Tomi X, 1531, Tomus IX, p. 50; cited in Van Werveke, p. 135).
50 Paris, Bibliothèque Nationale, ms. 9152, fol. 188 recto: *Clavier a carillonneur les cloches comme lon faict au pais bas et aultres endroicts et saccordent musicallement.*
51 Lübke, p. 119; Coleman, p. 194; Rice (1925), p. 325.
52 Burney, passim; Verschaffel, p. 57.
53 Rombouts (2002).
54 Bauters, p. 32-34.
55 Lehr (2005).
56 Van Doorslaer (1893), p. 4.
57 Felix (1990), p. 16-23.
58 Secular songs in Leuven, Bruges and Tournai: Van Even, p. 348; Gilliodts-Van Severen, p. 35; Portier, p. 39; Patart, p. 133; Vanderstraeten, part 5, p. 18.
59 Van der Weel (1998).
60 Original texts in Romita, p. 56-69;
Haarlem: *Item prohibemus, ne campanis abutantur, quibus earum custodia committitur, ad lascivarum ineptarumque cantionum tinnitum; quandoquidem illae ad convocandum populum ad audiendum Verbum Dei, et ut mysteriis intersint Divinis, avertendisque tempestatum cladibus consecratae sint; neutiquam, ut sonitu earundem, a pietatis contemplatione, ac ab iis, quibus pro salute sua intendere debent, avocentur homines, coganturque propemodum vel inviti ad lascivias dedecoraque (iam tunc postposita) memoriam revocare, quod sane nefas est Christiano.*
Cambrai: *Qui tintinnabula et campanulas ad harmoniam quandam pulsare solent, caveant omnino ut huiusmodi pulsatione cantiones turpes, inhonesta et vulgo iactatas imitentur: sed potius hymnorum et canticorum ecclesiae modulationes. Si quis non paruerit, puniatur; ut qui multis labendi occasionem praebuerit, et in re sacris dicata, spurca et inhonesta attulerit.*
Mechelen: *Cohibeant episcopi cantores, organistas, et campanarios, et alios quoscumque a lasciva, militari et quavis indecora musica in cantu, organis et campanis, sub poena decem stuferorum, ad pios usus arbitrio episcoporum applicanda. Et si semel puniti non abstinuerint, poena carceris ac alias arbitraria plectantur.*

61 Van der Weel (2009), p. 7.
62 Rottiers, p. 47.
63 Gustin; Hellemans.
64 General information on the robbery of bells at this time: Goris; Van den Bergh (1986); Van Doorslaer (1939).
65 On Mechelen bells abroad: Van Bets and Decoster, passim.
66 Van den Bergh (1986).
67 Donnet, p. 171-174.
68 Romita, p. 69: *Tintinnabula quoque et campanas ad harmoniam quandam pulsantes, eiusmodi pulsatione turpes, inhonesta vel scandalosas cantiones non imitentur, sed potius hymnorum et canticorum ecclesiae modulationes. Et sicubi necesse fuerit, cum magistratu desuper agatur.*
69 Deleu (2008); Van Eyndhoven.
70 Felix (1990); Van Eyndhoven.
71 Original text: *je vous diray qu'il y a un aveugle a Utrecht, fort renommé pour la Musique, qui jouë ordinairement sur les cloches (...), lequel j'ay vû faire rendre 5 ou 6 divers sons a chascune des plus grosses de ces cloches, sans les toucher, approchant seulement sa bouche de leur bord...*
72 Biographical information on the Hemony brothers principally can be found in Lehr (1959) and Id. (1960).
73 Chronology of the stay of the Hemonys in Zutphen: Looper.
74 On the Hemony carillons in Antwerp: Donnet, p. 74-75; Spiessens (2008); Verheyden (1925), p. 171-172.
75 On the Hemonys' tuning technique: Lehr (2000).
76 On Pieter Hemony in Ghent: principally Lehr (2004).
77 Year Mammes Fremy died: Lehr (1974a).
78 On Melchior De Haze: Donnet, p. 243-268; Lehr (1981b), p. 217-224; Vanderstraeten, part 5, p. 337-345, Van Doorslaer (1926-1927).
79 Fagot (1959), p. 204-206; Spies.
80 Meilink, p. 16.
81 Godenne (1960); Michiels; Price (1978); Williams.
82 Bossin (1991a), p. 53-75.
83 Elias; Guérin; Lehr (1984); Marques Da Gama and Lehr; Vanderstraeten, part 8, p. 333-343.
84 On Willem Witlockx: Lehr (1981a), p. 224-231; Spiessens (1992).
85 Dacquin and Formeyn, passim; Gilliodts-van Severen, p. 154-173.
86 Godenne (1960); Williams, p. 87.
87 In the 18th century, the family changed the spelling of their name from Van den Ghein to Vanden Gheyn.
88 Wauters, passim.
89 Vanhoof.

90 Dilis, p. 293-295.
91 Van Doorslaer (1923), p. 12-14, 19-20.
92 Debevere, p. 39-44.
93 Lehr (1981a), p. 241-245.
94 Huybens (1981a), passim; Van Elewyck.
95 Huybens (1981b), p. 63-69.
96 Huybens and Rombouts.
97 Roggen, p. 9-13.
98 Presented in full in Verheyden (1943).
99 Bijvank and Van de Veen, p. 44.
100 The original text is a chronogram:
    MYn sChor geLoeY op reYs, Voor dapperen Van noort
    kLinkt na een Lange rUst, thans in een fraaY akkoort.
101 Van der Zwart, p. 21-30.
102 Rombouts (1990b), p. 32-33.
103 Van Elewyck, p. 36-41, 70-79.
104 More information in Lehr (1993).
105 More information in Lehr (1985b).
106 Van der Weel (2008), p. 100.
107 Van der Weel (2008), p. 79.
108 Januszajtis, p. 48.
109 More information in among others Timmermans, p. 117; Van der Weel (2008), passim.
110 For example in the Brabant towns of Diest and Tienen: Diest (1714): each Sunday and holy day from eight thirty to nine, and a half hour in the evening before benediction; each Wednesday from eleven to eleven thirty or longer, each Thursday before the six-thirty Mass and in the evening before benediction; each Saturday, a half hour before benediction. In addition, on Shrove Tuesday and Rogation days, on Christmas eve, Christmas night and on the patron feast days of the crafts and trades (Di Martinelli, p. 392-393). Tienen (1723): each Tuesday, Thursday and Friday, twice on all Sundays and holidays, and three times on each first Sunday of the month; in addition, once or twice on the day preceding most holidays (Fagot (1959), p. 240-243).
111 De Brabandere and Deleu, p. 147; Rombouts and Huybens, p. XVII; Verheyden (1926), p. 127, 155.
112 A number of testimonials can be found in Uddin and Verberckmoes.
113 Burney, p. 290.
114 Verheyden (1926), p. 28-41.
115 Di Martinelli, p. 390.
116 D'hollander (2003), p. 119.
117 Van Doorslaer (1927), p. 41.

118 Gilliodts-Van Severen, p. 183.
119 General information about the confiscation of bells: Donnet, p. 180-199; Félix (1998); Frère; Remans; Sutter (1993), p. 193-218.
120 Original text: *les cloches, dont la superstition avoit surchargé les églises, nous offrent une ressource féconde, une sorte de mine assez abondante pour suffire à nos besoins*, in Instruction sur l'art de séparer le cuivre du métal des cloches.
121 Verheyden (1926), p. 32-40.
122 *(...) pour être emploiées à un usage plus utile en consolidant l'oeuvre sublime de la liberté du monde.*
123 Loosjes, p. 126.
124 Aarssen, p. 54.
125 De Krant van West-Vlaanderen 21/8/98, p. 11 (printed in *Jaarboek Roeselaarse Klokkengilde*, 1998, p. 76).
126 Hous, p. 95.
127 Van Doorslaer (1939), p. 15.
128 Huybens (1990), p. 28.
129 Rombouts (1990a), p. 16.
130 Van der Weel (1999).
131 Loosjes, p. 64.
132 De Saint-Hilaire, p. 118-121.
133 More information on the situation in the Netherlands: Brandts Buys; Van der Weel (2008), p. 128-130.
134 Maassen.
135 Lambin.
136 F.R. de Chateaubriand: *Génie du Christianisme*, part IV, book I, chapter I.
137 Translated from Hugo (1974), p. 121-123, 135-136.
138 Hugo (1986), passim.
139 More information in among others Vos.
140 Janssens (2009), p. 73-75.
141 Rombouts (1995); Verschaffel, p. 55-56.
142 *Kronyken der nijverheid in Belgien* (1839); J. Collin de Plancy, *Légendes des origines* (1850).
143 Cited in Coleman, p. 136-139.
144 Sabbe, p. 25-27, 96-109.
145 Citations from Rodenbach, p. 9, 14-15, 16-17.
146 Hullebroeck, p. 62, Van Doorslaer (1927), p. 46-47; Van Nuffel, p. 16.
147 More information on the bell-founders Van Aerschodt: Bearda, Sergeys and Teugels, p. 50-56; Vernimmen.
148 More information on 19th century carillon keyboards: Denyn (1925); Price (1933), p. 137-140; Verheyden (1926), p, 97-108.

149 Haweis, p. 455-477; Haweis wrote two versions of the second visit; see Rice (1925), p. 124-125; Verheyden (1926-1927), p. 25-27.
150 Simpson (1895); Id. (1896).
151 Jennings, p. 105-113, 125-133; Milsom.
152 Most of the information in this chapter comes from or can also be found in: Cosaert (1987); Godenne and Joosen; Hans; Price (1933); Rombouts (2009); Wachters. In addition, newspaper cuttings and program booklets from the Mechelen Monday concerts were used. Detailed references are provided below only for little-known facts.
153 Van Doorslaer (1893), p. 53.
154 Price (1933), p. 117; Hans, p. 20.
155 Collage from lectures by Jef Denyn: Denyn (1915); Id. (1922); Godenne and Joosen, p. 1-145; Rice (1925), p. 324.
156 De Coster (1962).
157 About William Gorham Rice: De Turk (1990); Rice (1914); Id. (1915); Id. (1922); Id. (1925).
158 Rice (1925), p. 115 ff.
159 Rice (1914), p. 7.
160 De Schaepdrijver, p. 54; Callewaert, p. 157.
161 Cited in Rice (1925), p. 162-164.
162 De Stoop, p. 24.
163 A systematic treatment in Watkins, p. 38-42.
164 Derez, p. 188-196.
165 Edwards, p. 37.
166 More information principally in Lehr (1981b), p. 307-321; Lehr (2006); Loosjes, p. 25-36; Van der Ven, passim.
167 Williams, p. 76.
168 Teugels, De Wet and Van Deventer, p. 84.
169 More information in among others De Coster (1962); D'hollander (1997); Nys; Cosaert (1998).
170 More information on the introduction of the carillon in North America: Barnes (1987); De Turk (1990); Johnston (2008); Keldermans (1996); Myhre; Rice (1922).
171 Bossin (1991b).
172 Rice (1925), p. 89.
173 Ewing; Shull.
174 Gilman (1972); Id. (1978).
175 Swager, p. 71; Jennings, p. 92.
176 On Rockefeller and Brees: Barnes (1987), p. 26; De Turk (1990), p. 25-26; Godenne (1972), p. 41; Johnston (2008), p. 41-67; Milford Myhre, oral information.
177 Jennings, p. 90-91.
178 On Lefévere and Cohasset: Rice (1925), p. 328-329.
179 Lefévere (1970), p. 47.

180 De Turk (1990), p. 27; Godenne (1980), p. 37; Semowich.
181 Johnston (2008), passim; Keldermans (2000), p. 154.
182 Schafer, p. 126-138.
183 On the life and work of Cyril Johnston: Augustus; Johnston (2008).
184 Price McCree.
185 Newspaper cuttings from documentation by Michel Lejeune.
186 De Raedt, p. 103-104.
187 Godenne (1972), p. 58-59.
188 Gebruers; De beiaard van Turnhout; Price (1933), p. 66.
189 Debevere, p. 119-120.
190 Rombouts (1990c), Id. (2008).
191 Van den Bergh (1985), p. 7-8.
192 Ippel, p. 105-113.
193 D'hollander (1996).
194 Aarssen, p. 59-67.
195 Baas and Callens, p. 13.
196 Lawson (1994).
197 Lehr (2003).
198 Danielson; Lawson (1989).
199 Cosaert (1998); D'hollander (1998); Godenne (1972).
200 McCabe, p. 95.
201 Elias, p. 161-168.
202 Johnston (2002); see also Johnston (2008), p. 141-156.
203 Halsted; Rombouts (2012).
204 Bigelow (1966), p. 43.
205 Raphael and Herberich-Marx, p. 247.
206 Espy, p. 325.
207 Nys, p. 97-98.
208 Johnston (2002), p. 113.
209 Bijtelaar, p. 166-167.
210 Bijtelaar, p. 174; Heijbroek, p. 56-58.
211 Frank, p. 30, 119.
212 't Hart, p. 30.
213 Boogert (1993), p. 7-8; info via e-mail Piet Boekestijn.
214 General information on the confiscation of bells in World War II: Kreps; Lambert-Avis; Lehr (1981b), p. 334-345; Lejeune; Price (1948); Schùermans.
215 Ambagts, p. 9.
216 De Coster (1972).
217 Schuermans, appendix 2.

218 Merry, p. 9-10.
219 Vercammen.
220 MacDonald, p. 92-100.
221 Lefévere (1970), p. 47.
222 Bossin (1984), p. 32-33.
223 Price (1948), p. 112.
224 Johnston (2002), p. 113.
225 Giesler, p. 216.
226 Nagai, p. 117-118.
227 General information about the return of the Belgian and Dutch bells: Kreps; Lambert-Avis; Price (1948).
228 Augustus-Kersten (1992b).
229 General information on developments in bell casting after World War II: De Waard.
230 Van Heuven.
231 -70°C is equivalent to -94°F.
232 Augustus-Kersten (1992a); Lehr (2002a).
233 Mulisch, p. 44-46 (on the location Haarlem and the exploratory visit: oral statement by Harry Mulisch to the author).
234 General information on the Carillon Americana: Bigelow (1952).
235 Buchanan.
236 Joos; *Bondsnieuws* nos. 6, 7, 9, 10 and 11; fragments of media articles and letters from L. Boogert and J. Sergeys files.
237 Ippel, p. 131-140.
238 General information on American carillon culture after World War II: Barnes (1987); De Turk (1990); Id. (1996); Keldermans (1996); Myhre.
239 Rombouts (2008).
240 Price (1972).
241 Price (1975).
242 Price (1947), p. 21-22.
243 Robins.
244 Timmermans, p. 8.
245 Price (1949), p. 5.
246 Lehr (1960); p. 64-102; Id. (1974b); Id. (1987) Id. (1992).
247 Lehr (1987b); Schoofs and Van Campen.
248 Winsemius.
249 Van Geuns and Scholte; Van Wely; Verhoef.
250 Carillons in Japan: oral information Mariko Matsue; Bodden; Zwart.
251 Williams, p. 214, n. 3.
252 Abbenes.

253 On the danger of cultural imperialism with respect to carillons: Sutter (1994).
254 Van der Weel (2008), p. 41.
255 Winter, p. 44.

Bibliography

AARSSEN, R., *Grimbergen & de beiaardkunst*, Eigen Schoon, Grimbergen, s.d. <1998>.
ABBENES, A., 'Grootste beiaard ter wereld in Korea', *Klok en Klepel*, 81 (December 2002), p. 7-8.
AMBAGTS, T., 'De renovatie van de Juliana-beiaard van Bergen op Zoom', *Klok en Klepel*, 86 (March 2004), p. 7-10.
AUGUSTUS, B., 'Een ontmoeting met Gillett & Johnston,' *Klok en Klepel*, 55 (December 1995), p. 19-26.
AUGUSTUS-KERSTEN, A., 'Tuur Eijsbouts: "Hemony-klokken waren niet te overtreffen"', *Klok en Klepel*, 48 (June 1992a), p. 41-45.
AUGUSTUS-KERSTEN, A., 'Hein Fritsen: "Als je zaken doet, moet je zorgen dat er twee lachen"', *Klok en Klepel*, 49 (December 1992b), p. 39-41.
BAAS, A. and CALLENS, C., 'La fonderie de cloches Michiels ou l'apogée de l'art campanaire tournaisien', *Le Bulletin Campanaire*, 55 (2008/3), p. 11-17.
BARNES, R., 'The North American Carillon Movement: The Instrument, Its Players and Its Music', *Bulletin of the Guild of Carillonneurs in North America*, 36 (January 1987), p. 20-36.
BAUDOT, J., *Les cloches*, Liturgie, Bloud, Paris, 1913 (Reprint Paris, 1974).
BAUTERS, P., *Kracht van wind en water. Molens in Vlaanderen*, Davidsfonds, Leuven, 1989.
BEARDA, T., SERGEYS, J. and TEUGELS, J., *Campanae Lovanienses. Het klokkenpatrimonium van Groot-Leuven*, Peeters, Leuven, 2008.
BETS, P.,' Byzonderheden over de Beijaerden van Thienen', in *Mengelingen voor de Geschiedenis van Braband*, Leuven, 1871, p. 133-150.
BIGELOW, A., 'And What About the Electronic Carillon?', *Etude*, July 1952, p. 14-15, 62-63.
BIGELOW, A., 'The Unwritten Prelude', *Bulletin of the Guild of Carillonneurs in North America*, 17,1 (May 1966), p. 38-43.
BIJTELAAR, B., *De Zingende Torens van Amsterdam*, J.H. Bussy, Amsterdam, 1947.
BIJVANK, J., and VAN DE VEEN, G., *De Grote Kerk van Nijkerk*, Nijkerkse Klokkenspelvereniging, Nijkerk, 2004.
BODDEN, G., 'Japanse ervaringen', *Klok en Klepel*, 49 (December 1992), p. 55-57.

BOOGERT, L., 'Een jubileum dat niet werd gevierd. De NKV in oorlogstijd', *Klok en Klepel*, 50 (June 1993), p. 3-17.
BOSSIN, J., 'The Berlin Carillon – 1706 to 1944', *Bulletin of the Guild of Carillonneurs in North America*, 33 (January 1984), p. 25-33.
BOSSIN, J., *Die Carillons von Berlin und Potsdam. Fünf Jahrhunderte Turmglockenspiel in der Alten und Neuen Welt*, Stapp Verlag, Berlin, 1991a.
BOSSIN, J., 'In Search of North America's First Carillon', *Bulletin of the Guild of Carillonneurs in North America*, (1991b), p. 35-38.
BRAND, P.J., 'Klokken en beiaarden in Hulst door de eeuwen heen', in *Oudheidkundige Kring "De Vier Ambachten" Hulst. Jaarboek 1976-1977*, De Vier Ambachten, Hulst, 1977, p. 27-98.
BRANDTS BUYS, M., 'Klokspelen en Klokkenspellen in Nederland', in *Beiaardkunst. Handelingen van het Eerste Congres Mechelen 1922*, L. Godenne, Mechelen, s.d., p. 31-45.
BUCHANAN, B., 'The Carillons of Belmont', *Bulletin of the Guild of Carillonneurs in North America*, 45 (1986), p. 18-44.
BURNEY, CH., *The Present State of Music in Germany, the Netherlands and United Provinces*, London, 1773.
CALLEWAERT, F., 'Klokken en beiaarden in werk van Abraham Hans', in *Jaarboek Roeselaarse klokkengilde 2006*, stad Roeselare, s.d., s.l., p. 157-163.
CHAMBERS, R.W., *Barbarians*, D. Appleton and Company, New York/London, 1917.
COLEMAN, S.N., *Bells. Their History, Legends, Making, and Uses*, Rand McNally, Chicago/New York, 1928 (Reprint Tower Books, Detroit, 1971).
COSAERT, K., *Jef Denijn. Grondlegger van een nieuwe beiaardkunst*, Campana, Mechelen, 1987.
COSAERT, K., 'De klokkengieterij te Mechelen. Een economische en culturele situering', in *Jaarboek Roeselaarse Klokkengilde 1995*, stad Roeselare, s.d, s.l., p. 33-47.
COSAERT, K., 'Uit de archieven van de Koninklijke Beiaardschool 'Jef Denyn' te Mechelen', *VBV-magazine*, 4,1 (1st quarter 1998), p. 2-13.
D'HOLLANDER, J., 'Jef Denijn en een nationale klokkengieterij in Mechelen', *VBV-magazine*, 2,4 (4th quarter 1996), p. 3-13.
D'HOLLANDER, J., 'Vijfenzeventig jaar Koninklijke Beiaardschool (1922-1997)', *VBV-magazine*, 3,4 (4th quarter 1997), p. 2-15.
D'HOLLANDER, J., 'Kamiel Lefévere (1888-1972), pionier van onze beiaardkunst in de U.S.A.', *VBV-magazine*. 4,3 (3rd quarter 1998), p. 2-17.
D'HOLLANDER, J., *Van klok tot beiaard. Met 'clocke Roeland' in de hoofdrol*, Mens & cultuur, Gent, 2003.
DANIELSON, E., 'Archives: "I Ring Only For Peace"', *Hoover Digest. Research and Opinion on Public Policy*, 2000,2.
'De beiaard van Turnhout', *Muziekwarande*, 11 (1 November 1924), p. 257.
DEBEVERE, E., *Grasduinen in de geschiedenis van de Nieuwpoortse beiaard*, VVV Nieuwpoort, Nieuwpoort, 2004.

DEBRABANDERE, P., and DELEU, F., 'De Kortrijkse stadsbeiaard', *De Leiegouw*, 30 (1988), p. 139-178.
DE COSTER, H., 'Drie jubilea in hetzelfde jaar', *Bondsnieuws*, 21 (July 1962), p. 8-12 and 22 (November 1962), p. 6-11.
DE COSTER, H., 'Pour servir à l'édification de l'Histoire', in W. GODENNE en H. JOOSEN, (edd.), *Jubileumboek 1922-1972. Koninklijke Beiaardschool «Jef Denyn» te Mechelen*, Koninklijke Beiaardschool Mechelen, Mechelen, 1972, p. 164-185.
'Deinze: een grote-tertsbeiaard', in *Beiaarden en klokkenspellen in Oost-Vlaanderen*, Provinciebestuur Oost-Vlaanderen, Gent, 1995, p. 91-94.
DELEU, F., 'Manuscrit Néerlandais 58: Het muziekschrift van Hendrick Claes', *VBV-magazine*, 14,1 (1st quarter 2008), p. 16-32.
DENYN, J., 'Technique et mechanisme du carillon' (Lecture for the Royal Society of Arts in London, 17 December 1915), in *Gedenkboek Jef Denyn, "Stadsbeiaardier en Meester van den Toren"*, Beiaardschool Mechelen, Mechelen, 1947.
DENYN, J., 'Wat zal de beiaard spelen?', in *Beiaardkunst. Handelingen van het Eerste Congres Mechelen 1922*, s.n., Mechelen, p. 101-112.
DENYN, J., 'Beiaardklavieren', in *Beiaardkunst. Handelingen van het Tweede Congres 's-Hertogenbosch 1925*, s.n., 's-Hertogenbosch, 1925, p. 126-147.
DE RAEDT, R., 'Bij den beiaardier van het koninklijk paleis', in *Alle klokken luiden*, Bosch & Keuning, Baarn, s.d., p. 101-107.
DEREZ, M., '"The Land of Chimes." De overzeese promotie van de Belgische beiaard', in M. BEYEN, L. ROMBOUTS and S. VOS (red.), *De beiaard. Een politieke geschiedenis*, Universitaire Pers Leuven, Leuven, 2009, p. 187-208.
DE SAINT-HILAIRE, E., *Les mystères de Sainte-Hélène*, Melines, Cans et Compagnie, Brussel, 1847.
DE SCHAEPDRIJVER, S., *De Groote Oorlog. Het koninkrijk België tijdens de Eerste Wereldoorlog*, Atlas, Amsterdam, 1997.
DE STOOP, C., 'Grote geruchten sterven niet', *Knack*, 12 December 1990, p. 22-25.
DE TURK, W., 'William Gorham Rice and the North American Carillon Movement', *Bulletin of the Guild of Carillonneurs in North America*, 39 (1990), p. 14-37.
DE WAARD, R., 'Restoration of Historic Carillons' in L. BOOGERT, A. LEHR en J. MAASSEN, *45 Years of Dutch Carillons 1945-1990*, Nederlandse Klokkenspel-Vereniging, Asten, 1992, p. 26-45.
DI MARTINELLI, V., *Diest in de 17de en 18de eeuwen*, A. Siffer, Gent en F. Uten, Diest, 1897.
DILIS, E., 'L'ancien carillon et la vieille horloge de Saint-Jacques, à Anvers', in *Académie Royale d'Archéologie de Belgique. Bulletin*, 1911 IV, Antwerpen, s.n., 1912, p. 275-316.
DONNET, F., *Les cloches d'Anvers. Les fondeurs anversois*, s.n., Antwerpen, 1899.
EDWARDS, G.W., *Vanished Towers and Chimes of Flanders*, The Penn Publishing Company, Philadelphia, 1916.
ELIAS, A., *I Want Two! Historical and Technical Study about the Carillons of Mafra*, diss. Lemmensinstituut Leuven, 2004.

ESPY, E., 'The Church's Debt to Hitler', *Religion in Life*, 11,3 (Summer 1942), p. 323-335.
EWING, H., 'A National Peace Carillon for Washington, D.C.', *Bulletin of the Guild of Carillonneurs in North America*, 45 (1996), p. 65-68.
FAGOT, D., 'Beiaard', in *Hulde-Album Prof. Dr. E. Blancquaert*, Gent, 1958, p. 371-379.
FAGOT, D., 'Enkele documenten over de beiaard van Tienen', *De Brabantse Folklore*, 142 (June 1959), p. 198-252.
FELIX, J.-P., *Le recueil d'hymnes et chansons arrangés par Théodore de Sany pour le carillon de Bruxelles en 1648*, own publication, Brussel, 1990.
FELIX, J.-P., 'Les saisies de cloches dans le département d' l'Ourthe', in *Cloches et carillons, Catalogues et monographies de la Collection Tradition wallonne*, 11, Brussel, 1998, p. 221-242.
FISCHER, J.P.A., *Verhandeling van de klokken en het klokke-spel*, Willem Kroon, Utrecht, 1738 (Reprint Klokkengieterij B. Eijsbouts C.V., Asten, 1956).
FRANK, A., *Het achterhuis. Dagboekbrieven 12 juni 1942-1 augustus 1944*, Bert Bakker, Amsterdam, 1993.
FRÈRE, H., 'Des cloches aux monnaies', in *Cloches et carillons, Catalogues et monographies de la Collection Tradition wallonne*, 11, Brussel, 1998, p. 395-400.
FRIEDRICH, A., 'Thomas Platter der Jüngere und das Glockenspiel der Kathedrale von Antwerpen', *Campanae Helveticae*, 4 (1995), p. 26-43.
GEBRUERS, S., 'Beiaard als Industrieartikel', journal title unknown, 28 februari 1925.
Gedenkboek Jef Denyn, "Stadsbeiaardier en Meester van den Toren", Beiaardschool Mechelen, Mechelen, 1947.
GIESLER, H., *Ein andere Hitler. Bericht seines Architekten Hermann Giesler. Erlbenisse, Gespräche, Reflexionen*, Druffel, Leoni am Starnberger See, 1978.
GILLIODTS-VAN SEVEREN, L., *Le carillon de Bruges. Recueil de textes et analyses de documents inédits ou peu connus*, Essais d'Archéologie Brugeoise, 1, Brugge, 1912.
GILMAN, M., 'Our Lady of Good Voyage Church Carillon', *Bulletin of the Guild of Carillonneurs in North America*, 23 (November 1972), p. 36-43.
GILMAN, M., 'Voices From the Carillon's Past', *Bulletin of the Guild of Carillonneurs in North America*, 27 (April 1978), p. 81-87.
GODENNE, W., *Cloches en URSS*, Koninklijke beiaardschool "Jef Denyn", Mechelen, 1960.
GODENNE, W., 'Historische kanttekeningen over de beiaardschool', in W. GODENNE en H. JOOSEN, (edd.), *Jubileumboek 1922-1972. Koninklijke Beiaardschool «Jef Denyn» te Mechelen*, Koninklijke Beiaardschool Mechelen, Mechelen, 1972, p. 9-60.
GODENNE, W., 'An Appreciation of William Gorham Rice', *Bulletin of the Guild of Carillonneurs in North America*, 29 (January 1980), p. 33-43.
GODENNE, W. and JOOSEN, H., (edd.), *Jubileumboek 1922-1972. Koninklijke Beiaardschool «Jef Denyn» te Mechelen*, Koninklijke Beiaardschool Mechelen, Mechelen, 1972.
GORIS, J., *Historiek van de Herentalse beiaard (ca. 1541-1965)*, VVV Herentals, s.l., s.d.

GUSTIN, J., 'Le De Tintinnabulis de Jérôme Maggi', in Cloches et carillons, Catalogues et monographies de la Collection Tradition wallonne, 11, Brussel, 1998, p. 27-40.

HAAKMA WAGENAAR, TH., 'De toren en zijn klokken', in C.A. BAART DE LA FAILLE e.a., Ergens beginnen de klokken hun lied. Zeven opstellen over de historie en de restauratie van de Utrechtse Domtoren, zijn carillon en zijn luiklokken, Bruna, Utrecht/Aartselaar, 1981, p. 13-35.

HALSTED, M., 'Arthur Lynds Bigelow: The Man and His Work', Bulletin of the Guild of Carillonneurs in North America, 44 (1995), p. 44-54.

HANS, A., De Mechelschen Toren en Jef Denyn, A. Hans' Kinderbibliotheek, 10, Hans-Van der Meulen, Kontich, s.d.

HAWEIS, H.R., Music and Morals, Isbister, Londen, 1874[5].

HELLEMANS, G., Klokken. De Tintinnabulis van Hieronymus Magius. Vertaling met aantekeningen, diss. Koninklijke Beiaardschool 'Jef Denyn', Mechelen, 2009.

HEIJBROEK, J., 'Het carillon van het Rijksmuseum', Bulletin van het Rijksmuseum, 54 (2006), p. 54-63.

HOUS, J.B., Leuvense Kroniek (1780-1829), (ed. J. de Kempeneer), Abdij van Park, Heverlee, 1964.

HUGO, V., De klokkenluider van de Notre Dame (Translation into Dutch by Halbo C. Kool), Veen, Wageningen, 1974[4].

HUGO, V., België (Translation into Dutch by Ernest van Altena), Op Schrijvers voeten, Veen, Utrecht/Antwerpen, 1986.

HULLEBROECK, E., Beiaarden, De Standaard, Brussel, s.d. <1924>.

HUYBENS, G., Bouwstenen voor een geschiedenis van de muziek te Leuven 17^e en 18^e eeuw, Reprint from Mededelingen van de Geschied- en Oudheidkundige Kring voor Leuven en omgeving, 21, 1981a.

HUYBENS, G., 'Willem Gommaar Kennis' oeuvre. Thematisch catalogus', in Arca Lovaniensis. Artes atque historiae reserans documenta, de vrienden van de Leuvense stedelijke musea, Leuven, 1981b, p. 41-113.

HUYBENS, G., Muziek te Leuven in de 16^e eeuw, own publication, Leuven, 1982.

HUYBENS, G., 'De Leuvense stadsbeiaarden en hun beiaardiers', in Stad met klank. Vijf eeuwen klokken en klokkengieters te Leuven, Leuven, 1990, p. 19-30.

HUYBENS, G. and ROMBOUTS, L., Preludia voor beiaard. Matthias Vanden Gheyn, Monumenta Flandriae Musica, 2, Alamire, Leuven/Peer, 1997.

IPPEL, S., Verhalen rond de Oostendse beiaarden, own publication, Oostende, 1992.

JANSSENS, G., '"Een echte nationale kunst." Koninklijke belangstelling voor de beiaardmuziek', in M. BEYEN, L. ROMBOUTS en S. VOS (edd.), De beiaard. Een politieke geschiedenis, Universitaire Pers Leuven, Leuven, 2009, p. 69-82.

JANSSENS, R., 'Van madonnabeeld naar nieuwe beiaard' in Beiaard stad Halle, s.n., s.l., s.d. <Stadsbestuur Halle, 1973>.

JANUSZAJTIS, A., 'Bell-playing in Gdańsk – a Historical Outline' in A. JANUSZAJTIS e.a. (edd.), The Gdańsk Carillons, The Historical Museum of the City of Gdańsk, Gdańsk, 2003.

JENNINGS, T.S., *Master of My Art. The Taylor Bellfoundries 1784-1987*, John Taylor, Loughborough, 1987.
JOHNSTON, J., *England's Child. The Carillon and the Casting of Big Bells*, Cadmus Editions, San Francisco, 2008.
JOHNSTON, N., *A Memoir* (ed. Jill Johnston), Print Means, New York, 2002.
JOOS, J., *Deelneming van de Heilige Stoel aan de Algemene Wereldtentoonstelling van Brussel 1958. Algemeen Verslag*, s.n., Brussel, 1958.
KELDERMANS, K & L., *Carillon. The Evolution of a Concert Instrument in North America*, Springfield Park District, Springfield, Illinois, 1996.
KELDERMANS, K., 'The Carillon Design Methods of the Bell-Founder Gillett & Johnston', in L. ROMBOUTS (ed.), *Proceedings of the 11th World Carillon Congress, August 9-13, 1998, Mechelen-Leuven*, Vlaamse Beiaardvereniging, Mechelen/Leuven, 2000, p. 153-156.
KOLDEWEIJ, J., *Geloof & geluk. Sieraad en devotie in middeleeuws Vlaanderen*, Terra Lannoo, Arnhem, 2006, p. 165-173.
KREPS, J., *La bataille des cloches* (Reprint from *La Revue Générale Belge*, 45, 1949), Ad. Goemaere, Brussel, 1949.
LAMBERT-AVIS, J., *Wie met klokken schiet, wint de oorlog niet. De klokkenvordering tijdens de Tweede Wereldoorlog*, Nationaal Beiaardmuseum, Asten, 1992.
LAMBIN, M., 'De tragische idylle van Edouard Manet en zijn Hollandse geliefde', *Gazet van Antwerpen*, 9-11 August 1973, p. 33.
LANDES, D.S., *Revolution in Time. Clocks and the Making of the Modern World*, The Belknap Press of Harvard University Press, Cambridge,MS/Londen, 1983.
LAWSON, J., 'I Ring for Peace. The Bells at Stanford', *Sandstone and Tile (Stanford Historical Society)*, 13,3 (Summer 1989), p. 3-6.
LAWSON, J., 'The Bells of San Simeon', *Bulletin of the Guild of Carillonneurs in North America*, 43 (1994), p. 14-23.
LEFÉVERE, K., 'De ontwikkeling der beiaardkunst in de Verenigde Staten van Amerika en Canada', *Vlaams muziektijdschrift*, 22 (1970), p. 44-48.
LEHR, A., *De klokkengieters François en Pieter Hemony*, Klokkengieterij Eijsbouts, Asten, 1959.
LEHR, A., *Historische en muzikale aspekten van Hemony-beiaarden*, Klokkengieterij Eijsbouts, Asten, 1960.
LEHR, A., 'Oefenklavieren in het verleden', *Klok en Klepel*, 4 (November 1964), p. 20-22.
LEHR, A., 'Hemony en Fremy', *Klok en Klepel*, 15 (February 1974a), p. 7.
LEHR, A., 'Elk jaar één kilogram lichter!', *Klok en Klepel*, 16 (November 1974b), p. 15-20.
LEHR, A., 'Het middeleeuwse klokkenspel van Bethlehem', *Klok en Klepel*, 27 (December 1981a), p. 1-111.
LEHR, A., *Van paardebel tot speelklok. De geschiedenis van de klokgietkunst in de Lage Landen*, Europese Bibliotheek, Zaltbommel, 1981^2b.

LEHR, A., *De twee klokkenspelen op het Nationaal Paleis te Mafra. Een verslag van de huidige toestand*, Athanasius Kircher-Stichting, Asten, 1984.

LEHR, A., *Klokken en klokkenspelen in het oude China tijdens de Shang- en Chou-dynastie. Een muziekhistorische studie*, Athanasius Kircher-Stichting, Asten, 1985a.

LEHR, A., '"Met losgemaakte ringkraag en in hevig zweet". Een oriënterende verkenning in oude beiaardtracturen', in *Jaarboek van het Vlaams centrum voor oude muziek*, 1 (1985b), p. 109-222.

LEHR, A., *The Designing of Swinging Bells and Carillon Bells in the Past and Present*, Athanasius Kircher Foundation, Asten, 1987a.

LEHR, A., 'Beiaarden en zure regen', *Klok en Klepel*, 39 (december 1987b), p.15-18.

LEHR, A., 'Restoration of Historic Carillons' in L. BOOGERT, A. LEHR and J. MAASSEN, *45 Years of Dutch Carillons 1945-1990*, Nederlandse Klokkenspel-Vereniging, Asten, 1992, p. 74-89.

LEHR, A., *Trommelspeelwerken in het verleden. De automatische uurmuziek van het klokkenspel*, Nationaal Beiaardmuseum, Asten, 1993.

LEHR, A., *Campanologie. Een leerboek over klank en toon van klokken en beiaarden*, Koninklijke Beiaardschool Jef Denyn, Mechelen and Nationaal Beiaardmuseum, Asten, 1996.

LEHR, A., 'De dubbeltonige Chinese klok tijdens de Shang-en en Chou-dynastie', *Berichten uit het Nationaal Beiaardmuseum*, 16 (February 1997), p. 14-18.

LEHR, A., 'De opschriften op de klokken van Medardus Waghevens (1530) uit de voormalige voorslag te Zoutleeuw', *Berichten uit het Nationaal Beiaardmuseum*, 24 (August 1999), p. 3-6.

LEHR, A., 'De stembank van François en Pieter Hemony', *Klok en Klepel*, 71 (June 2000), p. 5-9.

LEHR, A., 'De eerste beiaard die ging reizen: De Reizende Beiaard', *Klok en Klepel*, 79 (June 2002a), p. 20-23.

LEHR, A., *De klokkengieters Petit te Helmond, Someren, Eindhoven, Aarle-Rixtel en Gescher (D.) gedurende de achttiende eeuw en het begin van de negentiende eeuw*, Nationaal Beiaardmuseum, Asten, 2002b.

LEHR, A., 'Over een klokkengieter die klokken vervalste en over een universiteit die haar kritische zin verloor', *Berichten uit het Nationaal Beiaardmuseum*, 36 (November 2003), p. 6-19.

LEHR, A., *Een klokkengieter schrijft zijn opdrachtgever. De brieven van klokkengieter Pieter Hemony (Amsterdam) aan abt Antoine De Loose (Ename B.), 1658-1678*, Nationaal Beiaardmuseum, Asten, 2004.

LEHR, A., 'Bestond de 'schering' uitsluitend uit verticale draden?', *Klok en Klepel*, 90 (March 2005), p. 28.

LEHR, A., 'De Hollandse reis van Jef Denijn in oktober 1915, een keerpunt in de Nederlandse beiaardkunst', *Berichten uit het Nationaal Beiaardmuseum*, 42 (April 2006), p. 6-28.

LEHR, A., TRUYEN, W. and HUYBENS, G., *The Art of the Carillon in the Low Countries*, Lannoo, Tielt, 1991.

LEJEUNE, M., 'De klokkenroof in de Tweede Wereldoorlog (deel 1)', *Nieuwsbrief Campanae Lovanienses*, 22,2 (2009), p. 18-24.

LEJEUNE, M., 'De klokkenroof in de Tweede Wereldoorlog (deel 2)', *Nieuwsbrief Campanae Lovanienses*, 22,3 (2009), p. 61-65.

LEJEUNE, M., 'De klokkenroof in de Tweede Wereldoorlog (deel 3)', *Nieuwsbrief Campanae Lovanienses*, 22,4 (2009), p. 70-79.

LOOPER, B., 'The Hemony's in Zutphen', *Klok en Klepel*, 45 (December 1990), p. 5-7.

LOOSJES, A., *De torenmuziek in de Nederlanden*, Scheltema & Holkeman, Amsterdam, 1916.

LÜBKE, A., *Uhren, Glocken, Glockenspiele*, Verlag Müller, Villingen, 1980.

MCCABE, J., *Mr. Laurel and Mr. Hardy: An Affectionate Biography*, Robson Books, Londen, 1998.

MAASSEN, J., 'Netherlands Automatic Carillon Music in the 19th Century', in L. ROMBOUTS (ed.), *Proceedings of the 11th World Carillon Congress August 9-13, 1998, Mechelen-Leuven*, Vlaamse Beiaardvereniging, Mechelen/Leuven, 2000, p. 104-112.

MACDONALD, P., *Big Ben. The Bell, The Clock and The Tower*, Sutton Publishing, Phoenix Mill/Thrupp/Stroud/Gloucesterhire, 2004.

MARQUES DA GAMA, L. and LEHR, A., *Os Carrilhões de Mafra*, Direcção-geral dos edifícios e monumentos nacionais en Instituto Português do património cultural, s.l., 1989.

MEILINK-HOEDEMAKER, L, 'De Amsterdamse klokkengieterij onder Jan Albert de Grave, 1699 tot 1729', *Klok & Klepel*, 115 (December 2011), p. 14-17.

MERRY, E., 'Les cloches de Maredsous', *Le Bulletin Campanaire*, 41,1 (2005), p. 6-16.

MICHIELS, L., 'Klokken in de Sovjetunie', *Bondsnieuws. Tijdschrift van de Belgische Beiaardiersgilde*, 103 (September 1991), p. 6-19.

MILSOM, M., 'John Taylor & Co. and Canon Simpson', *Bulletin of the Guild of Carillonneurs in North America*, 32 (January 1983), p. 19-20.

MULISCH, H., *Het zwarte licht*, De Bezige Bij, Amsterdam, 1963.

MYHRE, M., 'The Development of the Art of the Carillon in North America', in W. GODENNE and H. JOOSEN, *Jubileumboek 1922-1972. Koninklijke Beiaardschool "Jef Denyn" te Mechelen*, Koninklijke Beiaardschool te Mechelen, Mechelen, 1973, p. 293-310.

NAGAI, T., *The Bells of Nagasaki*, Kodansha International, Tokio/New York/San Francisco, 1984.

NYS, L., 'Jef Denyn. Identiteit in veelvoud', in M. BEYEN, L. ROMBOUTS and S. VOS (edd.), *De beiaard. Een politieke geschiedenis*, Universitaire Pers Leuven, Leuven, 2009, p. 83-99.

PATART, C., *Les cloches civiles de Namur, Fosses et Tournai au Bas Moyen Age. Recherches sur l'historie de l'information de masse en milieu urbain*, Collection Histoire Pro Civitate, série in-8°, n° 44, Credit Communal de Belgique, 1976.

PORTIER, A., *Brugsche tooverklanken*, L. De Reyghere, Brugge, 1939.

PRICE, P., *The Carillon*, Oxford University Press / Hemphrey Milford, Londen, 1933.

PRICE, P., 'The Elements of Carillon Music', *Bulletin of the Guild of Carillonneurs in North America*, 2,1 (December 1947), p. 9-27.

PRICE, P., *Campanology. Europe, 1945-47. A Report on the Condition of Carillons on the Continent of Europe as a Result of the Recent War, on the Sequestration and Melting Down of Bells by the Central Powers, and of Research Into the Tonal Qualities of Bells Made Accessible by War-Time Dislodgment*, The University of Michigan Press, Ann Arbor, 1948.

PRICE, P., 'A Letter From the President in Europe', *Bulletin of the Guild of Carillonneurs in North America*, 3,2 (May 1949), p. 1-6.

PRICE, P., 'The Sound that Went Before', *Bulletin of the Guild of Carillonneurs in North America*, 23 (November 1972), p. 14-21.

PRICE, P., 'The Second North American Congress of Carillonneurs and the Foundation of the GCNA', *Bulletin of the Guild of Carillonneurs in North America*, 25 (May 1975), p. 1-20.

PRICE, P., 'The Carillons of the Cathedral of Peter and Paul in the Fortress of Leningrad', *Bulletin of the Guild of Carillonneurs in North America*, 27 (April 1978), p. 62-71.

PRICE, P., *Bells and Man*, Oxford University Press, Oxford/New York/Toronto/Melbourne, 1983.

PRICE MC CREE, D., 'Percival Price – His Life and Music', *Bulletin of the Guild of Carillonneurs in North America*, 50 (2001), p. 35-49.

RAPHAEL, F. en HERBERICH-MARX, G., 'Dieu mis au pas', *Revue des Sciences Sociales de la France de l'Est*, 23 (1996) p. 244-247.

REMANS, A., 'Klokkenroof in Limburg tijdens de Franse Revolutie', *Limburg*, 34 (1955), p. 101-107.

RICE, W.G., *Carillons of Holland and Belgium. Tower Music in the Low Countries*, John Lane, New York/Londen en Bell & Cockburn, Toronto, 1914.

RICE, W.G., *The Carillon in Literature*, John Lane, New York/Londen, 1915.

RICE, W.G., 'The Growth of the Interest in Carillons in the United States', in *Beiaardkunst. Handelingen van het Eerste Congres Mechelen 1922*, s.n., Mechelen, p. 21-30.

RICE, W.G., *Carillon Music and Singing Towers of the Old World and the New*, Dodd, Mead and Company, New York, 1925.

RICE, W.G., *Beiaarden in de Nederlanden* (Hollandsche bewerking door J.H. van Klooster), De Spieghel, Amsterdam, 1927.

ROBINS, D., 'The Aesthetics of the Carillon', *Bulletin of the Guild of Carillonneurs in North America*, 14 (November 1961), p. 45-51.

RODENBACH, G., *De beiaardier* (Translation into Dutch by Jan H. Mysjkin), Houtekiet, Antwerpen/Amsterdam, 2003.

ROGGEN, W., *De Hasseltse beiaard*, s.n., Hasselt, 1996.

ROMBOUTS, L., 'De abdij van 't Park: de wieg van de beiaard', in *Stad met klank. Vijf eeuwen klokken en klokkengieters te Leuven*, Leuven, 1990a, p. 12-17.

ROMBOUTS, L., 'De muziekdoos van Sint-Geertrui', in *Stad met klank. Vijf eeuwen klokken en klokkengieters te Leuven*, Leuven, 1990b, p. 31-36.

ROMBOUTS, L., 'Interpres variae vitae: de universiteitsbeiaard', in *Stad met klank. Vijf eeuwen klokken en klokkengieters te Leuven*, Leuven, 1990c, p. 37-41.

Rombouts, L., 'Over klokken en zotten in Aalst en Ronse', in *Beiaarden en klokkenspellen in Oost-Vlaanderen*, Provinciebestuur Oost-Vlaanderen, Gent, 1995, p. 27-36.

Rombouts, L., 'De oude Brabantse en Vlaamse jaquemarts', *Nieuwsbrief Campanae Lovanienses*, 11,3 (November 1998), p. 41-49.

Rombouts, L., 'In Search of the Origin of the Carillon – An Interdisclipinary Approach', in *Proceedings of the 13th World Carillon Congress, Cobh and University College Cork, Ireland, 28 July to 1 August 2002*, World Carillon Federation, s.l., s.d., p. 32-39.

Rombouts, L., 'Beiaarden in Vlaanderen. Leuven, Universiteitsbibliotheek', *VBV-magazine*, 13,4 (4th quarter 2008), p. 12-18.

Rombouts, L., '"Het Mechels wonder." De beiaard tussen cultus en city-marketing', in M. Beyen, L. Rombouts and S. Vos (edd.), *De beiaard. Een politieke geschiedenis*, Universitaire Pers Leuven, Leuven, 2009, p. 147-170.

Rombouts, L., 'An American in Louvain: Arthur Bigelow's Years in Belgium', *Bulletin of the Guild of Carillonneurs in North America*, 61 (2012), p. 25-40.

Rombouts, L. and Huybens, G., *Het liedeken van de Lovenaers. Een 18de-eeuws Leuvens beiaardhandschrift*, Universitaire Pers Leuven, Leuven, 1990.

Romita, F., *Ius musicae liturgicae. Dissertatio historico-iuridica*, Marietti, Turin, 1936.

Rottiers, J., *Beiaarden in België*, Beiaardschool Mechelen, Mechelen, 1952.

Sabbe, J., *Peter Benoit, zijn leven – zijne werken – zijne beteekenis*, De Nederlandsche Boekhandel, Gent/Antwerpen, 1902.

Schaepkens, A., *Des cloches et de leur usage*, J.-B. De Mortier, Brussel, 1857.

Schafer, K.A., G., *Remembering and Performing the Ideal Campus: The Sound Cultures of Interwar American Universities*, Ph.D. diss., The University of Texas at Austin, 2010.

Schatkin, M., 'Idiophones of the Ancient World', in H. Cronzel e.a., *Jahrbuch für Antike und Christentum*, 21 (1978), p. 147-172.

Schoofs, A., & Van Campen, D., 'Analysis and Optimatization of Bell Systems', in L. Rombouts (ed.), *Proceedings of the 11th World Carillon Congress, August 9-13, 1998, Mechelen-Leuven*, Vlaamse Beiaardvereniging, Mechelen/Leuven, 2000, p. 208-227.

Schùermans, H., *Les cloches dans la tourmente*, own publication, s.l., s.d., <1997>.

Semowich, Ch., 'Jef Denyn's 1927 Albany Concert', *Bulletin of the Guild of Carillonneurs in North America*, 46 (1997), p. 48-54.

Shen, S., 'Acoustics of Ancient Chinese Bells', *Scientific American*, 256 (May 1987), p. 94-102.

Shull, J.M., 'The Washington Peace Carillon', *The Boston Transcript*, 29 november 1918.

Simpson, A., 'On Bell Tones', *Nash's Pall Mall Magazine*, 7 (1895), p. 183-194 (Reprint in T. D. Rossing (ed.), *Acoustics of Bells*, Benchmark Papers in Acoustics Series, Van Nostrand Reinhold, New York, 1984, p. 27-39).

Simpson, A., 'On Bell Tones', *Nash's Pall Mall Magazine*, 10 (1896), p. 150-155 (Reprint in T. D. Rossing (red.), *Acoustics of Bells*, Benchmark Papers in Acoustics Series, Van Nostrand Reinhold, New York, 1984, p. 40-46).

SMITS VAN WAESBERGHE, J., *Cymbala (Bells in the Middle Ages)*, American Institute of Musicology, Rome, 1951.

SPIES, H., 'Geschichtliches über das Salzburger Glockenspiel', *Mitteilungen der Gesellschaft für Salzburger Landeskunde*, 86/87 (1947), p. 49-56.

SPIESSENS, G., 'Antwerpse documenten over klokkengieter Guillelmus Witlockx (Moergestel 1669-Antwerpen 1733)', *Musica Antiqua*, 9,2 (May 1992), p. 71-79.

SPIESSENS, G., 'De grote vernieuwing van de Antwerpse stadsbeiaard', *VBV-magazine*, 14,3 (3th quarter 2008), p. 7-19.

STEURS, F., *De toren van Sint-Rombautskerk te Mechelen*, Steurs-Bussers, Mechelen, 1900.

STINS, C.J., *Geschiedenis van Hoorns klokken en beiaarden*, s.n., s.l., 1946.

SUTTER, E., *La grande aventure des cloches*, Zélie, Paris, 1993.

SUTTER, E., 'Les carillons ambulants: un effet pervers?', *Le patrimoine campanaire*, 17 (2nd Semester 1994), p. 21-22.

SWAGER, B., 'The Evolution of the Carillon Art in America and Its Netherlandic Heritage', *Bulletin of the Guild of Carillonneurs in North America*, 44 (1995), p. 65-79.

TEUGELS, J., DE WET, T. and VAN DEVENTER, P., 'De Taylor-beiaard van Kaapstad', *Nieuwsbrief Campanae Lovanienses*, 25,4 (2012), p. 84-92.

'T HART, L. E.A., *Herdenkingsboek Vijfentwintig jaar Nederlandse beiaardschool 1953-1978*, Stichting Nederlandse Beiaardschool te Amersfoort, s.l., s.d.

TIMMERMANS, F., *Luidklokken en beiaarden in Nederland*, Allert de Lange, Amsterdam, 1944.

UDDIN, I, and VERBERCKMOES, J., '"Een totaal gebrek aan smaak". Reizigers over klokken in de Lage Landen voor 1800', in M. BEYEN, L. ROMBOUTS and S. VOS (edd.), *De beiaard. Een politieke geschiedenis*, Universitaire Pers Leuven, 2009, p. 41-49.

VAN BETS, M. and DECOSTER, K., *De Mechelse klokkengieters*, Koninklijke Beiaardschool Jef Denyn, Mechelen, 1998.

VAN DEN BERGH, G., 'De klokken- en beiaardgieter Omer Michaux', in *Stad Halle. Beiaardconcerten 1985*, s.n., s.l., s.d., <Stadsbestuur Halle, 1985>, p. 5-10.

VAN DEN BERGH, G., 'Het klokkenspel van abdij Rozendaal', *Uit de Historie en de Folklore van Waverland* 10 (1986), p. 5-22.

VAN DER STRAETEN, E., *La Musique aux Pays-Bas avant le XIXe siècle*, Brussel, C. Muquardt, 1867 (Reprint Dover, New York, 1969).

VAN DER WEEL, H., '»Het ureslach was Gaudeamus omnes in Domino». Haarlemse klokken en het beleg van Haarlem (1526-1573)', *Klok en Klepel*, 65 (December 1998), p. 12-19.

VAN DER WEEL, H., '"Het groot verlangen van veele voldaan!" Utrechtse klokken in de Bataafs/Franse tijd 1795-1813', *Klok en Klepel*, 68 (September 1999), p. 4-11.

VAN DER WEEL, H., *Klokkenspel. Het carillon en zijn bespelers tot 1800*, Verloren, Hilversum, 2008.

VAN DER WEEL, H., 'Calvijn tot in de top. De invloed van het Calvinisme op het luidklokken- en klokkenspelgebruik', *Klok en Klepel*, 106 (March 2009), p. 2-9.

VAN DER ZWART, J., *Het Carillon van Schoonhoven. Een onderzoek naar de historie van de stadhuisklokken*, Historische Vereniging Schoonhoven, Schoonhoven, 1975.

VAN DOORSLAER, G., *Le Carillon et les Carillonneurs de la Tour St.-Rombaut, à Malines*, L.& A. Godenne, Mechelen, 1893.

VAN DOORSLAER, G., 'Les Waghevens, fondeurs de cloches', in *Annales de l'Académie d'Archéologie de Belgique*, 60 (1908), p. 301-532.

VAN DOORSLAER, G., *Les van den Ghein, fondeurs de cloches, canons, sonettes et mortiers à Malines*, s.n., Antwerpen, 1910 (Reprint from *Annales de l'Académie royale d'Archéologie de Belgique*, 1910).

VAN DOORSLAER, G., *De beiaard van Steenockerzeel*, Reprint from *De Brabantsche Folklore* 12, 1923.

VAN DOORSLAER, G., 'Een Latijnsch Gedicht ter eere van den Antwerpschen klokgieter Melchior de Haze', in *Beiaardschool te Mechelen. Jaarverslag en Mededeelingen 1926-1927*, s.l., s.d., p. 28-46.

VAN DOORSLAER, G., *De beiaard van Aalst*, Beiaardschool Mechelen, Mechelen, 1927.

VAN DOORSLAER, G., *Verdwenen klokkenspelen in de Antwerpsche Kempen*, Reprint from *Oudheid en Kunst*, 1939.

VAN ELEWYCK, X., *Matthias Van de Gheyn et les célèbres fondeurs de cloches de ce nom depuis 1450 jusqu'a nos jours*, s.n., Paris/Brussel/Leuven, 1862.

VAN EVEN, E., *Louvain dans le passé & dans le présent*, Fonteyn, Leuven, 1895 (Reprint Peeters, Leuven, 2001).

VAN EYNDHOVEN, C., *A la recherche du temps perdu. Een artistieke reconstructie van de beiaardmuziek tussen 1600 en 1650 in de Zuidelijke Nederlanden op basis van historische versteekboeken*, Diss. Luca School of Arts, Leuven, 2012.

VAN GEUNS, S. and SCHOLTE, H., 'Het nieuwe Ricker-zevengelui in de Onze-Lieve-Vrouwetoren te Amersfoort', *Klok en Klepel* 77 (December 2001), p. 1-4.

VAN HEUVEN, E.W., *Acoustical Measurements on Church-Bells and Carillons* (Diss.), Van Cleef, 's-Gravenhage, 1949.

VANHOOF, F., 'Cellebroeder Peter VI Vanden Gheyn, klokkengieter van beroep', *Nieuwsbrief Campanae Lovanienses*, 4,3 (1991), p. 37-39.

VAN IMMERSEEL, F., *Manten en Kalle, de jacquemarts, de uurautomaten*, Studio Ros Beiaard, Antwerpen, 1963.

VAN NUFFEL, P., *Kermisklokken*, Aalst, Spitaels-Schuemans, 1920.

VAN SCHAIK, M., 'De cymbala van psalm 80: een symbolische interpretatie', *Klok en Klepel*, 38 (June 1987), p. 3-25.

VAN WELY, B., 'Een nieuwe beiaard voor de Onze Lieve Vrouwe-toren te Amersfoort', *Klok en Klepel*, 67 (June 1999), p. 10-16.

VAN WERVEKE, A., 'De ontwikkeling van het klokkenspel te Gent', in *Beiaardkunst. Handelingen van het Eerste Congres, Mechelen, 1922*, s.n., s.l., 1922, p. 124-135.

VERCAMMEN, L., *Eiland in het groen. Beknopte historiek Rouwmoershoeve, klooster – college*, College Essen, Essen, 1986.
VERHEYDEN, P., 'Ontwikkeling van de beiaarden te Antwerpen', in *Beiaardkunst. Handelingen het Tweede Congres 's-Hertogenbosch 1925*, s.n., 's-Hertogenbosch, 1925, p. 169-173.
VERHEYDEN, P., *Beiaarden in Frankrijk*, De Sikkel, Antwerpen, 1926.
VERHEYDEN, P., 'Hoe Adolf Denyn speelde', in *Beiaardschool te Mechelen. Jaarverslag en Mededeelingen 1926-1927*, s.l., s.d., p. 25-27.
VERHEYDEN, P., '"Triumphdicht over den nieuwen Carlejon", Hasselt, 1752', *Limburg*, 24,3-4 (1943), p. 45-73.
VERHOEF, H., 'De Hemony-beiaard van Amersfoort. Geschiedenis van het instrument en restauratie van 1994-1996', *Klok en Klepel*, 58 (March 1997), p. 3-13.
VERNIMMEN, P.-F., 'De klokkengieters Vanden Gheyn en Van Aerschodt', in *Stad met klank. Vijf eeuwen klokken en klokkengieters te Leuven*, Leuven, 1990, p. 43-62.
VERSCHAFFEL, T., 'Trots, melancholie en de juiste tijd. België als een land van beiaarden', in M. BEYEN, L. ROMBOUTS and S. VOS (edd.), *De beiaard. Een politieke geschiedenis*, Universitaire Pers, Leuven, 2009, p. 103-125.
VOS, S., '"De kus op de stenen slapen". Beiaard, ontwaking en verzet', in M. BEYEN, L. ROMBOUTS and S. VOS (edd.), *De beiaard. Een politieke geschiedenis*, Universitaire Pers, Leuven, 2009, p. 147-170.
WACHTERS, L., *Jef Denyn en de beiaard*, Davidsfonds, Leuven, 1938.
WATKINS, G., *Proof Through the Night: Music and the Great War, Volume*, University of California Press, Berkeley/Los Angeles, 2003.
WAUTERS, J., 'Een Thiense Klokgietersfamilie', *Hagelands gedenkschriften*, 1924, 1-2, p. 19-31.
WILLIAMS, E., *The Bells of Russia. History and Technology*, Princeton University Press, Princeton, 1985.
WINSEMIUS, B., 'De Zuidertorenbeiaard te Amsterdam', *Klok en klepel*, 52 (June 1994), p. 2-17.
WINTER, C., *Dank voor klank. Een onderzoek naar de appreciatie bij de bevolking van het beiaardspel tijdens reguliere beiaardbespelingen en de invloed daarop van beiaardier, lokale klokkenspelvereniging en lokale overheid*, Diss. Utrecht, 2007.
ZWART, B., 'Tussen kunst en kitch', *Klok en Klepel*, 48 (June 1992), p. 45-47.

Origin of the illustrations

The author has attempted to contact all holders of the copyright to the visual material contained in this publication. Any copyright-holders who believe that illustrations have been reproduced without their knowledge are asked to contact the publisher.

Anton Brees Carillon Library, Bok Tower Gardens, Lake Wales, Florida 288
Bundesarchiv, B 145 Bild-P016307 / CC-BY-SA 250
Gelders Archief, Arnhem 266
Gilbert Huybens, Leuven 110
Hubei Provincial Museum, China 21
Institut Européen d'Art Campanaire, L'Isle-Jourdain 300
Jacques Sergeys, Leuven 33
Jagiellonic Library, Kraków 44
KADOC-Archives, Leuven 282
Klok & Peel Museum Asten 16, 64, 87, 259, 272, 297
Luc Michiels, Mechelen 237
Municipal Archives Brussels 81
Musée de Saint-Germain-en-Laye 22
Musée d'Orsay, Paris. Legacy of Alfred Chauchard, 1910 37
Museum of Fine Arts of Lyon 141
National Library Paris, Ms. Fr. 9152 72
Palácio Nacional de Mafra/DGPC 106
Private Collection 167, 174
Royal Carillon School Jef Denyn, Mechelen 76, 135, 178, 188, 209, 217

Royal Library Albertina, Brussels, Ms. IV 111, fol. 13v 50
St. Austrégésile Church, Mouchan 42
University Library Utrecht, Ms. 400, fol. 1r. 63
University Archives Leuven 198
University of Pennsylvania, Rare Books & Manuscript Library, Paul Cret Papers 212
University of Sydney Archives 226

PHOTOS

Gideon Bodden 118
Geert D'hollander 122, 123
Jan and Wim Decreton 53
Carlos De Vasconcellos 106
Kim Hill 317
Tom Haartsens 16, 87
Laurence Hamonière 141
Joris Luyten 66, 92
Douglas Miller, 1955 245
Luc Rombouts front cover, 76, 95, 113, 135, 144, 234, 303, 311
Jean-Claude Salles 300
Utrecht Bell-Ringers' Guild 47
Cor van de Ven 64

Indices

Index of persons

The index of persons contains names of historic, fictitious and mythological figures, as well as names of companies.

Abrantes, Marquis of 105
Adams, Edward Dean 233
Addicks, company 229
Adriaansz, Job 128
Adriaens, Theo 243-244
Agatha, St. 30
Akelei, Maurits 273
Albert I, King 191, 196, 240
Albrecht, Archduke 80
Allard, Emilien 291
Allenby, Edmund 245
Alva, Duke of 75
Ambiorix 158
Amphion 90
Andrew, Piatt 211, 213
Andriessen, Louis 318
Anthony the Great, St. 24-25
Apollo 82
Arts, Jan 230
Assmus, family 130
Auber, Daniel 149
Augustus, Emperor 23

Bach, Johann Sebastian 115, 253, 292, 315, 318
Badings, Henk 318

Ball, Clifford 227
Bancroft, Hugh 217
Bancroft, Jane W. 217
Barbara, Infante 105
Barber, Llorenç 316
Barber, Samuel 221
Barbieux, Jean-Baptiste 116
Barker, Bryan 226
Barron, Clarence W. 217
Barron, Jessie M. 217
Baudelaire, Charles 154-155
Baudouin, King 240, 299
Beeckman, Isaac 85
Bellini, Vincenzo 172
Bender, Wilhelm 250, 254, 264
Benedict of Nursia, St. 27-29
Benoit, Peter 161, 235
Berghuys, Frederik 132
Berghuys, Jan 132
Bernard, Antoine 115
Beullens, Alphonse 235
Beullens, company 235
Bigelow, Arthur Lynds 185, 246-247, 276-277, 285-286, 292, 293, 313
Bikkembergs, Kurt 318

Bizet, Georges 181
Bok, Edward William 219, 221
Bollée, Amedée 168, 170
Bollée, Ernest 168, 170
Bollée, company 209
Borluut, Joris 163
Brand, Tita 197
Brandts Buys, Marius 201, 202
Bredero, Gerbrand Adriaensz. 80
Brees, Anton 216-217, 219, 221, 225, 231, 242, 281, 293, 313
Brees, Gustaaf 195, 208, 216
Brown, Arthur Jr. 240
Bruckner, Anton 266
Bruegel, Pieter I 158
Burney, Charles 112-113, 133-134
Buskes, Jan 254
Butendiic, Steven 79
Byrnes, Robert 291, 318

Cadbury, George 176
Caesarius of Arles, St. 28
Cage, John 318
Callixtus III, Pope 36
Calvin, John 75, 77, 78
Cammaerts, Emile 197
Canivez, Johanna 247
Carsseboom, Arnold 104
Casparie, J. 230
Causard, company 163
Causard, family 88
Celestine I, Pope 25
Cellier, Jacques 71, 72
Chambers, Robert 199-200
Charlemagne 28-29
Charles V, Emperor 74-75, 159
Charles Alexander of Lorraine 131
Charlotte, Princess 159
Chopin, Frédéric 172, 186, 218, 315, 318
Churchill, Winston 252
Claes, Hendrick 80-81
Claes, Mathéus 158-159
Clément, Géo 244, 282-283
Coecke, Bartholomew 159

Coecke, Pieter 159
Colfs, Jan Jozef 119
Collin, Armand-François 170
Confucius 20
Coolidge, Calvin 219
Courter, John 318
Courtray, Maryette 199-200
Cret, Paul 211, 212
Crowe, Olive Marjorie 224
Curtis Bok, Marie Louise 219

Daimler-Benz, company 311
Damman, Johannes Franciscus 123
Dante Alighieri 51
Dathenus, Peter 77
David, King 51-52, 75
Davies, Marion 238
Davis, Booth Colwell 239
De Beefe, Gilles 105
De Beer, Jozef 261, 267
De Borch, Henrick 79
Debussy, Claude 196
De Chateaubriand, René 152
De Coster, Henry 186-187, 260
De Coster, Theodoor 181, 186
De Croes, Hendrik Jacob 131
De Decker, Jozef 139
De Geyter, Pierre 205
De Grave, Jan Albert 102-102, 104, 107, 145-146, 166, 192, 236, 250, 251, 264, 265
De Gruytters, Amandus 123, 125, 130, 133, 143
De Gruytters, Jan 123, 125, 130-131, 133, 134, 135
De Haze, Maria 100
De Haze, Melchior 97-100, 107, 130
De Jong, Jan, Archbishop 257
De Keyser, Edward 182, 184, 187
De Keyser, Hendrick 90
De la Rue, Pierre 73
DellaPenna, Frank 316, 317, 318
Delmotte, Ephrem 282-283
De Loose, Antoine 94, 96, 146
Demeersseman, Rosalie 144
De Mette, Karel 163, 208

De Meyere, Jacob 71, 74
De Morgan, William 196-197
Denyn, Adolf 172, 177-178, 179, 180
Denyn, Jef 177-189, 191-192, 195, 199, 201-205, 208, 209, 211, 214, 215, 216, 218-219, 224, 225, 227, 229, 230, 231, 234, 235-236, 238, 240-244, 246, 247, 253, 256, 260, 274, 289, 293, 294, 298, 303, 304, 313, 315, 316
Derck, Johan Nicolaas 107, 307
De Prins, Frans 117, 132
De Renesse van Baer, Adriaan 117, 143, 144
De Roovere, Anthonis 59
De Saint-Aubert, Augustin 73
De Saint-Aubert, Philippe 73
De Sany, Jean 73
De Sany, Michel 83
De Sany, Theodoor 81, 82-83, 122, 125, 130, 291
Descartes, René 85
De Sevin, François-Didier 98
De Smet, Aloïs 181
Des Prez, Josquin 73
Dessain, Francis 187
Destrée, Jules 208
Devreese, Frédéric 318
D'hollander, Geert 318
D'hondt, Antoon 124
D'hondt, Jan 124
Donizetti, Gaetano 151, 163
Dow, Charles 217
Drouot, company 235
Dumery, Joris 107, 155, 239, 265
Dupont, André 132, 291

Eckart, Dietrich 249
Edward VIII, King 225
Edwards, George Wharton 198-199
Eggert, Johann Ephraim 130, 291
Eijsbouts, Bonaventura 203, 229
Eijsbouts, company 170-171, 203, 229, 271-273, 275, 281, 287, 295, 296, 298, 301, 304, 307, 312, 315
Eijsbouts, Tuur 271-272
Elgar, Edward 197, 215, 228
Elisabeth, Queen 196, 240

Elisabeth, Tsarina 107
Eliseus 60
Ensor, James 236
Espy, Edwin 250
Eugène of Savoye, Prince 131

Fabiola, Queen 299, 313
Farnese, Alexander 80
Feremans, Gaston 274, 293
Fétis, Edouard 159
Feyen, Jan 294
Fiocco, Joseph-Hector 131
Fischer, Johan 59
Fosdick, Harry E. 221
Förster, Johann Christian 102
Frank, Anne 254-255
Frank, family 254-255
Franssen, Benoit 274
Franz Ferdinand of Habsburg 191
Frederick I, King 103
Frederick William, King 103-104
Fremy, Claude 97, 99, 100
Fremy, family 88
Fremy, Mammertus 94, 96, 97
Fritsen, Hein 281
Fritsen, Henricus 165

Garibaldi, Giuseppe 171
Gebruers, Adrian Patrick 243
Gebruers, John 274, 280
Gebruers, Staf 232, 242-243, 280
Gerhardt, Ida 255
Gerken, Albert 291, 293, 318
Geysen, Frans 318
Giesler, Hermann 266
Gifanius, Aubertus 78
Gilbert, François 117
Gillett, William 213
Gillett and Bland, company 172
Gillett & Johnston, company 213, 215, 217, 218, 221, 223-224, 226, 229, 230, 233-234, 241, 245, 251, 273, 276, 277, 285
Glass, Philip 319
Godfrey, Frank 285

Godfrey of Bouillon 158
Goebbels, Joseph 249, 251, 253
Goemaere, J.P. 278, 283
Göring, Hermann 251, 257
Gregory the Great, Pope 28
Grieg, Edvard 186, 318
Grisar, Albert 158-159
Guillelmi, J.B. 100

Haazen, Jo 307, 315
Handel, Georg Frideric 173, 218, 253
Harding, Warren G. 213
Hardy, Oliver 243
Hardy, Thomas 195-196
Harmon, Arthur Loomis 244
Hathaway, Henry 285
Haverals, Gommaar 140
Haweis, Hughes Reginald 171-172, 173, 177, 180
Haydn, Joseph 252
Haydn, Michael 100
Hearst, William Randolph 238-239
Heer, Friedrich 29
Hemony brothers 97, 98, 99, 101, 107, 111, 119, 151, 167, 173, 175, 201, 202, 204, 214, 221, 258, 265, 267, 272, 273, 287, 294-296, 301, 304-305, 310, 315
Hemony, François Jr. 93
Hemony, François Sr. 86, 87-91, 94-96, 101, 111, 145, 170, 202, 251, 254, 255, 265, 273, 295-296, 304
Hemony, Margareta 93, 94, 96
Hemony, Pieter 86, 87-88, 91-96, 97, 109, 116, 139, 143, 146, 239, 265, 294
Henry III, King 71
Henry, Léon 244, 251
Hershals, Willem 62
Hess, Joachim 125
Heymans, Paul 278
Hitler, Adolf 249, 250, 252, 256, 260, 265-266
Hofdijk, W.J. 86
Hooft, Pieter Cornelisz. 80
Hoover, Herbert 200, 233, 240, 241, 308
Horacantus, company 275, 294

Horace 21
Hugo, Victor 153-155, 158
Hullebroeck, Emiel 207-208
Huygens, Christiaan 53
Huysmans, Camille 182
Hymans, Paul 207

Isaac, Heinrich 73
Isabella, Archduchess 80

Jacobi, Johann 103-104
Jan de bayardere van Aelst 60
Janzen, J.W. 258, 269
Jarvie, Amelia 245
Jarvie, James Newbegin 244
Johann Ernst von Thun und Hohenstein 99
John V, King 105, 222
Johnson, John Thad 218
Johnson, Roy Hamlin 289-290
Johnston, Arthur 213
Johnston, Cyril 213-214, 217, 221, 222, 223-224, 231-234, 244, 245, 273, 285, 304
Johnston, Jill 224
Johnston, Nora 213, 214, 244-246, 272
Joltrain, Hendrick 125
Joseph II, Emperor 139, 146
Josephine-Charlotte, Princess 240
Juliana, Queen 287
Jullien, Alexis 107, 122, 125, 145
Jullien, family 88

Kagel, Mauricio 318
Kane, Charles Foster 238
Keetell, Hendrik 147
Keldermans, Raymond 287
Kennedy, brothers 287
Kennis, Willem Gommaar 112-113
Kieckens, Jan Baptist 119
Kiliaen, Corneel 79
Kircher, Athanasius 47
Köhn, Dr. 260
Korngold, Erich 163
Koster, Assuerus 89
Koster, Gerard 97

Kreps, Joseph 263, 269

Ladeuze, Paulin 233, 234
Lady Gaga 319
Lannoy, Maurice 244
L'hermite, Jehan 79
Laurel, Stan 243
Lawson, James 293
Lee, Byung-Ik 307
Leenhoff, Carolus 151
Leenhoff, Suzanne 151
Lefévere, Kamiel 217, 218, 222, 225, 227, 233, 239-240, 241, 242, 263, 281, 293
Legros, Nicolas 116
Lehr, André 239, 272, 294-302
Lemaire, Simon 120
Lemmens, Nicolas 177
Lenaerts, Jeronimo 100
Lenin, Vladimir 205
Leopold I, Emperor 103
Leopold I, King 159
Leopold III, King 240, 252
Leopold, Prince 159
Lerinckx, Jos 274
Leroux, Xavier 163
Levache, Jean-Baptiste 111
Levache, Nicolas 105-107
Lindbergh, Charles 218
Liszt, Franz 151, 152, 172
Loder, Hendrik 51
Longfellow, Henry Wadsworth 155-157, 159
Longstaff, William 227-228
Loomis, George 285
Loomis, Rose 285
Loosjes, Adriaan 204, 207
Louis XIV, King 135
Louis Napoleon, King 147
Louis the Pious, Emperor 29
Louise, Queen 104
Louise Henriette, Countess 103
Lovaert, Leo 169, 182
Luther, Martin 75, 130
Lyon, Marianne 276

Maas-Rowe, company 276
Maassen, Jacques 318
Maeterlinck, Maurice 182
Magius, Hieronymus 78
Mahler, Gustav 318
Maisonnave, Canon 170
Manet, Edouard 151
Manneke, Daan 318
Manten and Kalle 53-54
Margaret of Austria 65, 74, 158
Marie-Antoinette, Queen 140
Marlborough, Duke of 131
Marriott, Frederick 222, 293
Martens, Dirk 159
Martin, company 276
Martini, Jean-Paul-Egide 132
Mary of Burgundy, Duchess 157
Massey, Chester 213
Maximilian, Emperor 157
Mayer, Frederick 214, 216, 221-222, 224, 233
McIntyre, Cardinal James Francis 279
Medary, Milton B. 219
Meeks & Watson, company 312
Mendelssohn-Bartholdy, Felix 151, 253
Meneely, company 214
Menotti, Gian Carlo 221
Mercier, Cardinal Désiré 187, 205, 209, 233
Merlin, François 71, 72
Mersenne, Marin 85
Metallica 319
Meulemans, Arthur 274
Meulenberg, P.J. 257-259
Michaux, Omer 235, 236, 239, 261, 262
Michelin, Maria 88
Michiels, Edward 235
Michiels, Marcel Jr. 235, 236-240, 252, 274, 275, 279, 280, 294, 298
Michiels, Marcel Sr. 235
Miller, Arthur 157
Millet, Jean-François 37
Monroe, Marilyn 285, 286
Monterey, Count of 99
Morgan, Julia 238
Mozart, Leopold 134

Mozart, Nannerl 134
Mozart, Wolfgang Amadeus 104, 134-135, 168, 318
Muir, Ernest Edward 227
Mulisch, Harry 273
Mussorgsky, Modest 101, 318
Myhre, Milford 293

Napoleon Bonaparte, Emperor 145, 147-148, 152, 202
Nauwelaerts, Antoon 195, 208
Nees, Staf 184, 217, 230, 241, 244, 253, 264, 274, 279, 281, 293-294
Nelson, Horatio 217
Neurenberg, Hans 64
Nieuwenhuizen, Frederick 147
Noorden, Claes 100-102, 145-146, 192, 236, 251

Obrecht, Jacob 73
Ockeghem, Johannes 73
Olmsted, Frederick Law Jr. 219
Olsen-Nauen, company 312
Oortkras, Barend 107
Orff, Carl 318
Ost, Alfred 183

Paccard, Alfred 285-286
Paccard, company 168, 209, 283, 312
Palestine, Charlemagne 316
Patrick, St. 25
Peeters, Elisabeth 109-111, 115
Peeters, Karel 111
Pei, Ieoh Ming 305
Pétain, Henri Philippe 257
Peter I, Tsar 100-102, 103, 107
Petit, Alexius 117
Petit, family 88
Petit, Henricus 260
Petit & Fritsen, company 165-166, 229-230, 270, 272, 275, 278, 280-281, 287, 296, 298, 307, 312
Philidor, François 132
Philip II, King 75, 79
Philip the Bold, Duke 54

Philippe, Prince 159
Pius VII, Pope 145
Pius XII, Pope 281
Platter, Thomas 65
Plumere, family 88
Poe, Edgar Allan 101
Potholt, Jacob 133-134
Pozdro, John 290, 291
Praet, Cornelis 60
Price, Frank Percival 213, 216, 218, 225, 244, 270-271, 277, 288, 289, 291, 292, 293
Pruyn, Harriet Langdon 187-188

Quasimodo 153

Rachmaninov, Sergei 101
Raick, Dieudonné 131
Ramel, Dominique 142
Reeder, Eggert 252
Rees, Thomas 287
Reger, Max 315
Rice, William Gorham 187-189, 197-198, 205, 208-210, 211, 218-219, 222, 241, 289, 312
Rieu, André 316
Rieulin, Jacques 68, 78
Rilke, Rainer Maria 157
Rimsky-Korsakov, Nikolai 101
Rincker, company 305
Robins, Daniel 292
Roccha, Angelo 76, 126
Rockefeller, John D. Jr. 214-216, 218, 221-222, 224, 225, 233, 241, 273, 292
Rockefeller, John D. Sr. 214
Rodenbach, Georges 161-163
Romke de Waard, Dr. 274, 280
Rosemann, Professor 262
Roosevelt, Eleonor 246
Roosevelt, Franklin Delano 187
Rossetti, Dante Gabriel 157
Rossini, Gioacchino 151
Rota, Nino 221
Rottiers, Jef 184, 243, 274
Rubens, Pieter Paul 110, 158, 161, 234, 235
Rubinstein, Anton 172

Rublev, Andrei 101
Rumbold, St. 184

Sabinian, Pope 28
Sax, Adolphe 168, 310
SBR, company 276
Schepers, Cornelis 140
Schiller, Friedrich 34, 152-153
Schlüter, Andreas 103
Scholl, Dirck 99
Schoofs, Bert 299-302
Schubert, Franz 186, 318
Schuller, Arvella 302
Schuller, Robert H. 302
Schulmerich, company 276-283
Schulmerich, George 276-283, 286
Schumann, Robert 186, 318
Segovia, Andrés 292
Sergeys, company 246, 262, 298, 305
Sergeys, Constant 235, 236
Sergeys, François 298
Sergeys, Jacques 298
Seyss-Inquart, Arthur 252, 257-258
Shirlaw, Walter 174
Shull, James Marion 210-211
Sigers, Pastor 115-116
Simpson, Arthur 173-175, 213, 271
Slegers-Causard, company 235, 252, 261, 282
Smulders, Frederik 169-170
Solomon, King 23
Somers, Désiré 179, 182, 243
Spelman, Laura 215, 222
Speyer, Lala 197
Sprakel, Juriaen 95
Speybrouck, Jos 160
Stalin, Joseph 249, 251
Steijns, Frank 316
Stevens, George 213
Steylaert, Adriaen 79
Starmer, William Wooding 195
Strauss, Richard (carillonneur) 312
Strauss, Richard (composer) 318
Suso, Heinrich 50, 51

't Hart, Leen 255-256, 264, 274
Tarkovsky, Andrei 101
Taylor, company 175-176, 211, 213, 214, 215, 216, 218, 219, 223, 224, 225, 229, 235, 242, 273, 285, 289, 312
Taylor, Denison 213, 214, 215, 216
Taylor, John William I 175
Taylor, John William II 175, 213
Taylor, Pryce 213
Ten Wege, Catharina 100
Thedieck, Franz 260
Theophilus 31, 43
Tilton, Theodore 159, 161
Timmermans, Ferdinand 230, 244, 293
Tolhuis, Jan 79
Tranströmer, Tomas 157
Truman, Harry S. 287
Tsjaikovski, Peter Ilyich 148, 318

Urban II, Pope 35
Uten, Eugeen 184

Van Aerschodt, André Louis Jean 166-168, 230
Van Aerschodt, company 166-168, 298
Van Aerschodt, Félix 192, 195, 235, 236, 242, 251, 261, 262
Van Aerschodt, Séverin 166-168, 169, 170, 181, 182, 209
Van Artevelde, Jacob 157
Van Balkom, Sjef 318
Van Beethoven, Ludwig 172, 253
Van Bergen, company 165, 229, 230, 258, 287, 296
Van Bevere, Jan 59
Van Call, Jan 123
Van Campenhout, Nicolas 260, 269
Van de Velde, Henry 239
Van den Broek, Piet 298
Van den Ghein, family 67, 109, 236
Van den Ghein, Peter I 67, 79, 147, 254, 298
Van den Ghein, Peter II 67
Van den Ghein, Peter III 67
Van den Ghein, Willem 67, 109, 298

Van den Gheyn, Gabriël 119
Van den Vondel, Joost 90
Van der Ende, Jaap 315
Van der Ven, Dirk Jan 204-205
Van Dyke, Henry 191-192
Van Elewyck, Xavier 112-115
Van Eyck, Hubert 119
Van Eyck, Jacob 85, 86, 88, 90, 91, 175, 301
Van Eyck, Jan 119
Van Frachem, Matheus 111
Van Geyseghem, Victor 244
Van Heuven, Engelbert 271-272
Van Hoof, Jef 208, 242
Van Lennick, Lucas 88
Van Immerseel, Frans 53
Van Noordt, Sybrand 101
Van Noort, Olivier 117
Van Nuffel, Petrus 191
Van Rijn, Rembrandt 253, 256
Van Rijswijck, Theodoor 152
Van Roey, Cardinal Jozef Ernest 260, 267
Van Spiere, Jan 55-56, 60-61, 308
Van Stappen, Jef 261
Van Tuldel, Theodoor 55
Van Waeyenbergh, Honoré 33
Van Wou, Geert 46-48, 55, 273, 305
Vanden Gheyn, Andreas Jozef 115-119, 120, 126, 136, 142, 143, 144, 167, 173, 176, 182, 193, 205, 214, 223, 231, 232, 236, 239, 246, 261, 264
Vanden Gheyn, André Louis 120, 166
Vanden Gheyn, Andries I 109
Vanden Gheyn, Andries II 109, 117, 145-146
Vanden Gheyn, family 109, 175, 298
Vanden Gheyn, Joost 119
Vanden Gheyn, Matthias 111-115, 117, 119, 128, 131-132, 133, 145, 171, 291
Vanden Gheyn, Peter V 109
Vanden Gheyn, Peter VI 109-111, 115, 145, 194, 232, 253
Vandeplas, Theo 208
Vandervelde, Emile 197

Vekenstyl, Henricke 64
Veldkamp, Aeneas 125
Verhaeren, Emile 182
Verheyden, Prosper 189, 219
Verlinden, Edmond 316
Vermaak, Jacques 256
Vincent, Jacob 201-202, 203-204, 230, 254, 316
Vliegen, Robert 305
Volckerick, Jan 152
Von Falkenhausen, Alexander 252, 260
Von Falkenhausen, Ludwig 205, 252
Von Weber, Carl Maria 151
Vox Campanae, firma 275

Wagenaar, Johan 203-204
Waghevens, family 67, 236
Waghevens, Hendrik 67
Waghevens, Jacob 67, 68, 92-93
Waghevens, Medard 67, 117
Waghevens, Peter 62
Warner, company 195
Warren, Whitney 232-234
Watkins, Gladys 227, 244
Wauters, Jan 261
Welles, Orson 238
Westcott, Wendell 293
White, Gary 290, 291
Whitechapel, company 214, 312
Wilhelmina, Queen 201-202
William I, King 147, 149
William V, Stadtholder 146, 147
William of Orange 158
Withers, Harry 213
Witlockx, Willem 105-107, 109, 143
Wyckaert, Filip 125, 130

Yamasaki, Minoru 305
Yi, Marquis 20-21

Zeelstman, Jan 79
Zita, Empress 253

Index of places

The index of places contains city names and the names of regions and countries that don't occur frequently in the book.

Aalst 59-60, 140, 159, 163, 168, 191, 208
Aarle-Rixtel 165
Aberdeen 168, 181
Alaska 211
Albany, NY 187, 218-219, 223
Alfred, NY 239
Alkmaar 99, 130, 203
Almelo 229
Amersfoort 203, 274, 280, 292, 295, 304-305, 312, 313
Amsterdam 52, 67, 80, 89-90, 91, 93-94, 97, 98-99, 100, 101-102, 103, 104, 133-134, 165, 189, 201, 203, 204, 229, 230, 253, 254-255, 256, 295, 297, 304
Andenne 193
Ann Arbor, MI 270, 301
Annecy-le-Vieux 168
Antoing 168
Antwerp 40, 41, 52, 59-60, 65, 68, 73, 78, 79, 80, 89, 93, 97, 98, 100, 105, 107, 110, 111, 123, 25, 126, 130, 134-135, 142, 143, 144, 145, 149, 152, 154, 158, 161, 170, 177, 182, 187, 188, 189, 191, 192, 193, 194, 195, 196, 198, 208, 216, 219, 232, 242, 243, 261, 264, 267, 269, 274, 296, 315
Antwerp-Kiel 242
Appingedam 176, 229, 269
Aranjuez 99
Arnemuiden 67, 79, 147, 254, 298
Arnhem 202-205, 207, 229, 265, 266
Asten 170, 229, 271, 298, 312, 313
Ath 68, 262
Autun 52
Averbode 90, 145
Avesnes 142, 264

Bad Hersfeld 30
Bailleul 136
Balkans, the 61, 264

Bassigny 87
Belgrade 36
Bergen-op-Zoom 258
Berkeley, CA 291, 304, 315
Berlin 103-104, 197, 250, 252, 254, 257, 260, 264, 265, 311
Bethlehem 52
Birmingham 176
Black Forest 54
Bloomfield Hills, MI 287, 308
Bonnefond 117
Borgerhout 216
Boston (E) 168
Boston, MA 211, 217, 224
Bourgh 170
Bournville 176, 208, 227
Braine-le-Comte 262
Brazil 105, 222
Breda 264
Brielle 128, 269
Broekburg 168
Brooklyn, NY 219
Bruges 36-37, 52, 59, 71, 73, 97, 99, 107, 124, 125, 140, 154, 155-157, 158-159, 161-163, 176, 177, 187, 195, 196, 208, 213
Brussels 73, 75, 78, 80-83, 90, 99, 111, 122, 129, 145, 149, 153, 163-164, 177, 178, 182, 189, 208, 260, 264, 276, 278-281, 293
Buffalo, NY 209

Cambrai 77, 136
Cambridge (E) 171, 173
Campania 27
Canino 30
Cape Town 206, 225
Cassel 136
Cattistock 168, 182
Charleroi 236

Chartres 52, 221
Chênée 235
Chicago, IL 222, 292
China 18-21, 22, 45
Cluny 52
Cobh 242-243, 280
Cohasset, MA 217, 219, 241
Cologne 167, 205, 264
Congo 298
Constantinople *see Istanbul*
Copenhagen 107
Cornwall 46
Croydon 172, 213-214
Cuba 211
Culver, IN 285, 292
Czechoslovakia 257

Daejon 307
Danzig *see Gdańsk*
Darmstadt 130, 257, 265
Deinze 56, 301
Delft 99, 125, 128, 132, 255-256, 264, 271
Den Helder 219
Dendermonde 112, 193, 194, 235
Denmark 79, 303, 309, 313
Deurne (B) 261
Deventer 51, 88, 128, 230
Diest 109, 129, 139, 140, 208
Diksmuide 194, 195, 236
Dinant 192, 193, 231, 261
District of Columbia 211
Dordrecht 315
Douai 136, 153, 312, 313
Drunen 272
Dublin 25
Dunkirk 59-60, 136, 168, 252

East Lansing, MI 293
Eaton Hall 168
Edam 67, 78
Egypt 21, 23, 24, 25
Eindhoven 299, 301
Ename 92, 94, 116, 146
Enkhuizen 170

Erfurt 47-48
Esquelbecq 136
Essen (B) 262

Fittleworth 173, 175, 176
Fleurus 140

Gallipoli 226
Garden Grove, CA 302
Gdańsk 107, 128, 130, 291, 307
Georgia 219
Ghent 73, 74, 78, 92-93, 119, 123, 130, 134, 139, 157, 159, 161, 169, 191, 215
Gloucester, MA 211, 214-215
Goes 116, 170
Goor 88
Gouda 4, 78, 128
Grimbergen 143, 236, 294
Groningen 165, 302, 312

Haarlem 77, 80, 203, 256, 273, 304
Halle (B) 54, 83, 235
Hamburg 90, 168, 170, 257, 259, 261-263, 267, 269-270
Harelbeke 239, 251
Hartford, CT 289
Hasselt (B) 64, 65, 115-116, 145, 305
Hawaï 211
Heiligerlee 165
Helmarshausen 31
Helmond 145, 298
Herentals 168
Herzele 275
Hessen 30, 31
Hilversum 259
Hiroshima 266
Hoensbroek 258
Hoorn 64, 107
Hove 107
Hulst 59-60, 280
Huy 145, 269

IJsselstein 103
Iran 15

Iraq 15
Ireland 25, 242-243, 313
Istanbul 36, 78
Italy 28, 43, 53, 132, 133, 171, 257
Itami 305
Izegem 205, 235

Japan 266, 305-307
Jericho 32
Jerusalem 35, 244-245

Kaliningrad 103, 249
Kampen 47, 95, 128, 151, 255, 295
Kent 195
Königsberg *see Kaliningrad*
Kortrijk 53, 54, 64, 168, 170
Kraków 44

Lake Wales, FL 219-221, 223, 225, 278, 293, 313
Langemark 144, 250
Lawrence, KS 285, 289-290, 291, 293
Le Creusot 142, 146
Le Mans 168
Leeuwarden 99
Leicestershire 175
Leiden 80, 128
Leuven 33, 55, 62, 64, 109-120, 131-132, 133, 139, 143, 144, 145-146, 159, 166, 167, 168, 177, 182, 192-193, 196, 198, 200, 207, 211, 232-234, 235, 236, 246-247, 251, 261, 262, 263, 264, 277, 298, 303, 313, 316
Levécourt 87
Liège (city) 105, 111, 116, 145, 191, 235
Liège (Prince-Bishopric) 64, 71, 74, 115, 140
Lier 122, 125
Liessies 117, 136, 142
Linz 266
Lisbon 79, 105, 243
Lokeren 275, 294
London 113, 167, 171, 172, 195, 196, 202, 213, 214, 227, 244, 263, 265, 267, 273
Lorraine 90, 94, 107, 115, 117, 131, 165
Loughborough 175, 215, 216, 225, 241
Luristan 15-16

Maaseik 145
Maastricht 68, 79, 93, 143, 145, 169, 170, 316
Mafra 105-107, 111, 222, 233, 243-244, 298, 310
Mainz 90
Malmaison 148
Maredsous 261
Maulbronn 249
Mechelen 55, 60, 62, 65-67, 73, 74, 77, 79, 80, 107, 109, 111, 112, 119, 140, 154, 167, 172, 176, 177-189, 192, 195, 199, 201-203, 204, 206, 208-209, 215, 216, 217, 219, 222, 224, 225, 227, 230, 231, 232, 233, 235, 236, 239, 240-247, 253, 256, 260, 261, 264, 274, 279, 280, 289, 290, 293, 294, 298, 299, 303, 305, 307, 312, 313
Mercersburg, PA 216-217
Middelburg 170, 251
Misono 305, 306
Monnickendam 66, 67
Mons 139, 153-154, 282
Monte Cassino 27-28
Montpellier 170
Moscow 101, 148, 205
Mouchan 42
Münster 82, 88

Nagasaki 266, 307
Namur 168
Nashville, TN 277
Nederbrakel 275
Neerwinden 140
New Haven, CT 285, 315
New York, NY (city) 101, 214, 216, 218, 219, 220, 221, 222, 224, 232, 239-240, 241, 264, 278, 293, 305, 310, 316
New York (state) 187, 219, 239
Newcastle-upon-Tyne 226
Niagara Falls 211, 233, 285, 286
Nieuwpoort 111, 194, 232, 274-275
Nijkerk 117, 203, 229
Nijmegen 111, 123, 264
Nivelle 199
Nivelles 65, 120, 166, 235, 244, 251
Norway 283, 312
Norton 175

Notre Dame, IN 209

Osaka 305
Ostend 196, 205, 235, 252, 282-283
Ottawa 218, 219, 25, 236, 288, 289, 293
Oudenaarde 55, 60-61, 92, 116, 182, 205, 231, 235

Palestine 21
Palo Alto, CA 240, 308, 310
Paris 37, 80, 132, 139, 146, 147, 148, 151, 152, 153, 158, 167, 170, 189, 198, 224, 264, 275, 278
Pearl Harbor 240
Persia 12, 15
Philadelphia, NJ 168, 198, 209, 219, 233
Philippines 211
Pittsburgh, PA 246, 286
Poland 257, 307, 313
Postel 145, 274
Potsdam 104, 249, 257, 265
Prague 99
Princeton, NJ 276-277, 287, 292
Puerto Rico 211

Reims 211
Rhenen 230
Richmond, VA 310
Riga 99
Roeselare 168, 169, 182, 205
Rome 168, 266, 278
Ronse 236, 282
Rotterdam 229, 230, 244, 251, 293
Rouen 170
Rwanda-Urundi 207
Rueil 148
Russia 61, 101-102, 107, 148, 173, 205, 251, 256, 265, 307, 318

's-Hertogenbosch 46, 60, 168
Salzburg 99-100, 134
San Francisco, CA 238, 240
San Simeon, CA 238-239
Santa Monica, CA 235
Schaffhausen 34

Scheveningen 147
Schiedam 151
Schoonhoven 117, 118, 203
Scotland 79
Sellersville, PA 276
Sewanee, TN 286
Sheffield 175
Shiga 305
Sint-Maartensdijk 67, 269
Sint-Truiden 109, 116, 170
South Korea 307-308
Southampton 224
Spain 43, 74, 75, 80, 99, 153
Springfield, IL 287, 315
St. Amand-les-Eaux 142, 244
St. Helena 148
St. Omer 132
St. Petersburg 102-103, 107, 307
St. Quentin 136, 231
Steenokkerzeel 111, 145, 252-253
Stockholm 93
Sussex 173, 175
Sweden 46, 79, 102
Sydney 225-226
Syria 21

Tamines 193
Tellin 163, 235
The Hague 97-87, 107, 125, 187-188, 189, 205, 256, 260, 267
Thebes 90
Tholen 269
Tielt 264
Tienen 109, 116, 129, 261
Tongerlo 91, 93, 119, 143
Torhout 205
Toronto 213, 214, 244
Tournai 68, 116, 154, 235, 236, 244, 274, 282, 298
Trafalgar 217
Trent 77
Tunbridge Wells 195, 202

Utrecht 47, 48, 55, 59, 65, 78, 85, 87, 93, 103, 147, 151, 203-204, 207, 295, 307, 313, 318

Val Saint-Lambert 145
Valais 61
Valencia 61
Valenciennes 73
Vatican 30, 32, 105, 147, 257, 270, 278-282
Veere 111, 187
Venice 155
Verdun 29, 211
Vermont 305
Versailles 146, 207, 276
Vézelay 52
Vienna 149, 319
Visé 193

Wadi Natrun 24
Washington D.C. 210-211, 212, 263, 285, 286, 287, 291
Waterloo 148, 149
Weert 107

Weesp 254
Wellington 226-228, 244
Wervershuizen 272
West Point, NY 214
Westrozebeke 54
Wilhelmsburg 257, 267
Willemstad 177
Windesheim 51
Wingene 168, 205, 231, 235
Wittenberg 75

Ypres 73, 144, 194-195, 236

Zaltbommel 151
Zeebrugge 163, 177
Zierikzee 67, 269
Zoutleeuw 67, 261
Zutphen 87, 88, 95, 201, 202
Zwolle 230

Index of subjects

abbey carillon 121, 132, 142, 145, 166
abuse of bells 36-37, 52
acid rain 294-296
American pedal board 224, 292-293
Angelus 35-36
apotropaic function 19, 23, 24-25, 32, 34-35
appeelkens 56
arpeggios 133, 172, 180, 320
arrangements 131-132, 135, 150, 291, 318-320
associations 207-208, 274, 312-313
atmosphere 17, 56, 71, 295-296, 320

Bancloque 40-41, 56
baptism of bells *see blessing of bells*
baton keyboard 59, 60, 64, 71, 168, 169-172, 179, 210, 261, 275, 310
beats 45, 69, 223, 294, 302
beehive profile 30, 43
belfry 39-40
bell-chamber 127, 180-181, 203, 222, 320-321

beyaert 61-62
bian zhong 20
blessing of bells 32-25, 270, 278
books about bells or carillons 59, 78, 126, 189, 197-198, 204-205, 287
brochette 87
broek system 126-127, 178, 201, 203, 230, 304

Calvinism 75, 77-78, 103, 151
campana 27
campanile 28
campus carillon 223, 287-288, 322
cannon 45, 89, 93, 107, 117, 124, 142, 147, 148, 210, 251
canonical hours 27, 28, 36-37, 39
capitularies 29
carillon 61-62
Carillon piano 169-182
carillonic bells 276-277
Carillon Plus 316-317

casting process 15-16, 19, 31-32, 45-46
cement 272
centaur 96, 153
change ringing 173, 175, 197
chime (USA) 210, 214, 216, 285
chimer (trad.) 42, 60, 61, 63, 101, 126
chiming (trad.) 42, 59-62, 79, 101, 148
church carillon 129, 142
clapper 16, 17, 18, 22, 28, 31, 32, 41, 60-62, 65, 126-127, 178-180, 193-194, 222, 287, 304
clay 15-16, 19, 31, 43, 45-46, 65, 272
clay ground 67, 165
clay mold casting method 19
clogga 25
collective character of carillon music 210, 321-322
compass of carillons 80, 82-83, 126, 215, 224, 287, 292, 308, 316
competition 62, 111-112, 119, 127-128, 162-163, 184, 201, 204, 230, 313-314
Compline 27
computer-aided design 296-302
confiscation of bells 74, 78-79, 141-146, 205, 256-263
cope 31, 43, 46
copper 15-16, 31, 46, 123, 141, 251, 257, 263, 275, 298
core 31, 43, 45
corrosion 295-296, 312
cost of carillons 105, 121, 239
counterreformation 77, 129
cowbell 23
crotal 15-16, 18, 21-24, 48
cuckoo clock 54
cuckoo motif 54-55
curfew 35, 40
cymbala 52, 210
cythara 71

death bell 34
decay 18, 19, 56, 96, 150, 175, 180, 270, 271, 288, 290, 291, 293, 301, 317, 318, 319, 323
Denyn system 179-180
descant 223

diminution 32
documentation centers 313
doubled treble bells 223, 226
drum of automatic carillon 64, 82, 105-106, 122-125, 128, 130, 136, 156, 302, 310
duet playing 316
Dutch pedal board 126
dynamic similarity 96, 119

echo effect 180, 229
education of carillonneurs 127, 186-187, 208-209, 240-242, 274, 313
electrolysis 263
electronic bells 275-276
equal temperament tuning 91, 150, 223
escape wheel 49
escapement 49
etymology 25, 27, 52, 54, 61-62, 73, 79, 101, 210, 307
exam *see competition*
exercise 173

false bell 31, 43, 45-46, 90, 298
fen-ling 18
festivals 287, 315
fifth 68, 69, 85, 175, 237
finger protectors 314
fire bell 41
Five-Tone Simpson Principle 213
Flemish pedal board 126
foliot 49, 53
forestroke 50, 54-56, 60, 62, 64-65, 67-68, 69, 73, 136, 151, 171, 291, 302-303, 322
frequency of automatic music 124, 151
frequency of manual music 129, 315
frieze 96
fundamental 17, 20, 48, 68-69, 173, 175, 237
funeral tolling 34

gate bell 40
Gloria toll 29
gothic profile 43
gu 21

halo 319
handbell 173
handbell choir 173
historical carillons 310
horsebell 22-23
huang zhong 18-19

interculturalism 322
internationalization 182, 309-310, 312-313

jaquemart 53, 54, 60, 307

kodon 24
kolokol 101

lath 125
Lauds 27, 28
lead 20, 35, 271
legato 172, 180, 202, 318, 320
listening test 213, 301
lost-wax technique 15-16, 31
Lutheranism 75, 130

machine à carillonner 170
magic 23-24, 35, 182-184, 317
major third 68-69, 91, 167, 299-302
major-third bell 167, 276, 299-302
malinovji zvon 307
Matins 27, 28, 36-37, 40, 49
mean tone temperament 91, 150, 296
Mechelen pedal board 224
melody note 17, 68-69, 223
metal fourth 221-222
minor third 21, 69, 85, 91, 95, 167, 223, 276, 286, 290, 299, 301-302, 304
mobile carillon 245, 272, 301, 307, 314, 316
modal keys 56, 274
museums 296, 307, 313

nationality of the carillon 153, 158-163, 197, 200, 240, 241, 253, 310-311
nomadic bell-founders 87-88, 165
None 27, 40

octave 68-69, 173, 175
octave stretching 223, 304
octatonic scale 290
original carillon music 114-115, 132, 152, 184-185, 242, 274, 289-291, 318
ornaments 133
oscillator 270, 271, 272
overtones *see partial notes*

partial notes 17-19, 20, 21, 56, 68-69, 85, 90-91, 175, 180, 222, 237, 270, 271, 290, 295, 299, 301-302, 317, 319, 320, 323
patina 295
peal 47, 62, 173, 175
pedal board see pedals
pedals 61, 64, 71, 73, 126, 130, 132-133, 134, 169, 172, 210, 224, 233, 290, 291, 292, 303, 312, 319
image of carillonneurs 314
image of carillons 314
piano keyboards 170, 172, 178, 209, 224, 239
pins 56, 64-65, 123, 124-125, 133, 195, 234, 302
political use of the carillon 77-78
preluding 115, 117, 133, 186
prime 69, 173, 175, 223, 286, 305
Prime 27, 40
protectionism 203-205, 231-232, 280
psalms 32, 51, 75, 77-78, 96, 104, 130, 132, 133, 147, 151, 157, 201, 204, 254
pure minor third 223, 304
pendulum clock 53, 154
physical efforts during carillon playing 133-134, 168-169, 172, 182, 246, 283, 314
pomegrenade 15, 16, 48
practice keyboard 65, 245
prayer bell 27-28, 32, 34, 35-37
programming the carillon 55-56, 64-65, 75, 82, 100, 104, 106, 117, 123-125, 128-130, 133-136, 151-152, 155, 302-303, 310
putti 96, 105
Pythagorean tuning 274-275

rammel 151
recital 315

reconstruction of carillons 304-305
recording of carillon music 184, 208, 227, 230-231, 247, 254, 264, 294, 316-317
reformation 75-78
repertoire 56, 75, 78, 80, 82, 114, 129-133, 151, 201, 225, 274, 289-291, 309-310, 318-319
resonance 85, 91
restoration of carillons 243, 287, 295-296, 297, 304, 312

scel 56
schering 73, 126-127, 178, 201
schools *see education*
secondary strike note *see metal fourth*
semantron 24, 28, 101
Sext 27
signum 24, 28-29, 266
societal changes 149-150
sound rim 30, 43, 85, 96
sounding bars 65, 245
spit 31
spring drum 105, 125
staccato playing 180, 318, 320
standard keyboard 179, 224, 292-293, 303, 312
status of carillonneurs 42, 127, 128, 151, 283, 292, 314
strike note 17-18, 19, 48, 69, 180, 221, 301
striking 17, 25, 28, 41-42, 54, 62, 79
sugarloaf model 43
sui 20
sulfur 295
summer concerts 181-184, 315
sundial 49, 53
swinging bell 17, 167-168, 195, 238, 249, 258, 261-262, 290, 305, 316
swinging rope 27, 30, 32, 43, 144, 173

tape system 302
Te Deum toll 29
template 31, 45
Terce 27, 40
thickening of treble bells 96, 119, 287
time dimension of carillon music 322
time indication 39-40, 49-56, 149

timing of carillon recitals 128-129, 202, 243, 315
tin 15-16, 20, 31, 45, 46, 251, 263, 275, 298
tintinnabulum 22, 24
toccata playing 291
tocsin 41, 93
tower clock 52-53, 56, 73, 128
tower watchman 40, 51, 53-54, 124, 154, 195
traveling carillon *see mobile carillon*
treble bells 96, 119, 223
tremolo playing 125, 180-181, 184-185, 186, 204, 229, 242, 274, 291, 293, 319
trézeler 62
trezvon 101, 307
tribouler 62
trychel 23
tumbler system 178-181, 224, 229, 230, 303-304
tumblers 124, 126, 178-179, 182, 202, 203, 304, 312
tuning bars 91, 96, 119
tuning forks 270
tuning lathe 91, 272
tuning machine 175, 213
tuning margin 91
tuning of bells 67-68, 85, 90-91, 94, 96, 103, 107, 166, 167, 175, 213, 223, 230, 237, 271-272, 277, 296, 299
turnbuckles 179-180
Turkish Bell 36
tuymelaer 124

vent 31
verge 49
Vespers 27, 36-37, 40, 56

water clock 49
wax 43, 45, 87, 298
weaving industry 73
weight of carillons 89, 93, 117, 221, 224, 233, 310
windmill construction 73
women playing the carillon 170, 172, 314
work bell 40, 52
World's fair 170, 239-240, 278-282

zhong 18-20
zvon 101, 173, 307

www.ingramcontent.com/pod-product-compliance
Lightning Source LLC
Chambersburg PA
CBHW021116300426
44113CB00006B/167